BLACK BUDDHISTS AND THE BLACK RADICAL TRADITION

Black Buddhists and the Black Radical Tradition

The Practice of Stillness in the Movement for Liberation

Rima Vesely-Flad

NEW YORK UNIVERSITY PRESS

New York

NEW YORK UNIVERSITY PRESS
New York
www.nyupress.org

References to Internet websites (URLs) were accurate at the time of writing. Neither the author nor New York University Press is responsible for URLs that may have expired or changed since the manuscript was prepared.

Library of Congress Cataloging-in-Publication Data
Names: Vesely-Flad, Rima, author.
Title: Black Buddhists and the black radical tradition : the practice of stillness in the movement for liberation / Rima Vesely-Flad.
Description: New York : NYU Press, 2022. | Includes bibliographical references and index.
Identifiers: LCCN 2021029462 | ISBN 9781479810482 (hardback) | ISBN 9781479810499 (paperback) | ISBN 9781479810543 (ebook) | ISBN 9781479810505 (ebook other)
Subjects: LCSH: Race relations—Religious aspects—Buddhism. | Racism—Religious aspects—Buddhism. | Buddhism—United States. | Buddhism and politics—United States. | African Americans—Religion.
Classification: LCC BQ4570.R3 V47 2022 | DDC 294.3/376—dc23
LC record available at https://lccn.loc.gov/2021029462

New York University Press books are printed on acid-free paper, and their binding materials are chosen for strength and durability. We strive to use environmentally responsible suppliers and materials to the greatest extent possible in publishing our books.

Manufactured in the United States of America

10 9 8 7 6 5 4 3 2 1

Also available as an ebook.

For Rev. angel Kyodo williams, Konda Mason,
Zenju Earthlyn Manuel, and Jozen Tamori Gibson.
Thank you for the wise counsel that you offer, the invitations you extend,
and the steady presence that each of you exudes.

For all of the organizers and participants in the retreats for
Buddhist Teachers of Black African Descent, "The Gathering I"
and "The Gathering II."
May you find yourselves mirrored in these pages.

And for all Black people who are drawn to the dharma.
May you be inspired by the wisdom of Black Buddhist teachers.
May you be liberated.

CONTENTS

Introduction

Drumming fills the meditation hall. On the altar behind the drummers sit figures of the Buddha and Quan Yin, Bodhisattva of Compassion. In the large space in front of the drummers sit three hundred Buddhist teachers and meditation practitioners of African descent. As the drumming grows louder, people get up to dance, clap, and shout. And then there is silence, stillness.

This book uplifts the distinctive voices and practices of Black people who embrace Buddhism, a religious tradition established in India twenty-six hundred years ago. Buddhism's encounter with the United States has been chronicled in hundreds of texts and articles, many of them particularly focused on the intersection of Buddhism with psychology. Yet, this literature is generally espoused without recognizing the larger context of white supremacy in the United States and the intergenerational trauma that consequently pervades Black communities. Furthermore, although Buddhism in the United States—as it has been practiced by Asian immigrants and their descendants, and as white Americans have adopted it—has been the subject of much study, the encounter of Buddhism with Black communities has yet to be broadly documented.[1] This book aims to partially fill that void, highlighting the history and social context of the United States as well as teachings and rituals practiced by Buddhists of African descent.

The central thesis of this book is that Buddhist teachings and practices liberate Black people from psychological suffering. Black liberation depends on healing intergenerational trauma, and forms of Buddhism facilitate the process of attaining inner freedom. More than half of the forty Black Buddhist teachers and long-term practitioners interviewed for this study identified healing racially induced trauma as a motivation for investing in the practice of Buddhism. Thus, a primary aim of this book is to illuminate teachings and practices for healing intergenerational trauma in Black communities. Inspired by Joy DeGruy's 2005 *Post Traumatic Slave Syndrome: America's Legacy of Enduring Injury and Healing*, contemporary research on intergenerational trauma recognizes that the specific realities encountered by Black people necessitate specific responses.

A second argument made by this book is that Buddhist teachings (known as the *dharma*) practiced by Black Buddhists emphasize different aspects of Buddhism than are experienced in white convert Buddhist communities. While Black Buddhists similarly embrace silent meditation, their additional spiritual practices adhere closely to indigenous rituals as well as forms of Buddhism practiced in Asian Buddhist communities (known as *sanghas*). This is especially witnessed in the practices of honoring ancestors—biological and spiritual—and in the prioritizing of community. Black Buddhists bring distinctive interpretations of the dharma to the community, in their embrace of ancestors, elders, and collective care. Scholars and dharma teachers assert that the dharma is always transmitted through culture,[2] and thus African and African American cultural traditions are key for how the dharma is transmitted in the West. Meditative practices that honor African ancestors are a conduit for transmitting the dharma, including drumming, chanting, teaching through African and African-American wisdom teachings, placing African-derived images on Buddhist altars, and practicing devotional bowing to pay respect to known and unknown ancestors.[3]

A third argument made by this book is that the socially vilified Black body is, for Black Buddhists, a profound and reclaimed vehicle for liberation. The racialized Black body is degraded in a white-supremacist society, and such denigration must be taken into account as a source of suffering. And yet the Black body, which is capable of anchoring spiritual practices of stillness, movement, and sensuality, serves as a vehicle for liberation.

A fourth and final argument of this book is that each of these core assertions supports the commitment to psychological liberation, as promulgated by the Black Radical Tradition. Black Buddhists are indebted to Black Freedom Movement activists, Black Church leaders, and Black Feminists, ancestors who, as author and singer Rachel Bagby quotes, have been "making a way outta no way."[4] Whether or not they consciously or explicitly embrace Black Radical thinkers and ideas, Black Buddhists stand in a long tradition of confronting white supremacist conditions and healing intergenerational trauma. In the practice of Buddhism, Black practitioners cultivate the capacity to deconstruct the false, degrading messages imparted in a white supremacist social order, cultivate compassion, and shift harmful habitual patterns. In the honoring of ancestors, there is an emphasis on collective liberation and community. In focusing on the Black body as a vehicle for liberation, Black Buddhist practitioners reclaim Blackness, sensuality, and joy.

Thus I argue that Black Buddhist teachings are highly congruent with Black Radical philosophies. Both Black Buddhist teachings and Black Radicalism seek to understand Black people on their own terms, rather than always in response to whiteness. In so doing, the Black Radical Tradition and Black Buddhism uplift political, psychological, and spiritual liberation. By cultivating the capacity to see internalized patterns of harm as well as the falseness of white supremacist narratives and to establish a nonreactive approach to white supremacy, the practice of Black Buddhism *fulfills* the Black Radical Tradition's emphasis on psychological liberation.

In sum, in their distinct interpretations of the dharma, Black Buddhists expand "American Buddhism." Black Buddhists recognize that contemplative spirituality cannot be explored without a forthright reckoning and analysis of the broader racialized social reality; they furthermore acknowledge that a dimension of embodied healing must take place for political, psychological, and spiritual liberation to occur.

Origins of This Book

This book was conceptualized in the wake of Black Lives Matter protests in Ferguson, Missouri, following the fatal shooting of a Black teenager, Michael Brown, by a white police officer in 2014. While joining the protests during two separate trips, I inquired into the relationship of the church to vanguard Black activists. The resounding response was that the vanguard activists felt disaffected, in part due to widespread homophobia on the part of Black clergy. Yet these activists—many of whom self-identify as queer—were deeply spiritual. Their responses illuminated an emerging "Healing Justice" framework in social activism that incorporates meditation, yoga, and other contemplative modalities.[5] Many Black Lives Matter activists were—and are—highly oriented toward spirituality and healing, but critical of the class-stratified, superficial "politics of respectability" that often take place in churches. They are seeking something else. While finishing my first book, on the U.S. penal system and the Black Lives Matter movement, I began asking whether U.S. convert Buddhism could provide a spiritual foundation for Black Lives Matter activists.

I was also asking questions about spirituality and activism for myself. At the time I had been meditating for more than ten years, but had struggled to maintain a steady practice since becoming a parent. I was wrestling with my identity and sense of belonging; I felt deeply isolated in the small southern city in which I found myself after taking an academic position. These were not new challenges. As a Black woman born into a white family in Chicago in 1975, I came of age in a racially divided city, forced to navigate white culture and Black identity largely on my own. My mother's family of origin, second-generation Eastern European immigrants, espoused their denigration of Black people repeatedly. My maternal grandparents raised my mother in Cicero, a "sundown" town infamous for its virulent hostility toward Martin Luther King Jr. during the six months he attempted to address housing segregation and poverty in Chicago's South Side slums. My mother, as a young rebellious activist, embraced the interracial cultural ethos of the 1960s, first by marrying a dark-skinned Puerto Rican member of the Latin Eagles (an organization loosely affiliated with the Young Lords) and later by having two children with a Black man. I am the elder of the children she bore.

My maternal grandparents did not want relatives or members of their white, suburban, middle-class community to know they had Black grandchildren and took steps to hide our existence by not displaying pictures of us in their home and not inviting us to large, important family gatherings (such as their fiftieth anniversary party). At nineteen years old I confronted them, letting them know that I knew they were ashamed of me. They responded by telling me that I did not help wash the dishes.

But there was no refuge on the paternal side of my family. My father—who did not live with me and had three children already—was struggling with drug addiction and poverty. He was not in a position to support two more children and had largely disappeared from our lives by the time my brother arrived, six years after my birth. I have not seen him since I was seven years old and have not had any contact with my paternal family members—with my Black heritage. I hold a few nuggets of knowledge. My father's father—as part of the Great Migration—had traveled from Mississippi to the South Side of Chicago with thirteen siblings. My father was one of three children born into a household in which domestic violence took place. When he was young, his mother left and moved to Massachusetts. He and his siblings were sent to live with extended family members. In the summer of 2018, while researching this book, I asked my mother about my paternal grandmother. "Oh, she loved you," my mother said. "I have met her?" I asked, amazed. "Yes," my mother said. "But you know, she had twenty-five other grandchildren." *What? I didn't know. I have twenty-five cousins on my father's side?* "What was my grandmother's name?" I asked my mother. But she didn't remember.

I illuminate parts of my story because the trauma described by Black Buddhist teachers and practitioners in this book is deeply personal. Rejection by a white world, along with the gaps in family history, produces an emotional landscape with which I resonate. For a long time I turned to activism to channel my trauma and rage. I performed valuable work—but even then I could tell that I was avoiding something, someone. I was avoiding myself. After burning out repeatedly, I, like so many teachers and practitioners uplifted in this book, turned to Buddhism—primarily to meditation, and more recently to movement and devotional practices—as a way of settling, entering my own inner architecture, holding my pain, seeking liberation from suffering.

Embracing Political, Psychological, and Spiritual Freedom: Black Buddhists and Black Radicalism

In making the connections between Black Buddhist practices and the Black Radical Tradition, this book does not suggest that Black Buddhists speak to all aspects of Black Radicalism, nor does the meaning of freedom within the political tradition of Black Radicalism squarely map onto the meaning of liberation within the religious tradition of Buddhism. Black Buddhists are focused on liberation of the heart, mind, and body. Living and teaching within the context of a white supremacist society, Black Buddhists are manifestly concerned with social conditions that impact the liberation of the mind, heart, and body of Black people: racism, poverty, police violence, and mass incarceration.

Black Radical thinkers analyze racially induced suffering through a political lens that centers critiques of imperialism, colonialism, neoliberalism, and capitalism, alongside anti-Blackness. A younger generation of Black Radical activists expands these critiques to include intersectionality, prison abolition, exploitation of the earth, gender-based violence, gender binaries, and cis-heteropatriarchy.[6] While there is direct overlap in the critique of white supremacy and the acknowledgment of the psychological impact of anti-Black racism, these two traditions diverge in multiple ways with regard to frames of analyses, meanings, terms, and reference points.

However, this book argues—drawing on interviews, dharma talks, and published writings—that Buddhism and Black Radicalism, *as these traditions are lived out among Black practitioners and activists*, mutually reinforce each other. The synergies are particularly evident with regard to intersectional commitments to psychological wellness, social justice, honoring ancestors, and uplifting the denigrated Black body as a vehicle for liberation. As Black activist communities increasingly recognize the impact of intergenerational trauma and correspondingly embrace healing modalities, Black Buddhist teachers elaborate the dharma to address racially induced harm. As this book outlines, Black Buddhist teachers and long-term practitioners are reinterpreting Buddhism in distinctive and important ways.

What is liberation? In this book I use the words "liberation" and "freedom" interchangeably and distinguish between political, psychological, and spiritual freedom, recognizing that there is overlap between all three. I define political liberation as freedom from oppression by the state (such as freedom from criminalization and violent policing norms) and by private corporations (such as freedom from financial exploitation and/or inconsistent schedules for employees). Political liberation relies on establishing basic conditions within a democratic order that ensure access to living-wage jobs, quality food and education, safe living situations, and mental and physical health care. Moreover, political liberation means having agency to act collectively to establish basic political rights and norms in one's social environment, through means such as elected representation and community activism. Charlene Carruthers, in her 2018 book *Unapologetic: A Black, Queer, and Feminist Mandate for Radical Movements*, writes, "Liberation is a collective effort in which, even after freedoms are won, continual regeneration and transformation are necessary. Liberation must entail resistance to the dominant oppressive systems that permeate our societies (e.g., capitalism, patriarchy, and anti-Black racism)."[7] These definitions draw on the analysis offered by Robin D. G. Kelley in his foreword to Angela Y. Davis's book *The Meaning of Freedom*. Kelley writes,

> Davis's conception of freedom is far more expansive and radical [than the concept of negative liberty][8]—collective freedom; the freedom to earn a livelihood and live a healthy, fully realized life; freedom from violence; sexual freedom; social justice; abolition of all forms of bondage and incarceration; freedom from exploitation; freedom of movement; freedom *as* movement, as a collective striving for real democracy. For Davis, freedom is not a thing granted by the state in the form of law or proclamation or policy; freedom is struggled for, it is hard-fought and transformative, it is a participatory process that demands new ways of thinking and being.[9]

Davis herself refers to the interlocking practice of transformation as one that is simultaneously outward-facing and inward-looking. In her lecture "Race, Power, and Prisons since 9/11," she states, "If I acknowledge that I am also implicated in the continued patterns of racism, I ask not only how do I help to change those whom I hold responsible for the structures of racism, I ask also: How do I change myself?"[10]

Davis's question bears on the quest of Black Buddhist practitioners for psychological and spiritual liberation. Psychological and spiritual liberation requires seeing the nature of impermanence (*anicca*) and the self clearly: that the ego and all phenomena are unstable and lack an inherent essence or stability. Mundane or constructed reality is understood as distinct from ultimate reality, a state of being in which the mind is freed from greed, hatred, and delusion.

For many Black Buddhists, then, psychological liberation arises from the practice of deconstructing mundane reality, a process of seeing the constructs of white supremacy as inherently false, empty, deluded, and unstable. Deconstructing oppressive white supremacist phenomena, moreover, is extended to seeing clearly the roots of misogynoir and cis-heteropatriarchal heterosexism (including homophobia and transphobia). In the process of deconstructing and seeing clearly the intersectionality between racism, misogyny, cis-heteropatriarchy, and heterosexism, Black Buddhists seek to establish healthy boundaries, empower themselves and their communities, and cultivate radical self-love.[11] Thus they speak of psychological and spiritual liberation as being free from internalized white supremacist narratives and reconstructing a sense of self that honors Black bodies, psyches, and communities.

Spiritual liberation similarly refers to awareness of impermanence and freedom from internalizing white supremacist, cis-heteropatriarchal messages rooted in greed, hatred, and delusion. Spiritual liberation, furthermore, refers to awakening: an awareness of impermanence of all phenomena that extends to the self. Thus, spiritual liberation includes the experience of non-self (*anatta*). In other words, spiritual liberation includes understanding the "self" as a compilation of Five Aggregates: body, feeling sensations, perceptions, mental formations, and consciousness. The experience of non-self is an experience of reality beyond the ego structure—which is informed and shaped by white supremacist systems—and rigid, constricting views. Buddhist practitioners relate to thoughts, constructs, and perceptions as inherently unstable, thus leading to inner attunement to one's inherent spaciousness and ultimately one's awakening.[12]

In sum, political, spiritual, and psychological liberation are all adjacent to one another and, while interlocking, refer to distinct philosophies and practices.

A Theory of Stillness in the Movement for Liberation

Increasingly, scholars of Black and feminist studies recognize the importance of prioritizing inner life while challenging violent institutions. These scholars identify the extraordinary and disproportionate toll enacted by mass protest, pointing to poor health rates—such as heart disease, infant mortality, anxiety, and depression—as well as sheer exhaustion and burnout that disproportionately burden Black Americans.[13] Furthermore, they note that white people have the privilege to disengage mentally, spiritually, and physically from racially induced suffering. However, Black people must constantly confront a degrading social landscape in which they are isolated, stigmatized, and identified as the sole representation of their race. Scholars and activists have begun to write about the importance of Black people cultivating their interior lives—working through trauma as well as practicing joy—as a way of standing on their own terms, resiliently.[14]

Kevin Quashie, a scholar who illuminates the importance of honoring the interior lives of Black people, writes in *The Sovereignty of Quiet: Beyond Resistance in Black Culture* that it is critical to honor the interior lives of Black people. In Quashie's analysis, such a commitment is long overdue. Black cultural discourse privileges public outcry over quiet observation. Indeed, the public activist lives of Black leaders and community members dominate discourse on Black lives, without acknowledging the complexity of Black people's experiences:

> The determination to see blackness only through a social public lens, as if there were no inner life, is racist—it comes from the language of racial superiority and is a practice intended to dehumanize black people. But it has also been adopted by black culture, especially in terms of nationalism, but also more generally: it creeps into the consciousness of the black subject, especially the artist, as the imperative to represent. Such expectation is part of the inclination to understand black culture through a lens of resistance, and it practically thwarts other ways of reading. All of this suggests that the common frameworks for thinking about blackness are limited.[15]

Quashie thus argues that much of the scholarship in the sciences and humanities overly emphasizes the social resistance of Black people without acknowledging their capacity for solitude, personal reflection, and "the integrity that arises from cultivating an inner life." He contends that it is both reductionist and racist to see Black people only as political and social agents when white actors can be valued for their quietude and personal reflections. Indeed, Quashie argues, what is lost is an attentiveness to the importance of Black people's interior lives: modes of reflecting and being that are not always in response to whiteness and the dominant culture. Furthermore, what is overlooked is a way of being in which an individual takes note of social forces and oppressive dynamics, including one's own experiences, but does not internalize the degrading messages inherent in those oppressive encounters. In quietness and stillness, one reflects but does not react; one observes but does not adopt the social forms available to actively counter oppression. Rather, the quiet subject creates her own forms, in her interior life; she pays attention to degradation and feels pain and anger deeply, but does not act from a place of woundedness or self-righteousness. This dignity—to perceive but not lash out, to feel but not impulsively react—informs an inner strength that lifts the quiet subject above the superficiality and violence inherent to white supremacy. It puts the quiet subject on her own terms. From that place of inner strength, the quiet subject refuses to engage the pettiness of the dominant culture; rather, the quiet subject wants something more: the wisdom and self-awareness that come from watching, observing, standing still. Far from being passive, Quashie argues, this quiet observation is, in fact, dignified action.

Quashie identifies several ways of illuminating Black people's inwardness by pointing to literature that emphasizes feelings, desires, imagination, creativity, self-expression, self-awareness, intimacy with one's own interiority, and surrender to emotional forces larger than the political and social landscape.

> Quiet is often used interchangeably with silence or stillness, but the notion of quiet in the pages that follow is neither motionless nor without sound. Quiet, instead, is a metaphor for the full range of one's inner life— one's desires, ambitions, hungers, vulnerabilities, fears. The inner life is not apolitical or without social value, but neither is it determined entirely by publicness. In fact, the interior—dynamic and ravishing—is a stay against the dominance of the social world; it has its own sovereignty. It is hard to see, even harder to describe, but not less potent in its ineffability.[16]

The "sovereignty" to which Quashie is referring is an interiority that is on its own terms, not in active relationship to the outside world, although of course it is informed by and informs social dynamics. Individuals are not isolated; personalities are shaped in union and opposition to other personalities and larger patterns. And further, cultivated quietness is a forceful stance against oppression. Still, Quashie writes, the social world is not the focus of the inner life; a depth of interiority can manifest as a noted strength against dominance, but the outer world, oppressive or inviting, is not the object of attention in the interior life:

> For sure, the interior can be approximated, hinted at, implied, but its vastness and wildness often escape definitive characterization. And yet the interior *is* expressive; it is articulate and meaningful and has social impact. Indeed, it is the combination of the interior's expressiveness and the inability to articulate it fully that makes interiority such a meaningful idiom for rethinking the nature of black expressiveness. . . . Quiet, then, is the inexpressible expressiveness of this interior, an expressiveness that can appear publicly, have and affect social and political meaning, challenge or counter social discourse, yet none of this is its aim or essence. That is, since the interior is not essentially resistance, then quiet is an expressiveness that is not consumed with intentionality, at least in regard to resistance.[17]

Quashie distinguishes between "quiet" and "silence."[18] For the purposes of this book, however, I use the terms "quiet," "silence," and "stillness" interchangeably. Most importantly, this book evolves Quashie's analysis in that it honors the long, slow process of Black people quieting their thoughts, delving into their own interior lives, and healing the fractures that have widened with intergenerational trauma and social degradation.

The Fierce Urgency of Now: Healing Intergenerational Trauma and Honoring Ancestors

Black people know suffering, the first tenet of the Four Noble Truths of Buddhism. Suffering due to craving—as described in the Second Noble Truth—is also familiar. Furthermore, Black people are concerned with imminent liberation—liberation in the here and now. This freedom is attainable, the Third Noble Truth espouses, if one follows the Noble Eightfold Path.

The Noble Eightfold Path—the Fourth Noble Truth—can be embodied in commitments to ethics (Right Speech, Right Action, and Right Livelihood), concentration (Right Effort, Right Mindfulness, and Right Concentration), and wisdom (Right View and Right Intention).

While adhering to the Noble Eightfold Path, Black Buddhists are concerned with liberation from social conditions: anti-Black racism, cis-heteropatriarchy and cis-heterosexism, homophobia, ageism, and ableism. The forty multilineage teachers and long-term practitioners interviewed for this book delineate between the three types of liberation—political, psychological, and spiritual—that are essential for the full experience of liberation in the United States, due to its long history of racial slavery and segregation and the fact that the United States remains a highly racialized context with overt and covert practices of discrimination.

Joy DeGruy, author of *Post Traumatic Slave Syndrome*, identifies trauma as

> an injury caused by an outside, usually violent, force, event or experience. We can experience this injury physically, emotionally, psychologically, and/or spiritually. Traumas can upset our equilibrium and sense of well-being. If a trauma is severe enough it can distort our attitudes and beliefs. Such distortions often result in dysfunctional behaviors, which can in turn produce unwanted consequences. If one traumatic experience can result in distorted attitudes, dysfunctional behaviors and unwanted consequences, this pattern is magnified exponentially when a person repeatedly experiences severe trauma, and it is much worse when the traumas are caused by human beings.[19]

This definition of trauma is further expanded in Peter A. Levine's *Waking the Tiger: Healing Trauma*. Levine writes that the standard accepted definition of trauma is the response to a stressful occurrence "that is outside the range of usual human experience, and that would be markedly distressing to almost anyone." Levine recounts specific events: "serious threat to one's life or physical integrity; serious threat or harm to one's children, spouse, or other close relatives or friends; sudden destruction of one's home or community; seeing another person who is or has recently been seriously injured or killed as the result of an accident or physical violence."[20]

Arisaka Razak, a Black Buddhist teacher in the Insight tradition—a lineage originating in the Southeast Asian countries of Thailand and Burma—elaborates these definitions of trauma in relation to people whose ancestors were displaced by the slave trade: "Trauma, by definition, attacks the individual's coping skills and threatens the organism's stability. It has been with us since humanity's beginnings as we experience death, illness, loss, and environmental catastrophe. However, sociocultural oppression enacts a burden that is in addition to the normal traumas of life."[21]

Several scholars define trauma as any experience that "threatens one's physical and psychological well-being, including ability to cope."[22] They recognize that traditional diagnostic measures cannot measure historical trauma, such as genocide, slavery, and systematic segregations enacted on one's ancestors. Razak quotes trauma therapist Thema Bryant-Davis, who writes, "Experiences of racism, discrimination, bias, and hate crimes are traumatic in and of themselves."[23] DeGruy locates these contemporary experiences of trauma in historical dehumanization:

> One hundred and eighty years of the Middle Passage and well over 300 years of slavery, rape, and abuse, followed by an illusory freedom. Black codes, convict leasing, and Jim Crow, all codified by our national institutions. Lynching, medical experimentation, redlining, disenfranchisement, grossly unequal treatment in almost every aspect of our society, brutality at the hands of those charged with protecting and serving. Being undesirable strangers in the only land we know. Since the first of our ancestors were brought here hundreds of years ago against their will, we have barely had time to catch our collective breath. That we are here at all can be seen as a testament to our willpower, spiritual strength, and resilience. However, 385 years of physical, psychological, and spiritual torture have left their mark.[24]

Scholars researching the effect of intergenerational trauma on African Americans today describe high rates of child and domestic violence; alcoholism; poor physical health, such as high blood pressure; and psychological disorders, such as chronic feelings of inferiority and low self-esteem.[25] The psychological impact of historical trauma results in "long-term impact on African Americans' cognitive schema of themselves and their social environment, and changes their ability to cope with future experiences."[26]

In light of the particular challenges facing people of African descent living in the United States, Buddhist teachers and long-term practitioners identify meditation practices, including sitting, bowing, and chanting, as practices that elevate spirituality as well as heal the damaged psyche. Black Buddhist teachers posit that dharma teachings and practices can be one path to healing intergenerational trauma.[27]

Healing Intergenerational Trauma in Buddhist Practice

Intergenerational trauma results from systemic conditions: colonialism, enslavement, laws, and institutions that perpetuate persistent poverty, racism, sexism, and misogyny. For many Black Buddhists, resistance to multilayered oppression cannot take place solely within systemically oriented organizing and activism. There must be space for internal healing from systemically inflicted harms as well as the damage inflicted by Black people *within* Black families and communities. Indeed, sixteen of the forty Black Buddhists interviewed for this project spontaneously—without prompting—identified the importance of healing from intergenerational trauma as a primary reason to invest in Buddhist practice. These interviewees described undergoing violence inflicted by authorities and community members; witnessing and experiencing domestic violence as women and children; feeling disconnected from familial roots due to the absence of family members or a lack of knowledge of their families of origin; and engaging in substance abuse and recovery. For these practitioners, systemic racism can be dismantled only with healing intergenerational trauma as a primary practice.

Many Black Buddhist teachers highlight intergenerational trauma as a pattern sometimes experienced as Black men harming Black women, and Black parents abusing Black children. Insight teacher Noliwe Alexander identifies interfamilial violence, substance abuse, and social isolation as three manifestations of intergenerational trauma. For Alexander, who cofounded the Deep Time Liberation retreat to foster intergenerational healing, Black families have had to discern different ways to survive, often at great cost to the parents and children. Alexander's insights are echoed by Gretchen Rohr, a Community Dharma Leader in the Insight tradition. Rohr speaks of entrenched social isolation in Black communities resulting from inadequate health care—especially mental health care—gentrification, the war on drugs, and intracommunity gun violence. "The experience of trauma is on multiple levels . . . a lot of healing is necessary, a lot of rest is necessary."[28]

Ericka Tiffany Phillips, a long-term meditator who was raised in a household steeped in Black Consciousness, describes her practice as a process for deconstructing internalized oppression and healing internalized trauma. Silence, alongside embracing African American communal rituals such as *Kwanzaa*, fosters interdependent (as opposed to individualistic) mentalities within Black communities that, Phillips notes, have been and continue to be essential for Black survival. In these collective, ritual-oriented spaces, dominant narratives fall away. For Phillips, lifting up Black culture was central to familial experiences in her household as a way to confront and contest white supremacist messages:

> When I encountered Buddhist practice it was the first time I felt, "Here is a practice for undoing, for uncovering, excavating, and transforming internalized oppression." It's one thing to know it and to see it, but it's another thing to actually heal. The practice didn't feel foreign to me. It didn't feel new. It felt very much like language being given to something that I was trying to figure out . . . here was a practice of liberation and practice of freedom.
>
> And even though I was learning from teachers who didn't have that language and who weren't really connecting it to my experience, because that experience is so in my body, and because I had the language internally, I think it just worked. The teachings spoke directly to my heart, directly to my body, directly to my mind.[29]

Buddhist teachings and practices furthermore serve as a refuge when countering systemic violence enacted by the police state. Devin Berry, a teacher in the Insight tradition, highlights racial profiling and violence against Black men and women as contemporary trauma-inducing situations that have historical roots. Berry recounts numerous incidents of racially induced trauma that for many years fueled his rage. He describes his ultimate commitment to meditation as a practice of healing:

> [While living in Marin County, California] I had thirteen interactions with the police over a three-year period and was never arrested for any-

thing, never charged with anything, but [I experienced] this as a constant attempt to humiliate me and not show me dignity or respect whatsoever. And it really felt like that's just what it was. They saw this really young black man driving an expensive car and that was reason enough. I had had a few interactions with the police previously but these interactions shook me as I felt quite isolated in the almost all white enclave I was living in during that period of my life.

Berry describes how his visibility was criminalized in the small Northern California town, especially after traditional work hours when he played basketball or went to the library:

There was a string of petty crimes that took place at one point, someone, not the police, made a sketch made of the person that they thought it was, the sketch was literally me! At that point, I couldn't live in the town. . . . I didn't have the tools to work with that, and so I just bounced from mistrust, resentment to anger and hatred and rage.

I had a similar incident in college where I had gone to a house party with a small multiracial group of friends. Two of us were black . . . the only black people there. We were assaulted at the door after exchanging words with the hosts and my boy got lost in the crowd and was attacked by a white mob. I ran off the property and made my way across the street to find help. . . . Somebody called the police. The mob then ran up the stairs, grabbed me and dragged me to the street. The police showed up just as my friends and I were fighting the mob and arrested us. So, I had this fire, this rage at what I considered acute antiblack oppression. I began to feel constantly under threat . . . real and perceived.[30]

The racial profiling Berry describes is echoed by other Black teachers and long-term practitioners. Ralph Steele, a teacher in the Insight tradition, remembers his father's assassination at the hands of the Ku Klux Klan in Georgia, a direct vestige of the white supremacy of segregation. Joshua Alafia, a Community Dharma Leader in the Insight tradition, recalls experiencing racial profiling from police officers as well as being targeted by members of a Black community in Los Angeles.

I think [the desire for meditation] comes from us wanting to heal ourselves. I was someone who had been traumatized by my parents' divorce, traumatized by my father's alcoholism and later crack [addiction]. Slight micro-traumas of just being of mixed heritage. Having an African American father and a mother from Texas with European and indigenous ancestry. Growing up in Texas, dealing with a lot of racism, dealing with police who put the gun to my head as an adolescent. A young gang member put his gun to my head as a teenager when I went to see my dad in South Central. And the guys who sold him crack got so jarred by seeing this guy they sold crack to walking with his son. They spat at him and I was like, "Yeah, what's up?" and they put a gun to my head.[31]

Alafia's practices of healing include somatic movements, such as qigong. For Alafia, as for many Black practitioners, incorporating movement practices into meditation practices facilitates the process of identifying trauma in the body and working to heal it.[32]

In addition to embracing meditation, somatic therapies, and devotional practices, Black Buddhists have engaged in street protests and online activism, such as Black Lives Matter, #SayHerName, and #MuteRKelly. Berry is conscious of the unwarranted violence against not only Black men but also Black women, who are often afflicted at the hands of family members. He recalls becoming exceedingly conscious of gendered and sexualized violence against Black women at a Deep Time Liberation retreat in 2018.

We are exploring the sources of trauma and where it extends into today. When you really look at where it extends, gender and intersectionality are there, without a doubt. We can't just have a huge ceremony and play the drums and speak about our Africanness and speak about the legacy of oppression and slavery and not bring the roles black men, women, black queer folks, trans folks play, and the weight of patriarchy. So even though we're all oppressed . . . many black men still play out old conditioning, both consciously and subconsciously perpetuating the same ole' same ole'. That happens over and over again to black women.[33]

The violence enacted against women takes multiple forms, including psychological, physical, and sexual. And not only is violence disproportionately directed at Black women, it is also a norm directed at children in many Black households. Psychologists suggest that corporal punishment against Black children was normalized during and after slavery, as Black people turned the punishments inflicted against them on their family members. Jozen Tamori Gibson, a Theravada Vipassana (Insight) teacher and Soto Zen lay student, remembers the unfolding of patriarchy in their childhood:

> In my elementary and teen years, there was just something that didn't feel right when it came to being told by my elders to act like a man, be a man, act a certain way. I always had this question in the back of my heart: what does that even mean? What are you talking about? . . . That language was not aligned with non-harming. For example, it could be violent. It could be aggressive and abusive. I grew up in a home in which I was witnessing domestic violence, witnessing adult on child discipline which was actually violent. As an adult today I joke with friends about when we had to go get the whip or the switch or whatever it was and we now laugh claiming that as a part of our healing as a community. Yet for me to be asked by an elder to go get the whip, the belt, and bring it back to the person who is then going to beat me with it, that whole sequence of things is not just receiving belts on the bottom, on the backside. But it's the being told to go get it, looking for it, taking a moment to see if I can get away with bringing the thin one, remembering that the thin one actually was more painful than a big one last [beating]. What was that about? And that whole process—looking at the various options that would then lead to my demise for that day—felt like a lifetime. And then *Dhamma* getting me to a point of recognizing that everyone in that moment was dealing with some pain. The adult was just living out once again what they experienced and were taught. And the idea that was popping up in my heart was that this has to end at some point. I'm going to have children. I'm not going to treat my children this way. So that being a form of a vow, if you will: "Let me remember this so that I don't perpetuate [violence]."[34]

Indeed, as Gibson describes, painful family dynamics spur much of the healing work undertaken by Black Buddhist teachers and long-term practitioners. Such commitment arises from suffering widespread inter-generational violence, which was a routine facet of life for Black people under slavery. Frederick Douglass describes in his *Narrative* how violence was meted out to slaves for both small and serious infractions or simply for the sadistic pleasure of whites who asserted their authority. Such corporal punishment was later extended within families. In *The Warmth of Other Suns*, journalist Isabel Wilkerson writes,

> The worst thing that could happen to a colored child in the South was for a parent to hear that a child was acting up. There would be no appeals, the punishment was swift and physical. The arbitrary nature of grown people's wrath gave colored children practice for life in the caste system, which is why parents, forced to train their children in the ways of subservience, treated their children as the white people running things treated them. It was preparation for the lower-caste role children were expected to have mastered by puberty.[35]

In short, Black Buddhist teachers describe how extensive violence from white people and white institutions was extended into Black families as normal and continues to function as routine in the present day. So too were family separations, due to the forced splitting of families on the auction block and migrations from the South to the North. These twin aspects—violence and separation—often took place within Black families upon emancipation and in many families and communities. Furthermore, these traumatizing facets of life continue to reverberate in the twenty-first century. Family separations remain a source of acute pain. Kabir Hypolite, a long-term practitioner in the Insight tradition, reflects on gaps within his family history, which were a primary motivation for him to attend the Deep Time Liberation retreat in 2018.

> I think we [attended the retreat] because we're haunted. Each of us, I think . . . were haunted by a series of questions and a yearning to know more about where we came from and who we were. And that's largely out of broken homes and untold histories and fractured relationships. . . . I have very little history about my family, beyond my grandmother, and very little almost just a couple of stories really about my grandfather. And so, I have always been kind of curious, like, you know, where do we come

from? Who are we? Who was he? . . . It's like there's this kind of haunting. Who are we? Where do we come from and what is our history, what's our story? And I felt like everybody in that room in Mississippi [during the retreat] was trying to answer that same question or trying to heal something, fill in some blanks, that kind of thing.[36]

Thus, as many Black teachers across multiple Buddhist lineages discuss, healing through spiritual practice is a necessary component of addressing systemic violence. Lama Rod Owens, a teacher in the Kagyu Tibetan tradition, states that in the quest for liberation, deep healing of trauma must take place:

I hear people talk about liberation positions, Black Lives Matter and other movements, and I'm always thinking, what liberations are you talking about? What do you really mean? So I'm thinking of psychosocial liberation. I'm thinking about social liberation and ultimate liberation together. I'm also thinking about the place of trauma, too. So if all of these oppressive systems were lifted in an instant, we would actually recreate them, because that's how trauma works. Trauma is about recreating and falling into cycles of experience. We have to start doing the work of undoing trauma right now.[37]

Owens speaks from the personal experience of working with dharma practices to heal long-term depression, an experience he recounts in the books *Radical Dharma* and *Love and Rage*. His ready acknowledgment of how intergenerational trauma impacts people of African descent has influenced other Black Buddhist practitioners, fostering a conversation about healing alongside activism. Breeshia Wade, author of *Grieving While Black: An Antiracist Take on Oppression and Sorrow*, reflected during the 2021 Black and Buddhist Summit:

I think about the losses that we, as Black folks have faced, are facing, as a result of what it means to be Black in America. I think immediately of how that is tied to impermanence, and to the losses that we're non consensually facing, whether it's the loss of a job opportunity or because of our name; whether it's the loss of safety when we are walking down the street in a Black body; whether it's the loss of feeling of connection to community, when we're walking through our own neighborhood and we feel other and out of place. . . . And then, how that gets siphoned back and pushed back onto us, into our bodies, and that's something we're constantly moving through and moving with. . . . And that just brings me back to the practice and why we're here.[38]

The centuries of trauma inflicted upon people of African descent, from the origins of the transatlantic slave trade to the brutal conditions of slavery and the present-day penal system and systemic racism, require forms and practices for intergenerational healing. For Buddhist teachers and practitioners of African descent, dharma teachings on liberation and practices of compassion form a path toward healing intergenerational trauma. Contemporary meditation-based practices of focusing the mind and not avoiding one's suffering but conversely looking directly at one's suffering as a practice of healing have facilitated Black Buddhists' interruption of cycles of trauma, rage, and internalized racism. As Owens states, liberation is not merely about lifting oppressive yokes. Rather, it includes healing intergenerational and internalized patterns of coping with trauma, ultimately to practice and live in such a way that release is actualized. Black Buddhist teachers and long-term practitioners, alongside psychotherapists, teach that confronting one's depth of suffering, rather than avoiding or masking it, fosters healing.

Buddhism and Psychotherapy: Spiritual and Psychological Integration

Employing dharma practices to heal trauma is integral to how the dharma has unfolded in the West. Indeed, as Black people are investigating the dharma, an extensive conversation on the merits of Buddhism for psychological healing is taking place. The conversation between the fields of Buddhism and psychology initially was documented in 1960, with the publication of *Zen Buddhism and Psychoanalysis*, cowritten by Erich Fromm, a prominent psychologist, and D. T. Suzuki, the Japanese master who brought Zen to the United States. Since this pioneering publication, contemporary practitioners of Buddhism and psychology and psychiatry continue to expound upon numerous overlapping approaches to psychological wellness.[39]

Not only does the practice of meditation allow the practitioner to steadily observe the processes of the mind, proponents of psychological healing and sitting practices declare that meditation also provides the practitioner with agency. Polly Young-Eisendrath writes that much of human suffering arises from a sense of isolation and fear. In response, therapy and meditation can foster mutually reinforcing impulses:

> Eventually, the patient discovers what Jung (1916/1969) has called the "transcendent function": an ability to contain tensions and conflicts without prematurely deciding that they are "good" or "bad." . . . This function allows the patient to keep an open mind in the face of momentary impulses, feelings, pressures, and so on. And finally, the patient finds that the skill of the transcendent function can be used in many life situations in which the patient had previously reacted through old destructive emotional habits. The interdependence of patient and therapist, in the discovery of meaning and the transcendent function, eventually allows the patient to "suffer with" self and others. Suffering-with is the essence of "compassion" in its ability to witness pain and adversity, and to help without judgment.[40]

In short, psychoanalysis, psychotherapy, and Buddhism foster understanding of unconscious motivations and developmental deficits in the self, thereby leading to an ability to tolerate suffering, feel compassion, and shift damaging patterns and reactions.[41] In an essay titled "The Encounter of Buddhism and Psychology," Franz Aubrey Metcalf acknowledges that the two fields of Buddhism and psychology are divided in numerous ways but that practitioners in both fields share similar assumptions and, even more importantly, mutual respect:

> The mainstream of this dialogue has been founded on powerful shared assumptions. Both traditions assume that they respond to similar human needs. They assume that they uncover and reshape dynamics inherent to the human mind. Further, they assume that they undermine and possibly eliminate defenses the ego or self creates for its survival. In all this, they share a therapeutic self-image. Both traditions assume that the person or mind develops through life, and is continually being created by experience and by its own reflexive thought. Both assume that the mind is

inherently self-corrective when provided with insights into its dysfunctional dynamics. They assume that their practices are able to provide such insights, and an ongoing path on which to interrogate them. What is perhaps most remarkable, though, and serves as a respectful dialogue between these traditions, is the assumption of each that the *other* follows a similar path and that if it does not provide the same insights it at least provides complementary ones. Such mutual respect provides the ground in which the field of *Buddhism and psychology* has taken root.[42]

Other scholars of psychology who are also practitioners of Buddhism similarly reiterate the overlap between the two fields. Jeffrey B. Rubin, in his text *Psychotherapy and Buddhism: Toward an Integration*, describes in great detail how "psychoanalysis and Buddhism are both deeply concerned with the problem of human suffering. One key purpose of psychoanalysis, according to Freud, was to eliminate neurotic misery. A central task of Buddhism is to achieve Enlightenment, which is said to eradicate suffering. Each tradition presents a highly sophisticated theory and methodology for attempting to alleviate human misery."[43]

The integration of psychology with Buddhism in the West is broader than academic discourse; indeed, it has reached deeply into sanghas in the United States. In a profile on Josh Korda, the leader of Dharma Punx NYC + Brooklyn, scholar Ann Gleig describes the "relational turn" employed in Western interpretations of Theravada teachings.[44] Similarly, the integration of psychology and Buddhism is also seen at prominent retreat centers such as Spirit Rock Retreat Center in Marin County, California.

Collectively, these scholars and teachers promote the integration of psychology and Buddhism. However, Black Buddhist practitioners declare that "decolonized" psychological approaches to healing intergenerational trauma—which includes recognizing the history of colonization and ongoing traumatizing violence—is a necessary component to healing. Furthermore, as greater numbers of therapists emphasize how intergenerational trauma is stored in the body, there is increasing awareness that somatic practices, in addition to meditation and psychological therapies, must be included in healing trauma. Black Buddhist teachers are increasingly focused on somatic practices alongside meditation to foster psychological wellness.

Race and Culture in U.S. Convert Buddhism: Illuminating White Supremacy

As Black people seek out dharma teachings in an effort to heal intergenerational trauma, they often encounter reiterations of white supremacy in predominantly white sanghas. A number of critical texts on convert Buddhism starkly illuminate the culture of white supremacy experienced by Black Buddhist teachers and practitioners. These texts make three overlapping critiques: (1) white supremacy functions as a dominant culture within "American Buddhism"; (2) "American Buddhism" distinguishes itself from "heritage Buddhism," privileging silence and solitude over sangha and devotional practices; and (3) white leaders in predominantly white sanghas fail to understand the need for culturally safe spaces, or "affinity groups."

The texts on the topic of Buddhism and race take a critical approach to the transmission of the dharma to the United States, in that white, middle- and upper-class practitioners who have flocked to sanghas inevitably reproduce white supremacist racial hierarchies in broader U.S. society.[45] Larry Ward, a scholar of Buddhism and teacher in Thich Nhat Hanh's Order of Interbeing, writes in his 2020 book *America's Racial Karma*, "To assume that our current racial dysfunction is disconnected from America's continental and Eurocentric past is a delusion of the highest order. Our racial past echoes through the air we breathe and permeates the ground on which we walk."[46] Without a critical analysis of white supremacy, and without practical attempts to build racially diverse sanghas from the outset, convert Buddhist community members reinforce dominant cultural norms, often without any communal understanding of the implicit and recurrent meanings of their behavior. As scholar Jasmine Syedullah writes in her essay "The Unbearable Will to Whiteness,"

Whiteness is more than an individual identity. It is more than an abstract category. It is a desire, a destiny, an investment in a future that partitions the presence of the past in the present to mirror its imagination of itself onto the world for all time. We sense it before we understand it. Whiteness walks into an American Buddhist community and announces itself without speaking a word. It calls our attention and orients our sense of place. We are accounting for it with our language, with our gestures. We anticipate all it means in an instant and yet it has its limitations. My own arrival into white spaces, as a black, dark skinned, woman signals to those that have already made themselves at home there that I must be in want of or require something, that I must require being welcomed or a pass to enter, to belong. It is an alienating sensation to say the least.[47]

In another text, *Radical Dharma: Talking Race, Love, and Liberation*, Syedullah—together with Rev. angel Kyodo williams and Lama Rod Owens—argues that the whiteness of and racism within mainstream Buddhist communities and organizations in the United States "amplify" rather than "deconstruct" systems of suffering. The internalization of hatred due to skin color is a particular form of suffering. It can be healed by dharma practice—yet the isolation experienced in predominantly white sanghas, along with microaggressions and an inability to relate to cultural perspectives, reiterate the very systems that initially created harm.

Thus it is critical, these writers argue, that Buddhist sanghas acknowledge the social conditions of racism and the unique perspectives of Black Buddhist practitioners. Owens states that in a racialized social reality there is not the possibility of Black people "being at home in whiteness," for it "goes hand-in-glove with the presumption that everything whiteness does must be best, right, noble, beautiful, moral, and productive."[48] Owens further writes, "Dharma practice called my attention to the deepest of my investments in white supremacy and made me feel, without sugar coats, without apology or redemption, how deeply destructive it is to live in the afterlife of slavery as the unembodied trauma of the white experience."[49]

This critique of whiteness has been acknowledged by a few academics and retreat leaders. There are developing efforts to train long-term Black meditators as sangha and retreat leaders and to highlight the emerging publications of Black teachers in trainings. At the same time, as scholar Sharon Suh articulates, "This invisible whiteness as the center and normative yardstick to measure nonwhites operates in many Buddhist sanghas and meditation centers where white privilege is shrouded in ignoble but seemingly golden silence, a gilded refusal to speak up lest one breaches the oneness that emptiness and interdependence connote. The silence venerated in the space of retreat halls echoes the silent refusal of white supremacy to lay bare its privilege."[50] Suh, a religious studies professor, critiques the white myopia of Buddhist scholars in the academy as well as practitioners in sanghas. Her sentiments are echoed by Hsiao-Lan Hu, a former doctoral student under the Buddhist feminist scholar Rita Gross.[51] In a 2019 essay, Hu illuminates the attitudes of racial superiority held by her dissertation advisor. Hu notes that Gross, while a sharply critical thinker, articulated comments indicating a sense of racial superiority, especially with regard to immigrant, or "heritage," Buddhist communities.

Hu and Suh's observations are reiterated by Gleig, author of *American Dharma: Buddhism Beyond Modernity*, and by Larry Yang, author of *Awakening Together: The Spiritual Practice of Inclusivity and Community*.[52] Yang, a teacher in the Insight tradition who self-identifies as a gay Chinese man, argues for greater awareness of the role of culture in predominantly white sanghas that are invested in transmitting the dharma.[53] To avoid wrestling with the implications of whiteness is to fail to see clearly, a core tenet within Buddhism. Yang writes,

> Shared experiences of marginalization and oppression within the dominant, European American, hetero-based, and able-bodied normative culture actually reinforce cultural values of interdependency among such groups: we strengthen our core identity in order to survive the unconscious impact of the dominant culture's oppressive unconsciousness. Cultural interpretations of the Dharma focused on individuality and personal experience by teachers of European American descent and their communities do not resonate with those of us who share a cultural inclination towards interdependent ways of living and being in the world. We often experience a subtle but impactful sense of exclusion when the dominant culture's interpretation of the Buddha's teachings is offered through a cultural lens that overlooks the value of togetherness in favor of personal, often solitary, practice.[54]

Yang describes how in each setting in which it arrived, Buddhism adapted to local cultural forms. This is especially noted in Chinese and Tibetan Buddhism. Indeed, as numerous Buddhist scholars elaborate,

Buddhism took on the cultural forms of the location in which it was embraced: trade, societal norms (including food and clothing), images, and spiritual practices. As Buddhism originated in India and spread throughout Asia, the tradition adopted the varying cultural forms the teachings encountered in Sri Lanka, Burma, Thailand, Japan, China, and eventually Tibet.[55]

As Buddhist teachings and practices were introduced to European and American would-be adherents in the nineteenth century, white communities claimed for themselves the teachings and practices, adapting them to a culture of white supremacy. Insight teacher JoAnna Hardy defines cultural appropriation as "the act of an individual from a particular, usually privileged or dominant culture, adopting cultural and religious elements of a marginalized culture. In doing so, cultural practices or symbols are overly simplified, stripped of their meaning and significance, and can replicate systems of oppression."[56] These predominantly white convert Buddhist communities have emphasized aspects of the dharma that appealed to them, especially solitary meditation, while ignoring other practices associated with "culture" (that is, people of color [POC]), such as devotional bowing. Convert Buddhist practices in the United States emphasize psychological understandings of the self, silence, solitude, and individualism above other "cultural" forms of practice.[57] Yet the emphasis on individualism can be particularly alienating for Black practitioners, many of whom have their roots in the collective experiences of the Black Church and value ancestors and community. The individuality and isolation in predominantly white sanghas can reinforce the need for "affinity groups"—smaller sanghas within a larger sangha. The development of such affinity groups is itself a critique of white hegemonic culture that dominates convert Buddhist communities.[58]

The cultural isolation within the dominant culture to which many Black practitioners refer is a theme throughout critical studies of convert Buddhism. Indeed, Ruth King's *Mindful of Race: Transforming Racism from the Inside Out* delineates broad cultural strokes within white and POC communities. King observes that white practitioners tend toward individualism—solitary meditation and limited contact—yet POC communities tend to embrace collective practices that strengthen a sense of community.

Sharing like experiences—for example, by crying together, drawing strength from one another, strategizing together, and healing together—are ways in which many POC cope with the pain inherent in racial oppression and internalized oppression. Racial suffering has united POC, and most tend to believe that racial survival and progress have largely been due to the racial group and its many sacrifices. Thus, they may think, *Should I experience any success, I owe it to the group that supported me.*[59]

The critical literature on Buddhism and race illuminates the dominant trends in Western convert Buddhism. As a result, the experiences of Black Buddhist practitioners are gaining attention. However, broader studies on the distinctive dharma interpretations and devotional practices of teachers and practitioners of African descent have yet to be written. This book speaks to the gap in the emerging field of critical Buddhist studies.

Methodology

I am, first and foremost, a scholar of critical race theory and religious ethics and a practitioner of the Insight (Theravada) tradition of Buddhism. Thus I approach this book as a scholar-practitioner. Methodologically, I combine ethnography, specifically in-depth interviews and participant observation, with discourse analysis. Over the course of two and a half years (April 2017 to December 2019), I interviewed forty Black Buddhist teachers and long-term practitioners (whom I defined as practitioners who have steadily practiced for at least ten years). Interviewees practice in different traditions, including Theravada/Insight/Vipassana, Kagyu Tibetan, Nichiren Shu, Order of Interbeing, Shambhala, Soto Zen, and Triratna. Twenty-two of my interviewees locate themselves within the Insight tradition,[60] although three also claim different lineages. Seven interviewees identify as Zen teachers and practitioners. Three teachers and practitioners are part of the Shambhala community. In addition to these three traditions, I interviewed one teacher or practitioner from the following traditions: Kagyu Tibetan, Nichiren Shu, Order of Interbeing, and Triratna. Four teachers or practitioners identify with different lineages and claim Buddhism as foundational to their spiritual identity but do not claim any one lineage as their spiritual home.

Seven interviewees use the term "biracial" in addition to "Black" to self-identify. At least half self-identify as LGBTQIA. This may correspond to the leadership of the Black Lives Matter national and local movements, in which queer and gender-nonconforming identities are validated and embraced. Addressing gender and sexuality alongside race is a core part of the BLM global network, which states, "We affirm the lives of Black queer and trans folks, disabled folks, undocumented folks, folks with records, women, and all Black lives along the gender spectrum. Our network centers those who have been marginalized within Black liberation movements."[61] Privileging Black trans, queer, gender-nonconforming, and intersex people is also a central policy commitment of the Movement for Black Lives, a coalition of fifty Black-led organizations and allies.[62] We do not have data on the movement as a whole, and it is possible that my sample reflects a greater proportion of people who self-identify as LGBTQIA than in the Black Lives Matter movement more generally, as the result of my solicitation of interviewees through existing contacts via networking. Yet many of the Black people who are drawn to Buddhism with whom I spoke feel exiled from the church due to their sexuality, and I suspect that the teachers and long-term practitioners reflect broader trends in the demographic of Black Buddhists, as is also seen in the leadership of the Black Lives Matter movement.

Interviewees were chosen via word-of-mouth networking. I am particularly indebted to the organizers of the Gatherings I and II, two retreats for Buddhist Teachers of Black African Descent, for allowing me access to names and email addresses of invitees for the purposes of researching this book.

Each interviewee gave informed consent. Each responded to seven open-ended questions, along with follow-up questions. Interviews ranged from forty-five minutes to an hour and a half in person or via Zoom. Interview questions and procedures were approved by the Institutional Review Board at Warren Wilson College.

Interviewees are identified by first and last name and/or their given dharma name. The interviews were transcribed and analyzed according to an inductive method process described in *The Practice of Qualita-*

tive Research (2011). The interviews were analyzed for descriptive codes, which are used to identify interviewees' thoughts, feelings, and motivations, as expressed in the conversations. I then developed analytic codes through a process of reviewing the data.

In addition to conducting forty interviews, I have included excerpts of dharma talks from ten Black dharma teachers as well as excerpts from two anthologies edited by Black Buddhists: *Dharma, Color, and Culture* (2004) and *Black and Buddhist* (2020). Furthermore, I have included excerpts of articles and essays by Black Buddhist teachers that have been published in academic books and in popular magazines such as *Lion's Roar*. In sum, in an attempt to represent the broader Black Buddhist community, this book uplifts the voices of more than seventy Black Buddhist teachers and long-term practitioners.

My participant observation included participating in two retreats for Black Buddhist teachers of African Descent: "The Gathering I," held in New York City at Union Theological Seminary, October 19–21, 2018; and "The Fierce Urgency of Now: The Gathering II," held at Spirit Rock Retreat Center in Marin County, California, October 7–15, 2019.

As a participant observer, I employed a methodology known as participatory action research (PAR).[63] Since June 2005, I have participated in two different dharma lineages, an American Zen Tradition influenced by Soto and Rinzai lineages, for one year, and the Insight tradition, since 2006. I maintain a daily sitting practice and regularly attend retreats. At the time of writing, I am participating in an online "Mindfulness Meditation Teacher Certification Training" led by teachers in the Insight tradition.

Outline of Chapters

Chapter 1, "The Tradition of Buddhism: Lineages, Culture, Race, and Liberation," provides a social history of Buddhism, including the story of the Buddha's enlightenment and the spread of Buddhism throughout Asia. It explains the emergence of three distinct lineages—Theravada, Mahayana, and Vajrayana—and uplifts the figure of the Bodhisattva. This chapter furthermore chronicles Western engagement with Buddhism, including the development of a nineteenth-century Orientalist lens, Buddhist monastics' resistance to colonialism, and a set of "streamlined" teachings on meditation adopted by adherents from the United States. This chapter also outlines how white Western practitioners married psychology with Buddhism while dismissing "cultural" practices, leading scholars to designate the emergence of "two Buddhisms" operating in the United States. Critical scholars, in turn, have identified practices of cultural appropriation in American Buddhism and complex dynamics among Asian and Black practitioners. This chapter concludes with the meaning of Buddhism for Black Buddhist writers, whose publications have significantly expanded since 2016.

Chapter 2, "From the Plantation to the Prison: The Causes and Conditions of Intergenerational Trauma," investigates the causes and conditions of contemporary Black trauma by providing an overview of colonialism, dislocation, slavery, segregation, and contemporary institutionalized racism. It illuminates the degrading constructs of Black bodies, the emotional trauma of separated families, the antebellum penal institutions that preceded mass imprisonment in the present day, the terror of lynchings, and the consequences of the Great Migration from the South to the North. This chapter further identifies numerous contemporary traumatic wounds disproportionately inflicted upon Black people, including mass incarceration, school pushouts, violence against Black women, and microaggressions, including within predominantly white Buddhist sanghas. In naming these numerous, overlapping traumatizing experiences, scholars and Black Buddhist teachers point to the tremendous threat and violence that continues to be enacted upon Black bodies. Black Buddhists turn to dharma practices and somatic therapies to heal multifaceted intergenerational trauma. This chapter concludes with acknowledgment of how meditation practices, supported by somatic therapies, can positively impact the nervous system to heal racially induced intergenerational trauma.

Chapter 3, "Honoring Ancestors in Black Buddhist Practice: Rituals of Devotion and Resilience," examines how Black Buddhists have embraced ancestral practices as they elaborate dharma teachings in convert Buddhist communities. Such practices include storytelling, devotional bowing, drumming, dancing, and chanting, as well as honoring African-derived images and ancestors on Buddhist altars. This chapter emphasizes the importance of honoring ancestors and the land within different lineages as well as practices for incorporating indigenous rituals into Buddhist practices. For indigenous-oriented Buddhist practitioners, the history of ancestors carries meaning for themselves, their family members, and their broader community. Furthermore, the courage, determination, and perseverance embodied by ancestors are mirrored in the resilience of the land to withstand natural forces. Even when African Americans acknowledge their complex relationship with the land of the United States—land they were violently made to work as enslaved peoples to garner profits for white slave owners—they acknowledge the importance of feeling located on land and honoring the presence of First Nation peoples who populated the land prior to colonization. The ability to see the land as sacred, beyond the history of European colonialism, has been incorporated into numerous African American healing initiatives.

Chapter 4, "Turning toward External Conditions: Political and Psychological Freedom in the Black Radical Tradition," uplifts Black Radical ancestors and examines the history of embracing psychological liberation in Black communities, drawing on three traditions within Black Radicalism: the Pan-African and Black Power Movements, the Black Church Tradition, and the Black Feminist Movement. Contemporary Black Buddhist practitioners are directly and indirectly indebted to the thinkers and leaders of these movements and organizations. The Black Power Movement emphasized communal uplift and care, particularly programs that offered free breakfasts for children, medical care for members of the community, and schools that taught messages of freedom. The Black Church Tradition emphasizes the Spirit and dance and remains important for Black Buddhists who were raised in church communities and often stay connected to the church even as they join sanghas. Finally, contemporary Black Buddhists are highly indebted to the Black Feminist Tradition, particularly its emphasis on gender, sexuality, class distinctions, and intersectionality, as well as acknowledging interpersonal dynamics between Black men and women, and violent state oppression. The writings of Audre Lorde, bell hooks, and Alice Walker are particularly influential.

Chapter 5, "Turning toward Internal Suffering: Dharma for the Practice of Psychological and Spiritual Liberation," investigates Buddhist teachings that speak directly to spiritual, psychological, and political liberation for Black Buddhists. This chapter outlines Buddhist teachings embraced by Black teachers and practitioners: the Four Noble Truths and the Noble Eightfold Path; the Three Marks of Existence; self and non-self; ultimate and relative reality; the *Satipatthana Sutta*; and awareness practices—particularly awareness of the body and how the Black body has been racialized. This chapter illuminates how Black Buddhists are both deeply invested in the tenets of their traditions and yet highly innovative in explaining seemingly obscure concepts to communities that have been historically dehumanized.

Chapter 6, "The Body as a Vehicle for Liberation: Gender and Sexuality in Black Buddhist Writings," illuminates differing understandings of embodiment within Buddhism, particularly in the Mahayana and Vajrayana traditions. This chapter explains the importance of gender even as sutras state that form is unimportant for liberation, thereby providing a foundation for understanding nonbinary identity through a Buddhist lens. This chapter furthermore explores the importance of female embodiment—particularly in the portrayal of Tibetan Buddhist deities—as well as Tantric teachings on cultivating sexual union as a path to enlightenment. Finally, this chapter explores implications for honoring female embodiment and sensuality for Black writers and Black Buddhist teachers. It extensively investigates Audre Lorde's writings on erotic power and James Baldwin's writings of sensuality in rejecting white supremacist norms and embracing life. It concludes with an analysis of three Black Buddhist writers who speak directly to the importance of honoring embodiment, sexuality, sensuality, and joy.

Chapter 7, "Love and Liberation: Collective Care and Refuge in Black Buddhist Communities," illuminates how love and liberation are at the heart of Buddhism and the Black Radical Tradition. This chapter speaks to working with rage, violence, and familial trauma while committing to core Buddhist teachings on Right Action, relating skillfully to suffering, and cultivating presence, inner spaciousness, and emptiness. Finally, this chapter argues that, in practicing the dharma, Black Buddhists *live into* the Black Radical aspiration to psychological liberation by practicing teachings that foster clearly seeing the false constructs of white supremacy, and cultivating love for oneself and one's community.

This volume concludes with an analysis of how forms of Buddhism practiced by Black people speak to grassroots organizers who are challenging systemic oppression in the present day. It speaks to the importance of healing inner conditioning even as Black activists seek to change external conditions, by practicing stillness in the movement for liberation.

1

The Tradition of Buddhism

Lineages, Culture, Race, and Liberation

When people from groups who have historically found
themselves socially, economically, and politically outside
the margins, hear that the Buddha taught liberation, nothing more needs to be said. There is no need to proselytize
or seduce. All our lives we thirst for freedom, and when we
recognize the path that will lead us there, our hearts validate
that recognition. To wake up is the task at hand. Not wishing that our lives are better, nor different, we wake up to the
reality of our lives, just as they are.

To see this reality clearly is the first step to freedom. Such
is the significance of the Four Noble Truths to the racially
and culturally excluded people living today in the United
States. Teachings of liberation heard clearly in a culture
driven by ignorance, fear, anger, and hate is like the breaking
of chains after centuries of subjugation. That is the gift the
Buddha Shakyamuni gave us.

—Ryūmon Hilda Gutiérrez Baldoquín[1]

In order to understand the meaning of liberation for Black Buddhists, it
is important to understand the evolution of Buddhism as a tradition—
including the spread and assimilation of dharma teachings throughout
Asia—and how encounters with Europeans shaped contemporary forms
of Buddhism practiced in the West today. Furthermore, it is critical to
contextualize the emergence of Buddhism in the United States. This
chapter explores the theory of "two Buddhisms" and dynamics among
Asian and Black Buddhists, and how Black Buddhists, through memoirs
and published essays, offer a distinctive interpretation of the dharma. In
short, this chapter provides an overview of Buddhism as it has emerged

over several centuries, with a particular view of its meaning for Black Buddhists in the twenty-first-century United States.

Buddha Shakyamuni and His Teachings

Black Buddhists are inspired by the historical person known as Siddhartha Gautama, a prince born into the Shakya clan who, upon his enlightenment, was identified as the "Buddha" (Enlightened One) and known as Buddha Shakyamuni (Enlightened One of the Shakyamuni clan). Joshua Bee Alafia, a Community Dharma Leader in the Insight tradition, upholds the Buddha as a warrior to emulate.[2] Pamela Ayo Yetunde, who trained as an aspirant in Thich Nhat Hanh's Order of Interbeing and is a Community Dharma Leader in the Insight tradition, affirms that despite the Buddha's wealthy, sheltered upbringing, Buddhism has much to offer Black people:

> Let's look at one Buddha story that is culturally irrelevant for most African Americans today. Siddhartha was born into a wealthy family. Most African Americans are not wealthy; in fact, many of us are poor due to generations of impoverishment created by wealthy people. Siddhartha's father protected him from knowing about the countless ways people suffer. African Americans are not protected from the suffering of economic disparities, racism, violence, injustice, mass incarceration, rape, lack of nutrition, and illness.
>
> Siddhartha . . . was shocked when he saw that people actually got sick, old, and died. African Americans encounter death well before they become teenagers and young adults. In fact, many die when they are teenagers.
>
> Siddhartha left his home, encountered a new reality, realized he had been lied to, and chose not to return home. Instead, he entered the forest to learn how to avoid illness, aging, and death. After years of spiritual practice in the forest, Siddhartha became enlightened. Then, as the Buddha, he proclaimed the first noble truth: there is suffering! This is not a profound insight from an African American perspective. *Yet hidden in this story of the Buddha's life is the substance of myth that can reconnect African Americans to a larger story and inspire them to advocate for their lives.*[3]

Indeed, the story of the Buddha is the story of a prince born in northeast India in the fifth century BCE.[4] As the son of a king of the Shakya clan, Siddhartha was cloistered behind palace walls until the age of twenty-nine, whereupon he ventured outside the gates and encountered human beings in various states of decay: old age, sickness, and death. He thereafter left the palace to seek spiritual enlightenment, practicing with rigorous Hindu teachers for six years. Unable to achieve enlightenment through strict, renunciate methods, Siddhartha recalled experiencing peaceful feelings in childhood while in nature. He eventually realized a "middle way" between strict renunciation and material comfort with its sensual pleasures.[5]

Legend describes that on the night of his enlightenment Siddhartha settled under a bodhi tree and began meditating. The forces of *mara*, a demon, attacked his mind relentlessly, attempting to sow greed, hatred, fear, confusion, and doubt. In response, Siddhartha calmly touched the earth, summoning her support. With the help of mother earth, mara's arrows could not harm Siddhartha; the arrows turned into flowers.

The Four Noble Truths

After his enlightenment, as an *arahant*—one who has gained awareness of the true nature of existence, and consequently become enlightened—the Buddha taught an initial sermon on the Four Noble Truths. The First Noble Truth is that life is dissatisfactory (*dukkha*) due to four aspects of existence: (1) physical conditions that are subject to decay, (2) painful mental and emotional experiences, (3) unpleasantness, and (4) not getting what one wants. Human beings seek what the Buddha called Three Forms of Thirst: (1) sensual pleasure, (2) ego-driven protection, and (3) aversion to unpleasantness.

The Second Noble Truth, the Buddha taught, is that dissatisfaction arises from grasping for lasting happiness that is, in reality, impermanent. The Third Noble Truth posits that there is a path to alleviate dissatisfaction. The Fourth Noble Truth is the way forward: the Noble Eightfold Path.[6]

Black Buddhists identify the Four Noble Truths as foundational for their gravitation toward Buddhism. A teacher in the Triratna tradition, Valerie Mason-John (also known as Vimalasara), states,

Rather than actually talking to Black people about love and hate, we need to be teaching the Four Noble Truths. In the Four Noble Truths we see that there is suffering. We of African descended people know what suffering is. It's in our DNA. We see it on the streets. We know what suffering is. Yes. We know the second truth, of just seeing how we can create extra suffering and how we as African descent people create extra suffering in our lives. We've done it the same way as white people, from greed, hatred, and delusion. We are creating extra suffering. So the third [truth] is that there is the end of suffering and the fourth [truth is that] there's a way out of suffering. That to me are the teachings at the heart [of liberation]. There were so many different teachings but the practical teaching of how to live your life [is most important]. . . . What do we place at the center of our lives? What influences what we do, breath by breath; influences what we do, step by step? It's becoming aware of what we place at the center of our lives.[7]

Charles Johnson, a Buddhist author of several books, echoes Mason-John's words. In "Reading the Eightfold Path," Johnson writes that the first teaching of the Buddha resonates with Black Americans: "From almost any angle that we view black American life, historically or in the post–Civil Rights era, we find the First Noble Truth: the presence of suffering."[8]

The Eightfold Noble Path encompasses teachings on wisdom, ethics, and concentration. Wisdom (proper view) refers to Right Understanding and Right Thought. Ethics (proper conduct) refers to Right Speech, Right Action, and Right Livelihood. Lastly, concentration (proper practice) refers to Right Effort, Right Mindfulness, and Right Concentration.[9] The Buddha taught that the practice of the Noble Eightfold Path leads to enlightenment.

While employing these core teachings over forty-five years, the Buddha established monastic communities throughout northeast India, often relying upon the patronage of wealthy merchants and rulers.

The Teachings of Early Buddhism

Upon the Buddha's death, Buddhism spread throughout the Indian subcontinent and was eventually established in Sri Lanka. Approximately one hundred years later, in the fourth century (ca. 350 BCE), Buddhist monastics developed the *Vinaya Pitaka* (monastic codes).[10] Subsequently, one hundred years after the establishment of the *Vinaya Pitaka*, an Indian Buddhist emperor, Asoka (272–236), claimed Buddhism as the formal religion of the Sinhala state. Asoka's patronage effectively made Buddhism the dominant religion not only in the northern half of India but in southeast India and Sri Lanka as well.[11]

Over the next two hundred years, interpretations of the dharma evolved, coalescing in schools of thought that later became known as Theravada (Doctrine of the Elders) Buddhism. Theravada Buddhism adhered to—and continues to follow—teachings on the Four Noble Truths and the Noble Eightfold Path; the Three Refuges—the Buddha, dharma (teachings), and sangha (community); Dependent Origination (interdependent causes and conditions); the inherent emptiness of all existence (impermanence); and the Five Aggregates (the human person is not a constantly existing self, but rather consists of an ever-changing body with shifting feeling sensations, perceptions, mental formations, and consciousnesses).[12]

Buddhist practitioners "take refuge" in the Three Jewels: Buddha, dharma, and sangha. By seeking refuge—emulating the wisdom of the Buddha, practicing the teachings of the Buddha, and belonging to the community of monastics and lay practitioners—"one receives these three treasured gifts."[13]

The Buddhist teaching on Dependent Origination (in Pali: *paticca samuppada*) elaborates twelve links of cause and effect that describe the causes and conditions of suffering. The four central links are experiential in nature: contact, feeling, craving, and clinging. Contact (*phassa*) refers to contact through the senses: sense organ (such as the nose), sense object (such as a rotten egg), sense consciousness (aversion to the bad smell of the rotten egg). Feeling sensation (*vedana*), also known as the second aggregate, refers to pleasant, unpleasant, or neutral feelings. Craving (*tanha*) refers to greed, hatred, or delusion—a yearning for something to be different. Clinging (*upadana*) refers to the activity in the mind that fixates on an experience and takes hold of it.

The *suttas* (discourses) in the Theravada tradition identify grasping as the origin of attachment, and clinging as the ongoing activity of attachment. In grasping and clinging, human beings create a "self" that is inherently changing, empty, and thus unstable. Consequently, Buddhism teaches that a Right Understanding of the "self" is an emptiness of self, or "non-self" (*anatta*). This teaching refers to the Five Aggregates (*khanda*): form, feeling tone, perception, formations, and consciousness. The first aggregate is form (*rupa*), which refers to the material body composed of bones, muscles, and flesh. The second aggregate is feeling tone (*vedana*), known by pleasant, unpleasant, or neutral sensations. The third aggregate is perception (*samjna*), the means by which human beings recognize, name, and categorize. The fourth aggregate (*sankhara*) refers to complex mental formations. The fifth aggregate of consciousness (*viññāṇa*) is the direct capacity to understand through hearing, touching, tasting, and thinking.

The essence of the teaching—that there is not a stable "self" but rather a self that is constantly shifting in an environment that is perpetually changing—arises from Right Understanding. In gaining mastery over the Three Defilements of greed, hatred, and delusion, and in ceasing to cling to the inherent emptiness of all phenomena, the early suttas taught that meditators could attain enlightenment, thereby achieving liberation from *samsara*, the world of suffering.

Sebene Selassie, a teacher in the Insight tradition, identifies the teachings on the Five Aggregates as liberatory, in that a Right Understanding of non-self uncovers how human beings perpetuate their own suffering.

> We act in these unconscious ways . . . but we have conscious ideas about who we are and what we think, how we act, what we say. I'm a bit of a geek in terms of loving to understand the roots of these words. And it's interesting for me that in Pali *samjna*, *vedana*, *viññāṇa*—perception, feeling tone, consciousness—all have the same root, the same as *paññā*, or wisdom, which is "to know."
>
> The form, *rupa*, knows the eye coming into contact with black skin. At the same time there's this knowing that comes with perception or naming, a feeling tone of pleasant/unpleasant/neutral, and *viññāṇa* or consciousness of it all happening. [These aggregates are] sort of answering the question: what is this? What's going on here? These are based on many experiences, so pulling from all of these past experiences to know, okay, what is this? . . . *Sankhara*, or mental formations, has the same root as *karma*. It's how we form our opinions, our thoughts, our emotions.

Here, you end up asking the questions: What do I do about this? How do I respond? Do I like or dislike it? Do I have fear or love, based on all of this perception and feeling about this? So, these *sankharas* are so important to understand. In your practice, your mindfulness and *metta* [loving-kindness] meditations, love and kindness are *sankharas* that you can cultivate. We can start to cultivate a different reaction to things.[14]

These teachings on liberation—the Four Noble Truths and the Noble Eightfold Path, the Three Refuges, Dependent Origination, Emptiness, and the Five Aggregates—are core teachings of Buddhism, even as they have been rearticulated in different cultural terms as Buddhism has spread throughout the continent of Asia and to the West.

Mahayana Buddhism: The Second Turning of the Wheel

The initial set of teachings, later identified with the lineage of Theravada Buddhism, informed the Mahayana tradition, the "second turning of the wheel," which is sometimes referred to as the "greater vehicle." Approximately six hundred years after the Buddha's death, scholars penned a series of sutras to clarify emerging Buddhist doctrines. Initially transmitted orally in Pali, the dharma was later articulated in Sanskrit, a sister dialect to Pali.

In the first century CE, Buddhism became established as the main religion throughout Asia, spreading throughout countries known today as Burma (also called Myanmar), Thailand, Laos, Cambodia, Vietnam, and Indonesia.[15] By the early second century, Buddhism spread across Central Asia to China.[16] Itinerant monks translated Sanskrit into Chinese and attempted to adapt a monastic tradition to a culture in which familial ties were paramount. In so doing, Buddhism took on the numerous cultural forms inherent to the places that traveling monastics encountered.

In China and elsewhere, Mahayana adherents distinguished their interpretations of the dharma from Theravada schools in two ways: they uplifted the figure of the Bodhisattva and elaborated the concept of Emptiness (*sunyata*).

The Bodhisattva was hailed as a meditator who, driven by great compassion for suffering beings, rejects enlightenment and returns to earth again and again. In so doing, the Bodhisattva commits to saving all sentient beings. Filled with *bodhicitta*—the energy of aspiration to relieve suffering—the Bodhisattva is another Buddha, an awakened one. To be sure, the figure of the Bodhisattva appears in an important text in Theravada Buddhism, the *Visudhimagga*, written by the fifth-century Sri Lankan scholar Buddhaghosa.[17] However, historically some scholars argued that, in the Theravada tradition, the Bodhisattva ideal is peripheral in the quest for enlightenment. Mahayana Buddhists, scholars ascertained, elevated the figure of the Bodhisattva as central to the practice of enlightenment.

In China, leading Mahayana scholars posited the way of the Bodhisattva—to reach enlightenment and subsequently return to help suffering sentient beings—as the primary aspiration for all who follow in the path of the Buddha.[18] The Bodhisattva is aligned with skillful means (*upaya*); thus the Bodhisattva takes a variety of forms to skillfully address the particular suffering experienced by human beings in different situations. The teachings on skillful means are found throughout Mahayana sutras. For example, in the *Lotus Sutra*, the Buddha teaches that there are different vehicles to entice hearers toward enlightenment; those who are realized must employ such different vehicles to lead human beings out of suffering. These skillful means can refer to uplifting cultural expressions of the dharma: in China, the Bodhisattva of compassion, Avalokitsvara, became known as Quan Yin.[19]

Alongside the figure of the Bodhisattva, Mahayana Buddhists also introduced a doctrine of Emptiness. The Indian philosopher Nagarjuna and his primary disciple, Aryadeva, established the Madhaymika school of thought, in which they taught the fundamental Emptiness (sunyata) of all existence as the voidness that constitutes ultimate reality and the true nature of things.[20] In the Mahayana *Heart Sutra*, "form is empty; emptiness is form." Sunyata, for Mahayana Buddhists, is not a negation of existence but rather acknowledges that all people and things are empty of permanent and separate existence. All apparent entities, distinctions, and dualities arise out of this Emptiness of existence, which is also described as an Emptiness within consciousness. Emptiness is present within each consciousness as an awakened nature, an enlightened awareness of temporary, changing phenomena. This is also referred to as

"Buddha Nature." Within this Emptiness, the mind accesses connection, wisdom, compassion, loving-kindness, even bliss.

Patronage of powerful leaders continued to advance Buddhist teachings. The fourth-century Gupta Empire (350–650) dominated India for two centuries, marking what noted historian Paul Williams calls "an environment of intellectual brilliance and sophistication."[21] Important Buddhist scholars Asanga and Vasubandhu, who articulated the Cittamatra-Yogacara doctrine of mind, flourished as influential philosophers. Buddhaghosa, a philosopher and translator, offered respected commentary. Buddhism influenced Hinduism in India as it continued to spread to Korea, Japan, and Nepal. Chinese adherents were particularly eager to evolve their understandings of Buddhist doctrine: in 414, Chinese pilgrims arrived in India in search of sutras to translate and bring back to China.[22]

In 520 CE, Indian scholar Bodhidharma arrived in China and founded the sect that later in Japan became known as Zen Buddhism.[23] Chinese Zen took on new characteristics as it continued to incorporate Taoism alongside the teachings of Bodhidharma.[24] Later in the sixth century, Mahayana Buddhism was formally incorporated into Japan and flourished due to patronage from political leaders. Many different forms of Buddhism arose, including Soto and Rinzai Zen, which are widely practiced in contemporary times. In the seventh century, Mahayana Buddhism expanded greatly, incorporating new cultural idioms. Buddhism arrived in Tibet, merging with already established indigenous practices as well as Chinese Zen sutras that were translated into Tibetan. Another set of teachings was brought to Tibet from India, through the renowned Indian scholars Santaraksita and Padmasambhava.

Vajrayana Buddhism: The Third Turning of the Wheel

As Buddhism was incorporated into Tibetan religious practices, a form of Mahayana Buddhism known as Tantra or Vajrayana arose. This new form of Buddhism greatly influenced artistic and scholarly expressions of the dharma. Tantric Buddhism, known as the "third turning of the wheel" and the "diamond vehicle," incorporated embodied practices that were understood to lead to the achievement of enlightenment in one lifetime.[25] An emerging dynamic between Indian and Tibetan Buddhism unfolded; for the next five centuries, Indian and Tibetan scholars evolved Tantric Buddhism in monasteries, universities, and temples.

In the thirteenth century, after the invasion of Muslim armies and the destruction of monasteries and universities, Buddhism in India was effectively wiped out. However, in Tibet Tantric Buddhism thrived. Similarly, even while undergoing domination by colonial powers in Burma and Sri Lanka, Theravada Buddhism continued to exist in Southeast Asia and remained the majority religion in Thailand (which was not subjected to Western colonialism). Various forms of Mahayana Buddhism continued to flourish in China and Japan as well as other Far East countries.

The three primary lineages of Buddhism—Theravada, Mahayana, and Vajrayana/Tantric—evolved into numerous different sects in different locations, far too many to explore briefly in this chapter.[26] For the purposes of this book, it is most important to identify the primary lineages that have been influential for Black Buddhists in the United States.[27]

Buddhism and Modernity

Scholars argue that across lineages the forms of Buddhism that practitioners in the United States know as Buddhism are actually a confluence of intellectual forces that have coalesced during modernity, particularly since the nineteenth century. David McMahan argues in *The Making of Buddhist Modernism*,

> What many Americans and Europeans often understand by the term
> "Buddhism," however, is actually a modern hybrid tradition with roots in
> the European Enlightenment no less than the Buddha's enlightenment, in
> Romanticism and transcendentalism as much as the Pali canon, and in
> the class of Asian cultures and colonial power as much as in mindfulness
> and meditation. Most non-Asian Americans tend to see Buddhism as a
> religion whose most important elements are meditation, rigorous philo-
> sophical analysis, and an ethic of compassion combined with a highly
> empirical psychological science that encourages reliance on individual
> experience. It discourages blindly following authority and dogma, has
> little place for superstition magic, image worship, and gods, and is largely

compatible with the findings of modern science and liberal democratic values. While this picture draws on elements of traditional forms of Buddhism that have existed in Asia for centuries, it is in many respects quite distinct from what Buddhism has meant to Asian Buddhists throughout its long and varied history. The popular western picture of Buddhism is neither unambiguously "there" in ancient Buddhist texts and lived traditions nor merely a fantasy of an educated elite population in the West, an image with no corresponding object. It is, rather, an actual new form of Buddhism that is the result of a process of modernization, westernization, reinterpretation, image-making, revitalization, and reform that has been taking place not only in the West but also in Asian countries for over a century. This new form of Buddhism has been fashioned by modernizing Asian Buddhists and western enthusiasts deeply engaged in creating Buddhist responses to the dominant problems and questions of modernity, such as epistemic uncertainty, religious pluralism, the threat of nihilism, conflicts between science and religion, war, and environmental destruction.[28]

McMahan is one of many scholars who point to multiple intersecting points of engagement between Buddhism and Western theologies and philosophies. One set of scholarship argues that white Buddhist sympathizers "orientalized" Buddhism, creating a Western gaze that exoticized aspects of Buddhism—especially meditation—while dismissing devotional practices as localized cultural affects. Scholar Joseph Cheah argues that "Buddhism, represented by the Orientalists, was therefore a fabricated construct: it does not exist outside of the rerepresentations made about it by those in the West."[29]

Another set of analyses describes the employment and adaptation of Buddhism to resist European colonialism in Asia. In this review, scholars chronicle the adaption of Buddhism that found itself under attack by Christian colonizers. For example, Cheah describes the context white U.S. citizens encountered when they arrived in Ceylon (now Sri Lanka) in 1880: "Singhalese Buddhism had been under assault by British colonialism: the tradition of royal patronage of the monastic order had been eliminated, children born to Buddhist parents were considered ipso facto illegitimate unless the parents were married in a Christian church, and Buddhist monastic schools were reduced to four, versus 805

Christian schools."[30] White sympathizers of Buddhism, including Henry Wykoff Olcott, Emily Steel Olcott, and Helena Petrovna Blavatsky, set out to support Singhalese Buddhism and, in the process, reform it. In so doing, Henry Olcott in particular created a version of Buddhism that came to be known as Protestant Buddhism.

> [The scholar] Gregory Schopen makes an insightful assertion that the ascription of primacy to textual sources in Buddhist studies by the Orientalists mirrors the Protestant value of "the primacy of the Word" and does not necessarily reflect the history and values of Indian Buddhism. . . . The reformers' distrust of religious objects, sculpture, relics, images, and their unwillingness to allow actual practices of religious people a meaningful place in the definition of "true" religion became so assimilated in the Western intellectual tradition that such a distrust is simply taken for granted. Schopen concludes it is possible that this conception influenced by the Protestant reformers' assumption of the locus for "true" religion "has determined the history of the study of Indian Buddhism and that—as a consequence—our picture of Indian Buddhism may reflect more of our own religious history and values than the history and values of Indian Buddhism."[31]

Among the reforms were uplifting the biography of Siddhartha Gautama as the founder of Buddhism, elevating textual study over devotional rituals, and prioritizing the laity while undercutting the status of monastic institutions—all of which are central to the institutionalization of Protestant Christianity.[32]

As the laity were upheld as recipients for meditation instruction, another shift in Buddhism took place: leading monastics simplified meditation practices that were taught to foster the path to enlightenment. This shift took place in the twentieth century at the initiative of Burmese and Thai monastics and lay leaders, not at the behest of U.S. and European-born sympathizers. Thus it is important to recognize that many modernizing influences came from *within* Asian Buddhist communities, rather than at the request of Westerners.[33] In short, the "modernizing" of Buddhism that took place in the late nineteenth century—in response to European colonialism, Orientalist scholarship, the forming of Protestant Buddhism, and the movements to uplift lay practitioners—

arose from within Asian countries as well as from European nations and the United States.

The initiatives of Buddhist monastics in Burma and Thailand are particularly important for understanding the forms of Buddhism that arrived in the United States, particularly with regard to the Insight communities that have arisen. Scholar Ann Gleig describes the student-teacher relationships to which Insight techniques are indebted: in Burma, the lineages of Ledi Sayadaw (1846–1923) and Mahasi Sayadaw (1904–1982); and in Thailand, the Thai Forest Tradition of Ajahn Buddhadasa (1906–1993) and Ajahn Chah (1918–1992).

In Burma, Ledi Sayadaw was known as a scholar of Buddhist texts as well as a meditation master who taught sutras and meditation techniques accessibly to the laity. He identified his approach as a subversive challenge to nineteenth-century colonialism. Several years later, a young monk, later known as Mahasi, initiated a "streamlined" style of Vipassana meditation. Gleig writes, "The primary aim of Mahasi's approach was to attain *sotapanna*, or stream entry, the first of the four stages leading to Nirvana. He believed that the laity could directly experience advanced stages of realization without studying the scriptures or renouncing the world. With his exclusive focus on Vipassana, Mahasi downplayed or eliminated many traditional Theravadin practices, such as scholarship, devotional exercises, and merit-making activities."[34] Mahasi Sayadaw established several meditation centers in Burma. His style of meditation was subsequently adopted by Theravadin communities in Thailand, Sri Lanka, Indonesia, and India as well as by white U.S.-based practitioners who, in turn, established meditation centers in the United States.

Unlike Burma, Thailand (formerly known as the Kingdom of Siam) was never colonized by a Western nation. The "modernizing" tradition of which McMahan speaks arose from attempts to reconcile Buddhism with modernity, including the spread of scientific inquiry, rational thinking, and Christian hegemony. Two monks, Ajahn Sao (1859–1941) and his student Ajahn Mun (1870–1949), sought to reform the monastic orders in Thailand by teaching rigorous meditation practices that could lead to enlightenment in the lifetime of a practitioner. Mun's student, Ajahn Chah, ordained the first U.S.-born monk, Ajahn Sumedho (1934–), as well as several other white, U.S.-born adherents.[35] Another monk, Ajahn

Buddhadasa, similarly had a profound impact on the emergence of U.S. Buddhism. Gleig writes, "Ajahn Buddhadasa began to systematically re-interpret Theravada Buddhism in the 1930s and came to national promi-nence in the 1970s. He demythologized Theravada Buddhism and made it compatible with scientific rationalism and social reform. Rejecting the traditional Buddhist separation of the mundane and supramundane realms, Buddhadasa located the everyday world as the true site of Bud-dhist practice and rendered its highest goals of realization accessible to ordinary people."[36]

In addition to influencing the development of Insight meditation centers, modern Buddhism had a tremendous influence on the cultiva-tion of Japanese Soto and Rinzai Zen communities in the United States. Scholars argue that modernizing forces led Western-oriented Japanese and Zen priests to create a "New Buddhism" that countered the influ-ence of Christianity but could accommodate scientific innovations.[37] Japanese elites described Zen as "pure experience": missionary monas-tics who arrived in the United States found a ready audience of U.S. practitioners who were already primed from reading Transcendentalist texts. Two Japanese Zen teachers, Shunryu Suzuki, founder of the San Francisco Zen Center, and Taizen Maezumi, founder of the Zen Center of Los Angeles, were of particular importance in the training of white U.S. dharma disciples. Soka Gakkai, a Japanese tradition without for-mal teachers (different from other forms of Japanese Buddhism), has flourished in the United States, not only among white practitioners but among Black and Latinx adherents as well.[38]

Tibet's engagement with the West is notably more recent than that of Japan and the countries of Southeast Asia, in that Tibetan lamas (teach-ers) did not engage with Western cultures until the Chinese government occupied Tibet in 1950. A popular Tibetan teacher in the United States, Chogyam Trungpa Rinpoche (1939–1987), advocated for a secular ap-proach to the dharma. A prolific writer, Trungpa Rinpoche became popular in Beat circles in the United States as he founded a series of meditation and publishing centers under the umbrella of Shambhala Buddhism. Furthermore, the spiritual and political leader of Tibet, the Dalai Lama—who was forced into exile in 1959—has embraced moder-nity and linked Buddhist teachings with science. The Dalai Lama also promotes universal Buddhist values in nonreligious rhetoric, fostering not only a link with secular values but also engagement with social and environmental causes.

Socially Engaged Buddhism

Indeed, an aspect of modern Buddhism that has emerged in Asia as well as the United States is the employment of Buddhist teachings and practices to address social conflicts and environmental destruction. This may be seen as early as 1956 with the conversion of Dr. B. R. Ambedkar, an Indian scholar born Hindu into the Dalit (ex-Untouchable) class, who was a primary architect of India's constitution. Scholar Aishwary Kumar refers to Ambedkar as "a prodigious 'untouchable' who, lifting himself against the exclusion and violence that surrounded him, became a revolutionary constitutionalist, a thinker whose laborious draftsmanship and exegetical rigor produced a new constitution for the free republic in 1950."[39] Ambedkar embraced Buddhism publicly as a traditional Indian faith (even though it had been largely extinct in India since the thirteenth century) and as a religion that could be practiced rationally, ethically, and apart from priestly Hindu authorities.[40] Ambedkar thought that Buddhism's emphasis on impermanence and ethical action fostered an approach to countering rigid social hierarchies that were institutionalized in Hindu Brahmanism. Ambedkar embraced these ideals as well as narratives of the historical Buddha's welcome of women and lower-caste members of Indian society into monasticism.

For Ambedkar, then, returning to Indian Buddhism to counter rigid social hierarchies was returning to a religious tradition that shunned a caste system and embraced a doctrine of no-self (anatta), in which all persons are fundamentally empty of a solid nature and are thus equal in a profound way. Furthermore, for Ambedkar, Buddhist narratives and ethical teachings are fundamentally focused on social relations and thus compel adherents to challenge social oppression.

Ambedkar's focus on the social ethics of Buddhism in the 1950s was taken up and elaborated a decade later by Vietnamese Zen monk Thich Nhat Hanh under the rubric of Socially Engaged Buddhism. Nhat Hanh wrote that Buddhist social engagement is "an effort to express the *ideals* of Buddhism—nonviolence, loving-kindness, and the rest—in practical action."[41] In his writings, Nhat Hanh has sought to adapt Zen teachings for an increasingly busy, chaotic social world in which the destruction of the earth is taking place.[42] Nhat Hanh writes simply, "Many of us become sick because we're alienated from our body and from the body of the Earth. So the practice is to go home to Mother Earth to get the healing and the nourishment we so desperately need."[43] Nhat Hanh continues, "Unless we restore the Earth's balance, we will continue to cause a lot of destruction and it will be difficult for life on Earth to continue. We need to realize that the conditions that will help to restore the necessary balance don't come from outside us; they come from inside us, from our own mindfulness, our own level of awareness. Our own awakened consciousness is what can heal the earth."[44] Nhat Hanh's approach to environmental healing is extended to social dynamics. As an antiwar activist who fled Vietnam during the Vietnam War, he advocates for an awakened consciousness that finds peace first in oneself. Inner equilibrium, then, is extended in peace movements. Nhat Hanh writes, "Can the peace movement talk in loving speech, showing the way for peace? I think that will depend on whether the people in the peace movement can be peace. Because without being peace, we cannot do anything for peace. . . . The peace movement is filled with anger and hatred. It cannot fulfill the path we expect from them. A fresh way of being peace, of doing peace is needed."[45]

Thich Nhat Hanh's approach to peacemaking in situations of conflict and war echoes the approach of the Dalai Lama, who similarly teaches that economic, political, and environmental conditions lead to great suffering and that an end to suffering is distinctly located in ethical actions. Thus, Buddhist leaders must ethically address the social factors that perpetuate war, violence, and repression that lead to extensive psychological and physical pain. The Dalai Lama states in his autobiography, *Freedom in Exile*, "Religion and politics do mix and both agree that it is the clear duty of religion to serve humanity, that it must not ignore reality. It is not sufficient for religious people to be involved with prayer. Rather, they are morally obliged to contribute all they can to solving the world's problems."[46]

Indeed, the Dalai Lama has experienced and witnessed atrocities committed by the Chinese government against the people of Tibet since the Chinese invasion in 1950. In his writings and speeches, the Dalai Lama describes "arrests without justification, beatings and torture,

prison sentences and even execution by trial [that] characterise the be-
haviour of the Chinese authorities."[47]

For the Dalai Lama, the goal of communist economic prosperity is
not, by itself, a worthy goal: he believes that religious sentiment and
practice are the foundations for harmony and that religious and secular
ethics, not solely economic prosperity, will lead to widespread nonviolence and peace.[48] The tenets of Buddhism and the practice of meditation foster compassion and goodwill, the best of human beings. Thus
contemplative practice and prayer are inseparable from creating social
conditions in which all sentient beings can thrive. The Dalai Lama identifies the Bodhisattva ideal as a path to helping all sentient beings:

> According to Buddhist thought, a Bodhisattva is someone on a path to
> Buddhahood who dedicates themselves entirely to helping all other sen-
> tient beings towards release from suffering. The word Bodhisattva can
> best be understood by translating the *Bodhi* and *Sattva* separately: *Bodhi*
> means the understanding or wisdom of the ultimate nature of reality, and
> a *Sattva* is someone who is motivated by universal compassion. The Bo-
> dhisattva ideal is thus the aspiration to practise infinite compassion with
> infinite wisdom.[49]

The Dalai Lama emphasizes that it is not just sentient beings but also
nature that thrives with committed Buddhist practice. Indeed, Socially
Engaged Buddhists state that as all sentient beings live in nature, it is
important to protect earthly resources. This is an approach similar to
that of Maha Ghosananda (1913–2007), a Cambodian forest monk and
peace activist, and Sulak Sivaraksa (1933–), a Thai social activist and professor. These spiritual and social justice leaders have forged connections
between meditation, ritual, and working toward a more humane and
just world.

Buddhism, Culture, and Race in the United States

As modern Socially Engaged Buddhism has evolved in the United
States, predominantly white, Buddhist adherents have sought to live out
their contemplative practices with a commitment to alleviating social
problems. Their intentions are reflected in numerous publications under

the rubric of Socially Engaged Buddhism. For example, one of the foremost white teachers of Socially Engaged Buddhism, Bernie Glassman, published *Instructions to the Cook: A Zen Master's Lessons in Living a Life that Matters*. Glassman states that meditation practice fueled his commitment to Right Livelihood, the fourth pillar of the Noble Eightfold Path. Meditation practice fosters doubt, faith, and determination, "ingredients" that are "like air, water, and heat."[50] From this foundational practice of clear seeing without judgment, one is able to move into a life of social action. In what Glassman calls the "Five Courses," he delineates "Recipes for Social Change" in the fourth course. "If I meet starving people, I first give them food. That's where they are. If I were hungry, I'd want to eat first. If I were homeless and cold, I'd want shelter. . . . The point is to identify with the people you're working with, in order to discover their needs."[51]

In his reflections, Glassman chronicles his commitment to alleviating joblessness and homeless in the predominantly Black city of Yonkers, New York. He and fellow community members founded a bakery to provide employment and purchased buildings to provide housing, child care, and community centers. He reflects briefly on being a visible white leader in predominantly Black communities: "When I went to talk to Afro-American coalitions, for example, I was always introduced as 'Bernie, the guy who makes all those great cakes.' Then we could talk about politics and housing strategy and so on. I was still white, but I was more accepted because of my role in the bakery they all loved."[52]

Glassman writes about his approach to Socially Engaged Buddhism from the perspective of a white Jewish man who was able to access enough resources to purchase property, start a business, and network with wealthy entrepreneurs throughout the country. He approached Socially Engaged Buddhism from a position of privilege, attempting to make Zen Buddhism relevant to people whose are struggling with survival. As the founder of Zen Peacemakers, he influenced a generation of Zen practitioners who identify suffering not only as a result of personal desire but also as a result of external conditions.

Glassman's acknowledgment of race and class within American Buddhism is part of a broader context of the evolution of Buddhism in the United States, in which the construction of race and the lived experience of racism are increasingly acknowledged as paramount social conditions within Buddhist academic and practice communities. In academic spheres, scholars argue, white myopia has elevated a set of discourses that inadvertently reinforce white supremacy. Known as the two Buddhisms theory, scholars of Buddhism in the United States have distinguished between predominantly white "convert" Buddhism and predominantly Asian "heritage" Buddhism. A number of leading scholars, among them Charles Prebish, Paul David Numrich, and Richard Seager, have distinguished between forms of Buddhism in the United States that are based on ethnicity and race.

The origins of the two Buddhisms framework lie in the writings of psychologist Emma McCloy Layman, who in the late 1970s described U.S.-based immigrant communities as differing in terms of style. Layman identified three different categories of communal practice. Shortly thereafter, scholar Charles Prebish noted two broad categories of Buddhist sanghas based not primarily on practice style but rather ethnicity. Academics studying Buddhism in the United States seized upon the term "two Buddhisms" coined by scholar Paul David Numrich. The term was identified as a salient distinction between modern Buddhism—particularly a distinct "American Buddhism" that weds Buddhism to psychotherapy and is often secularized into "mindfulness"—and immigrant communities that practice devotional rituals.

As Numrich expanded the categories of two Buddhisms from ethnicity to race, many scholars adopted the term as useful for understanding the phenomenon of Buddhism in the United States.[53] Numrich's term—while limited—acknowledged a context in which "heritage" immigrant communities and white "convert" communities practiced Buddhism in different ways. Wakoh Shannon Hickey, who critiques embedded racism in identified scholarly approaches to the study of Buddhism in the United States, quotes Numrich in noting that Buddhist temples serve different functions for immigrants than do Buddhist centers offering space and teachings to predominantly white practitioners, in part because white practitioners generally have more access to social, financial, and institutional power.[54]

Critiques of Two Buddhisms

However, many scholars argue that the coining of the term "two Buddhisms" does not allow for the diversity within sanghas and meditation
centers in the United States. Hickey and Cheah both note that "immigrant" and "Asian" are terms far too broad to encompass the complexity
of Buddhist identity and practice in "heritage" Buddhist communities.[55]
Additionally, the term "convert," as it is associated with whiteness, does
not convey the emerging numbers of self-identified Buddhist practitioners of African descent, nor does it allow for fluidity when U.S.-born
Asian practitioners join "convert" communities.[56] Hickey writes,
"Because we cannot link nationality or ethnicity to religion so tidily,
we cannot assume that any ethnically Asian person who begins to practice Buddhism in the United States is reverting to a heritage faith. Of
course, it is also very problematic to speak of 'Asians' and 'Asian Americans' as if they were homogenous. 'Asian' is a broad, racialized category,
just as 'white' is, and both contain great ethnic, cultural, and religious
diversity, with associated tensions."[57] In addition to critiques of the two
Buddhisms framework, many self-identified Buddhists expressed alarm
at a 1991 editorial by then-*Tricycle* editor Helen Tworkov: "The spokes-
people of Buddhism in America have been, almost exclusively, educated
members of the white middle class. Meanwhile, even with varying statistics, Asian-American Buddhists number at least one million, but . . . so
far . . . they have not figured prominently in the development of something called American Buddhism."[58] Tworkov later followed her written
comments by stating, "White Buddhism evolved essentially independent
of Asian communities."[59] Rev. Ryo Imamura, an eighteenth-generation
Buddhist priest in the Jodo Shinshu tradition and a professor of psychology at Evergreen State College in Washington State, responded with a
letter to the editor:

> I would like to point out that it was my grandparents and other immi-
> grants from Asia who brought and implanted Buddhism in American
> soil over 100 years ago despite white American intolerance and bigotry. It
> was my American-born parents and their generation who courageously
> and diligently fostered the growth of American Buddhism despite hav-
> ing to practice discretely in hidden ethnic temples and in concentration

camps because of the same white intolerance and bigotry. It was us Asian Buddhists who welcomed countless white Americans into our temples, introduced them to the Dharma, and often assisted them to initiate their own Sanghas when they felt uncomfortable practicing with us.[60]

The divisions between white "convert" and Asian "heritage" Buddhists deepened. White Buddhists were castigated as individualistic, myopic, focused on their own liberation but expressly disinterested in addressing white supremacist systems of power. Asian Buddhists were dismissed as preoccupied with rituals, hierarchy, and foreign cultural traditions rather than enlightenment. In the conversations and debates that ensued, the fact of white supremacist social, political, and economic hegemony within convert Buddhist communities was acknowledged and named explicitly. Hickey describes several aspects of white supremacist power: "So although cultural and linguistic continuity is an important need *internal* to an immigrant group, we should not overlook *external* forces that create both a need for places of refuge and ambivalence about practicing alongside white converts."[61] Hickey further notes that white people often assert the privilege of naming what American Buddhism is for everyone. Cheah expands this argument by stating directly, "What is implied, according to Asian American critics, is that Buddhism becomes truly American only when white Americans become seriously involved."[62]

Hickey furthermore elaborates another narrative expressed by white Buddhists: the idea that white Buddhists practice an authentic Buddhism that originates directly from the Buddha's enlightenment, whereas Asian Buddhists, in their devotional practices, are participating in foreign rituals in the United States. Chanting and bowing are seen as un-American, whereas solitary sitting on retreat is hailed as true Buddhist practice. Cheah argues that this distinction rests upon "racial rearticulations"—in this case, "an Asian meditative practice has been rearticulated into a specific but deliberately chosen form that helps preserve the prevailing system of racial hegemony."[63] Cheah elaborates,

> These are the people who had the power to speak, categorize, and determine what is considered authentic Buddhism. These are the people who selectively appropriate certain kinds of ideas (such as Buddhist phi-

losophy and textual Buddhism) and practices (such as meditation) and repackage them according to Western, and often, Orientalist frameworks because they believe their interpretation of certain sutras of their understanding of particular practices to be better or more true to the Buddhism of the Buddha than those of Asian Buddhism. This value judgment shows that some of the Euro-Americans' appropriation of Asian Buddhist ideas and practices into the American context is not the usual run-of-the-mill adaptation process. Deeply embedded in this process is the arrogance that comes from the racial ideology of white supremacy that asserts, "We know your tradition better than you do."[64]

Cheah acknowledges that the white supremacist arrogance embedded in such orientations toward Buddhism is invisible to many white practitioners who embrace Buddhism through a meditative process of attempting to heal psychological trauma.[65] At the same time, Cheah, like Hickey, notes that white supremacy fosters the dominance of a certain type of Buddhist practice, in large part because white Buddhists have access to institutions such as retreat centers, magazines, and publishing houses, which allow them to disseminate Buddhist teachings packaged in particular discourses that are familiar to white practitioners.[66]

Buddhism, Culture, and Appropriation

The phenomenon of white supremacy in convert Buddhism has prompted conversations in Buddhist organizations such as Buddhist Peace Fellowship (BPF), which in 2017 initiated a series of conversations on whether Buddhism is being culturally appropriated by white practitioners. Funie Hsu, in an article posted to the website of BPF, wrote,

> [Acknowledging the response of Rev. Imamura] It is evident that the cultural appropriation of Buddhism operates on a framework that holds that our spirituality can only be made safe through white ownership.
> To be clear, Buddhism belongs to all sentient beings. Even so, Asians and Asian American Buddhists have a rightful, distinct historical claim to Buddhism. It has been rooted in our cultures for thousands of years. When it is said that Buddhism has been practiced for over 2,500 years, it is important to consider who has been persistently maintaining the

practice for millennia: Asians, and more recently, Asian Americans. It is because of our physical, emotional, and spiritual labor, our diligent cultivation of the practice through time and through histories of oppression, that Buddhism has persisted to the current time period and can be shared with non-Asian practitioners. This is historical fact.

To not acknowledge the labor and contributions of Asian American Buddhists in the development of American Buddhism is simply cultural appropriation.[67]

Hsu advocates for white convert practitioners to incorporate reflections on cultural appropriation into their dharma practice, using the five precepts to guide meditators on cultivating proactive, intentional recognition of the origins of Buddhism.[68] She points explicitly to not harming and not stealing as ways to practice giving gratitude and recognition for what Buddhism, founded in Asia and transmitted by Asians, has offered convert practitioners:

> Dana as gratitude might include intentional efforts to center the histories of Asian and Asian American Buddhists in your sanghas; that work might be informed by facilitating reading groups or inviting Asian American Buddhist scholars and practitioners to speak. A white practitioner could choose to attend an Asian-dominant sangha and learn from a teacher who is not white. And we can all actively assert the need for consistent incorporation of Asian and Asian American Buddhist perspectives and leadership roles in popular Buddhist magazines, organizations, and conferences.
>
> Advocating for the centrality of Asian and Asian American Buddhists is definitely not to say that we practice the most authentic, perfect form of Buddhism; in fact, a different form of racism can also exist in Asian sanghas, one that's directed at non-Asian People of Color. Dana, then, might also look like a mutual fostering of conversations about how we can combat interpersonal racism toward each other in our communities and sanghas.[69]

Hsu points to the BPF as an organization that addresses the cultural appropriation of Buddhism with integrity. As part of a "Radical Rebirth" process that includes establishing principles and intentions to guide

BPF's work, Hsu uplifts a set of practices to "mobilize against systemic oppression, grow compassionate direct action, and actively seek racial justice, among other engaged projects."[70]

In addition to naming the cultural appropriation of Buddhism by white convert practitioners, Hsu points to the need for reckoning with complicated dynamics *within* Buddhist communities of color.

Dynamics among Asian and Black Buddhist Practitioners

As the critique of cultural appropriation has been directed toward white convert Buddhist practitioners, Black Buddhist practitioners are also engaging the ways in which Asian and Asian American sangha members have been disregarded in the spaces created by mainstream American Buddhism. Cross-racial support between Black and Asian community leaders can be seen historically as well as in the present day. In the nineteenth century, African Americans and Asians were two groups deemed polluted by mainstream society.[71] While Black people in the South were emerging from centuries of chattel slavery and the Civil War, Chinese immigrants in the West labored for companies, particularly on railroads. Religion scholar Duncan Ryūken Williams describes how Chinese immigrants were known as "the 'heathen Chinee,' a group of people racially unassimilable and religiously unacceptable."[72] Williams uplifts, in particular, the support voiced by Frederick Douglass in 1869, when he openly supported citizenship and voting rights for Chinese immigrants:

> I have said that the Chinese will come, and have given some reasons why we may expect them in very large numbers in no very distant future. Do you ask, if I favor such immigration, I answer I would. Would you have them naturalized, and have them invested with all the rights of American citizenship? I would. Would you allow them to hold office? I would. . . . The voice of civilization speaks an unmistakable language against the isolation of families, nations, and races, and pleads for composite nationality as essential to her triumphs.[73]

Williams, in turn, describes the importance of Douglass's advocacy for Chinese immigrants at a time of systemic exclusions: "I thought it was amazing to hear that kind of voice have a different vision of America than one of singularity and supremacy, one that said America is essentially a white and Christian nation. It is a very different vision that he had in that era, during the Chinese Exclusion Act that targeted one group of people for racial and religious exclusion, that had someone who spoke up to provide a different vision in my community."[74]

Williams celebrates solidarity between Black and Asian members of society who exist in marginalized spaces and promote a similar vision of a racially and religiously diverse, expansive society. His narrative is part of a larger conversation about white supremacy and racism amongst people of color within sanghas. Hsu, for example, points to dynamics among people of color, in which anti-Blackness is present within Asian communities. This was an especially poignant conversation in the wake of George Floyd's murder in May 2020, during which a Hmong police officer in Minneapolis stood by while his white colleague knelt on Floyd's neck and killed him. Scholars identify an anti-Black conditioning among Asians, who aspire to be a "model minority."[75] This critique was articulated in social media in the call to support Black Lives Matter protests. Several South Asian scholars published public calls to action and initiated an internal dialogue within Asian communities on internalized racism and anti-Black sentiments. Nanjini Rathi wrote in *Indian Express*,

It is no secret that South Asians grapple with various measures of anti-blackness that manifest in banal preferences for lighter complexions, prevailing negative associations in pop culture, and languages with all things black. Sometimes it is unleashed as verbal and physical attacks against Africans. Once in the US, immigrant families often continued to mingle within their own caste and regional associations and strongly discouraged children from dating or marrying African-Americans. Even when many of them gained economic and cultural capital, old patterns and prejudices lingered.[76]

Similarly, in response to widespread Black Lives Matter protests in June 2020, Professor Reshmi Dutt-Ballerstadt wrote,

While it would be too reductionist to claim that everyone belonging to the Asian American diaspora is affected by anti-Blackness, it is fair to assert that most Asian / Asian Americans have been brought up with some notion of colorism and casteism, whether they belong to the working class or hold the model minority status. . . . The relationship here between gendered colonialism, anti-Blackness and racism is deeply woven into the consciousness of many postcolonial subjects. Many Asian Americans also think of themselves as "honorary whites," based on their per capita income and occupational status. Their almost nonexistent contact with other working-class communities of color (including their own) often prohibits them from understanding racial and economic disparities faced by these communities on a daily basis.[77]

While highlighting anti-Black racism, these scholars simultaneously uplift the presence of Asian protestors in the streets in the wake of Floyd's murder.[78] Similarly, Williams, in his March 2021 Harvard lecture, "The Karma of a Nation," described many acts of solidarity in which he, as a Japanese Buddhist priest, has engaged. Many more Asian and Asian American demonstrators have posted support online, arguing for a full embrace of Black Americans and the cause of racial justice. Within Black Buddhist communities, there is an emerging conversation about practicing Buddhism without appropriation; acknowledging racism broadly—from whites as well as Asians—while seeking to remain inclusive; and cultivating rituals, such as devotional practices similar to those practiced in Asian sanghas, to honor African and African American ancestors.

The confluences between the forms of Buddhism practiced by Black people and the forms of Buddhism practiced by Asian and Asian American Buddhists have prompted the question of why the majority of Black Buddhists are affiliated with predominantly white sanghas rather than Asian Buddhist communities. Indeed, Black Buddhists and Asian Buddhists share numerous commitments and forms of practice.[79] As noted, Socially Engaged Buddhism arose in Asia, in the activism of Thich Nhat Hanh and the Dalai Lama. One of the most noted Indian social reformers, Ambedkar, renounced Hinduism and embraced Buddhism as a path toward social equality. Black Buddhists, too, are committed to antioppression activism, particularly with regard to racial, gender, sexual, and class oppression. While race, class, and gender are not primary categories for social activism in Asian countries—where deforestation, poverty, authoritarian rule, and war create immense suffering—Black Buddhists and

Asian Buddhists similarly point to socially induced causes and conditions of suffering.

Furthermore, Black Buddhists and Asian Buddhists honor ancestors through devotional practices, ceremonies, and altars. Black Buddhists identify ancestors, known and unknown, as spiritual and biological forebears who "made a way out of no way." The history of survival and the continuing commitments to perseverance and leadership prompt Black Buddhists to uplift ancestors as worthy of respect, honor, and gratitude. Similarly, ancestral devotional practices are central to Asian forms of Buddhist practices that flourish within multigenerational communities. Within these sanghas, ancestors are honored as matriarchs and patriarchs of expansive clans.

Little published research exists on the topic of why greater numbers of Black Buddhists exist in predominantly white sanghas. However, interviews with Western Buddhist teachers gesture toward possible reasons for complicated dynamics among white, Asian, and Black Buddhists. Larry Yang, a teacher within the Insight lineage, speculates that Asian teachers brought to the United States not only teachings but also cultural practices within the sanghas they established. Zen temples model and mimic Japanese form. Similarly, Tibetan rituals adhere closely to their culture of origin. Embedded in these cultures of origin are often patriarchal hierarchies that are inconsistent with U.S. cultural notions of equality, egalitarianism, and gender equity. Furthermore, Asian teachers have little, if any, experience with the cultural nuances in the United States, particularly with regard to race and racism. Yang's thoughts are echoed by Kate Lila Wheeler, a white, female-presenting teacher in the Insight tradition who was a nun in Burma and for many years also practiced in a guru-centered Tibetan tradition. Wheeler suggests that patriarchy within Asian lineages and white supremacy within Western sanghas often support one another."[80]

Yang furthermore speculates that the Insight tradition has drawn significant numbers of Black practitioners due to its reliance on teachers' interpretations of Buddhist teachings, which depend heavily on Western psychology. He suggests that Insight teachers have to determine how the teachings could become relevant to suffering in a Western context. Yang asks,

What does African American Buddhism look like without the constraints of a dominant culture? What does Asian American Buddhism look like without the constraints of what white Western Buddhism says it is? This is the cutting edge. And that edge will be resisted by white-centered spirituality. I have no doubt. It will be diminished by the dominant culture's claims of impurity of the "original" teachings, misunderstandings of the Dharma by inexperienced practitioners, and sugary interpretations of spiritual bypass. That's when we need to remember the solidarity of our diverse cultural experiences as a counterpoint to the imposition of white supremacist ideologies.[81]

Yang uplifts the potential for Asian and Black Buddhist solidarity—even as he recognizes the existence of anti-Black racism in Asian communities—alongside solidarity with queer Buddhists, as the orientation toward community. Affinity-based sanghas and culturally specific forms of Buddhist practice serve the broader commitment to solidarity and ultimately, liberation.

Buddhism and Black Liberation

A plethora of publications and a few organized gatherings on Buddhism and Black identity illuminate how Buddhism serves the liberation of Black people. Since 2000, with the publication of Rev. angel Kyodo williams's *Being Black: Zen and the Art of Living with Fearlessness and Grace*, Black Buddhists have reflected on their embrace of Buddhism as a path toward freedom. Part personal reflection, part advocacy for healing through Zen practice, williams writes, "the Zen principles . . . can give us direction for addressing our innermost spiritual questions and experiencing their relevance to our lives."[82]

Williams's focus on spreading Zen teachings among Black people was joined by Tibetan Buddhist teacher Lama Choyin Rangdrol, who wrote *Black Buddha* in 2001, and by Tibetan Buddhist scholar Jan Willis, who also in 2001 published *Dreaming Me: An African American Woman's Spiritual Journey*.[83] Willis's memoir chronicles her travels in India during her college years, when she encountered Tibetan monks. Willis eventually embraced a Tibetan monk, Lama Yeshe, as her teacher, feeling that he understood the parallels between being exiled from Tibet and the oppression experienced by Black Americans. Willis writes, "I should have told him the truth . . . that I suffered; that I was often frustrated and angry; that slavery and its legacy of racism had taken their tolls on me; that I had come seeking help in coping with feelings of inadequacy, unworthiness, and shame. I should have told him that I felt a certain kinship with the Tibetans because they, too, had suffered a great historical trauma and yet seemed able to cope very well and, indeed, even to be quite joyful."[84] In witnessing the resilience of Tibetans, Willis was inspired to heal an internal suffering that was wrought, in part, by the conditions of racism in the United States. Indeed, Willis was keenly aware of the social conditions that led to Black people's suffering. She could become peaceful and *still* experience a deep anger triggered by white people who exhibited racism.

Yet even in a racist context, Willis concluded, the suffering of Black people could not be overcome *only* with marches and activism; she was deeply aware of the resentment and anguish that resided in her heart. The way forward for her was in meditation practice: sitting with painful feelings and, over the course of time, befriending them. Silent practice under the guidance of a skilled teacher was a means to heal the mind and heart.

Willis describes particular forms of suffering that are personal, interpersonal, and systemic. Like many Black dharma teachers and long-term practitioners, she embraces practices that speak directly to self-hatred: thus the importance of cultivating a practice of stillness and a sangha rooted in love. In 2002, Willis joined a multilineage group of Black dharma teachers at Spirit Rock Meditation Center to uplift the presence of Black teachers in American Buddhism. Led by Marlene Jones and Lewis Woods, numerous teachers from the Theravada/Insight, Zen, Vajrayana, Pure Land, and Soka Gokkai International traditions joined the gathering.[85] Many of these teachers participated in two later retreats—in 2018 and 2019—for Buddhist Teachers of Black African Descent, at Union Theological Seminary and at Spirit Rock Meditation Center, respectively.

A number of publications by Black Buddhists have picked up and expanded the themes discussed in Black Buddhist retreats and in personal narratives. In 2003, the Buddhist magazine *Turning Wheel* elevated the perspectives of Black dharma practitioners. A 2004 anthology edited by Ryūmon Hilda Gutiérrez Baldoquín, *Dharma, Color, and Culture: New Voices in Western Buddhism*, includes several personal narratives by African American practitioners. In 2010 and 2016, Acharya Gaylon Ferguson published *Natural Wakefulness* and *Natural Bravery*, respectively.

Since 2015, a plethora of literature by Black Buddhists has illuminated racialized traumas that induce enduring psychological suffering. Zenju Earthlyn Manuel, in her meditation *The Way of Tenderness: Awakening through Race, Sexuality, and Gender*, writes evocatively of the trauma inflicted on Black children in state institutions: "When I got home [from school], I asked my mother why I wasn't chosen [for a program], and watched her eyes drop. That night, I cried in my bed until it finally became clear to me. I wasn't white. I had moved from the black school where my identity was closely tied to our culture. My innocence vanished, and I learned that for some, love is conditioned. Once a talkative child, I grew quiet in the struggle to regain my balance. I felt a keen sense of loss, living in a world that favored white people."[86] Through rituals and concentration practices, Manuel deconstructed the derogatory social messages that shaped her earliest cognitive experiences. She was able to recognize that the hatred directed at her was part of a larger, oppressive social consciousness. Rejection was a response not to her personal deficiencies but rather to the ways in which she was constructed within the white myopic and cognitive dysfunction of systemic white supremacy. Manuel's 2018 meditations *Sanctuary* further illuminate her journey from externally driven actions to internally grounded solitude.

For Black practitioners, the social meanings of the Black body must be acknowledged, reconstructed, and embraced. This process is deeply internal and solitary and overtly external and communal. These Black teachers and practitioners emphasize the primacy of the *body*: a material body composed of flesh and blood that is socially constructed in degrading ways. For Black people, these social constructs lead to enduring psychological and often physical suffering. Buddhist practitioners must reckon with the forces of racism that denigrate the body and that have led to rejection, misery, and self-hatred. Manuel writes, "I am a survivor of the same hatred my parents experienced. The body I inhabit has experienced nearly every category of hatred that exists within this society, directed toward the various unacceptable differences that characterize its appearance. Perhaps it is a result of these experiences that I have paid fierce attention to liberation."[87]

The Black Lives Matter movement surfaced insidious targeting and exploitation of Black people at the hands of police officers and state officials and a level of systemic oppression that, as a pervasive force, causes relentless suffering against Black people. In their coauthored 2016 book *Radical Dharma*, Rev. angel Kyodo williams and Lama Rod Owens, with scholar Jasmine Syedullah, illuminate "profoundly liberating teachings and practices that have the power to sever at their very root the destructive behaviors and thought processes that we inherit by way of our birth into human bodies."[88] But, williams argues, the liberatory message of dharma must be applied to systems:

> The police force is the state institution carrying out a specific
> mandate. . . .
> That mandate is to control Black bodies. . . .
> Your compliance maintains the system.
> You are policed, too.[89]

As structures are dismantled, williams writes, healing is a priority; externally oriented activist work to dismantle structures of oppression must correspond with a commitment to inner clarity and ease: "Our healing cannot wait until the structures acquiesce, are dismantled, or come undone."[90]

Williams, Owens, and Syedullah uplift the spectrum of racism, from interpersonal interactions to systemic brutality. Blackness, laden with socially constructed negative connotations, brings suffering. For williams, there is a "third space"—internally oriented *and* externally facing—in the ongoing struggle to protect Black lives.

Indeed, it is the practice of stillness that prompts Black Buddhist teachers to practice the dharma in their movement toward healing. Black Buddhist teachers embrace the dharma as a set of teachings that illuminate the causes and conditions of suffering. Buddhism, in acknowledging context as well as providing instructions for wellness, is enduringly relevant to Black people who face violence and microaggressions in the U.S. context. The unfolding genre of Black Buddhist literature illuminates trauma as well as psychological and spiritual healing.

Cultivating inner well-being through the practice of dharma teachings resounds throughout Black Buddhist texts. Charles Johnson, in his 2014 collection of essays *Taming the Ox*, uplifts Buddhist practices as refuge as he mourns police violence against young Black men.[91] Sheryl Petty synthesizes Lucumi and Buddhist practices in her 2016 book *Ocha Dharma*. Triratna teacher Valerie Mason-John's 2017 meditations *Detox Your Heart* offer a set of Buddhist-based practices for healing emotional trauma.[92] Insight teacher Spring Washam, in her 2017 book *A Fierce Heart*, writes with sorrow as well as buoyant clarity of the conditions that led to her embrace of Buddhism.[93]

Such awareness, awakened in silent meditation practice, is "medicine," says Insight teacher Ruth King.[94] In her 2018 book *Mindful of Race*, King declares emphatically, "Racism Is a Heart Disease, and It's Curable!"[95] King's confidence arises from a fundamental optimism in a religious tradition that announces as its First Noble Truth "There is suffering in life" and subsequently proposes a way forward. King writes that it is possible to acknowledge ingrained patterns and shift inner dispositions. If human beings can understand themselves through mindfulness practices, they can move toward recovery and healing.

It is possible, writes Angela Dews in her 2018 edited volume *Still, in the City*, to find refuge as well as to awaken from the illusion of separation. Reinterpreting the Three Jewels as Buddha (awareness), dharma (truth), and sangha (love), Dews advocates for practicing stillness and compassion in the midst of gritty urban life.[96]

These narratives are similarly mirrored in Black Buddhist texts published in 2020: Sebene Selassie's *You Belong*, Lama Rod Owens's *Love and Rage*, Larry Ward's *America's Racial Karma*, Zenju Earthlyn Manuel's *The Deepest Peace*, Jarvis Jay Masters's *Finding Freedom*, Jan Willis's *Dharma Matters*, and the collection of essays *Black and Buddhist*, edited by Pamela Ayo Yetunde and Cheryl Giles. These texts are followed by a volume published in July 2021, *Afrikan Wisdom: New Voices Talk Black Liberation, Buddhism, and Beyond*, edited by Mason-John.

These writings illuminate new forms of Buddhism, practiced by Black people, that are arising in the United States. These emerging iterations of

Buddhism reckon with systemic and interpersonal racism within society as well as convert sanghas; they furthermore evolve the intersection of psychology and Buddhism by highlighting the experience of intergenerational trauma. Black Buddhists embrace ancestors and devotional practices alongside solitary meditation, honor the body as a practice of liberation, and invest deeply in community. Their published works declare: Black people can be liberated.

2

From the Plantation to the Prison

The Causes and Conditions of Intergenerational Trauma

We are created by our conditions. Shaped by our oppression.
—Assata Shakur[1]

The Buddha taught that the minds of human beings are beset by greed, hatred, and aversion. Known as the Three Defilements (Theravada tradition) or Three Poisons (Mahayana tradition), this teaching illuminates the causes of patriarchal white supremacy and the resulting conditions. The greed underlying European colonialism—the theft of land and resources and the enslavement of bodies—has culminated in exploitation of the earth and annihilation of peoples. The hatred of Black bodies—dislocated from land and community, compared to white bodies, and denigrated as less than human—has resulted in generations of suffering. And delusions of white supremacy—rooted in European Christian narratives of racial superiority and conquest—continue to perpetuate deluded thinking in the twenty-first century.[2]

In addition to expounding upon the Three Defilements, the Buddha illuminated that suffering (*dukkha*) arises from certain conditions. In a teaching known as Dependent Origination (in Pali: *paticca samuppada*), the Buddha taught that particular conditions lead to the arising of identifiable circumstances. The Buddha stated that comprehending one's conditions—that is, the causes for one's suffering—is essential for awakening.[3] In a white supremacist context, awakening includes cognizance of how the Three Defilements—greed, hatred, and aversion—have led to violent degradation, enslavement, and exploitation of Black people. These conditions furthermore manifest in generations of ill health, poverty, and internalized racism. In short, the Three Defilements, and the conditions caused by white supremacy, have resulted in intergenerational trauma.

The Trauma of Colonialism

The European colonial enterprise, beginning in the Spanish and Portuguese nations in the fifteenth century, enacted enduring trauma on peoples living on the continents of Africa, North, Central, and South America, and Asia, as well as the islands of the Caribbean and the South Pacific. The scale of colonialism expanded far and burrowed deep. European colonialism encompassed material conquest: seizure of lands, material resources, and people, brutally enforced work, and genocide of native populations. European colonialism furthermore sweepingly destroyed the cultural foundations of conquered peoples: it replaced the foundational contexts in which native peoples understood themselves—land, worship, music, language, and relationships with ancestors, family, and clan—with destabilizing European narratives of religious, intellectual, and physical superiority. European colonialism stripped native peoples of their physical locations and their identities, identified native peoples as commodities, and set into motion interlocking traumatizing experiences that continue to impact Black and indigenous, and other people of color, throughout the world.

While this book does not seek to replicate numerous other texts that describe in detail the traumatizing institutions established during European colonialism, it is important to note the psychological impact of European narratives of superiority on the minds and nervous systems of indigenous peoples and their descendants. The earliest known text to compare the skin colors of captured African peoples appeared in the fifteenth century. Gomes Eannes de Azurara, the royal chronicler of Prince Henry the Navigator of Portugal, reflected on the various colors (and relative beauty) of a group of captured Africans:

> On the next day, which was the 8th of the month of August, very early in the morning, by reason of the heat, the seamen began to make ready their boats, and to take out those captives, and carry them on shore, as they were commanded. And these, placed all together in that field, were a marvelous sight; for amongst them were some white enough, fair to look upon, and well proportioned; others were less white like mulattoes; others again were black as Ethiops, and so ugly, both in features and in body, as almost to appear (to those who saw them) the images of the lower hemisphere.[4]

The native peoples of the "lower hemisphere" were labeled "barbarians," and "like talking animals" who were considered depraved and natural servants.[5] Thus their enslavement was rationalized, creating psychologically traumatic frameworks that were internalized by conquered and conquering peoples alike. The multiple levels of subjection that would be enacted upon the indigenous peoples of the Americas and Africa emphasized their difference from Europeans in appearance and behavior, body and spirit, simultaneously. Influential voices espousing the degradation of Black people were heeded during this period. In 1493, Pope Alexander VI literally divided the world into spheres of influence for the nascent Portuguese and Spanish empires.[6] Their expeditions would affirm, and in fact cement, the natural philosophies of the era. Indeed, Columbus wrote in his chronicles, "The inhabitants of the north and south are unfit for exercising power."[7]

Columbus was only one representative of the racial imagination that had taken hold in Portugal and Spain in the fifteenth century. The influential sixteenth-century Jesuit Alessandro Valignano, a prominent authority in the Church's missionary endeavors, noted that Africans, like other reprobates, exhibited degenerate characteristics: they went around half naked, had dirty food, practiced polygamy, showed avarice, and displayed "marked stupidity."[8] These deluded identifications continue to be propagated in the twenty-first century.

In the analysis of religion scholar Willie Jennings, white Europeans saw themselves as embodying holy effects and saving grace, while also possessing a unique capacity to detect such presence (or absence) in others.[9] In degrading Black peoples and their cultures, Europeans simultaneously associated themselves with divinity.[10] The European logic posited that Black people were incapable of achieving election due to their inferior nature and thus were inherently degenerate. The Catholic classification of dark-skinned people as inferior, and European Christians as superior, influenced eighteenth-century Enlightenment philosophers who elevated science and rational thought, as well as Protestant theologians who sought to model their image of a holy society. Deluded narratives of Black inferiority spread to other shores.

The Degradation of Black People in Post-Reformation Protestant Europe

European natural sciences and philosophers established pseudo-scientific racial narratives that created enduring psychological trauma for people of African descent. While the concept of race did not come into common parlance until the late eighteenth century, racial constructs abounded within theological discourses. In the eighteenth century, natural scientists and philosophers expanded the narratives. None of the accepted systems of natural history used the concept of race—the prevalent theory was of a single humanity divided into varieties that were explained referencing differences in climate, customs, and government—but these theories were discarded by new discoveries in the West Indies and by the explanations of Carl Linnaeus (also known as Carl von Linné) and Georges-Louis Leclerc, Comte de Buffon.

Linnaeus and Buffon were prominent scientists whose highly regarded theories enshrined deluded taxonomies of bodies and character within the halls of academia. They published in the mid-eighteenth century, when the authority of science promoted the activities of observing, comparing, measuring, and ordering the physical characteristics of human bodies.[11] Linnaeus wrote:

Mammalia
Order I. Primates
Foreteeth cutting: upper 4; parallel teats 2, pectoral

HOMO
Sapiens. Diurnal; varying by education and situation

1. Four footed, mute, hairy. *Wild man.*
2. Copper-coloured, choleric, erect. *American.*
    Hair black, straight, thick; *nostrils* wide; *face* harsh; *beard* scanty; obstinate, content, free. *Paints* himself with fine red lines. *Regulated* by customs.
3. Fair, sanguine, brawny. *European.*
    Hair yellow, brown, flowing; *eyes* blue; gentle, acute, inventive. *Covered* with close vestments. *Governed* by laws.

4. Sooty, melancholy, rigid.

Hair black; *eyes* dark; *fevere*, haughty, covetous. *Covered* with loose garments. *Governed* by opinions.

5. Black, phlegmatic, relaxed.

Hair black, frizzled; *skin* silky; *nose* flat; *lips* tumid; crafty, indolent, negligent. *Anoints* himself with grease. *Governed* by caprice.[12]

For Linnaeus, then, the characteristics associated with the European body indicated superior European character. Indeed, Linnaeus's taxonomy demonstrated a racial scale in which physical appearance represented inner character. These descriptions of character represented by physical appearance were rearticulated over time and indeed survive in the twenty-first century, leading to internalized racism and psychological suffering.

Indeed, upon publishing *The System of Nature* in 1735, Linnaeus became one of the most influential scientists in eighteenth-century Europe. Half a century later, the Prussian-born moral theorist Immanuel Kant became known as "the father of race." When Kant first wrote on race in the 1770s and 1780s, the modern pseudobiological theory of race did not yet exist.[13] Kant's theories of skin color, environment, and essential character set the foundation for modern understandings of race.

Kant argued for four different races of the human genus: (1) the white race, (2) the Negro race, (3) the Hun race (Mongol or Kalmuck), and (4) the Hindu or Hindustani race.[14] He was not only interested in classifying races, however: he primarily sought to provide a teleological explanation for the reality of different races; in other words, he sought to explain *why* there were different races rather than simply providing mechanical explanations.[15] Scholars agree that his desire to provide a teleological explanation for racial difference provided the foundation for his later text, *Critique of Judgment*.[16] Indeed, Kant insisted that nothing happens by chance, that everything in nature has a purpose.[17]

Kant argued that the four races were the products of seeds (*Keime*) and natural predispositions (*Anlagen*) rather than the result of chance or mechanical laws alone. Thus, the seeds of all the races were latent from the start in all persons, and the appropriate seed was actualized to serve a purpose that arose from the circumstances.[18] The seeds or predispositions, then, could not be undone by differences in climate or environment: they must be permanent. In his interpretation, transpiration of elements is the most important bodily response to climate, and thus skin is the most important organ. Kant focused exclusively on color as a racial marker—"the race of the *whites*, the *yellow*, Indian, the negro and the *copper-red* American."[19]

The dark skin of non-Europeans had particular meaning, over and above the very aspect of complexion. For Kant, as for other Europeans at the time, it was not only the color of Africans but the hues of various peoples encountered by explorers that needed to be accounted for.[20] Nonetheless, Kant was particularly challenged by the darkness of Africans, whom he considered a "base race" along with whites.[21] Iron content in skin and humid warmth produced a "thick, turned-up nose and thick, fatty lips. . . . In short, all of these factors account for the origin of the Negro, who is well-suited to his climate, namely, strong, fleshy, and agile. However, because he is so amply supplied by his motherland, he is also lazy, indolent, and dawdling."[22] He referred to Black people as "born slaves"[23] and in the same notes a few lines later wrote: "Americans and Blacks cannot govern themselves. They thus serve only for slaves."[24] Indeed, seeds inherent to all peoples meant that Black people could never achieve civilization. Kant wrote, "The Negro can be disciplined and cultivated, but is never genuinely civilized. He falls of his own accord into savagery."[25] Scholar J. Kameron Carter argues that for Kant, at this point, whites were no longer described as a race (even if they are thought of as one).[26] With Kant's philosophical system, the concept of whites as raceless had emerged. His narrative of racial essentialism provided a framework for racial hierarchy that is still in effect in the twenty-first century.

The Transatlantic Slave Trade and the Institution of Chattel Slavery

The transatlantic slave trade took place over 366 years; an estimated 12.5 million Africans were captured and forcibly shipped to the New World. Volumes have been written on the enduring destruction resulting from the slave trade, including death, displacement, disconnection, dehumanization, and the trauma inflicted on the auction block.

The institution of slavery in the United States undergirded every aspect of life in the antebellum United States: familial, social, religious, political, and economic. Slaveholders emphasized the "social death" that resulted from the status of slavery. Slaves were dishonored and dishonorable beings[27]—a stigma that was conferred on all Black people by virtue of the fact that as chattel slavery expanded from indentured servitude, only people of African descent were enslaved. Black people were enslaved on large and small plantations in the South and in cities, small towns, and rural areas in the North. They underwent varying degrees of subjugation depending on the characters of their owners. As property, field hands in the South were usually treated poorly: adequate food, clothing, shelter, and sleeping mats were withheld. They were mandated to do hard physical labor from sunup to sundown. They spoke painfully of severe physical abuse, particularly the lash and the whip, which was often inflicted randomly and served as warning messages to other enslaved persons.

The trauma of violent force was but one affliction experienced by enslaved people. In addition to corporal punishments ranging from whippings and beatings to withholding of food, Black women experienced the enduring trauma of sexual violence and exploitation. Angela Y. Davis writes,

> Slavery relied as much on routine sexual abuse as it relied on the whip and the lash . . . Sexual coercion was . . . an essential dimension of the social relations between slavemaster and slave. In other words, the right claimed by slaveowners and their agents over the bodies of female slaves was a direct expression of their presumed property rights over Black people as a whole. The license to rape emanated from and facilitated the ruthless economic domination that was the gruesome hallmark of slavery.[28]

Black women testified to unwanted sexual advances and rape by their owners; the children born of rape were also enslaved, as under law the child inherited the slave status of the mother. Furthermore, Black women were often mated to Black men in order to bear enslaved children, thereby increasing the property of their owners. Not least, Black women disproportionately endured the trauma of the auction block, in which they were sold away from their children or their children were sold away from them.

Enslavement resulted in unspeakable trauma in the perpetual separation of families as children were auctioned away from their parents and spouses were permanently parted. The selling of enslaved Black people on the auction block inflicted generational trauma for all Black families. Even if Black families on large plantations did not personally experience the auction block, the threat of the sale of a loved one was always present, rendering in all Black people during the antebellum period a perpetually vulnerable psychological and physical state.[29]

Frederick Douglass, in his *Narrative* of his life as a slave, recounts two incidents in which the auction block severely impacted the lives of enslaved Black people. In one case a slave on a large plantation truthfully told his owner, whom he had not previously met, that he was treated poorly. The owner promptly sold him. Douglass writes, "He was immediately chained and handcuffed; and thus, without a moment's warning, he was snatched away, and forever sundered, from his family and friends, by a hand more unrelenting than death."[30] Douglass himself later describes when he himself was put on the auction block:

> We were all ranked together at the valuation. Men and women, old and young, married and single, were ranked with horses, sheep, and swine. There were horses and men, cattle and women, pigs and children, all holding the same rank in the scale of being, and were all subjected to the same narrow examination. Silvery-headed age and sprightly youth, maids and matrons, had to undergo the same indelicate inspection. At this moment, I saw more clearly than ever the brutalizing effects of slavery upon both slave and slaveholder.
>
> After the valuation, then came the division. I have no language to express the high excitement and deep anxiety which were felt among us poor slaves during this time. Our fate for life was now to be decided. We had no more voice in that decision than the brutes among whom we were ranked. A single word from the white men was enough—against all our wishes, prayers, and entreaties—to sunder forever the dearest friends, dearest kindred, and strongest ties known to human beings.[31]

Douglass's testimony of the deep anxiety experienced on the auction block is mirrored in other written narratives of that period. Journalistic documents from 1859, during an auction of more than four hundred slaves who had lived for generations on the Gullee Islands of the state of Georgia, illuminate the devastation wrought by the selling of loved ones:

> At exactly 11:55am on March 3, 1859, Dorcas, chattel number 278, was sold away from her first love, Jeffrey, a twenty-three-year-old "prime cotton hand." She stood on the auction block motionless—emptied of words, emptied of tears. She spent the greater part of that cold and rainy Thursday morning contemplating their final separation. Now the moment came and she stood still as a bronze cast, her head covered with a beaded gray shawl. She stared vacantly at the auctioneer, who with one stroke of his gavel, declared a death knell on her future.
>
> Jeffrey, a tall, strapping field hand with soft eyes, who was sold earlier for $1,310 to another master, pulled off his hat, dropped to his knees, and wept. Just the day before, he had cherished high hopes. . . .
>
> [Jeffrey said to his new master] ". . . Please buy Dorcas, Mas'r. We're be good servants to you as long as we live. We're be married right soon, young Mas'r, and *de chillum will be healthy and strong, Mas'r, and dey'll be good servants, too.* Please buy Dorcas, young Mas'r. We loves each other a heap—do, really true, Mas'r. . . . Dorcas a prime woman—A1 woman, sa. Tall girl, sir; long arms, strong, healthy, and can do a heap of work in a day. She is one of de best rice hands on de whole plantation; worth $1,200 easy, Mas'r, an' fus'rate bargain at that."
>
> These words seemed to move his new master, who looked at him obligingly and indicated he would consider his proposal. He approached Dorcas with white-gloved hands and first opened her lips to check her age. He turned her around, as if spinning a top, and bade her take off her turban. As she turned, his white-gloved hand would alternately brush against her back and breasts. He examined her limbs one by one and put his hands around her ample waist. Yes, these hips might be worth something. They might, in fact, breed a few children, all to his profit.[32]

Dorcas and Jeffrey were sold to different masters, thereby breaking up their union. Indeed, the auction block served as a place in which families were split apart, never to be reunited, even after the conclusion of the Civil War. In the same auction in which Dorcas and Jeffrey were separated, thirty babies were also sold.

The trauma of the auction block took place in two different types of slave auctions: private and public. Oftentimes, private auctions were such that family units were sold together, sometimes for lower prices. But public auctions took place when a slave owner possessed tax delinquencies, bad debts, or bankruptcies or was selling his or her estate.[33] In such cases, slaves were sold as individuals, away from their families.[34] Katherine McKittrick refers to the auction block as a site of violence, subjugation, and humanness, "a place where race is made known in multiple ways."[35] She writes,

> Human sale took place in town centers, on local plantations, at fairs, in formal auction houses, in fields, and in community buildings. Slaves could also be bartered, inherited, rented, given away, and stolen. The differing locations for the sale of slaves, as well as state and national differences, reveals that the prices of slaves varied and the reasons for sale were attached to local, community, familial, and personal interests. Increasing home or field labor, bankruptcy, sex and rape, reproducing the slave population, selling "unruly" resistant slaves, breaking apart slave allegiances—these reasons for sale, among others, show that the auction block and the point of sale were underpinned by variable interests.[36]

Those variable interests would periodically take into account familial bonds, largely to prevent running away. Slave owners speculated that emotional investment in other slaves secured their property: mothers and fathers, daughters and sons, were unlikely to leave the plantation if their family members remained.

But the trauma of tearing away of children from parents, and the hypersexualization of Black women's bodies, rendered the most vulnerable enslaved persons even more exploited on the auction block. As seen in Dorcas's situation, Black women were ultimately observed as bodies that could reproduce more enslaved bodies, as slave status was inherited through matrilineal lines. McKittrick writes that "the public auction and the auction block displayed and scrutinized black women's sexual bodies in response to the need to reproduce the slave population. In many cases, women were put on display partially nude or fully nude; slave buyers kneaded women's stomachs; doctors publicly and privately examined their breasts, stomachs, and reproductive organs."[37]

The trauma of sexual exploitation and of families separated by the selling of children, husbands, and wives haunted families during the antebellum period. Although the auction block is not the only facet of slavery to manifest in the vestiges of contemporary Black life, generational trauma originating in the breakup of families during the antebellum period carries symbolic vestiges. Konda Mason, a teacher in the Insight tradition, reflects,

> When I think about where black women are right now and I think about the Black Lives Matter movement, which is run by black women . . . black women are showing up in this time and place in deep leadership. We lost our children, when our children got taken away and sold. I think we're still finding our children. I think we're still looking for each other. And I think that the pain that black women have suffered—black men have suffered as well—but that particular pain is catalytic to the healing now that I find black women leading on a political level, on an interpersonal level, on community level, on a society level . . . that's where the wisdom is coming from.[38]

The trauma of the auction block was one aspect of the violence of slavery. Yet another dimension of slavery was the violence inflicted by slave patrols, and later convict leasing and chain gangs.[39] The worldview and practices used to criminalize Black bodies in the postbellum period continue to be institutionalized in the penal system in the twenty-first century.

Criminalizing Blackness

In the postbellum southern penal system at the conclusion of the Civil War—between 1866 and 1867—criminal laws known as Black Codes, aimed at curtailing Black mobility, exploiting Black labor, and maintaining white supremacy, were enacted in every southern state. Although the Thirteenth Amendment abolished forced labor for free persons, it permitted involuntary servitude as a punishment for a crime.[40] The Thirteenth Amendment and its concurrent state-based laws effectively perpetuated the trauma of the institution of slavery. A key aspect of the Black Codes was a series of laws against vagrancy, which ensured the continued availability of cheap or free Black labor. The crime of "vagrancy" was defined in such a broad and ambiguous way that the statutes perpetuated de facto slavery.⁴¹ Every former Confederate state passed a vagrancy law. Black Codes forced freed slaves onto plantations and railroads and into mines, thereby formalizing exploitation of Black labor in an era when laborers were ostensibly free. But these laws served another function as well: remodeling the image of the recalcitrant Black slave into that of the thieving Black convict.

The construct of Black criminality functioned symbolically as well as materially. Symbolically, it cast Black people as suspect, untrustworthy, and dangerous. Materially, the construct of Black criminality undergirded an emerging "New South" in which the vast majority of prisoners were leased to private industrialists to labor on railroads as well as in the coal, steel, and cast iron mines. By the end of Reconstruction in 1877, every formerly Confederate state except Virginia had adopted the practice of leasing Black prisoners into commercial hands. By the end of the 1880s, at least ten thousand Black men were slaving in forced labor mines, fields, and work camps in the formerly Confederate states.⁴² Company guards were empowered to chain prisoners, shoot those attempting to flee, torture any who wouldn't submit, and whip the disobedient—naked or clothed—almost without limit.⁴³ There was little outcry, as the white public relied upon convict leasing to contain the constructed threat posed by Black freemen.

Brutally severe conditions led to high rates of mortality. The narrative that unfolded posited the Black convict as expendable, in contrast to the Black slave, who was viewed as a commodity by whites. In the eyes of white authorities, incarcerated Black lives were worth very little. White authorities espoused the prevailing sentiment of "if one dies, get another."⁴⁴ Convicts were routinely starved and beaten by farmers, government officials, corporations, miners, and small-town businessmen intent on achieving the most lucrative balance between the productivity of captive labor and the cost of sustaining them.

For eight decades, the white public turned a blind eye to the terrible conditions of convict leasing.

On many railroads, convicts were moved from job to job in a rolling iron cage, which also provided their lodging at the site. . . . The prisoners slept side by side, shackled together, on narrow wooden slabs. They relieved themselves in a single bucket and bathed in the same filthy tub of water. With no screens on the cages, insects swarmed everywhere. It was like a small piece of hell, an observer noted—the stench, the chains, the sickness, and the heat. "They lie on their beds, their faces almost touching the bed above them. . . . On hot days . . . the sun streams down . . . and makes an oven of the place, and the human beings in it roast."[45]

The human beings who were subjected to postbellum criminal legislation, arbitrary arrest, and brutal convict leasing conditions were considered fundamentally expendable and unworthy of protection or care. Indeed, this general approach to Black lives traumatized those who experienced the brutality of convict leasing and their families, as well as Black people in the South who lived in constant fear of arbitrary state violence. The trauma of the southern penal system—the random cruelty and systemic dehumanization alongside increasing white vigilante violence in the form of lynchings—prompted a wide range of responses from Black people.

The Trauma of Lynchings, Dislocation, and Segregation

Black female journalist Ida B. Wells calculated that more than ten thousand lynchings took place between 1865 and 1895.[46] Similarly to the randomness of the southern penal system, lynchings—by white citizens rather than state authorities—invoked terror throughout the Black South. Angela Y. Davis writes that "lynching was undisguised counterinsurgency, a guarantee that Black people would not be able to achieve their goals of citizenship and economic equality."[47] After 1872, when Black men were increasingly constructed as hypersexualized beings who threatened the purity of white women, lynching was rationalized as a method to avenge the white South.[48]

The threat of random lynching by organized white supremacist organizations such as the Ku Klux Klan as well as masses of hostile whites traumatized Black people who already faced intimidation in numerous ways. Whereas poor whites and poor Black people might have sought to build bridges based on common economic interests after the Civil War, union organizer A. Philip Randolph explains lynching as a consequence of capitalism, in which poor whites and poor Black people were pitted against each other, resulting in greater wealth and power for the industrialists who benefitted from interracial strife.[49] Seeking to establish whiteness as a currency to enshrine social superiority, southern whites enacted violence and discrimination against Black people with impunity.

Lynching and other arbitrary acts of violence became a norm. So too was the system of comprehensive social segregation that became known colloquially as Jim Crow.[50] All aspects of social life were routinely segregated: transportation, schools, stores, restaurants, swimming pools, drinking fountains, and more. If a white person was walking down a sidewalk, Black people were expected to move into the street. If Black people went to a white person's home, they entered through the back door; they did not dare presume social equality by knocking on the front door. Black professionals such as schoolteachers were paid a fraction of what white professionals earned.

Black people responded to the rigid social codes and arbitrary violence of the South. Over six decades, from approximately 1915 to 1975, six million Black people fled the South for northern cities in what became known as the Great Migration.[51] The trauma of living in fear and the humiliation of being treated as less than human was overwhelming. Black people in all sorts of economic situations—rural sharecroppers, craftsmen, domestic workers, and middle-class professionals—sought safer, more prosperous opportunities. In her book *The Warmth of Other Suns*, Isabel Wilkerson describes the social realities that every Black family in the South was forced to confront: stay at the bottom of the social rung in a rigid society or join the first mass independence movement undertaken by Black people. Wilkerson notes that the Great Migration did not end until the 1970s, when formal integration in the South resulted in biracial schools, color-free drinking fountains, and a Black middle class that could live without fear of lynching and without socially ingrained deference.

Prior to the Great Migration, segregation existed in northern cities, but the numbers of Black people were relatively small and many approximated middle-class means.[52] Scholars note that race relations were generally stable even in the midst of visible inequality. The first wave of the Great Migration resulted in a large influx of Black southerners: for example, Black residents in Chicago numbered approximately 44,000 in 1910, growing to 109,000 by 1920.

In response to the influx of Black Southerners, Chicago officials sharply segregated housing during the first wave of the Great Migration during World War I. Northern cities legally restricted where Black people could live.[53] Chicago was not alone: cities such as New York, Brooklyn, Boston, Philadelphia, Cincinnati, Cleveland, St. Louis, Pittsburgh, and Detroit were alarmed at the numbers of arrivals and reacted by creating legal barriers—such as restrictive covenants and redlining—as well as inflicting targeted violence and steering potential homeowners only to Black neighborhoods, to deny housing availability to Black people.

The trauma of being brutally kept in place by the rigid social norms of the South, risking arbitrary violence, including lynching, and being sequestered in squalor in northern ghettos—even as Black migrants accessed jobs in skilled labor industries during the two world wars—deeply impacted the well-being of Black families. Being relegated to crowded tenement housing, in which tenants suffered from rats and leaking roofs amongst other terrible conditions, impacted the physical and psychological health of newly arrived Black people. Northern whites, and northern Black people as well, interpreted southerners as lazy, ignorant, and dangerous. Newly arrived persons were blamed for crime, alcoholism, disease, and breakdowns in family relations.[54]

Furthermore, even as Black southerners accessed skilled labor, they still competed with immigrants and native-born whites, who in the North, as in the South, were seen as more socially desirable. In short, in the North Black people had access to higher wages but still occupied the bottom rung of the social ladder and still experienced arbitrary violence and segregation.

Black migrants responded to northern discrimination in numerous creative ways: by seeking formal education and becoming literate, joining increasing numbers of organizations seeking civil and political rights for Black people, organizing with Black immigrants from the Caribbean and Africa, and expressing themselves artistically in cultural movements such as the Harlem Renaissance (1918–1937).[55] The ability to express grief and articulate narratives on their own terms, in their own cadence, brought a measure of relief and insight into the trauma of living in dark skin in a comprehensively segregated society. Yet the widespread trauma of constantly navigating deeply embedded cultural and institutional racism continued to take a toll on those who migrated from the South to the North, on those who stayed in the South, on those who grew up in the North, and on their descendants.

Intergenerational Trauma in the Twenty-First Century

Constructed as degraded, Black people suffered the institution of chattel slavery, including corporal punishments, the auction block, and social death. They were exploited as fodder for the postbellum system of punishment in the "New South." They suffered discrimination, violence, and humiliation under Jim Crow segregation and lynchings, prompting tens of thousands of Black people to leave their families and migrate to the North, where they were sequestered in dilapidated housing. In the twenty-first century, Black people in the United States continue to encounter multifaceted racism—within the penal system, including policing and prisons, and in public schools that are often an extension of the penal system. Black women experience disproportionate harm, both by the state as well as by male violence. Finally, all Black people, regardless of age and embodiment, experience persistent microaggressions: messages of not belonging within the dominant culture group in which they find themselves. The results of trauma are so great that, as Black Buddhist teacher George Mumford writes, "the focus needs to be on me, on my internal conditioning."[56] Bushi Yamato Damashii, lead resident teacher of Daishin Zen Buddhist Temple in North Carolina, elaborates: "Outside of myself there is only opinion. Inside of myself there is only me. If I bring outside opinion in, then I corrupt me."[57]

Aggressive Policing and Mass Imprisonment

As the Movement for Black Lives—a coalition of fifty Black-led organizations and hundreds of allies—illuminates, aggression against Black people has continued unabated into the twenty-first century.[58] Policing practices that disproportionately target Black people have resulted in what Black Feminist scholar Beth E. Richie terms a "prison nation" that relies upon punishing violations of norms, encoding intimidation by writing extensive regulations, fostering exclusive ideological standards such as heterosexism, creating fear of scapegoated groups, and defining enemies.[59]

The U.S. prison nation expanded rapidly in the 1970s and remains the largest carceral system in the world. It has relied on recurrent images of violent Black people, well-funded and militarized policing forces, and harsh crime laws. In 1973, New York State legislators signed legislation that became known as the Rockefeller Drug Laws, which stipulated a fifteen-year-to-life sentence for selling two ounces or possessing four ounces of a narcotic. The images of people using narcotics depicted Black men in urban environments.

Mandatory minimum sentences for drugs created one of the most dramatic changes in the U.S. penal system.[60] After the passage of the Rockefeller Drug Laws, every state enacted mandatory minimum sentencing laws. In the 1980s, the federal government also enacted mandatory minimum drug laws. As a result, the prison population doubled between 1972 and 1984, and again between 1984 and 1994.[61] Although statistics revealed that Black and white people engage in drug offenses—possession and sales—at comparable rates, in every year from 1980 to 2007, Black people were arrested nationwide on drug charges at rates 2.8 to 5.5 times higher than whites.[62] In sum, drug laws disproportionately impacted Black individuals.

Sentencing guidelines have mandated harsher and longer sentences that the federal courts are required to follow without exception, such as mandatory minimums, drastically increased punishments for repeat offenders, and longer periods of incarceration.[63] The result has been an unprecedented increase in the prison population, primarily of poor Black people, at a time with fewer job opportunities for workers without college degrees.[64] Yet the rationale for disproportionately incarcerating Black people was attributed to shiftless and violent demeanors and actions rather than lack of jobs.

Since the end of the 1990s, on average one million Black people have been in prison on a daily basis, and Black men in their thirties are more likely to have been to prison than to have graduated from college with a four-year degree.[65] These staggering rates of incarceration of Black men—and increasingly Black women—have continued into the twenty-first century.

School Pushouts

An extension of the penal system is the public education system, an institution that journalist Ta-Nehisi Coates describes as serving twin functions of Black bodily control:

> I came to see the streets and the schools as arms of the same beast. One enjoyed the official power of the state while the other enjoyed its implicit sanction. But fear and violence were the weaponry of both. Fail in the streets and the crews would catch you slipping and take your body. Fail in the schools and you would be suspended and sent back to those same streets, where they would take your body. And I began to see these two arms in relation—those who failed in the schools justified their destruction in the streets. The society could say, "He should have stayed in school," and then wash its hands of him.[66]

Indeed, for Coates, as for scholars of education policy, public schools further the aim of the U.S. penal system, to control Black bodies and dehumanize Black students. Monique W. Morris, in *Pushout: The Criminalization of Black Girls in Schools*, illuminates how Black girls are disproportionately penalized in schools that increasingly rely on law enforcement to monitor children. Whereas previously professionals trained in managing children oversaw conduct issues, in the twenty-first century armed guards surveil students. Furthermore, the punishment-oriented educational system relies upon suspension, expulsion, detention centers, house arrest, electronic monitoring, and other forms of social exclusion.[67] The result, Morris says, is an educational system reliant upon inflicting punitive measures rather than helping children thrive.

The school-to-confinement pipeline, which has historically been designated as the school-to-prison pipeline, gives students a right to be hostile, argues Erica Meiners.[68] Indeed, the continuum between schools and prisons is founded on "zero-tolerance policies . . . [that] place disagreements between students and teachers, regulation of classroom behavior, and enforcement of rules in the hands of armed police officers stationed in public schools."[69] The aggression enacted against Black children in schools is routinely violent when applied to differently gendered bodies and yet is highly sexualized when administered to female-bodied persons. Gendered punishment is overt not only within schools, police systems, and prisons but in homes and communities as well.

Violence Against Black Women

Black women experience disproportionate harm within the penal system and within private spheres.[70] A component of the Black Lives Matter movement, #Say Her Name, uplifts the lives of Black women who are killed by police violence. The driving-while-Black police incident targeting Sandra Bland, who was later found hanging in a Texas police precinct, illuminates state violence against Black women. Andrea J. Ritchie points attention to numerous situations of violence against Black women in her book *Invisible No More: Police Violence Against Black Women and Women of Color*. Bland's case, she argues, illuminates policing patterns that cause disproportionate harm to Black women and women of color, including situations in which police officers commit sexual assault. Aggressive policing patterns are furthermore evident when officers violently surveil gender-nonconforming appearance and transgender persons. Furthermore, there are repeated patterns of aggressively policing sex workers, mothers, and victims of domestic violence.[71]

State violence enacted against Black women takes place in other domains of the penal system, most notably the prison. Angela Y. Davis and Beth E. Richie recount in graphic terms the routine practices of sexual assault and harassment in carceral settings, including cavity searching and taunting.[72]

Systemic violence against Black women is not the only specter of violence; indeed, many more women undergo *interpersonal* violence by men. Harm takes place in the forms of physical and sexual assault, threats and emotional manipulation, financial exploitation, confinement, isolation, and more.[73] Richie describes how, among young people dating their peers, "physical and emotional abuse are common, which distinguishes African American women from their peer groups."[74] She notes that the vulnerability of Black women increases when they have low incomes, in that many Black women find themselves trapped by hostile environments. Indeed, they are disproportionately located in public housing and often unprotected. Richie writes,

> When domestic relations are characterized by power exercised by one person's extreme and persistent tension, dominance of their needs over others, chronic irritability, and irrational agitation that escalates over time, then a pattern is set that is abusive and controlling. The relationship becomes shaped by a cruel dynamic whereby the controlling partner can deploy a set of psychological, emotional, and/or verbal tactics that result in fear, anxiety, or at the very least confusion as a response.[75]

Recent documentaries—and the #MeToo movement—have brought the alarming rates of violence against Black women to the forefront. Buddhist practitioner Aishah Shahidah Simmons's *NO! The Rape Documentary* (2006) focuses on rape committed against Black women and girls, noncarceral accountability, and healing in Black communities. The #MuteRKelly movement led to the production of a six-part Lifetime series documenting, in excruciating detail, the harm inflicted upon teenagers and young women by R&B singer R. Kelly. Kelly's accusers name physical and sexual assault, withholding food, confinement, and isolation as patterns they endured, often for years. Although a film of Kelly urinating in the mouth of a fourteen-year-old girl during sexual intercourse was widely circulated, in 2008 he was acquitted of fourteen counts of child pornography. It was not until 2017, when Black women initiated a #MuteRKelly social media campaign, that radio stations and concert venues responded. In the words of Mikki Kendall, interviewed in the *Surviving R. Kelly* documentary, "No one cared because we were Black girls."[76] Jerhonda Pace, a survivor of Kelly's abuse, further stated, "It's the Black community that bashes the Black women who speak out about abuse."[77]

Violence is enacted against Black women in community contexts. Richie describes how Black women are disproportionately raped, harassed, and coerced into sexual acts within their immediate surroundings.[78] Intimidation can take place within the neighborhood; so, too, in the work environment. During the unfolding of the #MeToo movement, Drew Dixon, Sil Lai Abrams, and Sheri Hines documented their experiences of rape and sexual harassment by Russell Simmons, cofounder of Def Jam Records. They are three of twenty women who have accused

Simmons of sexual assault, acknowledging that it is deeply painful to accuse a successful Black man of crime.[79] Other Black women commentators discuss the public pressure to stay silent and refrain from naming harm enacted by Black men.

This message of "letting down the Black community" or staying in "the trap of loyalty" to the Black community is often used to manipulate Black women who have been harmed by Black men. Indeed, for Black women historically and in the twenty-first century, publicly naming harms committed by Black men has often come at the excruciating price of isolation and hostility from those who argue for racial solidarity first. Numerous scholars describe Black women's orientation toward family, social roles, respectability, and advancement to uplift of the Black community. The tremendous fear of alienating Black people by adding to the stereotype of Black men as violent, criminally prone, and shiftless prompts many abused Black women to self-silence.

Microaggressions: Everyday Exclusions

The violences of the education system and the carceral system, and the harms enacted within many Black families and communities, are historical continuums of oppressions against Black people. Furthermore, while many Black people may not be victims of institutional or interpersonal violence themselves, *all* Black people—regardless of gender identity or class—experience microaggressions: different treatment that is normalized in a white supremacist society. Scholars identify racial microaggressions as "brief and commonplace daily verbal, behavioral, or environmental indignities, whether intentional or unintentional, that communicate hostile, derogatory, or negative racial slights and insults toward people of color."[80] Racial microaggressions impair mental health and wellness and can result in trauma.

Unwanted physical touches, insults, and invalidating remarks are the most common microaggressions. These practices bear upon what diversity consultants Tiffany Jana and Michael Baran describe as "subtle acts of exclusion" that insult and harm: "Subtle acts of exclusion, because they serve to diminish people, are critical to understand, identify, and address."[81] Subtle acts of exclusion foster a sense of invisibility, inadequacy, and abnormality; victims view themselves only as a member of a marginalized group, a curiosity, a threat, a burden, and as not belonging.

Numerous Black Buddhist teachers and practitioners interviewed for this book spoke of their experiences of subtle acts of exclusion in predominantly white sanghas. A number of academic research projects, as well as reports from individual sanghas, highlight the white, middle- and upper-class composition of Buddhist convert sanghas.[82] These communities often fail to honor the Indian roots of Buddhism, challenge the whiteness of their community's composition, or understand the layered experiences of people of color in predominantly white settings.[83] Indeed, it is difficult to embrace dharma teachings and practices in the culture of a community that feels hostile, isolating, and alienating. Spring Washam, a teacher in the Insight tradition, recounts in her book *A Fierce Heart*,

> In the early days of my meditation journey, I traveled to retreat centers throughout the U.S. I loved the teachings and the practices, but I always felt like an outsider. Groups were almost a hundred percent white and consisted mostly of middle-aged people or seniors. All the teachers were white, mostly from upper middle class backgrounds. Consistently, I would walk into a room and be the youngest practitioner and the only person of color, and this would trigger a feeling in me that I was in a community I felt excluded from. The racism and pain I had experienced growing up would arise in me constantly during that time.[84]

In an effort to practice the dharma, predominantly white sanghas can often fall into "spiritual bypassing": the use of spiritual practice to circumvent personal developmental issues.[85] Such an emphasis on spirituality often comes at the expense of acknowledging social realities, including oppression due to racial, gender, class, and sexual identity, and how microaggressions operate in predominantly white settings.[86]

As Black Buddhists initiate nuanced conversations about spiritual, psychological, and political liberation, they are propelling forward an important conversation about the cultural dominance of whiteness. One of the foremost critics of whiteness in convert Buddhist sanghas, Rev. angel Kyodo williams, reflects on the isolation experienced by dharma

practitioners of African descent. She recounts one marginalizing experience at the Shambhala Center in New York City.

> I went to Shambhala New York and I just could not bear it. There's white-
> ness as a racial construct, there's whiteness as we talk about white folks. I
> come from New York, where whiteness shows up in such different ways.
> It wasn't the sort of massive thing that I felt was overwhelming. There
> are Jewish and Irish and Italian [folks]. My dad was a fireman and his
> dad was a fireman, so [we had] lots of contact with Irish and Italian folks
> in the fire department, and Polish people, so my range of white-skinned
> people was quite vast. And Shambhala New York was a kind of form, a
> particular strain of upper-middle-class whiteness that had a feeling of
> being oppressive, where people turned around and looked at you, and I
> had a strong feeling that I was not welcome.[87]

Conversations with teachers and practitioners of African descent as well
as studies on racial relations in individual sanghas and retreat centers
verify that williams's experience is, in fact, widespread. The dominant
whiteness williams experienced at Shambhala New York is but one
example of the cultural exclusivity expressed in homogenous Buddhist
sanghas. In williams's book *Radical Dharma*, coauthored with Lama Rod
Owens and Jasmine Syedullah, she describes attending a retreat of fifty
people, forty-seven of whom were white:

> One woman looked at me and asked, "Do you know that they're going
> to have a *Martin Luther King* Day retreat here?" She put great emphasis
> on "Martin Luther King." The color of my skin was both something to be
> called out and yet something to be utterly undealt with. . . . The real ques-
> tion remains: How can we address the barriers for people like me when
> the predominant culture cannot acknowledge its privilege? We are born
> into a particular body, and this can be a great source of pain, depending
> on how society views the identity [associated with it]. And yet, commu-
> nities in power pretend the difference, and the pain, is not there, which
> causes the individuals in that skin to question our value.[88]

Convert Buddhist sanghas are still overwhelming white, middle and
upper class, and resistant to recognizing how their structures and cul-

tures arise from and reinforce white supremacy. Teachers and practitioners of African descent report experiencing isolation, hostility, and microaggressions. Communities that have established people of color sitting groups report that they are generally separate from the rest of the community, with practitioners of color reporting consistent discomfort with the larger sangha. Critical reflections by teachers of color in convert sanghas reiterate the experiences of practitioners of color.

Yet Black people still embrace Buddhism. As Tibetan scholar and practitioner Jan Willis describes in her 2020 collection of essays *Dharma Matters: Women, Race, and Tantra*, practicing the dharma is a path of healing intergenerational trauma.

> It is the trauma of slavery that haunts African Americans in the deepest recesses of their souls. This is the chief issue for us. It needs to be dealt with, head-on—not denied, not forgotten, not suppressed. Indeed, its suppression and denial only hurts us more deeply, causing us to accept a limited, disparaging, and even repugnant view of ourselves. We cannot move forward until we have grappled in a serious way with all of the negative effects of this trauma. Tantric Buddhism offers us some tools to help accomplish this task, since it shows us both how to get at those deep inner wounds and how to heal them.[89]

Willis names Tantric Buddhism as a particular practice, and—as many Black Buddhist teachers describe throughout this book—Buddhist practices within the Theravada and Mahayana lineages also facilitate the healing of intergenerational trauma.

Trauma Stored in the Body: Healing Neural Pathways through Dharma Practices

Psychotherapist Resmaa Menakem, in his book *My Grandmother's Hands*, notes the wide array of physical illnesses that result from racialized intergenerational trauma:

> As many researchers now believe, the ongoing violations of the Black body and heart have resulted in widespread trauma. This racialized trauma shows up as an array of adaptive but dysfunctional behaviors, in-

cluding hypervigilance, heightened anxiety and suspicion, ADD/ADHD, Obsessive-Compulsive Disorder, and addiction. It can also appear as dysfunctional and non-adaptive behavior such as disordered thinking, difficulty concentrating, panic attacks, learned helplessness, self-hatred, hopelessness, depression, and a survival reflex that tends to involve violence. As Joy DeGruy and others have noted, all of these are common symptoms of a pervasive and persistent stress disorder.

In many African American bodies, this trauma has led to a variety of physical problems, the most common of which are high blood pressure, diabetes, obesity, compromised immune systems, heart problems, digestive disorders, chronic inflammation, and musculoskeletal disorders. . . . For anyone to genuinely address these health issues, the person needs to address the trauma that fuels them. Without that foundational healing, all other healing becomes difficult or impossible, because the body is still stuck in the trauma.[90]

A plethora of research illuminates how trauma becomes stored in the body. Several influential studies detailed by psychiatrist Bessel van der Kolk in his book *The Body Keeps the Score: Brain, Mind, and Body in the Healing of Trauma* demonstrate that after traumatic experiences, bodies reexperience terror, rage, helplessness, and the urge to fight or take flight.[91] Van der Kolk notes that all trauma is preverbal and therefore is akin to the experience of a stroke when it is difficult to speak. He notes that the brain captures images that return as nightmares and flashbacks. Unprocessed sense fragments from the traumatic experience—such as sounds, smells, physical sensations—register separately from the story itself. Time, then, does not matter: the trauma can be experienced one day as if it had happened the prior day, even if the actual experience took place in the previous decade.

Van der Kolk's research shows that images of past trauma activate the right side of the brain and deactivate the left. The right side of the brain, colloquially known as the "emotional brain," develops first in the womb: it carries memories of touch, sound, smell, and even intuition. It is associated with art, visual images, spatial understanding, and tactile movements, what van der Kolk refers to as "the music of experience."[92]

The left side of the brain, conversely, is associated with remembering facts, statistics, vocabulary, sequencing, and executive functioning.

It is denoted as the "rational brain," logical, analytical, able to name, compare, understand, communicate subjective experience.[93] When the left brain is deactivated and the right brain is activated, the right brain acts as if the traumatic event were happening in the moment. Van der Kolk's research demonstrates that trauma causes the left, rational brain to deactivate and the right, emotional brain to become highly activated.

When the right brain is activated by trauma and relives traumatic experiences as if they were happening in the moment, the body responds by increasing its production of adrenaline—"fight or flight" stress hormones that are present in the body to help individuals respond to danger and threat. This increase in adrenaline results in attention problems, irritability, sleep disorders, and long-term health issues that are sometimes called "underlying conditions." Much of the body's energy focuses on suppressing inner chaos in the aftermath of trauma.

Not only do individuals store trauma in their bodies, thus resulting in physical ailments and suppressed capacity for joy, but biological studies show that trauma is passed on to subsequent generations through changes in the brain, the maternal egg, and the paternal sperm. This passing of intergenerational trauma, known as "transgenerational epigenetic inheritance," is seen in both biological changes as well as behavioral shifts of offspring.

Increasingly, publications by Black Buddhist teachers are identifying the impact of intergenerational trauma on Black people's nervous systems. Gyozan Royce Andrew Johnson writes, "I learned that healing through meditation was as much about the central nervous system as it was about the mind. I understand now that the two are not separate."[94] Cheryl Giles, coeditor of the 2020 volume *Black and Buddhist: What Buddhism Can Teach Us about Race, Resilience, Transformation, and Freedom*, writes of the experiences of sexual violence enacted against Black women and the practice of taking refuge, particularly in meditating and calling on ancestors:

> We know trauma lives in the body. We carry it every day. Trauma cannot be buried, ignored, pushed aside, or denied. As long as we breathe, trauma reminds us it is with us and rises to the surface. Transforming trauma means being willing to address it in our lives. Developing a daily practice helps us to be with whatever comes up and not shut down. . . . By

learning to sit with discomfort, you develop an ability to be with whatever feelings, sensations, and thoughts arise within the body with presence and the courage to be with yourself just as you are in each moment.[95]

Order of Interbeing teacher Larry Ward also acknowledges the importance of healing embodied trauma. He writes in his 2020 book *America's Racial Karma*, "Our bodies hold the retribution energies of America's racial karma. No one escapes this fear and trembling deep in our bones. Whether we were or are victims, perpetrators, or witnesses, we are unavoidably biologically destabilized and dysregulated by our sensory experience or the memories of America's racial karma."[96]

Indeed, a plethora of research illuminates how traumatic experiences change the hormones and cells in the body and are subsequently passed down through cells—the maternal egg and the paternal sperm—to future generations. A body of scientific research that originated in cell biology and is now known as "epigenetics" illuminates that stress inherited from fathers and mothers through DNA is still present in the hormonal reactions of descendants three generations later.[97] Psychologist Mark Wollyn explains, "When your grandmother was five months pregnant with your mother, the precursor cell of the egg you developed from was already present in your mother's ovaries. This means that before your mother was even born, your mother, your grandmother, and the earliest traces of you were all in the same body—three generations sharing the same biological environment."[98]

While the mother's placenta nourishes the fetus, she also releases hormones and information signals generated by her feelings. These chemicals activate cells that, in turn, change not only the mother's body but also her fetus's. Wollyn writes that chronic responses to the environment, such as repeated anger and fear, can imprint her child, essentially preparing or "preprogramming" how the child will adapt to its environment. Stress hormones experienced by the mother can also trigger "fight or flight" mode in the fetus. Thus a child who has experienced a stressful in utero environment can become reactive in a similarly stressful situation.[99]

Of each person's DNA, 98 percent is called "noncoding DNA." The emotional, behavioral, and personality traits that human beings inherit from their parents and grandparents as well as responses to environmental toxins and poor nutrition are found in noncoding DNA. Scientists note that the cellular-level changes passed through generations help people to meet challenges and copy with traumas. However, the changes to DNA also impact a child's sensitive reaction to seemingly innocuous events and could predispose a child to stress-related diseases. In short, the external environment impacts the internal environment, leading to gene changes and varying reactions to stress over generations.

Studies on gene changes in mice have been particularly informative: newborn mice who are separated from their mothers encode DNA changes that are apparent in their offspring three generations later: the egg and sperm cells, as well as the brains, were impacted by the stress of being separated.[100] Similar stress patterns were observed with rats who received low levels of maternal care: they were anxious and more reactive to stress in adulthood than rats who received high levels of maternal care. Other studies have shown that even when DNA changes—such as high sensitivity to stress or sound—are not present, offspring exhibit the same *behavioral* challenges are their parents. Changes in DNA as well as behavior are, together, known as "transgenerational epigenetic inheritance."

Practicing dharma teachings facilitates healing neural pathways that are ingrained as a result of intergenerational trauma. Ward illustrates how a ramped-up nervous system leads to debilitating illnesses and proposes that Black people cultivate awareness of their bodies.

> Notice in yourself how the racial hierarchy has affected you and your nervous system. Observe not only your thoughts, but also, how your body has been responding. Have you noticed your own hypervigilance? Have you noticed your own fatigue? Have you noticed your own sense of overwhelm, or panic, or even hopelessness? All these issues, feelings, and sensations rise in us, but shame also rises in us. It's the shame of not being valued as a human being. It's the shame of the experience of not being worthy of love. This is our work, this is my work as an elder in my community, to witness and transform our collective experience of the pain of the last five hundred years, so that it will no longer continue to be transmitted.[101]

Indeed, the impact of intergenerational trauma is multifold. And yet psychologists, psychiatrists, and Black dharma teachers—including those who are particularly attuned to the intergenerational traumas experienced by people of African descent whose ancestors were enslaved—remain hopeful. Ward states directly, "We are blessed with a brain and nervous system that possess qualities of neuroplasticity: the ability for the brain's neurons to learn, adapt, and change, and we thus always have an opportunity to nourish the aspects of our consciousness that are joyful, wise, and free."[102] Ward and other scholars point to various studies that have shown that trauma symptoms can be reversed. For example, mice who live in low-stress environments as adults can experience a reverse in childhood traumatized symptoms.[103] In short, studies show that it is possible to change the patterns in the brain—to cultivate new pathways for healing. Buddhist and secular practitioners of mindfulness agree that the dharma offers a roadmap for understanding the roots of suffering and working mindfully with the body to calm the "emotional brain," also known as "the limbic system."[104]

Van der Kolk writes that the body is the seat of pleasure, purpose, and direction.[105] Indeed, Ward and other Black Buddhist teachers identify embodied practices—including ancestral devotions, connecting with nature, practicing yoga, walking, and dancing—as helpful for moving trauma through the body. Not least, Black Buddhist teachers practice the dharma as a method for healing intergenerational trauma and living into liberation.

3

Honoring Ancestors in Black Buddhist Practice

Rituals of Devotion and Resilience

To be deeply of a place and of a people means knowing their
seasons and languages, speaking their tongues, singing their
music of growing things, knowing and loving their names.
—Rachel Bagby[1]

Ancestors venerated in Black Buddhist practice are upheld as those
who embodied courageous responses to suffering. In their capacity to meet patriarchal white supremacy with resilience, while they
were alive, Black ancestors demonstrated fortitude, perseverance, and
embodied inspiration. As interviews with Black Buddhist practitioners attest, it is a central aspect of their practice to honor ancestors
with devotional rituals. For many, venerating ancestors is one part of
the Three Jewels: sangha—a sense of belonging, connection, family,
and community.

African-descended ancestors embraced by Black Buddhists cel-
ebrated, rather than denigrated, the dark-skinned body. They furthermore embraced African cultural expressions, including ritualized
traditions and customs, such as healing practices, song, and dance.[2] This
chapter illuminates an aspect of Black Buddhist practice that is emerging: honoring known and unknown, spiritual and biological ancestors,
often in connection to land.[3]

Buddhist teachers of African descent recognize that many indigenous peoples throughout the world have practiced the essence of the
dharma without calling it as such. In one example, Bhante Buddharakkita, a Ugandan monk ordained in the Theravada tradition, uplifts the
practice of *dadirri*—deep listening—as an essential practice of dharma.
Buddharakkita reflects,

About deep listening: I spent a lot of time in Australia. Basically I was tracking down indigenous wisdom because when I talk about African wisdom, indigenous wisdom, I know that the Aboriginals came from Africa. So then I went to their place. First I was in the library as I was writing my dissertation and I landed on a book. It is called *Healing Transgenerational Trauma*. And this author actually had done a lot of work with the aboriginals. Then in a library, I read the book and I read a term called dadirri. Dadirri is a practice of the Aboriginals. Then I kept on reading more. They said this what the dadirri means: deep listening awareness. I just said, "wow." These Aboriginals are the people nobody paid attention to in the society. I met their elder who actually collaborated with me in research. She told me: "This is meditation, this is mindfulness. Deep listening awareness."[4]

Deep listening, along with stories of ancestors, locate human beings in the social world, creating a sense of lineage and connection. Recognizing ancestors has prompted teachers and long-term practitioners to innovate practices to honor blood and spiritual forebears in Black Buddhist communities. Black Buddhist teachers note that such practices expand the breadth of sangha—the community—primarily in the acknowledgment that the community's values and rituals arise from practices established by forebears.

Moreover, ways of life modeled by ancestors are intricately connected to the land: ancestors on the continent of Africa lived close to earth, trees, and rivers. They depended upon the rhythms of the natural world—such as the rising and setting sun, periodic rainfalls, and weather shifts—to grow crops, hold ceremonies, and honor members of the community. Honoring the land, then, has been an essential part of honoring ancestors. Land connects ancestors to the living. Judy Atkinson, in her study of indigenous peoples in Australia, describes land as "a story place": "Land holds the stories of human survival across many generations. Land shapes people, just as people shape their countries. . . . For those people who have lived and loved here since the creation times, the land is more than a physical place. It is a moral sphere, the seat of life and emotions, and a place of the heart."[5]

Atkinson quotes Deborah Bird Rose, an anthropologist who describes the indigenous worldview: in Aboriginal cultures, there is a conceptual essence of the land and its people who are connected across genera-tions by "interacting, relating, moving, growing, nourishing and being nourished, transforming and being transformed, in this evolutionary process."[6]

Being connected to ancestors, then, involves participating in ongoing, ritualized practices that are intimately connected to land.[7] In some belief systems, ancestral beings humanized the natural world.[8] In other indig-enous cosmologies, spirit ancestors made humans.[9] Atkinson writes that "to know the country is to know the story of how it came into being," for people rely on the land and cultivate the country.[10] Thus, it is impera-tive to recognize those who have gone before. For indigenous-oriented Buddhist practitioners, the history of ancestors carries meaning for themselves, their family members, and their broader community. Fur-thermore, the courage, determination, and perseverance embodied by ancestors is mirrored in the resilience of the land to withstand natu-ral forces. Even when African Americans acknowledge their complex relationship with the land of the United States—land they were vio-lently made to work as enslaved peoples to garner profits for white slave owners—they acknowledge the importance of feeling located on land and honoring the presence of First Nation peoples who populated the land prior to colonization. The ability to see the land as sacred, beyond the history of European colonialism, has been incorporated into numer-ous African American healing initiatives.

The simultaneous process of venerating ancestors and honoring land has deep roots in indigenous healing practices throughout the world.

Land has recuperative aspects that are essential to Aboriginal well-being. Our land also has an important role to play in healing. The land is a power-ful healer, as is the sea. When your ancestors have walked these places for millennia, they hold an energy of timelessness that invokes serenity and the feeling that one is not alone, but in the presence of these ancestors, who are able to communicate via the senses and convey the feelings and thoughts that are most conductive to healing. When we are able to sit on our land in contemplation and hear, feel or see the spirits of our old people, then we have been to a place within ourselves of great depth and connectedness. It is this place that we need to go to in order to truly heal ourselves; and once we have learnt how to do that, then we can move forward.[11]

The healing practices of Aboriginals—particularly a training method known as Indigenous Focusing-Oriented Therapy (IFOT) for complex trauma, a decolonized intervention that arises from an indigenous world view—has been highly influential for healing the legacies of dislocation, chattel slavery, segregation, and institutional racism historically and presently experienced by Black people.[12] Furthermore, as described by Bhante Buddharakkita, Black Buddhist teachers note the synergy of the Australian concept of dadirri—"deep listening"—with Buddhist meditative practices of watching the breath, observing the mind, and attuning to the surrounding environment in stillness.

Miriam-Rose Ungunmerr Baumann, the founder of an Australian Aboriginal foundation that teaches the practices of dadirri, says,

> To know me is to breathe with me. To breathe with me is to listen deeply. To listen deeply is to connect. This is the sound, the sound of deep calling to deep. *Dadirri*: the deep inner spring inside us. We call on it, and it calls on us. We are river people. We cannot hurry the river. We need to move with the current and understand its ways. We wait for the rain to fill our rivers and water our thirsty ears. We watch our fish and wait for them to open before we gather them. We wait for our young people as they grow. The time for rebirth is now. If our culture is alive and strong and respected, it will grow. It will not die, and our spirit will not die. I believe that the spirit of *dadirri* that we have to offer will blossom and grow, not just within ourselves, but within our whole nation.[13]

Ungunmerr Baumann's embrace of her indigenous roots—in her love of the land, her ancestors, and her culture—is embodied primarily in ceremonies that promote healing through the senses, thoughts, and feelings.[14] "Ceremonies are a time to communicate with ancestral beings, creation powers, and other beings."[15] Ceremonies connect the ancestors with the present and with the descendants who are yet to be born. Such ceremonies are based on deep listening to the rhythms of the land. Through creating sacred objects and other art forms, as well as singing, dancing, and performing rituals, humans connect to ancestors who release their power into the community and foster future life. Indeed, such ceremonies were themselves created by the ancestors; thus, the living and the ancestors cocreate their way of being and their future commitments. In aboriginal culture, the ancestral past is called "the time before morning" and "the Dreamings."

Seeing and hearing ancestors in dreams is similarly a common experience within African American communities in the South.[16] Nancy Fairley's studies of two North Carolina communities illuminate how ancestors who appear in dreams communicate requests and advice to their family members.[17] Furthermore, Fairley describes how newborns are uplifted as filling a void created by a recently deceased person, and elders assess characteristics of children as showing the traits of elders.[18] The reverence for these ancestors and the reverence for new life are thus held together in a practice of communal honor.

Revered ancestors are those who have loved their families and communities well by modeling ethical actions. Not all ancestors are chosen as conduits; they must have been seen as exemplary to achieve the status of venerated ancestor. Bryson C. M. White's research into ancestor veneration in Africa identifies ancestors as a "divine community of the noble and exemplary dead."[19] White, summarizing Robert Hood's research, describes ancestor veneration as providing five important community strengthening bonds that take place in ancestor veneration: "(a) ancestorship and parenthood are highly prized in African social status; (b) veneration of the ancestors is really the 'ritualization of filial piety'; (c) observing the ancestors maintains communal living between the living, as well as between the living and the dead; (d) ancestors are safe guardians of communal ethics, family traditions, and community customs; (e) ancestors are also spirits that communicate with their survivors through dreams, reincarnation, and visions."[20]

Similarly to African and other indigenous leaders, African American spiritual elders highlight the importance of dreams, rituals, and ceremonies in connecting to ancestors. Yeye Luisah Teish, who has studied numerous spiritual traditions, including Zen, Church of the Science of Mind, and Bahá'í, and who now practices as a Yoruba priestess, describes how "ancestor-reverence" is central to African-derived belief systems that flourish in the United States. "Through reverence for [ancestors] we recognize our origins and ensure the spiritual and physical continuity of the human race."[21] For Teish and other elders who call on ancestors for psychic and spiritual well-being, ancestors continue to be influential in the spirit world. Furthermore, they can choose to be reborn at the right time and place.[22]

Ancestors serve as intermediaries between the human and natural world; they furthermore act as intermediaries between the conscious mind and the subconscious mind. Teish describes African-derived traditions in which the divine spirit—God or Goddess—communicates to the ancestor, who filters the idea to the human's subconsciousness. The idea then emerges in the human's conscious mind as a "burst of inspiration." Building altars to honor the ancestors and communicating with them through meditative practices facilitate a mode of being in which practitioners can quiet their minds enough and gaze upon visual images as they hear the guidance from their ancestors. Teish, for example, highlights the intuition as a primary way to hear the voices of the ancestors.

The spiritual quietness that allows the voices of the ancestors to surface is particularly important to a people whose ancestors' names are not known. The horror of the transatlantic slave trade and the auction block resulted in family disconnections and dislocations, so that the names of generations of ancestors are lost. People of African descent brought to and raised in the Americas were forced to take the names of their oppressors. Finally, many ancestors have traumatized spirits, due to the tragedies that they endured, and need healing before they can offer wisdom.[23]

Various African-derived traditions in the United States inspire numerous rituals and ceremonies for connecting to the ancestors. Contemporary rituals to connect to ancestors include offering food, calling upon names, pouring libations, meditating, smudging, dancing, asking specific questions from a quiet mind, and listening carefully for answers.[24]

The Wisdom of Ancestors in the Context of Colonialism

Ancestors, then, bestow guidance and wisdom on subsequent generations. In ceremonies, they transmit practices of the past; in meditation, they guide through intuitive sensing and feeling. Atkinson writes,

> In [making meaning], there is recognition of those who have gone before
> and their contribution to the whole of who we are, of the connections

and communications between people down the generations, between people and country, and between the corporeal and non-corporeal world. These are the inter-relationships, interdependencies, interconnections and continuities that form the whole. These inter-relationships must be considered in any developing understanding of the traumatic impacts of colonisation where irrevocable intrusion has occurred, and continues to occur, into the soul and fabric of the relationships that people had with each other and their country.[25]

The indigenous approach to understanding traumatized responses not as individual pathology but as part of a broader legacy of violent domination, dehumanizing institutional mechanisms, and degrading psychological narratives illuminates the conditions of nearly four million people of African descent who were captured and forcibly taken to the New World to work the land as slaves.

In short, the trauma experienced by people of African descent is part of a broader trauma inflicted on indigenous peoples globally. Similarly, Black Buddhists' rituals of honoring ancestors who provide wisdom, direction, and collective identity are practiced by indigenous peoples worldwide.

Scholars of indigenous traditions speak of the importance of remembering one's own story as well as the story of one's people. Numerous scholars acknowledge that trauma is greater and more severe when caused by human beings, in large-scale practices such as colonization, than when caused by natural disasters such as hurricanes.[26] Thus the trauma that has resulted from colonialism and enslavement has impacted the collective African American psyche in unique and identifiable ways. Such acknowledged trauma calls for an approach to healing that acknowledges the broader context and employs rituals that interweave African ancestry with personal psychological wellness.[27]

The violence of European colonization in Africa, Asia, North America, Latin America, and the Caribbean perpetuated systems of domination that continue to pervade bodies and human relationships to the land, community, and spiritual practices. DaRa Williams, a psychotherapist and teacher in the Insight tradition, reflects that there is both sacredness to uphold as well as terror to acknowledge in the specific history of African Americans' relationship to land in the United States:

Part of why we're still here is that we did a good job with externalizing grief, because the body couldn't hold all of it. And the other piece that comes up is the relationship to land. Land is representative. It's not just the physical land but it is representative of language, of movement, of food. It's representative of so many things that go into making a racial identity. One of the reasons why I think Indigenous Focusing-Oriented Therapy (IFOT) is so transferrable to African Americans or people of African descent is because it's the opposite side of the same coin. Native Americans were here and had their land absconded and stolen from them. They were placed on these little controlled pieces of land. And that started them down the rabbit hole of disenfranchisement and non-connection to ancestry and history, although there's a reclamation going on now, to some degree. And the African was removed from the land but brought to another land, where their main purpose was to work the land. There's this interplay of land and culture and connection that IFOT brings which supports the healing of these bodies. . . . This culture of identifying with land is something that African Americans don't have, because there's so much terror in the land here.[28]

Elaborating Williams's analysis, Sebene Selassie, a teacher within the Insight tradition, points out the history of the Middle Passage and the institution of enslavement in the United States as part of worldwide patterns in which Europeans colonized African, Latin American, Caribbean, and Asian lands by seizing territories, enslaving native peoples, and importing Africans. The domination of land and indigenous peoples took place simultaneously. Selassie notes,

Systems of domination stem from our disconnection from the earth. That's the patriarchal wound. And so [there are] practices that bring us back into connection with sort of natural rhythms and natural cycles. . . . [But] we've chosen very specific practices and we've left out others. What is the domination of bodies but the domination of nature? We are nature. And that kind of dominance shows up as patterns in lots of configurations. And so it's [domination] of the racialized body, but it's also of the earth. And the concept of race and racial superiority grew out of the need to enslave people so that they could take more from the earth. It's so interconnected. [Colonization took place] not because they just wanted to dominate the bodies. They wanted to dominate the bodies because they wanted to extract more and more and more [from the land].[29]

To heal the trauma and anguish due to dislocation, family separation, and violence, new initiatives in Buddhist convert sanghas uplift ancestral wisdom and reimagine the path to awakening that was seized and disfigured during colonialism. Selassie further reflects, "A lot of Western Buddhist thinkers and teachers dismiss [ancestral rituals] as sort of cultural baggage and not real practice, because it doesn't fit into a rational understanding of what is most efficacious and what is the quickest technology. And we tend not to study things that are mysterious or beyond our rational understanding."[30] Yet these ancestral practices, across Buddhist lineages, make the dharma personally meaningful for African-descended Buddhists. Thus honoring ancestors is a pivotal practice for many Buddhist teachers and long-term practitioners of African descent.

Connecting to Ancestors through Ceremonies

Selassie—along with Lama Rod Owens and Larry Ward, all of whom write from different Buddhist lineages—acknowledges the importance of connecting to ancestors through ceremonies.[31] Ralph Steele, a teacher in the Insight tradition who grew up speaking Gullah on the islands off the shores of eastern Georgia, simply states, "I'm always bringing my ancestors with me."[32] Similarly, Shanté Paradigm Smalls, a teacher in the Shambhala tradition, says that the emphasis on lineage and ancestors is incorporated into dharma gatherings of Black Buddhists because such an emphasis is innately understood. Black people stand on the shoulders of Black leaders who embody tenacity and resilience. Like Selassie, Smalls observes a disconnect from ancestors in many predominantly white convert communities. African Americans, conversely, innately understand the importance of venerating ancestors. Smalls says, "The emphasis on community, the emphasis on lineage and ancestors—we get it. White folks don't get that, as far as I can see it. . . . We have an embodied relationship to ancestors, not just the guru."[33]

Accessing Buddhism through ancestral cultural practices, in addition to the meditation practices accentuated in Western convert Buddhist sanghas, has been particularly meaningful for Black practitioners who connect to familial lineages in other countries. Myokei Caine-Barrett, Bishop of the Nichiren Shu Order of North America and Chief Priest of Myoken-ji Temple, draws from the traditions of her Japanese mother and her Black father. She notes the importance of ancestors and community in both lineages: "It's absolutely critical to true Buddhist practice to help your community. And that is one area in which I think Black folks in particular have deep, deep understanding. . . . Who else do you know that talks about taking care of your name, taking care of your community, being tied to the ancestors? It's present in both cultures."[34]

Jozen Tamori Gibson, who similarly shares Japanese and Black ancestry, describes the importance of Japanese Zen culture for their Buddhist practice. A Vipassana teacher and Soto Zen student with a Japanese grandmother, Gibson spent three years in Japan as an adult. They link their adherence to Zen to the celebration of ancestral ceremonies, in particular Obon ceremonies that take place annually in August. Gibson reflects,

> There are huge Obon ceremonies where you have your alter and have a picture of the ancestors. If you have the remains of the ancestors, the urns, you can place them there. In those practices, while I was living in Japan, ceremonies had become very powerful for me. At that time, I was physically reconnecting with my Obaachan (お婆ちゃん, grandma), and it was through those practices, those ceremonies where there was a lot of movement, a lot of dancing, a lot of drumming. I haven't been able to reconnect to that fully here even though I'm a part of Zen communities here. But the difference is that in living in Japan, those ceremonies take place not only in temples, but they also have parades in the streets and the towns shut down. And everyone is involved in the ceremonies. Having that felt sense in the embodiment of ceremony, that tradition, and bringing it into an embodied place, now, no matter where I am, I practice Obon within every step, in everything that I do. Obon is a reminder, all the elements earth, wind, air and fire are sensed within the lighting of the candles, within the breath, within the earth-body felt sense. That's all important for me. Also within Zen, the full moon ceremonies [every month] are a part I have been able to cultivate and benefit from, through being a part of a Zen center here where within community and chanting we enter full ceremonies.

They say taking the vows again and again, precepts—for example, right intention—is like a restatement. And for me it's a deep ceremony: it's taking the precepts and the vows again, the Bodhisattva vows in particular. It's re-engaging with them and engaging with them in a new space and time in your life, through ceremony, every month. You can feel depth and a broader sense of connection and expression of the vows at a point in time that's connected with the universe, the full moon and the stars, where you know that there are millions of people around the world doing the same thing and it's not just tied to Zen, but all Buddhist practices, dating back centuries where we had no [digital] clocks. We had the moon as our time piece, we had stars as our timepieces. The full moon ceremony takes us out of our worldly technological ways and reminds us of our embodied technologies. We have an integrated reminder of that on a monthly basis, [as well as] a moment to moment basis.[35]

Being attuned to nature is yet another aspect of indigenous approaches to spiritual healing. Gibson, who is trained in IFOT approaches to teaching the dharma, describes the importance of uplifting lineages that link land and people in holistic, intertwined ways of being. To know the natural world and one's ancestors is to know one's own place in the universe; to take vows under a full moon is to connect to all of the spiritual and blood ancestors who have gone before.

Ancestors are guides who are present to assist daily living and the cultivation of wellness. In her book *Daughterhood*, author and vocal artist Rachel Bagby writes, "Without the guidance of elders, and with our instincts impaired, how do we face what could be a fatal unknowing of how to come 'round to more restorative ways of living?"[36] Similarly, Claudelle Glasgow, a teacher in the Shambhala tradition, maintains that guides, including ancestors, exist to help manifest intentions. Glasgow describes how their writing channels the ancestral guidance:

The ancestors are saying, don't be distracted by the ways in which our bodies are used: that the Black body is used for entertainment, historically for service, for labor, for being the container. . . . Seeing Black people being senselessly killed has become the new entertainment in the absence of sports and all our other usual distractions. And so, when I think about coming back to ground, to coming back to what matters, that coming back is the practice of meditation. It's the practice of coming back to who are we, who are we at our roots. And we are far more, black people are far more than the bodies and the labels and the attributes that are given to us; these unilateral contracts to other people. We are the very soil that produces the fruits of this earth.[37]

The guides who appear and assert the fundamental goodness of practitioners are recognized during liturgical practices. As a teacher in a Tibetan tradition, Glasgow reflects,

> I don't really feel like recognizing my ancestors in dharma practice is planned. . . . I may be orienting my mind to [Tibetan ancestors], but I'm also remembering the rest of the mother lineage in my own lineage. I'm remembering my mother, remembering my grandmother, my great grandmother. And even in just remembering them, that calls them into this space. In some ways it's so ordinary to understand that we're not alone in this space and to understand planes of existence. And so for me growing up there were always multiple planes of existence coexisting in any given moment, whether we recognize it or not . . . there's a possibility of you being able to see into [the moment] and have access to all realms of existence in that particular moment. And so that includes for me by default one's ancestors. I think it also allows for an interconnectedness, one informed by Beings in other planes of existence. It becomes less like ego clinging to, "I'm doing this and creating this thing to happen, right?" It's like I'm in with all of these beings, including the ones I'm invoking, the ones that are in this space, the ones that have passed, the ones that are in this moment, the ones that are yet to arise. All of that is in concert in order to be able to see, move. It's not about me, it's not about just me.

Glasgow describes the supportive ancestral presence that arises in Buddhist practice:

> We have such a negative connotation of faith, but *you're not alone in this endeavor.* I'm not alone in this conversation. On some level, my opening is allowing somebody else to help me out. I may or may not see them, but I know that they're there. And when I'm in practice and doing for-

mal practice, a *sadhana* [spiritual exercise] or even something that I have memorized, I am remembering these beings of other realms who have passed before, who had the ability to be able to see the truth of this existence or they had the ability to magnetize or they had the ability to be compassionate. Whatever it is that we're calling into that moment, we need guides to be able to do that. . . . There are those who have passed who have a certain type of, if you will, magic, who are able to see, who have more of a bird's-eye view about, "Oh, how else can that manifest in this moment beyond your human capabilities? Oh, let me offer now that you've asked me, let me offer you some assistance and show you something else that could be of benefit." So, [guides are] how [the ancestors are] connected to practice for me.[38]

Glasgow uplifts ritual as a means to connect to the guiding ancestors. Indeed, the importance of ritual was brought up repeatedly as central to Buddhist practitioners of African descent. Those who spontaneously discussed the importance of ancestors highlighted the primacy of the body in ritual: by bowing and dancing, the body communicates connection to ancestors. Konda Mason, a teacher in the Insight tradition, notes that it is important to connect dharma teachings to ancestral rituals. Mason advocates for ceremony and ritual as a way to create community bonds in sangha.

I think that spiritual practice is way more than sitting and then being quiet and meditating. Meditation is a wonderful tool, but that's just one tool alongside rituals and ceremonies. We are ritual, human beings are ritual. And when we deny ritual, I think we deny part of ourselves. It's almost like soil that's been depleted. You got to sink deeper into where the actual richness is. Our spiritual practices, our indigenous spiritual practices, and our ancestors' spiritual practices, support all of that. . . . I bring [white and Black] people together [and do] deep ancestral work and building of altars, of our ancestors' altars.[39]

Mason reflects on the power of ritual for those whose families were enslaved and for those who were enslavers. She describes the ritual as a "catalytic transformational source" in that "for the deep soul work, we have to go into ritual."[40]

Ritual connects everyday, temporal experiences of the world with the individual soul and with ancestors. Ritual engages the body and the senses and allows for a knowing that connects the relative to the absolute. Selassie reflects on how indigenous rituals connect practitioners to a dimension of existence that is accessed through connecting to the relative, temporal conditions of the body. Ancestors speak through sensory experiences. Thus the body, which is made up of flesh, bones, and skin and which is subject to sickness, decay, and death, is a primary conduit for guidance from forebears. Selassie asks,

Can I access freedom through the relative? Of course. It's only through the relative, through my experience, that I can. It's only *through* this body that I can become free—it's not despite this body that I become free. But in what ways am I clinging to the relative and is that holding me back from freedom? Do white people need more access to the relative and do brown people need more access to the absolute? And did we lose that [access to the absolute] when we lost our connection to indigenous ways of knowing?

I was raised in a kind of de-indigenized, political, postcolonial Marxist revolutionary mindset of Africanness or Blackness, and in a lot of ways had lost that connection to what is interconnected and universal. I feel like a lot of my practice these days is really trying to connect to what is a deeper knowing that is ancestral.

[I have sensed] connections with the ancestors and with my ancestors and have had sensory experiences of that. I was on retreat at the Forest Refuge recently and my grandmother came to me in the form of smell. I didn't know my grandmother, my mom's mom. After we left Ethiopia, when I was three, she only came once to America. I have very fuzzy memories of her. But I had this sense memory or visitation. I don't know how to put it. It was really vivid and really real, that I smelled her.

And so where that smell was very distinct, it was very specific to a place and a culture and a history and all that she brought with her, all that she was carrying in her body. For me there's a way in which this connection to sort of deeper knowing is specific. So it's relative, it's related to my history and my experience. It's through this body but it's connecting me to something much bigger which is what I would put in lay terms as like the other dimensions of reality that I feel that my mother and my ancestors are within. And in this sort of secularized version of the dharma that we've been given through Western teachers and teachings, they're like oh, there's not enough proof for reincarnation or spirits. There's not enough proof for all of these things that are spoken about in the metaphysical aspects of the practice.

And it's like well, I had the proof in my nose and I wasn't only in my nose. It was a full sensory awareness experience. I can't say where that was but it's in the body.[41]

Selassie describes a spiritual bypassing class she coteaches, which deconstructs Western emphases on the technology of meditation over and against embodied practices such as chanting and bowing in honor of ancestors. Devotional practices, she asserts, connect the relative to the absolute. Selassie, like many other people of color on Vipassana retreats, incorporates rituals that support the practice of breath meditation and *metta* (loving-kindness) meditation. She further reflects,

We have a group in New York of women of color who are leaders in the Insight community here. We call it the Feminine Dharma Conspiracy. I remember one of our early meetings, we talked about how we survive on retreat, how we take care of ourselves. Most of us brought stuff to our rooms, like we brought color because the rooms are so drab. I always bring multiple cloths and I cover my bed in a pretty cloth. And most of us set up our own altar and usually involve some ancestral kind of connection. Some people listen to gospel music in their rooms on their headphones. What are the ways that we rebelled against the structures that have been given to us and that have been stated as being "the way," not recognizing that that way happens to correlate very closely to whiteness.[42]

Selassie notes that the meditation practices introduced to the United States are taught in a substantially different cultural context:

It's not the way from Asia. These Burmese teachers handed that down but there are a lot of questions as to whether the Burmese model, the way it was created, was a response to colonialism as a way to hold on to their teachings. . . .

And so what do we lose when we take these technologies and we say "oh, this [Buddhist practice] is going to help liberate us, as Black people this is going to help us liberate us." And it's like, what Buddhism? And what does it look like? And why did they take this particular strand and leave out these others that are very different? One thing that I've asked about this: did they practice a little differently in Asia? And [I was told "yes"] because the culture was very yin, the culture was very relational. And you could probably say that about a lot of the Asian practices and traditions: they were embedded in a culture where these monks or these monastic communities were in relationship to all these women who fed them or the children who were crawling around the floor when the festivals or the ritual days were on. And yes, the monasteries were very yang when that wasn't happening. It was like a yang practice inside a yin culture, and we took this yang practice and we dropped it in a yang culture.[43]

Critiques of the yang culture of whiteness were pervasive throughout the process of interviewing teachers and long-term practitioners of African descent. Black Buddhist practitioners articulated that whiteness appears as individualistic, isolated, preoccupied with psychological interpretations of the mind, and dismissive of indigeneity. Conversely, yin culture emphasizes feminine concern and care for family, household, and community. For Selassie, ancestral practices are located in yin culture as a fundamental aspect of community connection.

Like Selassie, Kate Johnson, a teacher in the Insight community, embraces ancestral remembrance and practices specifically on retreats:

For me, what's been really helpful in my practice is to remember that even though I might not know the names of or the exact locations of those ancestors, that they are actually present in my body and in my breath at this moment. So when I practice mindfulness of body or my passive breathing, I think of that as a way of connecting with my African ancestry, and I talk to them. Sometimes, I envision those ancestors, especially at my back. There's this way of connecting in the Black body to ancestors and to the beings that literally have our backs. So, I often will imagine them standing with their backs against mine or their hands on my shoulders. I don't draw on that practice at home as much, but when I have been on retreat and I have been one of the very few people of color, there have been microaggressions that I can't report because we are in silence for months at a time. And I only have fifteen minutes to talk to a teacher, a few times a week. I really want to talk about practice. . . . I know that those teachers may or may not be able to help me. And so just that's the way that I try to support myself and bring my ancestry and community to the present.[44]

The incorporation of spiritual ancestors alongside blood ancestors into ancestor veneration is a common practice among Buddhist teachers of African descent. Kaira Jewel Lingo, a teacher in the Order of Interbeing, says, "Each of us is a continuation of the Buddha, of our teachers, of all spiritual ancestors, blood ancestors. We're each a piece of the enlightened consciousness. And our practice is an opportunity to dig deep within ourselves to find more of what we're used to getting from others, to find that within ourselves. So that's possible. That's what the Buddha invited us to do."[45]

An ancestral practice that has been particularly important to Insight teacher Devin Berry draws its origins from the founder of the Order of Interbeing, Vietnamese Zen teacher Thich Nhat Hanh (also known as "Thay"), who has adapted numerous teachings for Western audiences. Nhat Hanh embraces the Touching the Earth ceremony as a means to involve the body in the present moment, while drawing in beings that support one's practice.[46] Berry similarly embraces the Touching the Earth ceremony as a way to connect to ancestors while tracing his roots to ancestors who lived on plantations. Thus the Touching the Earth ceremony is a way to acknowledge suffering: to look at the past directly, without flinching, and to name and recognize what is happening in the present. Berry says,

I've always felt a deep sense of spiritual urgency to engage the ancestral realm. There was a flavor of sorrow and of strength that I felt within me growing up, and it felt like it ran through my family across generations. My Grandfather called himself the "KinKeeper" One who gathers the family in all manner of ways. That's me now, only I gather the ancestors. I gather by deep looking and listening. I learned this from Thay's teachings. I was fortunate enough to know and hear directly from all four of my grandparents and even be in the presence of two great grandparents. I was steeped in family stories at a young age and had some sense, though very disjointed and ephemeral, of where many of the habits, patterns and behaviors of the family stemmed from. The tentacles of woundedness and signs of deep trauma were all around. I've long felt the deep desire to reconcile and untangle all the karmic knots. I couldn't clearly identify those tentacles until years after diving deeper into dharma practice and particular meditative practices, first with my teacher Lyn Fine and later during a retreat with Thich Nhat Hanh. He led a "Touching the Earth" ceremony. It was the first time that I was able to connect my ancestors with this meditation practice. I resonated with bringing in the ancestral . . . explicitly. So bringing in all of these folks that were my family, historical people and not just limited to black people but abolitionists, suffragists, spiritual ancestors, pulling them all in, like these are all my family, like really all my family. This deeply resonated with me.

The "Touching the Earth" ceremony was a practice I took up every day for a long time. I've adapted the versions I learned from both Thay as well as Larry Ward's adaptation for my own practice. I've since incorporated jhana practice, the brahmaviharas, dream yoga, four elements meditation and kasina work into my ancestral dharma toolbox. The Touching the Earth practice itself involves a deep bow or prostration. It was in completely giving myself to the ancestors, to the earth, that really opened me up. The humility and humbleness in that ceremony was profoundly heart opening for me.[47]

Berry acknowledges the inspiration of Bernie Glassman, the late Zen teacher and founder of Zen Peacemakers, as a role model who brought the dharma to groups of people suffering from intergenerational trauma. At one point, Glassman took a group of Jewish people to Auschwitz and chronicled their experiences of confronting intergenerational trauma. This practice of collective healing struck Berry as one that Black dharma teachers could replicate on southern plantations. He stated, "I decided at that point that yes, I wanted to do this with those who ancestors were enslaved on land here.[48]

Berry traveled to Virginia, to the land of a friend whose family had owned a plantation, to perform *Tonglen* (a practice that means "sending and receiving"),[49] Touching the Earth, and Vipassana practice. Thereafter, he went to a three-month retreat at Insight Meditation Society (IMS).

Knowing that I now had the capacity and depth of practice to center blackness, to center the ancestors while the mind is quieting, the body softening and the heart opening and being able to practice directly with all that comes into my purview was profound. I shifted from believing I was protecting myself and calling in ancestors with altars, divinations with someone else leading or guiding me to knowing that I can be in touch with my ancestors directly within my practice. I'm not criticizing those methods I explored before, I just discovered that I am my own healer. That was a profound shift in my life. I knew I was suffering with transgenerational trauma and I felt compelled to bring my ancestors into practice. Turns out that was skillful means. The "Touching the Earth" practice allowed me to see through collective trauma and connect my ancestors with the teachings and the practice. For the first time I realized I didn't need anything other than me sitting looking and listening deeply, to be in touch with my ancestors. It was the direct experience of the meditative process, observing and quieting the mind, knowing sensations in the body. I touched some deep places of historical wounding, broke down familial stories and habitual patterns. It's been an onward leading path to healing since then and Insight meditation has been my vehicle of choice. I was now able to touch the resilience of my ancestors embedded in DNA and hiding in plain sight in my body, via the direct experience of the Insight practice.[50]

Berry, who cofounded the Deep Time Liberation retreats, spoke of his personal experience delving into his family's history and reaching out to descendants of the family that had enslaved his ancestors. Having worked with a number of practices over the years to help heal his intergenerational trauma and ground his emotional turbulence, Berry was able to shift his focus to Vipassana (clear seeing) meditation and awareness of non-self:

I did what I called Deep Time Liberation self-retreat. I actually didn't need anything other than the meditation and the meditation instruction. The bringing in of the ancestors via family stories, culture and who we are as a people is an essential part of it. I did an extensive amount of genealogy work, and part of it, the forgiveness work, was both finding my African and my European ancestors. I was able to have a conversation with a descendent of one of the folks that enslaved my ancestors. Having that conversation—not necessarily the content of the conversation but just finding each other and being able to engage each other—led to pieces of armor dissolving, just washing away. Nothing was fixed, but the possibilities born of that were just absolutely incredible. And I realized from the conversation that one of things that I was holding, a karmic knot perhaps, was the deep shame I was carrying across generations.[51]

The practice of Vipassana facilitates an ability to be deeply present with the pain of descending from a lineage that was subjugated and forcibly dehumanized. Breathing through the pain in deeply compassionate, nonjudgmental gentleness, initiates a new legacy of healing, a liberation narrative of sorts. Berry averred,

> This is within this black body . . . I have the capacity to be with whatever arises . . . whatever. And I also translate that into: "my ancestors are with me, and this is a way for them to be in the room and so to see this, to bear witness and to know that I have their support and they have my support." It allows me to be anywhere. People have said, "Oh, my god how could you go to IMS, and there's like a hundred people, there's no other POC in the room," I tell people it's the work I've done, the explorations and perceptual attainments. I've practiced on the grounds of the places my ancestors were enslaved, the source of trauma, and flipped it. Those places are sacred to me. I honor my ancestors' legacy and I collect post-memory while there in the enslaved quarters, the plantations, the fields. The sacred places have become an altar. There isn't anywhere that I actually feel unsafe in ways I previously had as I have my ancestors with me always.[52]

Berry's experience of healing the trauma caused by intergenerational trauma initiated a series of conversations with other dharma teachers, which resulted in the manifestation of a Deep Time Liberation retreat in 2018.

Deep Time Liberation

Three teachers and a drummer held the first Deep Time Liberation (DTL) retreat for twelve participants in May 2018. They began with a focus on venerating ancestors, dharma practices, African healing systems, and indigenous complex trauma therapeutic intervention work. The sixteen group members represented peoples whose origins arose from the African Diaspora and African American, African Caribbean, and African Latinx traditions. They sought to create sangha and connection through laughter, conversation, and food at the beginning of the retreat in New Orleans. After arriving in New Orleans, they made their way to Magnolia, Mississippi, and settled into the large Victorian houses of the Flowering Lotus Retreat Center. For five days they sat, bonded, and held community space for each other with deep embraces of gratitude for each other's presence and commitment to DTL as a transformative and healing retreat.

Periodically throughout the retreat, the retreatants danced to drumming. The rhythm and the movement of sixteen Black bodies coming together around the intention and aspiration of healing trauma called forth anticipation, joy, anguish, and a deep sense of ancestral lineage. Drumming evoked the traditions and memories that were forcibly taken away over generations of capture, the Middle Passage, and two hundred forty years of enslavement in the United States. At the same time, the drumming opened up a space of honoring the resilience of a people, of acknowledging their capacity to heal and move forward unhindered by the past.

Kabir Hypolite, a meditation practitioner from the Bay Area who attended the first DTL, states, "Liberation is not when someone opens the door and tells you to go. There are intergenerational wounds and trauma. You have to touch the thing that you're being liberated from. You have to sit with it, you have to witness it, you have to touch it and taste and smell it. When you're walking around with unconscious trauma, you're doing things and holding things that shape you, and you do not even know exactly what it is that's actually running through you."[53] The dharma teachers who conceived of Deep Time Liberation are trained in the Insight tradition and are also deeply influenced by indigenous, feminine, and shamanic wisdom traditions, slave narratives, trauma psychology—

including post traumatic slave syndrome (PTSS)—and indigenous focusing oriented complex trauma (IFOT).

DTL was conceived over the course of several conversations. Berry and Noliwe Alexander, another Insight teacher, envisioned a retreat for meditators of African descent who suffer from intergenerational trauma. Berry and Alexander initially offered DTL as three separate daylong retreats for people of color over several months at East Bay Meditation Center in Oakland, California. The daylong retreats were structured around the themes of "Honoring the Ancestors," "Bearing Witness," and "A Portal to Healing." In offering these daylong retreats, Berry and Alexander realized that every group that has suffered collective trauma also suffers particular trauma and that as a team they were best equipped to speak directly to people whose ancestors had been enslaved in the United States.

They invited Rosetta Saunders, a teacher of American history and a drummer in West African and Afro-Cuban traditions, into the leadership team. Saunders reflects,

> It is such a powerful shift in our psyche when we begin to recognize those places of trauma within us. You have to be honest about [trauma], where you hold it in your body, and how to work with it to begin the process of releasing the cellular memories. For me, it is drumming, the heart beat which has been my medicine in working with and healing my own personal trauma. My meditation practice started eighteen years ago. I am not a dharma teacher per se, albeit I've spent the past twenty-five years as an educator focusing on the histories of people of color in the United States. These two practices, drumming and meditation, along with the knowledge of my race history, have conjoined and expanded my ancestral healing journey.[54]

As it became more evident that there was a missing piece to the activity of historical trauma healing, Alexander, Berry, and Saunders invited in Williams, whose psychotherapy training in indigenous-oriented trauma healing provided a language and framework for working with people of African descent. Together they designed the curriculum for a contiguous DTL retreat. Williams says,

The Deep Time Liberation retreat is the manifestation of a pinnacle of the hope for being Black and Buddhist. There is a particular history to African Americanism. You know, that's a particular experience. It's not the same experience [as other enslaved peoples], although it is related to the Afro-Caribbean or Afro-Latino experience. It has to do with being on the land of terrorism and atrocity.

When I went to Brazil, I saw a map of the slave trade. We don't get this in school, so unless you have somebody that knows the details of this journey in the Americas. So, I saw a map of the slave trade. It was an old map and it was one of the most clear, distinctive maps I've ever seen of the slave trade. And something clicked for me when I visually saw that people that were dropped here were on those ships for days and weeks taking the longest journey. The ancestors were just on those ships and in those conditions for weeks. One of the things that spoke to me about that was the resilience and fortitude and will to live of those people in terms of being able to tolerate and be able to be with those circumstances and situations of being moved across the oceans even amidst all the suffering and fear. When I saw that, I thought . . . our cultures have evolved, depending on where we were dropped, where we were enslaved to the land and the product.

And then the other thought that I had is, the African American is a particular iteration of African descent. In that at some point, the African American could disappear, like that experience could disappear as we continue to intermarry or have children cross racially and cross ethnically if we don't hold the African American culture as precious and a source of our resilience and joy. That experience could eventually become nonexistent and that history could eventually become nonexistent or very covered over. So, part of the DTL retreat for me was also perhaps similarly to the way the Jewish community thinks "lest we not forget because this is integral." This [history of enslavement is] an integral memory and integral understanding in terms of what, why, and how we are today, and the remembering that is not unlike mindfulness. The remembering is actually a place of strength and resource for being able to live in a well way in the present day. We were speaking, not to actually cover [the trauma] up, but to actually be aware of and with the suffering.[55]

Williams's emphasis on re-memory is a critical aspect of recognizing intergenerational trauma through an indigenous perspective and an orientation to decolonizing the dharma: "The components of coming to know your own mind and heart and then applying that to whatever the conditions and circumstances and situations gives me a great deal of belief and faith that dharma practice and wisdom is a doorway or a vehicle for transformation for Black folk."[56] She further reflects,

> It's important to have someone holding that role of psychologist, therapist, mental health healer, but it requires someone who has an understanding of a mind that has traveled through the terrain of decolonization and integrated it. Just Western psychology, just understanding of Western psychology is not going to do it all because for me it's a matter of what we've been saying but not overtly, that process of holism. A holistic intervention which includes all body, mind, spirit. . . . What makes DTL so impactful is that it creates the container and conditions for the grief to come forward. This is holistic. We're working with the body because that's also part of the drum whether you're moving to it or not. It reverberates within the body, so it is moving energy, it is grounding us in awareness, in our bodies and opening and taking care of our hearts. So, working holistically and acknowledging suffering and acknowledging grief. We're good at acknowledging all the anger, anxiety, and all the various manifestations of that history, but we're not so good at acknowledging and then engaging a process to deal with the grief. And a lot of times you can't really move beyond until you really engage the grief. . . . Like this turning away from that or somehow the expression of sorrow and grief, as sung in a lot of our hymns, the Black spirituals. There's a lot of sorrow and grief and we externalize it, which serves a purpose. I think that's why we're still here.[57]

For many Buddhist practitioners of African descent, there is an organic movement to acknowledge the genocide of Native peoples and honor their historical and contemporary presence by naming the peoples who had once walked the land. Such ritual is important in DTL as well. The first DTL retreat began with ritual and ceremony. The practitioners, along with the facilitators, set up an altar to honor their ancestors. Participants were asked to bring pictures and other small items that called to them from their ancestral roots. They transitioned to mindful meditation, silent walking reflection, dharma talks, and community-building exercises. The journey into honoring and calling forth ancestral legacies, to uncovering harmful histories and seeing clearly, to coming face-to-face with resilience, compassion, and healing unfolded over the course of the five days. Alexander reflects,

> We imbued Buddhist cosmology, mindful meditation, and compassion practices to ground the healing journey. In this particular Theravada lineage, there are places within my practice where I've been able to rest, generating a calming presence amidst an array of complex and painful circumstances. In over twenty years of Buddhist practice I have found an opening in my awareness that enables me to ask: can I sit right here in and with this body? This is a very difficult thing when you still are filtering through unspoken, unseen, and unaddressed trauma. Thus, we intentionally grounded Deep Time Liberation through the lens of self-compassion, in order to allow each participant their own agency through this process.[58]

The retreatants spent the first two days of the retreat in silence, practicing meditation and listening to dharma talks by Berry, Williams, and Alexander, who contextualized the retreat in Theravada teachings on the Brahmaviharas—loving-kindness (*metta*), compassion (*karuna*), empathetic joy (*mudita*), and equanimity (*upekkha*)—along with teachings on self-compassion, and being present with the feeling tones in the body.

The teachers spoke personally of their own journeys to encounter the narratives and places of their ancestors. Berry spoke of his journeys to Virginia. Saunders spoke to the group about her journey to Camilla, Georgia: "There was so much pain in the one story my mother would tell. I had to go to that place where the pain had occurred and festered within her. I was seeking to find my maternal great grandparents, and they did not disappoint. We met in an old dilapidated cemetery for Black folks in Pelham, Georgia, not far from Camilla. [I felt that] my great-grandparents were seeking me as well."[59]

Williams, who is also from the South, points to the specific trauma caused by the history of enslavement, segregation, and migrations—in short, violence, dehumanization, and dislocation. Both of her parents are originally from the South and were a part of the Great Migration, from the South to the North. For Williams, who describes herself as "a true believer in the Bodhisattva way," liberation is particularly tied to the liberation from suffering in general and more specifically the suffering caused by historical trauma.

> I spent many years of my youth traveling down South from Brooklyn with my mom, my dad, and my aunties, listening to the stories of my people and the history of southern living. I remember us having to make sure we left at the right time of day to not get caught out there driving through Virginia and North Carolina to our destination in the middle of the night, and to always make sure we had enough gas to make it through. I remember the fried chicken and potato salad made to eat on the road—which was delicious and fine—but the adults knew it was to make sure we did not have to stop and be unable to purchase food or eat at certain restaurants or roadside eateries.[60]

Holding the retreat in the South was particularly salient, given the scale of slavery for two hundred forty years and the institution of segregation for one hundred years. On the third day of the retreat, the group of sixteen traveled to the Whitney Plantation in Louisiana, the sole plantation in the country that narrates the horrors of slavery from the perspective of the enslaved people. The visit allowed the DTL participants to sit with memorials to infants, children, and adults who lived and died on the plantation as well as a monument to the largest slave uprising in U.S. history.

Hypolite was particularly struck by the monuments to this slave uprising. As he walked by rows of black heads made of ceramic on poles commemorating those beheaded in the uprising, Hypolite came upon his surname. He reflects:

> I was just completely, completely devastated, completely blown away. I didn't know anything about the uprising and didn't know it was the largest one. And I certainly didn't know that I would see the figure of a man with my last name who very well could be a relative. So I just stood there. I was in a state of shock and paralysis. I was taking it in, trying to take it in just the enormity of it all and wondering, what was this, what happened? Who were these people? And how is it that my name is on this

monument? I remember just being flooded with all these different feelings, shock and surprise and outrage and anger. And then through the process of practice and community connection with the group after we came back, all of that changed to me having a sense of pride.[61]

Upon returning to Flowering Lotus Retreat Center, the DTL teachers created a safe space to share their experiences at the plantation, acknowledge the stories that were told, and remember their legacies. Participants drew genograms to trace their family histories and did an exercise to explore their internal and external conditioning, which helped them to see how various traumas had manifested in physical illness, psychological disease, heart pain, and other forms of suffering. Berry reflects,

> The combination of sharing the stories, the sound of the drum and the sitting there in silence or looking at each other—it felt like generations of tears were being shed. A deep sorrow was coming up, and a deep joy and relief. So that's the drum, the storytelling: being able to just sit and witness the stories of other folks of African descent, and the pain and harm we've caused each other. This isn't about pain and harm that's just been caused to us. This is the whole shebang. Family dynamics over generations. The women that have suffered through generations of harm via black men who lacked the tools to work with their shame, fear, and rage, who within the privileged hierarchy took it out on their wives, sisters, and daughters. That's all there as well. And the community altar, seeing all of our ancestor's pictures and documents, etc., is all somehow connecting and healing.[62]

Beli Sullivan, a retreat participant, describes how her "bizarre" ailments had culminated in life-threatening illnesses that mirrored her mother's physical illnesses, which were undeniably connected to ancestral trauma: "Without any teachings, I've always said that the health problems that my family has experienced are ancestral. Not knowing my grandparents and cousins is an emptiness. It is trauma based. In the silence, and the walking meditation of the retreat, it came to me that all my illness was a spiritual manifestation of pain. I had gone so deeply into myself that I didn't know if I could come out of it. The retreat allowed me to center on self-admission. I was holding in family secrets."[63]

Buddhist teachings and practices are particularly useful for mapping physical trauma, says Alexander. She explains that the primary reason to hold DTL as a Buddhist retreat is to bring dharma teachings of compassion, self-compassion, and awareness to the participants:

We're going to be starting to peel back the layers of what has hardened within us. And for all the right reasons. There's no judgment around the hardening. But, there's a way in which you have to kind of crack open. And through dance and drumming and looking at our histories, people begin to soften and people begin to gather trust. And then, we can rest in Buddhist practices. We are calming the mind. We are touching the heart. We are unearthing our identities. We are piercing the veil of the manifestations we've been attached to in order to use our direct experience to heal collective wounds. We meet each participant exactly where they are, be it vulnerable, wounded, longing for connection, or merely curious about the patterned nature of their lives. I think people were able to bond with who they are, through common ancestral language and stories and the desire to experience healing on a cellular level. For many, being able to hear, "I see you," began a cycle of compassionate responses needed to embody these deep discoveries.[64]

After mapping their trauma, the retreatants embarked upon a two-day return trip to New Orleans, home of one of the first slave ports established in the British colonies. The group visited Congo Square—where slaves were able to rejoice with drums and dancing and singing on Sundays—as well as a well-known Black-owned restaurant and the Tomb of the Unknown Slave at St. Augustine's Church. The teaching team describes the retreat as a process:

The arc of the retreat is finding out where we actually feel the ancestral trauma in our bodies, examining the felt sense of unease and how we experience our responses and reactions to present day conditions. We are not escaping our bodies, but what may have felt like terror, could be a deeper wisdom speaking truth. We are walking onto the ancestral lands as the enslaved had, sensing that experience, reflecting then peeling back the layers of where our own history and our own family stories connect to our present-day experiences. Going to many of the historical sites of New Orleans let us know that this is who we are. We actually are extremely resilient. The DTL journey calls forth that resilience and helps to reveal our true nature that has been lost, stolen, and forgotten over generations of historical harm, and collective and multigenerational ancestral trauma.[65]

DTL is a specific container for collectively starting to heal intergenerational trauma through dharma and somatic practices, drumming, and ancestor veneration. The teachers acknowledge the importance of the retreat experience but also advocate for continuing such healing in daily practice and sangha as well. Sitting before altars, dancing to drumming, and performing ancestor veneration such as Touching the Earth support healing practices in daily life.

Venerating Ancestors in Daily Life

Building home altars to symbolize the sacred persons, rituals, and practices is common for Buddhist teachers and long-term practitioners of African descent. Interviewees speak of incorporating aspects of their particular Buddhist lineage as well as their African American, Caribbean, and African heritage into their shrines. Furthermore, they point to the importance of integrating spiritual and familial ancestors into their visual reminders of sacredness. Smalls, a senior teacher in the Shambhala tradition, explains,

At home in Brooklyn, I have my shrine. It's a Tantric shrine, as particular implements are on it. Below it, which is actually at my eye level when I'm sitting, is my ancestor shrine. My ancestor shrine has a couple things. It has Harriet Tubman . . . when she's in her last days, all in white, sitting in that chair. So that's framed. She is really a *Bodhisattva*, she is like *my* Bodhisattva. The more I think about and read about and research her life, [I am awed]. I've known about Harriet my whole life, but what she was able to achieve [was profound]. I couldn't achieve that now, let alone during chattel slavery. So I think about her as someone who was disabled, and who was illiterate, and who was really short, and just freed thousands and thousands of people, being a general and wielding that shotgun. She was the Moses of her people.

Also on my shrine, I have my mother, who passed away. I have a two candles—one for James Baldwin and the one for Harriet Tubman. And I have some earth elements, seeds, a little piece of a tree. I have the ashes of my dog who died last year. I have various implements of Black indigenous culture. I have a quote, some poetry from my teacher, and various lineages in kinship and ancestor implements. And so that's a huge part of keeping [Buddhism] alive for me and keeping it relevant for me personally. Yes, my teachers and the shrine that they pass down is very important, but having something that hits me right in the gut and the heart is really important.

I have different things that are on that shrine that connect me. And also part of my practice as I burn, there is some water, but also I burn juniper. And so I find that the juniper practice—the smell of the juniper, more so than incense—really does feel like it connects me with my ancestors. So the visualization practices I do bring me in touch with the *dralas*, or the ancestors.[66]

Alexander similarly has a meditation altar in her home that incorporates traditional Buddhist elements, such as a statue of the Buddha and flowers. To complement her Buddhist altar, she created a shrine to honor spiritual and blood ancestors. She reflects,

I have the ancestor altar close to my meditation altar. It has several things on it, including a small Buddha and candles and so forth. What having the ancestral altar does, it almost shrouds me in a cloak of being held. Oftentimes we use these shawls and these pashminas and so forth, but for me this feels like this is what the ancestors do for me. They warm me when I'm cold, they cool me when I'm hot, they hold me when I cry, they answer oftentimes questions that I didn't even know I had.

And the ancestor altar grows. I lost my mother about twenty-three years ago, so she's on my altar. I lost my brother about twenty-three years ago, and I lost my father last year, and other people in my life who are not just family ancestors, but family of choice ancestors.[67]

As Teish and other spiritual leaders of African-based spiritual traditions elaborate, ancestor veneration is central to the spiritual lives of people of African descent, in that ancestors support the psyche and foster resilience for the living, who often face enormous hurdles in daily life. Thus, visual representations of ancestors on altars bring forth remembrance of their strength, fortitude, and encouragement: they serve as reminders that it is possible to "make a way out of no way."

Interweaving Non-Buddhist Traditions into Dharma Practice

Oftentimes, altars represent not only Buddhist and ancestral images but also symbols of different religious traditions that have been incorporated into Buddhist practice. Zenju Earthlyn Manuel, a Soto Zen teacher, acknowledges the importance of making a religious tradition familiar and personally meaningful through practices such as creating altars. In her book *Sanctuary*, she writes of a Zen ceremony in which she incorporated images from Haiti:

> In a twenty-one day Zen Buddhist ceremony that begins in the home, I included three Haitian Vodoun deities that match in role to Zen's gatekeepers, protectors, and bodhisattvas. As I lit a candle at each altar, I called forth the Haitian spirits with their chants along with hymns to the Zen deities, and I touched a distinct and ancient place inside of me. I could feel my blood ancestors, who had been forced from their homes and taken up Christianity, still having the need to invoke their own lineage and deities. I felt myself touching *home* saying Legba Atibon, Ayizan Velèkètè, and Erzulie Jan Petro, invoking at the same time Avalokiteshvara and Bodhidharma. As I invoked the name of Shakyamuni Buddha as a great teacher, I invoked the sky by blowing an eagle whistle. Incorporating Vodoun deities into the Zen ceremony created a familiarity I found deeply resonant with home and therefore my heart.[68]

The sense of safety, refuge, and belonging that is fostered in ritual and ancestor veneration is sometimes judged by external authorities in familiar and isolating ways. Manuel further reflects,

> At the same time, I felt afraid that I'd be admonished for altering a Zen tradition that can appear set in stone. This, too, had an ancestral resonance, because Africans had to hide the things they added to their Christian rituals. As the fear subsided, it became clear that to shape religions

to my own sense of home is to create sanctuary. Dogen Zenji took the practice of Ch'an he'd experienced in China and created Japanese Soto Zen. For all of us, our worship or our practice has to feel like home for us to embrace it.[69]

For many Buddhist teachers of African descent, interweaving other religious traditions into Buddhist rituals is commonplace. Larry Ward, a teacher in Thich Nhat Hanh's Order of Interbeing, holds a doctorate in religious studies with an emphasis on Buddhism and the neuroscience of meditation. He incorporates indigenous rituals into retreats he leads. In Ward's view, the underlying wisdom of each tradition supports universal teachings on truth. The particularities of each tradition simply provide cultural access. Ward says,

> I feel commonality with the Christian tradition in the best sense of the Christian tradition, as well as the best sense of the Buddhist tradition and the Shamanic tradition, which I've also studied experientially but as well as theoretically both in Africa and with Native Americans over the years, and with Hindus in caves. I'm old, so I have had a great chance to experience a lot of the wisdom of humanity. It's how I would describe it. And so, in our wisdom school on "Great Action" in Mexico, five of our students are indigenous women from Chiapas. [At our last gathering], we invited them to create and lead us in a ritual to help us as bodhisattvas. We all did reflections, writing in a journal what from our ancestors we wanted to keep, cherish, and nourish so it grows in us. We also wrote down what from our ancestors we needed to let go of. . . . The wisdom from thousands of years ago was [this]: put both what you want to keep and what you want to let go of into the fire. To me, that's the teaching of the *Heart Sutra*. It was the second time [these five indigenous women leaders] had created rituals for our retreats; we had done one two years ago on the Day of the Dead. We integrated the indigenous Day of the Dead ritual with Buddhist practice.
>
> When we were in Africa and Botswana earlier in the year, we had a whole evening of African dance integrated into our retreat. People came up to say, "this doesn't seem like a normal Buddhist retreat." These things aren't as discretely separate in terms of both their development and depth experience. So, I think we must integrate indigenous wisdom and

practice into the liveliness [of Buddhism]. Does this help me come alive? And if it helps me come alive, it can help other people come alive. We teach sutras. We integrate Shamanism. My wife has a background in therapy. We integrate trauma work, which we have both been trained and certified in because one of our biggest issues everywhere is that so many of us are traumatized without skills to work with that trauma.[70]

The broader question of how to help people live into wholeness inspires many teachers of African descent to incorporate Christianity and indigenous wisdom into Buddhism. Sheryl Petty writes in *Ocha Dharma* of the synthesis between Lucumi beliefs and practices and Tibetan Buddhism, particularly with regards to drumming, singing, and chanting in ceremonies that include rituals to honor ancestors and elders.[71] Psychotherapist Justin Miles performs libation practices, libation ceremonies, and prayers influenced by different traditions, including Kemetic spirituality. He states,

We need to come to the understanding that spirituality is not about adopting a set of dogmatic rules or pledging fealty to a system. Our individual mandate is to be present with the realities of my first person (individual mind/experience), second person (experience of and with others) and third person (nature, objective reality) perspectives. In that way our view of and practice experiencing reality is whole. Buddhism has helped primarily with my first-person sense of sacredness. It primarily deals with the individuals mind, even though the view evolves to include other sentient beings and all of reality. I was raised a Christian and became an atheist at the age of twelve. Studying Christianity as an adult has helped me understand a second-person sense of sacredness; that I could connect with a love that exists outside of me. Practicing in the Lakota tradition has helped with a third person sense of sacredness by connecting me with the Earth, sky, animals and nature. In truth, the Buddha Dharma contains all those things. Actually, most of the world's wisdom traditions contain those three aspects of reality in terms of study and practice. However traditions tend to emphasize one perspective over another. The contemplative and mystical aspects of Christianity have been around for two thousand years, they're just not taught. In terms of kind of piecemealing things throughout my life, [these three traditions] really helped me to have a wholly lived sense of spirituality and to be able to work with the realities of the people I hope to be of benefit to in my community and work.

In writing a "Black Power Meditation Liturgy," Miles also incorporates libation practices and adapted prayers. These practices and prayers are deeply rooted in ancestor veneration. Miles says,

> The libation practice that I first learned, maybe twenty years ago, was kind of the backbone for one of the practices that I created for the Shambhala community. The idea of pouring libations is that our ancestors are still here, contain intelligence, wisdom, guidance and can be called upon when needed. All that's missing is for us to willingly choose to relate to them. The libation ceremony is an opportunity to remember our lineage, but also to remember that the ancestors are just a call away. The inspiration for the practice for the Shambhala community was the idea of being a Shambhala Warrior. The qualities of the warrior are fearlessness, gentleness, and unshakeable, fundamental confidence that comes from trusting in your nature. We have all these warriors in our lineages, but the problem was that when I came to Shambhala, I came to understand that we were appreciating Tibetan, Japanese, Chinese and European lineages and their warriors. I think we should do that. But I would look around and say, "Well, where are my people? Where are my ancestors? Where's their wisdom and their gentleness, their fearlessness? Where are those things? And how are you inviting them in here?" So I decided to create a practice that invited all of our warrior ancestors; mine and theirs. They said everyone should come here so I invited everyone to the party.
>
> So that was actually the first practice I created. It is called "Libation in Celebration of the Unbroken Universal Lineage of Warriorship." The idea is that all of our ancestral lineages are connected in the same way that we're connected today. We're all members of the family of awareness, so that everyone has it, no matter who you are, where you come from and those ancestors and warriors live and exist as that awareness. They knew what to do, when to do it. They knew when to fight, when not to fight, when to nurture children and when to let them let them go. They knew all these things, because they were deeply tuned in to their humanity. We have that capacity, just like they had that capacity. But the point is that

because we're all family members, if we're talking about building a kingdom—literally building enlightened society, which is basically the Shambhala mandate and the mandate of our hearts—then there ain't enlightened society if my ancestors ain't there. If my people ain't there, it's not enlightened society. So I began to ask the question, well, how long do you sit around and wait for somebody to invite your ancestors to the kingdom then? Or, how long do you sit around and wait for somebody to take these teachings outside of here and make them available to more than the middle and upper class whites in Baltimore? We're in a predominantly black city.[72]

Miles's adaptation of Shambhala liturgy to incorporate spiritual ancestors of African descent illustrates how Black Buddhist teachers are interpreting dharma teachings in unique and innovative ways. Not only does Miles interweave different liturgies and traditions, within the chants of the Black Power Meditation Liturgy, he also links Buddhist practice to the Black Radical Tradition. This incorporation of Black Freedom Movement rituals is also practiced by Smalls, who like Miles practices Vajrayana Buddhism in the Shambhala lineage. Smalls incorporates music and dance:

[In my personal practice], I actually sing gospel music before I practice. I just started doing it a few years ago, listening to gospel. I do yoga before I sit, and then the gospel. It was like: "I need Black stuff." And, when I do visualization practices, I visualize these deities as Black people. This is meaningful to me. And some people would say, "No, you can't do that because each color means something in each thing." And guess what? Yeah, their skin color means something to me too. So I really do feel that as a Black person and as a Westerner who's practicing Tantra, I [need to] figure out ways to make these practices meaningful to me. Of course, I do the forms as they were taught. And then after a while, I begin to play with them a little bit, because that's actually part of the introduction. If I don't play a little bit and make them really meaningful, then I'm lying, then it's like I'm always trying on a suit that doesn't fit me. And the test for me is always the result. If the result is that it doesn't feel so great, okay. But if the result is "whoa, let's investigate this more," I go for it.[73]

For Smalls, as for Miles, cultivating Black identity in dharma community is central to making the rituals feel like homecoming: a source of grounding, refuge, and belonging. For these teachers, the dharma can be fully expressed only in the context of sangha. It is not enough to clear the mind of greed, hatred, and aversion; liberation is knowing the mind and releasing compulsive energies and simultaneously cultivating communal support and identity, which Small links to indigenous practices:

> I love community. It's been denigrated. But there's the group, which is great. And within the group you learn so much about difference. There's also a kind of care that can happen in your group responsibility for each other. And I know that's antithetical to capitalism, but good. So this idea that the group is just a blob that subsumes you is a real lie of white supremacy. It's a way to turn us away from our indigenous knowledge and our indigenous ways which are about caring for each other, as a form of caring for ourselves. And this emphasis now in the secular world on community care, not just self-care, I feel is so important.[74]

Images used in First Peoples indigenous practices have also been meaningful for teachers and practitioners of African descent. Manuel embraces the image of the eagle, which for different Native communities has symbolized wisdom, strength, and courage. In some Native communities, eagles are identified as spiritual messengers to divine beings. Manuel says,

> The eagle is heavy. It's a big bird. So, it takes a lot of energy to lift off the ground and it's a struggle, and then eventually it gets up to a certain part in the sky and then it takes off. And the only reason that that bird can take off is because the bones are hollow. . . . There's a sense of emptiness so you can allow something to come through. I have an eagle bone that's used only in ceremony. You blow into it [like a flute]. You make it from the bone. It's very hard to make this. It was very hard for me to make. [The bone] was gifted to me. When you blow through that, it is to bring back that original song, that original flight of the bird. And so, a hollow bone means it's open in that something can come through, or even if there's still marrow in that bone, it is soft enough in there for something to come through.[75]

The practice of emptiness upheld in different Buddhist traditions and often interchangeably referred to as silence and stillness pervades the indigenous practices that are increasingly incorporated into Buddhist retreats. The settled energy of emptiness, silence, and stillness creates a sense of reverence for indigenous ancestors and for the land. Manuel's emphasis on emptiness is echoed by Petty, who is ordained in Lucumi and Tibetan Nyingma lineages and who writes of the luminosity and clarity inherent in the Dzogchen level of Tibetan Nyingma Buddhism, as practitioners access their innate nature and wisdom.[76]

Honoring the Land

Miles, who has adapted numerous rituals and litanies in the Shambhala tradition to honor the specific ancestry of African Americans, recognizes that people whose ancestors were violently compelled to work the land of the United States need rituals to reconnect to the land:

> A practice that I wrote was called "Contemplation of Nature" to bring in our relationship with the environment, to cut through there being a sense of separateness between our relative and absolute sense of existence. We are dependent on nature. We don't exist without each other. How we treat nature is how we treat ourselves, and how we treat ourselves is how we treat nature. . . . It's remembering that nature, again, is ubiquitous. It's everywhere. And so we're talking about being fully present and connected with all things. But we need a practice that helps us to do that.[77]

Connecting to ancestors on the land, and revering the ancestors by honoring the land, is a ritualized practice in indigenous communities and for many Black Buddhist teachers as well. Alexander speaks of a deep familial love that is rooted in love expressed by the ancestors.

> Love is a value. . . . It's a compassionate love and it's a tender love and it's a fierce love. It's a love that keeps me motivated to get up every morning. It's a love of family and of community and of my Blackness. And it's universal. And it's earth love, it's earthbound love. . . . And so, when I am now speaking of love, it's soul, body, it's all of that; the essence of it also draws out from the earth just as the ancestors' love draws out from the

earth for me. So, I'm held. I know I'm held. . . . I did a little bit of study around indigenous cultures [in present-day Colorado]. And I still have a lot of that in my practice, around some chanting and some drum work with the native drum.[78]

Alexander and Williams simultaneously understand the importance of honoring ancestors and recognizing the nuanced complexity of connecting to land. Ericka Tiffany Phillips, a long-term meditator living in Georgia, acknowledges the seeking of ancestral wisdom and connection for African Americans, especially in the South, where the majority of enslaved peoples labored on plantations:

> The South is where our journey in this country began, for those of us whose ancestry goes back to the Middle Passage. There's a certain energy and power that this land has here, in man-made buildings, roads, and all of those things. But there is also the natural world, nature. Here in Savannah, the trees and nature have witnessed so much here. I feel a resonance and a deep connection with seeing those things, seeing the places that my ancestors saw in Georgia. . . . I have always felt this deep connection with the South.[79]

To decolonize is to deconstruct the material power dynamics and mythological symbols constructed by colonizers and to reclaim a sacred relationship with the land and with ancestors. Lama Rod Owens, a Tibetan Buddhist teacher who has studied liberation theology and embraces his United Methodist Church roots, internalizes Buddhist wisdom to heal his suffering. Embracing ancestors and land is fundamental to his well-being: "I want to reawaken and reignite our wisdom that was displaced by Christianity, the slave trade, slavery, everything. I don't want to get rid of Christianity, but I want us to understand what our ancestors did and why they did it. Most importantly, I want us to reconnect to the land, to honor and respect the earth and the land. Instead of just feeling as if we are in debt to the land, I want us to celebrate the land."[80]

In sum, Black Buddhist teachers and long-term practitioners venerate ancestors and honor land as devotional dharma practices. Rituals and ceremonies invoke sacred practices in which community members listen for the presence and guidance of ancestors in their contemporary existence. The wisdom of ancestors is also heard in dreams and practices of *dadirri*—deep listening. Land shapes people, just as people honor and cultivate the land.

Striving to connect with ancestors by uplifting practices of deep listening can be challenging for peoples whose ancestors have been stripped from their lineages, due to the transatlantic slave trade and the auction block. Furthermore, many African Americans whose ancestors were enslaved in the United States have fraught, complicated relationships with the land: the land can symbolize the dispossessed, dehumanized status of chattel slavery, during which Black people were forced to work under the threat of the lash and the gun.

At the same time, Buddhist practitioners of African descent look to the land and to ancestors as guides, thereby living into resilience and belonging.

4

Turning toward External Conditions

Political and Psychological Freedom in the Black Radical Tradition

The most potent weapon in the hands of the oppressor is the
mind of the oppressed.
—Steve Biko[1]

The ancestors located within the Black Radical Tradition—freedom
fighters who confronted degrading conditions wrought by white
supremacy—promoted psychological liberation in their commitment
to liberation. In this way, Black Radicalism and Buddhism share an
orientation toward suffering: in Buddhism, the courage to turn toward
psychological suffering, rather than avoid or ameliorate it, is a practice
of spiritual liberation. In Black Radicalism, the courage to turn toward
degrading conditions and struggle for justice is foundational to political
freedom. For some thinkers, such as Martin Luther King Jr. and Malcolm X, psychological freedom is inseparable from spiritual identity in
Christian and Islamic traditions, respectively. For other thinkers, such as
Black Feminists, psychological freedom is bolstered by turning toward
internal suffering and naming intersectional oppressions while cultivating spiritual and artistic practices.

This chapter illuminates Black Radical writings on psychological and
spiritual liberation as integral to Black Radical challenges to capitalism,
patriarchy, cis-heterosexism, misogyny, and anti-Black racism. Indeed,
Black radical thinkers—historical and contemporary—have confronted
systemic oppression and promoted Black nationalism, international-
ism, anticapitalism (including socialism and communism), reparations,
prison abolition, and intersectionality. Black thinkers who locate themselves in the Black Radical Tradition critique the exploitation of Black
bodies under white supremacist institutions of slavery, colonialism, policing, and the prison-industrial complex. And as this chapter argues,

alongside political liberation, Black Radical thinkers have correspondingly emphasized psychological—and in some cases spiritual—liberation through Black Liberation Theology, Black Feminism, Womanism, and Buddhism. In proposing new ideas of Black agency, nationhood, international political solidarity, female bodies, and queer identity, adherents to the Black Radical Tradition also uplift the central commitment of healing intergenerational trauma. For many contemporary adherents of Black Radicalism, such healing is rooted in spiritual practices.

A Brief Overview of Psychological Liberation in the Black Radical Tradition

The Black Radical Tradition is illuminated in the antebellum era with texts such as David Walker's *Appeal* and Frederick Douglass's *Narrative*, the narratives of Harriet Jacobs and Sojourner Truth, and the leadership of Harriet Tubman. Stories of resistance to white supremacy were conveyed in written and oral works as well as in covert gatherings of slaves who interpreted the Bible from a liberationist point of view. In the aftermath of slavery, Black people continued to rely on freedom narratives in the Bible while they established independent Black schools, churches, and community institutions. In the late nineteenth century, for example, journalist Ida B. Wells challenged violent racism by publicizing the violence of lynchings in public forums.[2]

In the early twentieth century, Pan-Africanism—the belief that all Black people throughout the world exist in a colonial state and that the continent of Africa should gain independence from colonial rule—gained widespread attention in the United States through the mass movement led by Marcus Garvey, a Jamaican who arrived in New York in 1916. Garvey was drawn to separatist ideas espoused by Booker T. Washington in the early twentieth century.[3] However, unlike Washington, Garvey attacked white racism and white colonial rule. To grow his movement, he recruited from among the Black poor, the working class, and rural workers, identifying Black people as a "mighty race" and linking organizing efforts and institution building in the United States to Black people in the Caribbean. Perhaps most importantly, he viewed Africa as a mother nation.[4] He announced: "Day by day we hear the cry of 'AFRICA FOR THE AFRICANS.' This cry has become a positive, determined one. It is a cry that is raised simultaneously the world over, because of the universal oppression that affects the Negro."[5]

Garvey preached self-respect, the necessity for Black people to establish their own educational institutions, and the cultivation of religious and cultural institutions that uplift Black families. "Let us in shaping our own Destiny set before us the qualities of human JUSTICE, LOVE, CHARITY, MERCY, AND EQUITY. Upon such foundation let us build a race, and I feel that the God who is Divine, the Almighty Creator of the world, shall forever bless this race of ours, and who to tell that we shall not teach men the way to life, liberty, and true human happiness?"[6]

The institutions Garvey founded in 1918—the African Communities League and the Universal Negro Improvement Association (UNIA)— were unprecedented. The African Communities League established commercial houses, distribution houses, and wholesale and retail businesses, including the Black Star Line, a steamship company backed by Black people who bought tens of thousands of shares worth five to ten dollars. The UNIA was the first Black mass organization of its kind, an organization that set up chapters throughout the United States to teach that Black people were a global race with a common destiny and therefore constituted a "nation." The UNIA further preached that racial separation was essential for Black nationalism. For Garvey, communal commitment arose from self-respect and a sense of belonging; community was the development of a common vision and an identifiable Black culture, which he referred to as "cultural nationalism." Garveyites sponsored literary activities, debates, concerts, parades, colorful pageants, and musical activities. Garvey wrote, "When the Negro by his own initiative lifts himself from his low state to the highest human standard he will be in a position to stop begging and praying, and demand a place that no individual, race or nation will be able to deny him."[7]

Garvey's emphases on psychological freedom and communal uplift were perhaps the most enduring aspects of his legacy. While the institutions he built did not sustain—Garvey was convicted of mail fraud in 1925 and sentenced to five years in prison, effectively collapsing the African Communities League—his message of Black fortitude influenced subsequent generations. Malcolm X's parents were vocal Garveyites, as were other influential organizers across the United States.

Garvey was often at odds with his well-known contemporary W. E. B. Du Bois. Du Bois, a scholar and public intellectual, was the first Black graduate of Harvard University's doctoral program in sociology and later the editor of *The Crisis*, the public mouthpiece of the National Association for the Advancement of Colored People (NAACP). Garvey was hailed for influencing the Black masses, while Du Bois was honored for writings uplifting the intellectual and artistic voices of Black people.

Both Garvey and Du Bois illuminated the unique gifts possessed by Black people. Du Bois wrote, "It is our duty to conserve our physical powers, our intellectual endowments, our spiritual ideals; as a race we must strive by race organization, by race solidarity, by race unity to the realization of that broader humanity which freely recognizes differences in men, but sternly deprecates inequality in their opportunities of development."[8]

Du Bois, like Garvey, advocated for separate Black institutions: colleges, newspapers, businesses, schools of literature and art, and an academy. He furthermore envisioned a "cooperative state" in which Black thinkers and technicians would plan and build together and Black farmers would feed Black artisans. Du Bois's vision was akin to the socialist politics of his contemporary in the labor movement, A. Philip Randolph, who founded the first Black union, the Brotherhood of Sleeping Car Porters. In 1962, in a speech addressing Black unemployment, Randolph identified building the self-esteem of Black youth as a top priority. Such endeavors included cultivating the self-image of Black youth, identifying their economic requirements, and inspiring them. "*What is to be done?* The first step is to awaken, inform, arouse, and mobilize Negro workers in and out of the unions, and transform them into a militant and massive movement. . . . Youth of minority groups, and especially Negro youth, have particular problems that must be realistically met."[9]

Randolph was joined by Harlem-born writer James Baldwin, who similarly critiqued capitalism and was deeply concerned with the negative messages of inferiority internalized by Black people throughout the United States. Baldwin's 1962 book *The Fire Next Time* outlined the dimensions in which Black people "are taught really to despise themselves from the moment their eyes open on the world."[10] But such self-denigration need not be the final word. Baldwin argued that Black people possess the capacity to illuminate the myopia of the white world, reclaim their own self-worth, and embody the strength of inner authority that arises from facing suffering.

Spiritual Practice in the Black Freedom Movement: Martin Luther King Jr. and Malcolm X

Baldwin and Randolph were contemporaries of numerous activists who led the 1950s and 1960s Black Freedom Movement, which incorporated Black Nationalist and Pan-African commitments to psychological, political, and economic independence. Two leading figures—Baptist preacher Rev. Dr. Martin Luther King Jr. and Muslim minister Malcolm X (later known as El Hajj Malik El Shabazz)—merged spiritual devotion and psychological liberation to the quest for Black political freedom.

As a leading spokesperson for the Civil Rights Movement, King preached extensively on the psychological harm inflicted on Black people in white supremacist America. In his 1963 essay "Letter from a Birmingham Jail," King articulated the damage wrought by degrading messages of white supremacy:

> I guess it is easy for those who have never felt the stinging facts of segregation to say, "Wait." But when you have seen vicious mobs lynch your mothers and father at will and drown your sisters and brothers at whim; when you have seen hate filled policemen curse, kick, brutalize and even kill your black brothers and sisters with impunity; when you see the vast majority of your twenty million Negro brothers smothering in an air tight cage of poverty in the midst of an affluent society; when you suddenly find your tongue twisted and your speech stammering as you seek to explain to your six-year-old daughter why she can't go to the public amusement part that has just been advertised on television, and see tears welling up in her little eyes when she is told that Funtown is closed to colored children, and see the depressing clouds of inferiority begin to form in her little mental sky, and see her begin to distort her little personality by unconsciously developing a bitterness toward white people; when you have to concoct an answer for a five-year-old son asking in agonizing pathos: "Daddy, why do white people treat colored people so mean?"; when you take a cross country drive and find it necessary to sleep night

after night in the uncomfortable corners of your automobile because no motel will accept you; when you are humiliated day in and day out by nagging signs reading "white" and "colored"; when your first name becomes "nigger" and your middle name becomes "boy" (however old you are) and your last name becomes "John," and when your wife and mother are never given the respected title "Mrs."; when you are harried by day and haunted by night by the fact that you are a Negro, living constantly at tip-toe stance never quite knowing what to expect next, and plagued with inner fears and outer resentments; when you are forever fighting a degenerating sense of "nobodiness"; then you will understand why we find it difficult to wait.[11]

King's sensitive eloquence clarifying the psychological toll of living as a Black person in segregated America and his vision for justice for the most dispossessed were rooted in his prayerful commitment to agape love. This concept of love, King argued, emphasizes "the love of God working in the lives of men. . . . Here we rise to the position of loving the person who does the evil deed while hating the deed he does."[12] In practice, *agape* love is illuminated through the spiritual practice of nonviolence.

King rooted his philosophy of nonviolence in a theological tradition known as "personalism," which stresses that God is personal and loving for individuals as well as communities, that human beings possess inherent worth and dignity as "sons of the living God," and that humans are called to protest injustice and social evil to create conditions for the establishment of "beloved communities." Indeed, a moral society consists of conditions that support the collective well-being of beloved communities as well as individual initiatives to cultivate *agape* love.

In the first ten years of the Civil Rights Movement, culminating in the 1963 March on Washington, the 1964 Civil Rights Act, and the 1965 Voting Rights Act, Black Freedom activists primarily focused on desegregation and integration. But after riots broke out in Watts in August 1965, mere days after the signing of the Voting Rights Act, King and his colleagues in the Southern Christian Leadership Conference began to focus on urban poverty and militarism, in addition to racial integration. King protested the violence and economic resources escalating the Vietnam War and called for a restructuring of U.S. society, in which impoverished people would be guaranteed sufficient income, quality housing, and health care.[13]

King's shift toward antimilitarism and redistribution of wealth to eradicate poverty foreran the agenda of younger Black Power activists who organized in the wake of the Watts riots. Although many younger members of Black political organizations did not embrace his spiritual or practical approach to nonviolence nor call for integration, they exhibited tremendous respect for King's capacity to expand the Civil Rights Movement agenda to include urban poverty in the United States and violence in formerly colonized countries. They furthermore emphasized psychological liberation as central to the Black Freedom Movement.

Psychological freedom alongside devotional practices similarly anchored the political approach of King's contemporary Malcolm X. An adherent to Elijah Muhammad's Nation of Islam for thirteen years— and later to Orthodox Sunni Islam—Malcolm X consumed books and prayed daily to illuminate and refine his work for Black liberation. Indeed, for Malcolm, reframing Black existence by emphasizing violent white supremacy was integral to attaining psychological freedom. Performing devotional practices in the tradition of Islam facilitated submission to Allah's divine will. Committing to Black political representation and economic freedom as a Black Nationalist and Pan-Africanist was inseparable from psychological and spiritual freedom: indeed, Malcolm's speeches suggest that, for Malcolm, psychological and spiritual liberation *preceded* political independence.

Malcolm's psychological transformation took place during eight years of incarceration in the Massachusetts prison system. He knew the trauma of white supremacy intimately. After the violent death of his father at the hands of white supremacists and the institutionalization of his mother after her mental collapse, he spent his youth in white foster homes. At the age of fifteen, he moved to Boston and later New York, hustling in various facets of the underground economy and battling addiction. Imprisoned for burglary at the age of twenty, Malcolm met a mentor in prison who exposed him to the teachings of Elijah Muhammad and the Nation of Islam: the white man is responsible for Black people's suffering. To liberate themselves, Black people must practice rigid self-discipline and devotion to Allah as they strive to unshackle themselves from white economic rule. Books and prayer exposed Malcolm to spiritual and psychological liberation, simultaneously. He bent his knees in submission even as he identified the causes and conditions of Black self-hatred and dispossession.[14]

In 1963, as a minister for the Nation of Islam, Malcolm X gave one of his most renowned addresses, in which he highlighted the primacy of cultivating Black Consciousness in the most impoverished, down-trodden Black people—those like himself, prior to his conversion. He distinguished between the distinct consciousnesses of house and field Negros,[15] leading him to espouse in 1965: "Once you change your philosophy, you change your thought pattern. Once you change your thought pattern you change your attitude. Once you change your attitude it changes your behavior pattern. And then you go on into some action."[16] Indeed, throughout the stages of his political and spiritual evolution, Malcolm X uplifted Black self-esteem and spiritual discipline as foundational for uprooting internalized white supremacy. Even as he embraced Pan-Africanism and critiqued capitalism, Malcolm emphasized the central work of decolonizing the minds of Black people.

Psychological and Political Freedom: The Black Power Movement

Malcolm's militancy deeply impacted the evolution of the Student Nonviolent Coordinating Committee (SNCC), which in its initial stages had embraced nonviolence alongside Martin Luther King Jr. and the Southern Christian Leadership Conference (SCLC). After Malcolm's assassination, SNCC leader Stokely Carmichael embraced "Black Power" as a slogan and the Black Panther as a symbol. Carmichael sought to uplift Black Consciousness through political organizing: "We are now engaged in a psychological struggle in this country about whether or not black people have the right to use the words they want to use without white people giving their sanction. We maintain the use of the words Black Power—let them address themselves to that. We are not going to wait for white people to sanction Black Power."[17] Carmichael and other leaders of SNCC, along with Malcolm X and other revolutionary leaders, inspired the evolution of the Black Panther Party for Self-Defense (BPP), which integrated the language of Black Power into its operations and adopted the symbol of the Black Panther for its organizational representation.

Cofounded by Huey Newton and Bobby Seale on October 15, 1966, the BPP promoted psychological freedom alongside Black economic and political independence.[18] Like Garvey and Malcolm, the BPP understood Black people as colonized and connected the plight of Black people to emerging independence movements in Africa and Asia.[19] While denouncing global white hegemony and advocating for the right to bear arms for self-defense, the BPP leadership simultaneously sought to develop programs and uplift impoverished Black communities.

As a cofounder of the BPP, Newton emphasized the importance of psychological liberation of Black people who, for centuries, had internalized white supremacist values. In a 1967 essay titled "Fear and Doubt," Newton reflected at length on the low self-esteem afflicting Black men as a population:

> As a [Black] man, he finds himself void of those things that bring respect and a feeling of worthiness. He looks around for something to blame for his situation, but because he is not sophisticated regarding the socio-economic milieu and because of negativistic parental and institutional teachings, he ultimately blames himself. . . . It is a two-headed monster that haunts this man. First, his attitude is that he lacks the innate ability to cope with the socio-economic problems confronting him, and second, he tells himself that he has the ability, but he simply has not felt strongly enough to try to acquire the skills needed to manipulate his environment. If he openly attempts to discover his abilities he and others may see him for what he is—or is not—and this is the real fear. . . . Society responds to him as a thing, a beast, a nonentity, something to be ignored or stepped on. He is asked to digest a code of ethics that acts upon him, but not for him. He is confused and in a constant state of rage, of shame, of doubt. This psychological state permeates all of his interpersonal relationships. It determines his view of the social system. His psychological development has been prematurely arrested.[20]

Newton suggests that this state of psychological deprivation and despair begins in childhood, in part as the Black male child observes his environment and feels its hostility, and in part because the Black male child does not have a role model who mirrors him and assists in personal development. In the same essay, Newton further reflected, "As a child [the Black man] had no permanent male figure with whom to identify; as a man, he sees nothing in society with which he can identify as an extension of himself. His life is built on mistrust, shame, doubt, guilt, inferiority, role confusion, isolation and despair."

In empathizing with the psychological plight of the Black male, Newton contrasted such despair with the white man's privilege. He argued that it is imperative, therefore, to give the Black man the psychological tools for "awakening." In 1967, as he advocated for building a mass organization to confront the violence of white supremacy, Newton wrote, "The main function of the [BPP] is to awaken the people and teach them the strategic method of resisting a power structure which is prepared not only to combat with massive brutality the people's resistance but to annihilate totally the Black population."[21] Awakening, for Newton, centered on politically analyzing the violence of white supremacy and adopting a militant stance that involved taking up arms in self-defense. Newton further wrote, "The main purpose of the vanguard group should be to raise the consciousness of the masses through educational programs and other activities. The sleeping masses must be bombarded with the correct approach to struggle and the party must use all means available to get this information across to the masses."[22]

For Newton and BPP cofounder Bobby Seale, psychologically liberating oneself through analysis and taking up arms against police aggressors was only one factor in determining independence. They also advocated for self-scrutiny as a means to liberation, for constant self-betterment. Furthermore, Newton, Seale, and many male and female BPP activists advocated for developing community programs to meet the needs of impoverished Black residents of Oakland's destitute neighborhoods. The free breakfast, grocery, health, and education programs became enduring emblems of the BPP. The Oakland Community School was its longest lasting institution; it operated as a nonprofit organization until 1982. Educating Black children at their own paces, with extensive support systems in place, was emphasized as the foundation for psychological liberation and, in turn, revolution. Newton stated,

> The schools we go to are reflections of the society that created them. Nobody is going to give you the education you need to overthrow them.

> Nobody is going to teach you your true history, teach you your true he-
> roes, if they know that that knowledge will help set you free. Schools in
> amerika are interested in brainwashing people with amerikanism, giving
> them a little bit of education, and training them in skills needed to fill the
> positions the capitalist system requires. As long as we expect amerika's
> schools to educate us, we will remain ignorant.[23]

Newton defended the community programs as vehicles for awakening
consciousness. In defending the community-based "survival" organizations as ways to provide basic resources for impoverished community
members while raising their political awareness of white supremacy,
BPP members advocated for action and reflection simultaneously. By
providing free breakfasts, BPP members could talk to children about
why they were poor. By providing free health clinics, BPP members
could talk about the disproportionate health statistics between white
and Black people and why Black people suffered from heart disease,
stroke, cancer, high blood pressure, and infant mortality rates in starkly
higher numbers. Thus the "survival" programs were cast as an institutional integration of revolutionary ideology and practical support for
the most impoverished members of Black communities. Supporting
day-to-day basic livelihood captured the attention of community members who might have otherwise dismissed the BPP.

The BPP's advocacy for psychological uplift through community programs emerged as other Black-oriented political organizations emphasized Africanist cultural uplift. As in California, New York activists in
the BPP and other organizations embraced Black hair and phenotypes,
African-based garb and musical expressions, and African-originated
names. The adoption of African cultural expression directly refuted
white supremacist messages of the superiority of European values.

Assata Shakur, a member of the New York chapter of the BPP and
later the Black Liberation Army, describes how African-based cultural
expressions factored into community building within multiple, interlocking freedom organizations in New York City:

> The first time i attended a Republic of New Afrika event, i drank in the
> atmosphere and enjoyed the easy audacity of it all. The surroundings were
> gay and carnival-like. A group of brothers were pounding out Watusi,

Zulu, and Yoruba messages on the drums. Groups of sisters and brothers danced to motherland rhythms until their skins were glazed with sweat. Speeches were woven between songs and poems. Vibrant sisters and brothers with big Afros and flowing African garments strolled proudly up and down the aisles. Bald-headed brothers, wearing combat boots and military uniforms with leopard-skin epaulets, stood around with their arms folded, looking dangerous. Little girls running and laughing, their heads wrapped with gales, tiny little boys wearing tiny little dashikis. People calling each other names like Jamal, Malik, Kisha, or Aiesha. Sandalwood and coconut incense floated through the air. Red, black, and green flags hung from the rafters alongside posters of Malcolm and Marcus Garvey. Serious-looking young men, wearing jeans and green army field jackets, passed out leaflets. Exotic-looking sisters and brothers, decked out in red, black, and green, sat behind felt-covered tables and sold incense, bead earrings, and an assortment of other items.[24]

The emphasis on prioritizing psychological liberation and self-scrutiny, on uplifting the beauty of the Black body and building community, and on creating solidarity with colonized peoples throughout the world pervaded the organizations that arose even as the BPP and other Black Power organizations were infiltrated and attacked by the Federal Bureau of Investigation (FBI) and, as a result of the government onslaught, eventually shut down. Yet even as organizations did not sustain, the messages of Black liberation were incorporated into existing community institutions such as the Black Church.

Black Liberation Theology and the Black Church Tradition

The Black Power Movement influenced the theology of the Black Church—"the most important and dominant institutional phenomenon in African American communities"[25]—in the late 1960s and 1970s. In the wake of the Civil Rights Movement (1954–1968), in which Black clergy assumed community leadership as masses of Black citizens fought for social, political, and economic rights, theologians in the Black Church expounded Black Radical theologies. The Black Power Movement inspired Black Consciousness sermons such as those found in Albert Cleage's *The Black Messiah* (1968).[26] Black Power activists furthermore inspired the founding of Black Liberation Theology, as articulated in James H. Cone's *Black Theology and Black Power* (1969), *A Black Theology of Liberation* (1970), and *God of the Oppressed* (1975).

Cone wrote in the introduction to *A Black Theology of Liberation*,

> It is my contention that Christianity is essentially a religion of liberation. The function of theology is that of analyzing the meaning of that liberation for the oppressed so they can know that their struggle for political, social, and economic justice is consistent with the gospel of Jesus Christ. Any message that is not related to the liberation of the poor in a society is not Christ's message. Any theology that is indifferent to the theme of liberation is not Christian theology.
>
> In a society where persons are oppressed because they are *black*, Christian theology must become *black theology*, a theology that is unreservedly identified with the goals of the oppressed and seeks to interpret the divine character of their struggle for liberation.[27]

The confluence between Black Power ideologies of psychological, political, and economic freedom with liberation narratives of the Christian Bible reignited a long-standing theological tradition of lifting up the humanity, self-respect, and self-confidence of Black people while critiquing the psychological and economic damages wrought by white supremacy.

The Black Church Tradition finds its first iterations in underground Christian communities formed during two hundred forty years of chattel slavery. As early as 1750, enslaved Black preachers baptized Black congregants, establishing congregations upon plantations. Later, free Black preachers established Baptist churches in urban areas in Georgia, Virginia, and the Carolinas. Interpretations of biblical liberation messages continue to be pervasive; indeed, there is a centuries-old practice of enslaved Black people hearing biblical interpretations and identifying themselves as chosen by God. The Exodus narrative, of God leading the enslaved Israelites from slavery to freedom, remains particularly influential. Hebrew Bible prophets who condemned elite leaders for failing to care for the poor were heard as criticizing antebellum slave owners who profited from exploiting Black bodies. Finally, the Gospel messages of Jesus walking among the most marginalized members of Hebrew society—demon-possessed men, tax collectors, and bleeding women—spoke to the hearts of suffering, enslaved Black people. Men, women, and children who were legally defined as chattel property could hear their own stories of anguish in the Bible and find hope in the narratives of chosenness and salvation.

The Black Baptist Church traces its origins to these congregations of enslaved and free Black people in the South as well as northern urban churches established in the early nineteenth century.[28] The Black Baptist Church formed national institutions, even as local congregations remained independent. Alongside Black Baptist churches and institutions, Black Church leaders founded separate denominations within the Methodist Church. In the eighteenth and early nineteenth centuries, the African Methodist Episcopal Church (AME), the African Methodist Episcopal Zion Church (AMEZ), and the Christian Methodist Episcopal Church (CME) were created as separate denominations after a series of degrading, racist acts took place within the national, white-dominated Methodist Church.[29] The charismatic male leadership of these denominations preached social uplift of former slaves even as they theologized a message of spiritual salvation.

For many Black Buddhist practitioners, the church was initially a spiritual home—and indeed a number of Black Buddhists continue to engage church communities even as they claim Buddhism. Nearly half of all interviewees spoke of church community, church activism, and Christian theological roots as influential for their spiritual identities and practices.

Theology: An Emphasis on Spirit and Liberation

Many Black Buddhists retain a spiritual affiliation with particular aspects of Christian theology, particularly the image of the Holy Spirit as a vehicle through which God communicates, and the messages of liberation in the divine figure of Jesus of Nazareth.

In the Christian tradition, the presence of God—God making God known to humankind—is known in the presence of the Holy Spirit, one aspect of the trinity that makes up Father, Son, and Holy Spirit. As stated in 1 John 4:13, "This is how we know that we live in him and he in us: He has given us of his Spirit." Indeed, the Spirit is the energy that turns people toward each other and prompts expressions of love, compassion, and care. Similarly, the Spirit is the moving force that propels humans toward renewal and revitalization in God. Jeffrey Barbeau and Beth Felker Jones write that in the biblical creation narrative, "here is the Lord Holy Spirit. Standing distinct from his creation, unencumbered by any rival, he is lord over the works of his own hands. He is wind, but he is Spirit; he is breath, but he is God."[30]

The Holy Spirit might most accurately be identified as an invisible force that comes upon certain persons and events. Biblical leaders are seen as being anointed—that is, blessed—by the Spirit to declare the message of God and to lead God's people. Certain events, such as the Pentecost described in the Book of Acts, describe the Holy Spirit as descending upon Jewish disciples gathered in a house; after this event, the followers of Christ began missions to non-Jews known as Gentiles.

In the Christian tradition, to embrace the Spirit is to embody the Spirit; the human person is a dwelling place for the Spirit.[31] Moreover, the Holy Spirit is a prominent entity in the worship of Black Christians.[32] Black worshippers share a belief that "the Holy Spirit is personally accessible to the individual believer and that that brings a measure of empowerment and heightened spirituality as well as an openness to the Spirit's expressed presence and manifestation in the community's life and worship."[33]

Estrelda Alexander writes that in Black Pentecostal and Charismatic churches, deliverance from evil spirits "can only come by totally yielding oneself to another spirit: the Holy Spirit."[34]

Music is a corporate endeavor; everyone in the community participates in some way. . . . In its rawest, most spirited form, there are no professional musicians, no hymnals and no overhead screens . . . the most prized instrument is the human body: clapping time to the beat, stomping out the meter or swaying in time with the tempo.

Everyone dances: young and old, men and women, new convert and seasoned believer, high class and lowbrow, leader and congregant. . . . The holy dance is distinctive from all other dancing. . . . The true believer can discern when the individual is dancing "in the Spirit," that is, under the Spirit's influence or in direct response to some spiritual prompting.[35]

The Spirit, in the Christian tradition, leads believers to the joy of God. In quiet moments of feeling grace as well as ecstatic praying and dancing, the Spirit moves believers to transcend thinking, thus feeling divine presence within them. This liberatory feeling of being filled by holiness, personally and especially in collective worship, is a compelling experience of Black Buddhists who worship in Christian communities.

Liberation in Community: An Emphasis on Collective Rituals and Care

Christian liberation narratives emphasize two dimensions—personal salvation and social justice. In "conservative" and "liberal" hermeneutic wings that span the Christian tradition, the identification of Jesus of Nazareth as God's Son, who came to earth to liberate humankind, is interpreted as God's commitment to human liberation.

For the Black Buddhist teachers and long-term practitioners who were raised in or still attend Christian churches, community connection is a priority.[36] Many remain active members of Christian churches, in which the collective community support, and rituals such as praying and singing, elevate feelings of joy and belonging. Interviewees contrast the emphasis on collectivity in church with the prioritizing of silent meditation that is the norm in many convert sanghas. Whereas immigrant Buddhist sanghas often include collective devotional practices, convert sanghas have prioritized solitude with minimal group rituals. The structure of gatherings in convert sanghas can be isolating for many Black Buddhists, who were raised with experiences of collective rituals, especially creating music, that is central to Christian worship. Many have also noted that collective care is prioritized in church communities. Lama Rod Owens, a teacher in the Kagyu Tibetan tradition, writes,

> Growing up in church, I never really understood Christianity or Jesus. . . . Yet, as I remember, I recall that it was something deeper that drew me to church. Like most Black folk now and since slavery, I was drawn to the Black church because it was the only place I felt protected, affirmed, and seen. The Black church was, among many things, a strategy to negotiate the brutality of systemic racism and the unrelenting

demands of white supremacist culture to forget centuries of psychological trauma. My mom's insistence that I be present was part of how both she and the church loved me. It was and still remains invaluable for the community. It was how I survived. My church upbringing was my first lesson in what a spiritual community was and its power in shaping the lives of all its members.[37]

The safety of the church community was reiterated by numerous Black Buddhists who fondly recalled their childhood experiences of sanctuary and belonging. Zenju Earthlyn Manuel, who describes the Black Church as "sanctuary of [her] past" and "a foundation for sustaining the life of our community, our families, and our personal lives,"[38] writes,

> When Dr. Martin Luther King, Jr. spoke of the "beloved community," it was not the first time I'd heard of such a thing. I was raised in one. Every Sunday morning, my family dressed in our finest, and we gathered with the tribe that had migrated to Los Angeles from Texas and Louisiana. We arrived in our Buicks, Lincolns, Fords, and Chevrolets. It was our time to see each other eye to eye, time to sing, time to let loose from bearing yet another week of blatant discrimination.
>
> I would be in the backseat of our Buick with my younger sister, feeling beautiful, my hair slick and wearing my shining shoes and a dress reserved for Sundays. I was headed to the beloved community where love was guaranteed.
>
> To come to the beloved community was to head home, a place where you walk through the doors and are instantly hugged simply because you are alive. You might come to cry about what was lost or to eat homemade rolls or lemon meringue pie like they made back home. You might come to hear that song that lifts you from distress or just because you had nowhere else to go.[39]

The sense of belonging articulated by Manuel and Owens is affirmed in the scholarship of Christian ethicists who chronical communal traditions in churches. Jualynne Dodson and Cheryl Townsend Gilkes describe how sharing food is a central way in which church communities, particularly Black Church communities, care for each other. Dodson and Gilkes locate such food traditions in African rituals brought to the

Americas during the transatlantic slave trade. In many African cultural practices, feasts are central to community gatherings that honor African deities as well as the Christian God. Dodson and Gilkes argue, "African American church members feed one another's bodies as they feed their spirits—one another's 'temples of the Holy Spirit.'"[40] The practice of feeding the "flock" is, in Dodson and Gilkes's estimation, an ethic of love and hospitality in which community members care for the "community of saints." To connect to the Spirit of God, church community members care for one another's bodies.

Offering food as well as other practical care, Black churches help members navigate a racist society. Manuel writes,

> The church was the first place black sharecroppers and farmers went when they migrated north from the rural south. There they could find out about housing, employment, and schools where church members were teachers. The church also was the place to receive orientation to the big city. It would have been dangerous in the 1940s, '50s, and '60s to go north and not connect with other black people. Since church was where everyone gathered, it was the place for political movements, rejuvenation, and the non-acceptance of the objectification of black people. The church was the holy ground for grieving, speaking openly, talking loud, loving hard, and disagreeing in the name of God. We could be fully ourselves.[41]

The church, then, has been—and continues to be—the lifeblood for many people of African descent. Thus numerous Black Buddhist teachers and long-term practitioners continue to participate in church communities while embracing dharma teachings and practices. As Buddhist scholar Jan Willis writes, "I can use *Buddhist* methods to help me practice *Baptist* ideals."[42]

At the same time, many Black Buddhists have shunned the conservative teachings on sexuality that prevail in many Christian denominations. Owens and Manuel self-identify as queer and are conscious of the patriarchy and homophobia that prevail in many Black Church cultures. At least half of the interviewees for this book project are LGBTQIA-identified, and many have experienced rejection due to their sexual and gender identities. The judgment of LGBTQIA persons as sinful and hellbound has prompted many to name the discomfort they feel in church settings, and in some cases to flee the church and find refuge in convert Buddhist sanghas. Owens reflects,

> I slowly began to notice and accept my overwhelming sexual attraction to other men. I barely remember any anti-queer sentiments openly expressed growing up, but what I do remember was the silence [in church] that pertained not only to queerness but also to sexuality. The silence was constricting, and it spoke just as loudly as any sermon on the sin of homosexuality. It wasn't until I graduated from high school that I was able to gain distance from the community in order to start articulating my inner experience of my sexuality and body as it related to other male bodies.
>
> This particular movement [in my life] was one of remembering love but privileging the need to speak my own truth.[43]

The silences experienced by Owens are named within the Black Feminist Tradition, which not only critiques systemic racism, but also cis-heteronormative patriarchy and homophobia. In addition to critiquing oppression, many prominent Black Feminists also embrace a range of contemplative spiritual practices.[44]

Black Feminism

Black Feminists illuminate how racism, sexism, homophobia, cis-heteronormativity, and classism intersect to institutionally and psychologically oppress Black women on multiple levels. Beginning in the early 1970s, as the Black Power Movement unfolded and the white feminist movement gained attention, Black Feminists critiqued fellow activists on two fronts: Black male patriarchy and white feminist microaggressions.

Within the Black Power Movement, Black women began to name the hypocrisy of Black men, who announced publicly and privately that Black women were subservient and supposed to serve Black men sexually. Michelle Wallace describes the level of aggression that Black men directed toward Black women:

> [During the Black Power Movement] as I pieced together the ideal that was being presented for me to emulate, I discovered my newfound free-

doms being stripped from me, one after another. No I wasn't to wear makeup but yes I had to wear long skirts that I could barely walk in. No I wasn't to go to the beauty parlor but yes I was to spend hours cornrolling my hair. No I wasn't to flirt with or take shit off white men but yes I was to sleep with and take unending shit off Black men. No I wasn't to watch television or read *Vogue* or *Ladies' Home Journal* but yes I should keep my mouth shut. I would still have to iron, sew, cook, and have babies.[45]

In choosing to struggle alongside Black men to achieve Black liberation, Black Feminists had to acquiesce to patriarchy or leave the struggle. In the 1960s and 1970s, they were designated not only as inferior to Black men but as the Black man's oppressor. Whereas white men and white women held economic and political reins, Black women were in close proximity and subjected to intimate abuse—physical and verbal. As Wallace writes, the sheer willingness of Black women to commit to the Black Freedom struggle rendered them deeply vulnerable:

In the [National Black] theatre's brand of a consciousness-raising session I was told of the awful ways in which Black women, me included, had tried to destroy the Black man's masculinity; how we had castrated him: worked when he didn't work; made money when he made no money; spent our nights and days in church praying to a jive white boy named Jesus while he collapsed into alcoholism, drug addiction, and various forms of despair; how we'd always been too loud and domineering, too outspoken. . . . The message of the Black movement was that I was being watched, on probation as a Black woman, that any signs of aggressiveness, intelligence, or independence would mean I'd be denied even the one role still left open to me as "my man's woman," keeper of house, children, and incense burners. I grew increasingly desperate about slipping up—they, Black men, were threatening me with being deserted, with being *alone*. Like any "normal" woman, I eagerly grabbed at my own enslavement.[46]

In addition to acknowledging and subsequently resisting Black male patriarchy, Black Feminists furthermore acknowledged racist microaggressions from white women, who prioritized reproductive rights and sought to liberate "all" women, but who tokenized, exploited, and excluded Black women in the process of building a movement. In her essay "The Master's Tools Will Never Dismantle the Master's House," Audre Lorde writes, "If white american feminist theory need not deal with the differences between us, and the resulting difference in our oppressions, then how do you deal with the fact that the women who clean your houses and tend your children while you attend conferences on feminist theory are, for the most part, poor women and women of Color? What is the theory behind racist feminism?"[47]

In 1973, a statement publicized by a group of Black women who identified themselves as the Combahee River Collective articulated a broad vision for Black Feminism. In addition to identifying intersectionality as the pivotal point from which they articulated their analysis, the Combahee River Collective contested physical and sexual oppression by men, white and Black. They stated that the primary place from which one must act is from one's own identity. "Above all else, our politics initially sprang from the shared belief that Black women are inherently valuable, that our liberation is a necessity not as an adjunct to somebody else's way because of our need as human persons for autonomy. . . . We realize that the only people who care enough about us to work consistently for our liberation are us. Our politics evolve from a healthy love for ourselves, our sisters and our community which allows us to continue our struggle and work."[48] As did leading thinkers in the Black Power Movement, the Combahee River Collective named psychological oppression as a central force against which to struggle. Their identification of "identity politics" springs from the fact that the intersection of race and gender result in marginalization and abuse. They acknowledged,

> The psychological toll of being a Black woman and the difficulties this presents in reaching political consciousness and doing political work can never be underestimated. There is a very low value placed upon Black women's psyches in this society, which is both racist and sexist. As an early group member once said, "We are all damaged people merely by virtue of being Black women." We are dispossessed psychologically and on every other level, and yet we feel the necessity to struggle to change the condition of all Black women.[49]

The Combahee River Collective furthermore illuminates the isolation that Black Feminists experience, as they form small numbers in different parts of the country. Yet the experiences of oppression by Black men and exploitation by white women are common. So too is the experience of violence at the hands of the state.

Essayist and poet June Jordan reiterates the perspectives of the Combahee River Collective. Writing from California, she names loneliness and isolation as a pervasive experience, particularly during periods in which she was parenting as a single mother and in the aftermath of being sexually assaulted by men. Chronicling her second experience of rape, this time by a Black man, Jordan reflects, "I freaked out from that experience of brute domination. I lived terrified, completely. I refused even to contemplate sex with anybody. I denied the possible help of therapy. *I wanted nobody to touch me ever again.*"[50]

The importance of community for sustaining resistance to oppressive forces is central to the feminist writings of Jordan's comrade Angela Y. Davis, who writes not only on the intersections of race, gender, and class but also on the destruction of hegemonic capitalism and the militarized prison-industrial complex.[51] A former member of the BPP and the Communist Party USA who was incarcerated as a political prisoner in the 1970s, Davis has published numerous academic books highlighting the distinctive experiences of Black women in multiple spheres, including political movements. Davis's 1981 *Women, Race, and Class* was one of the first books to chronicle the historical and contemporary experiences of Black women in a racist, capitalist system who navigate a predominantly white feminist movement. She describes the multiple levels of exclusion and resulting efforts by Black women to organize themselves on their own terms.

Davis, with scholar Joy James, deconstructs racialized, gendered oppression interpersonally as well as systemically. James points to the capitalist state as an institution that wields significant economic power over the lives of Black women:

> Black feminist liberation ideology challenges state power by addressing class exploitation, racism, nationalism and sexual violence with critiques of, and activist confrontations with, corporate state policies. The "radicalism" of feminism recognized racism, sexism, homophobia and patriarchy, but refuses to make "men" or "whites" or "heterosexuals" the problem in lieu of confronting corporate power, state authority and policing. One

reason to focus on the state, rather than on an essentialized male entity, is that the state wields considerable dominance over the lives of non-elite women. The government intrudes upon and regulates the lives of poor or incarcerated females more than bourgeois and non-imprisoned ones, determining their material well-being and physical mobility, and affecting their psychological and emotional health.[52]

One way in which the state has intervened in the lives of Black women is in the matter of reproductive health. Davis writes in "Racism, Birth Control, and Reproductive Rights" that the state intrudes on women's desire to control their own bodies, including their reproductive systems. Such intrusion has made it more difficult for poor and racially oppressed women to seek out the resources they need to make healthy choices for themselves; moreover, women of color have been disproportionately forcibly sterilized.[53] State-influenced manifestations of patriarchy and sexism institutionalize oppression, alongside interpersonal abuses by Black men and microaggressions by white women.

As Black Feminists have named—and continue to name—the interlocking personal and systemic impacts of racism, capitalism, and cis-heteropatriarchy on the intricacies of their lives, poets and essayists have uplifted sensual and spiritual practices to heal residual trauma. The writings of Audre Lorde, bell hooks, and Alice Walker offer reflective accounts of finding joy through sensually moving the body, committing to meditation and prayer, and cultivating belonging in community *even as* they critique oppressive social systems. Their writings convey that Black people's capacity for well-being does not overtly depend on changing systemic oppression *first*—although they each, respectively, seek to dismantle systemic oppression. For each of these writers, contemplation fuels their capacity for confronting oppression without succumbing to the ravages of trauma.

The Dharma of Audre Lorde

The movement toward psychological wellness and reclamation of joy is expounded upon by Black Feminist poet and essayist Audre Lorde (1934–1992). As a Black woman writer who elaborates many teachings of the dharma—even if she does not name it as such—Lorde embraced the practice of turning toward suffering and knowing it fully.[54] Lorde reflects on the importance of self-scrutiny, even as she indicts white feminists for their racism and Black men for their sexism. In her writings, she simultaneously turns inward toward herself and turns outward toward oppressive social conditions. In her essay "Poetry Is Not a Luxury," Lorde writes,

> The quality of light by which we scrutinize our lives has direct bearing upon the product which we live, and upon the changes we hope to bring about through those lives. It is within this light that we form those ideas by which we pursue our magic and make it realized. . . . As we learn to bear the intimacy of scrutiny and to flourish within it, as we learn to use the products of that scrutiny for power within our living, those fears which rule our lives and form our silences begin to lose their control over us.[55]

Lorde uplifts internalized power as a way for Black women to gain control over their lives. In this essay and other writings, Lorde repeatedly redefines power as that which can be accessed by fearless confrontation with the intimidating messages and authority figures that have garnered strength by violent means. In confronting those internalized voices that women have been taught to fear, women evolve their capacity to define power on their own terms, distinct from the white, Western, patriarchal definitions of ruling. The patriarchal model uplifts ideas, thinking, and rationality. It privileges analysis and external structures. Lorde contests this definition of power by uplifting the importance of *feeling*. Power, for Lorde, revolves around not intellectual presumptions but rather creative, emotional expressions that privilege one's interior life. In her focus on inner excavation, Lorde writes,

> Within these deep places, each one of us holds an incredible reserve of creativity and power, or unexamined and unrecorded emotion and feeling. The woman's place of power within each of us is neither white nor surface; it is dark, it is ancient, and it is deep. When we view living in the European mode only as a problem to be solved, we rely solely upon our ideas to make us free, for these were what the white fathers told us were

precious. But as we come more into touch with our own ancient, non-european consciousness of living as a situation to be experienced and interacted with, we learn more and more to cherish our feelings, and to respect those hidden sources of our power from where true knowledge and, therefore, lasting action comes.[56]

Lorde, then, connects creativity and power with the examined life, with self-scrutiny and the willfulness to know one's interior being. She is highly political—she routinely critiques white feminists, domination imposed by the U.S. government, and the corporate pursuit of profit at the expense of human well-being. Yet at the same time she fervently advocates for a commitment to one's process of self-reflection. Her focus on knowing one's feelings, regardless of how excruciating or vile they might seem, is in tandem with the mindfulness teachings espoused in all Buddhist traditions. For Lorde, as well as practicing Buddhists, the embrace (rather than rejection) of difficult emotions evolves a powerful embodiment of fearlessness and growth. Lorde writes, "As they become known to and accepted by us, our feelings and the honest exploration of them become sanctuaries and spawning grounds for the most radical and daring of ideas. They become a safe-house for that difference so necessary to change and the conceptualization of any meaningful action. . . . We can train ourselves to respect our feelings and to transpose them into a language so they can be shared."[57]

Giving oneself permission to *feel*, for Lorde, is liberation. And, like Buddhist teachers, she advocates for training oneself to honor one's own emotions. Such training involves staying with one's feelings and allowing them to be articulated in language, rather than repressing them out of fear. Pain, Lorde muses, surfaces in dreams. And dreams, she believes, point the way to freedom. The recognition and honor of suffering is the foundation for liberation—just as articulated in the Four Noble Truths. In short, honoring one's feelings, including pain, ultimately fosters the experience of liberation, for women, for queer persons, for Black people who have been oppressed by a white, capitalist, cis-patriarchal social system.

bell hooks's Buddhist-Christian-Feminist Love

Lorde's contemporary, cultural critic bell hooks, similarly embraces the path to healing woundedness in acknowledging pain and embracing it, rather than turning away from it.[58] For hooks, the way forward within the context of a racist, capitalist, cis-patriarchal system is to embrace an ethic of love, which she defines as extending oneself to nurture one's own and another's spiritual growth, "a combination of care, knowledge, responsibility, respect, trust, and commitment."[59] For hooks, loving others is rooted in self-love, "the foundation of our loving practice."[60] In her 2000 book *All about Love*, she writes, "Giving ourself love, we provide our inner being with the opportunity to have unconditional love we may have longed to receive from someone else."[61] In *Salvation: Black People and Love*, she expands this definition of love to include care for the Black body: "We must work hard to love our black bodies in a white supremacist patriarchal culture."[62]

A self-identified Buddhist practitioner who also roots herself in Christian teachings,[63] hooks rejects the accumulation of wealth as a path to happiness, instead advocating for Right Livelihood—a tenet of the Noble Eightfold Path—as a practice of living into a love ethic. Right Livelihood references a way to relate to materialism, yet for hooks it fundamentally rests upon cultivation of a spiritual path. In an interview with *Tricycle* magazine, hooks reflects, "If I were really asked to define myself, I wouldn't start with race; I wouldn't start with blackness; I wouldn't start with gender; I wouldn't start with feminism. I would start with stripping down to what fundamentally informs my life, which is that I'm a seeker on the path. I think of feminism, and I think of anti-racist struggles as part of it. But where I stand spiritually is, steadfastly, on a path about love."[64]

For hooks, the path of love is rooted in daily disciplines—the practices of contemplation and self-interrogation as well as the practice of writing. Although a formidable voice within the genre of Black Feminism, hooks readily acknowledges that adhering to feminist theory is secondary to practicing contemplation. She states bluntly, "Feminism does not ground me. It is the discipline that comes from spiritual practice that is the foundation of my life. If we talk about what a disciplined writer I have been and hope to continue to be, that discipline starts with a spiritual practice. It's just every day, every day, every day."[65]

It is the daily discipline of contemplative practice that allows Black people to cultivate the capacity to love Blackness, an embodied form—hair, phenotype, and skin—that has been denigrated in white supremacist culture. In her book *Salvation: Black People and Love*, hooks states that "it is by now common knowledge that the trauma of white supremacy and ongoing racist assault leaves deep psychic wounds."[66] She identifies multiple dimensions in which such trauma has escalated. She points to abandonment that resulted from dislocation, enslavement, and the auction block and furthermore describes the dynamics within Black families, in which violence and authoritarian restrictions rather than tenderness and affection are norms. As noted with Right Livelihood, she rejects the valuing of materialism and wealth over community connections. And, fundamentally, hooks empathically illuminates how damaging it is for Black people to internalize shame of their Blackness.

The consequences of living through these multiple layers of trauma reside in Black bodies and spirits, leading to mental illnesses and community decay. To prioritize health, hooks argues, Black people must commit to "Valuing Ourselves Rightly: loving blackness as a form of political resistance":

> To end white supremacy we must create the conditions not only for black people to love blackness but for everyone else to love blackness. All black folks who love blackness recognize that it is not enough for us to be decolonized, that the non-black folks we work with, who teach our children, and so on, need consciousness raising that will enable them to see blackness differently. . . . Collectively, black people and our allies in struggle are empowered when we practice self-love as a revolutionary intervention that undermines practices of domination. Loving blackness as political resistance transforms our ways of looking and being, and thus create the conditions necessary for us to move against the forces of domination and death and reclaim black life.[67]

Therefore, hooks says, activists who are committed to sustaining Black lives must practice a different form of activism, infused with love for Black people and explicitly opposed to replicating the forms of power embraced by the dominant culture. As Lorde argues in her essay "The Master's Tools Will Never Dismantle the Master's House," hooks similarly advocates for a different way of being in relationship to one another in the struggle for health, well-being, and justice. In June 2020, during mass Black Lives Matter protests sparked by the murder of George Floyd, hooks reflected,

> Because of the awareness that love and domination cannot coexist, there is a collective call for everyone to place learning how to love on their emotional and/or spiritual agenda. We have witnessed the way in which movements for justice that denounce dominator culture, yet have an underlying commitment to corrupt uses of power, do not really create fundamental changes in our societal structure. When radical activists have not made a core break with dominator thinking (imperialist, white supremacist, capitalist patriarchy), there is no union of theory and practice, and real change is not sustained. That's why cultivating the mind of love is so crucial. When love is the ground of our being, a love ethic shapes our participation in politics.[68]

For hooks and other Black Buddhist practitioners, a love ethic is rooted in daily practices of self-interrogation, awareness, and generosity. From such inner spaciousness and openness, it is possible to offer attention, affection, and tenderness to activists working to confront violent, white supremacist vigilante and institutionalized forces. Fostering love within activist communities leads to sustained commitment to struggle and to personal well-being. Indeed, turning inward to tend to one's heart is upheld as central to resistance movements as speaking truth to racist, capitalist, patriarchal power.

Buddhism, Womanism, and Honoring the Earth: The Meditations of Alice Walker

The commitment to tending one's heart is foremost in the writings of Alice Walker, who coined the term "womanism" to distinguish Black women's differing lived realities from the norms taken for granted in the predominantly white feminist movement. Walker, like hooks and Lorde, writes that turning toward suffering and *making art* involves a set of practices that heals and confronts white supremacy. She uplifts an interior fortitude and capacity for spaciousness that prompts Black women to persevere—not only in the struggle against patriarchy and white supremacy, but also in the cultivation of an interior life. She disavows activists who only turn toward oppressive external forces rather than seeking to know their own interior lives, including their wounds.[69] For Walker, as for hooks and Lorde, healing and engagement is not choosing contemplative life over activist life but rather practicing meditation as part of the commitment to protect suffering peoples. Walker situates herself among "those of us humans who have stood up, wherever we could stand up, in defense of children, animals, the earth."[70] She acknowledges ancestors "who have done the same."[71] Standing up includes embracing personal pain. The process of caring for one's own inner life must be honored alongside the commitment to confront oppressive, harmful forces.

In her 1983 collection of essays *In Search of Our Mother's Gardens*, in an essay by the same name, Walker celebrates the Black woman's continued push to create art, through hands or words or song. Creating is, for the Black woman, a way forward. Walker writes,

> Black women are called, in the folklore that so aptly identifies one's status in society, "the *mule* of the world," because we have been handed the burdens that everyone else—*everyone* else—refused to carry. We have also been called "Matriarchs," "Superwomen," and "Mean and Evil Bitches." Not to mention "Castraters" and "Sapphire's Mama." When we have pleaded for understanding, our character has been distorted; when we have asked for simple caring, we have been handed empty inspirational appellations, then stuck in the farthest corner. When we have asked for love, we have been given children. In short, even our plainer gifts, our labors of fidelity and love, have been knocked down our throats. To be an artist and a black women, even today, lowers our status in many respects, rather than raises it: *and yet, artists we will be.*[72]

The artist honors an inner quietude that allows for expression and vision to come forth. For Walker, as for hooks, meditation in the tradition of Buddhism has facilitated such inner spaciousness. Walker claims Buddhism as a spiritual tradition that has taught her to practice "taking the arrow out of the heart," a reference to a Mahayana sutra on skillfully working with grief and loss. Rather than screaming at the archer who is inflicting pain—thereby remaining attached to one's own suffering and avoiding one's own grief—she seeks to know "How to take the arrow out of the heart? How to learn to relieve our own pain? That is the question."[73] For Walker, teachings and practices in the tradition of Buddhism foster healing and growth. She writes, "A better way is to learn, through meditation, through study and practice, a way to free yourself from the pain of being shot, no matter who the archer might be."[74]

Walker's writings over several decades, beginning with her Pulitzer Prize–winning novel *The Color Purple*, emphasize her commitment to standing on "the side of the poor, the economically, spiritually and politically oppressed, 'the wretched of the earth.'"[75] Interweaving stances against the ravages of global capitalism, war, environmental destruction, illiteracy, racism, and the poor health of impoverished children, Walker simultaneously uplifts Buddhism as a practice to sustain the heart: "This compassionate, generous, life-affirming nature of ours, that can be heard in so much of our music, is our Buddha nature. It is how we innately are."[76]

While Walker self-identifies not as Buddhist but rather as a practitioner of meditation who seeks to embody the teachings of the Buddha, she writes repeatedly of the importance of taking refuge in the dharma. She furthermore roots her spiritual practice to a connection with Mother Earth. For Walker, loving all aspects of nature—grass, trees, water, wind, along with sensual expressions of the body, including dancing—connects her to Spirit. In the depth of meditation, in love and care for the earth, in moving her body sensually, she encounters the energy to actively resist the degradations of white supremacist, capitalist, patriarchal culture.

And indeed, Walker has inspired marginalized women throughout the world, among them Christian-identified Womanist scholars within the United States. Influenced by Walker's Buddhist meditation practice, several Womanist theologians and ethicists have embraced Buddhist-Christian dialogue.[77] Womanist theology and ethic derive their definition of "Womanist" from Alice Walker's 1983 book of essays *In Search of Our Mother's Gardens: Womanist Prose*. Walker elaborates a four-part definition of "Womanist":

1. A black feminist or feminist of color. From the black folk expression of mothers to female children, "You acting womanish," i.e., like a woman. Usually referring to outrageous, audacious, courageous or *willful* behavior. Wanting to know more and in greater depth than is considered "good" for one. . . . 2. *Also*: A woman who loves other women, sexually and/or nonsexually. Appreciates and prefers women's culture, women's emotional flexibility (values tears as natural counterbalance of laughter), and women's strength. . . . 3. Loves music. Loves dance. Loves the moon. *Loves* the Spirit. Loves love and food and roundness. Loves struggle. *Loves* the Folk. Loves herself. *Regardless*. 4. Womanist is to feminist as purple to lavender.[78]

Uplifting invisible, disregarded women's voices in both Christian and Buddhist canonical texts is of fundamental importance for Womanist scholars. Furthermore, Womanist scholars emphasize Spirit and embodied practices—identified in Walker's definition—as pivotal. Finally, the commitment to working against systemic oppression while honoring ancestors who have persevered is central to Womanist literature.

Buddhist practices of embracing suffering to attain liberation compel Womanist scholars to engage Buddhist voices. Keri Day uplifts the theme of freedom as central to Walker's works, scholarly Womanist literature, and early Buddhist nuns' poetry.[79] In Day's interpretation, freedom is the capacity to *do* and *be*—a process of self-actualizing that rests fundamentally in spiritual practice. Day, like Walker, insists that social conditions matter, in that poverty, sexism, and racism often determine the extent of a woman's ability to thrive. She remains inspired by Walker's meditation on how to relate to pain, to take the arrow out of one's own heart.

In addition to illuminating the healing practice of embracing suffering, Walker has inspired creative *intellectual* practice for Womanist scholars who embrace interreligious textual exchange.[80] In this vein, Buddhist and Womanist scholars seek "fertile" global exchange. One way in which such global exchange is most identifiable—for both self-identified Black Buddhists as well as Womanist scholars—is in the reverence for ancestors, known and unknown. Indeed, uplifting literature by marginalized women of color and performing devotional practices that honor the fortitude of ancestors are central to Black Buddhist and Womanist commitments. Carolyn Jones Medine writes that for Walker—as for other Black Buddhists and people of color globally—the practice of ancestor veneration is "a form of memorialization, also a form of care and of healing, and a way to stand firm in the face of violence."[81]

Walker herself writes, "And, as always, I thank the ancestors, those who have gone on and those who are always arriving. It is because our global spiritual ancestors have loved us very dearly that we [are] practicing ways to embody peace and create a better world. I feel personally ever bathed in that love."[82]

The spiritual practices and sophisticated political analysis of Black Feminists, the spirit-filled, communally oriented traditions of the Black Church, and the emphasis on psychological and political freedom in the Black Freedom Movement influence the liberatory practices of Black Buddhists. As the next chapter details, Black Buddhist teachers evolve the Black Radical Tradition in distinctive interpretations of the dharma that incorporate Black Radical orientations toward political and psychological freedom.

5

Turning toward Internal Suffering

Dharma for the Practice of Psychological and Spiritual Liberation

Everything is practice, a very sacred and personal experience. There is freedom in the silence of practice, in the
stillness as well as in the movement of the practice of life.
The greatest teaching for me has been practicing compassion, first for myself, then for other individuals, and for all
beings in all directions. It is here that I have found true
freedom. Ache.
—Marlene Jones[1]

Black Radical thinkers, as ancestors and elders who promoted psychological freedom for people of African descent, embodied a practice of
turning toward the causes of externally wrought suffering and addressing harmful conditions. They illuminated the Three Defilements
undergirding European colonialism: greed undergirding exploitation of
land and enslavement of peoples, hatred of Black bodies, and delusions
of white supremacy. Several Black Radical thinkers, in addition to critique and activism, also embraced—and continue to embrace—spiritual
practices as a path toward psychological liberation.

This chapter argues that the practice of dharma teachings is a means
to cultivate psychological and spiritual liberation from white supremacy
and patriarchy. Particular teachings have been especially effective for
the liberatory practice of Black Buddhists: the Four Noble Truths and
the Noble Eightfold Path, the Three Marks of Existence, Relative and
Ultimate Reality, the Brahmaviharas, and the *Satipatthana Sutta*. This
chapter outlines the interpretations of Black Buddhist teachers and their
experience of dharma practice as a path to psychological and spiritual
liberation in the broader Black Radical Tradition.

The Four Noble Truths and the Noble Eightfold Path

The first teachings the Buddha gave were of the Middle Way between indulgence and prosperity and the Four Noble Truths, including the Noble Eightfold Path. The Four Noble Truths provide the core teachings for the different lineages found under the umbrella of Buddhism. The First Noble Truth articulated that life is dissatisfactory (*dukkha*) due to four aspects of existence: (1) physical conditions that are subject to decay, (2) painful mental and emotional experiences, (3) unpleasantness, and (4) not getting what one wants. Human beings seek what the Buddha called Three Forms of Thirst: (1) sensual pleasure, (2) ego-driven protection, and (3) aversion to unpleasantness. The Second Noble Truth is that dissatisfaction arises from grasping for lasting happiness that is, in reality, impermanent. The Third Noble Truth is that there is a path to alleviate dissatisfaction. The Fourth Noble Truth is the way forward: the Noble Eightfold Path.

The Noble Eightfold Path, as noted previously, includes eight teachings that emphasize wisdom, ethics, and meditation: Right View, Right Intention, Right Speech, Right Conduct, Right Livelihood, Right Effort, Right Mindfulness, and Right Concentration.

The Four Noble Truths and the Noble Eightfold Path provide an analysis and a roadmap that is particularly compelling for people whose ancestors have been enslaved: suffering is a part of life, and there is a path of liberation from suffering. Gretchen Rohr, a Community Dharma Leader in the Insight tradition, remarks, "Part of the initial attraction of Buddhism was this First Noble Truth of suffering. I know suffering. . . . There's such an attraction to being amongst people who recognize their suffering."[2]

But Rohr acknowledges that naming the perpetual existence of suffering can be challenging for activists, for such a recognition suggests that organizing against oppression will not ultimately end oppression. "[The First Noble Truth] forces one of two options: either what you're doing is not really working towards the end, or [suffering is] not going to end while you're alive."[3]

Yet Black Buddhist teachers and long-term practitioners embrace the nuances of human existence alongside a strident critique of social oppression. The long history of racial slavery, segregation, and discrimination has led to particular forms of suffering—separation of Black families, violence and rape, poverty and housing discrimination, patterns of symbolic racism that denigrate the beauty of Black bodies and intelligent Black minds—that Black practitioners acknowledge as core aspects of their suffering. In these widespread experiences of historical and contemporary trauma, Black teachers and long-term practitioners take into account the aspects of their social conditioning as well as the mental formations that perpetuate their suffering, as lived experiences that must be deconstructed, known, and transformed for liberation to take place.

Ryūmon Hilda Gutiérrez Baldoquín, editor of the anthology *Dharma, Color, and Culture*, elaborates that the Second Noble Truth teaches the causes of suffering: greed or desire, hatred or aversion, and delusion or ignorance—the Three Poisons. Baldoquín states, "When we get stuck in any of these three, we confuse our inherent wholeness and the wholeness of others and spend our lives swimming—or, for those of us less skilled, drowning—in the river of suffering."[4]

Leaning into suffering is the way forward, says Insight teacher Sebene Selassie:

> We are going to use these teachings of the Buddha which ask us to come face-to-face with and be intimate with our suffering and the suffering of others. That means asking us to let go of our usual strategies of trying to escape or fix our suffering. These teachings again insist that we need to face our suffering, internally, externally, and both internally and externally. We need to face the suffering of the world or we will not truly be free. So we are not going to find freedom by resisting our suffering, by hating it or trying to get rid of it. And we are not going to find freedom by avoiding it, by turning only to what pleases us. And we are not going to find our freedom by distorting our suffering, by getting caught up in or by trying to control or manipulate our experience.
>
> These teachings about suffering and the end of suffering are asking us to take an honest look internally at ourselves and externally at our world. And also to understand the ways in which we distract, avoid, also the ways we distort our experience. These come because we are not willing or we are afraid to meet our pain, our fear, our disappointments, our trauma. . . . And again, we are using our practice of cultivating this skill

for both internal and external awareness to help build the capacity to see clearly what's happening and to meet it with wisdom and compassion.[5]

Turning toward suffering, rather than avoiding it, is central to the story of the enlightenment of Siddhartha Gautama—later known as Shakyamuni Buddha. In this narrative, Siddhartha Gautama meditates under a Bodhi tree and faces internal demons until they subside. This narrative is uplifted as relevant for healing the particular suffering experienced by Black people. Pamela Ayo Yetunde, who trained as an aspirant in the Thich Nhat Hanh Order of Interbeing and is a Community Dharma Leader in the Insight tradition, suggests that locating Siddhartha's narrative in the conditions of the transatlantic slave trade and intergenerational trauma poses reflective questions for Black meditators:

... What noble truths arise when Siddhartha sees the suffering of racism?

Siddhartha's first truth could be "People, including loved ones, try to protect you from the truth of other people's harmful delusions." The truth of racism is too much to bear early in life, so being deluded early on is an experience many of us share.

A second truth could be "there is racism." Why is there racism? ... [Humans] are born without a perspective. Then, sometime after birth, ignorance, anxiety, and aggression begin to form our perspectives. Racism is a manifestation of ill-formed perspective-making processes.

Siddhartha's third truth could be "I am impacted by racism." Racism hurts the heart, as well as the ways it impacts people on a physical level.

A fourth truth could be "There is no refuge from racism." Yes, one can experience temporary relief from others' attacks, but racism still remains. Emerging from that "refuge" is a setup for the suffering that occurs when the reality of racism is inevitably faced again.

A fifth truth could be "This suffering I feel is felt by those who look like me." It is this truth that begins to reconnect us with others.

A sixth truth might be "Since this suffering is shared, the transformation of this suffering will also be shared."[6]

Yetunde further describes the agency Buddhism elevates in the teaching on the Third Noble Truth in particular. Indeed, there is communal knowing and experience of suffering, and there is also personal motivation ignited by the assertion that a suffering person and community can alleviate their suffering. Yetunde writes,

> The Third Noble Truth, which states that the causes of suffering are knowable to the sufferer, takes the mystery out of knowing oneself. Not only does it take the mystery out, it empowers, inspires, and motivates the believer. The potential for healing from universal existential angst lies within humans themselves. A woman can heal herself from the pain of sexism, a black person can heal from the pain of racism, a lesbian can heal from homophobia, and a person with these intersecting identities can heal from them all through Buddhist practice. When the First, Second, and Third Noble Truths begin to ring true, it gives rise to faith (a spiritual faculty) in one's self and the teachings that come thereafter, the Fourth Noble Truth, outlines an eightfold path to work with the knowable causes of suffering so that one does not needlessly suffer from the universal existential situation.[7]

For Yetunde and other Black Buddhists, the fundamental agency taught in Buddhism arises from the practice of internalizing new perspectives and worldviews.

Right Understanding: The Three Marks of Existence

One of the tenets of the Noble Eightfold Path is the teaching on Right Understanding. The original teachings on Right Understanding are found in the *Dhammapada*, a central text in the Pali Buddhist canon whose title can be translated as "Verses on the Buddhist Doctrine" or "Way of Truth." It contains teachings on the Three Marks of Existence: *anicca* (impermanence), *dukkha* (unsatisfactoriness or suffering), and *anatta* (non-self).

Anicca conveys the understanding that arose when Siddhartha Gautama first left his palace gates at the age of twenty-nine and ventured into the broader society, encountering inescapable suffering in the stages of sickness, old age, and death. He later articulated a central truth in his first teaching of the Four Noble Truths: all phenomena, including the human body, are impermanent. The Buddha extended the realization of impermanence to mental formations and states of mind: every thought that arises will pass away.

Alongside impermanence, the Buddha highlighted the experience of perpetual dissatisfaction (dukkha). He taught that dissatisfaction and suffering are found in every aspect of life. The teaching on dukkha elaborates the teaching of the First Noble Truth: it explains suffering as a consequence of craving or "thirst" to get what one wants, and aversion to receiving something undesirable. The Buddha taught that craving and dissatisfaction are intimately related: when one ceases craving, dukkha also evaporates. Dukkha is so pervasive that the Buddha distinguished between three different kinds: *dukkha dukkha* that arises from craving that the circumstances of our lives will be different; *sankhara dukkha* that relates to mental formations that arise when suffering is present, such as "shoulds" and judgments; and *viparinama dukkha*, which is related to impermanence: human beings seek to perpetuate pleasant experiences and experience dukkha when those pleasant experiences change.[8]

The doctrine of anatta (non-self)[9] asserts that, unlike in the European worldview—in which a personal self is identified and articulated—there is not a permanent, underlying substance that is identified as a personal self. Rather, each person is composed of five *khandhas* (in Sanskrit: *skandhas*) that are constantly in flux, in relation to environment, context, and interpersonal interactions. The five khandhas, sometimes translated as "aggregates," include *rupa* (form), *vedana* (feeling), *samjna* (perception), *sankhara* (mental formations), and *vinnana* (consciousness). Form refers to physical phenomena. Feeling refers to pleasure, pain, and neutral sensations. Perception refers to the process of mentally labeling and identifying objects. Mental formations refer to active processes in the mind, including attention and evaluation. Consciousness refers to the six senses, including the intellect.

The Buddha explained that the five khandhas constantly shift and lack inherent stability. Yet as Black Buddhists have argued, this doctrine should not be interpreted as negating self-dignity and human rights. Rather, the doctrine of non-self—if articulated with nuance and sensitivity in a racialized social context that arises from a history of denying Black personhood—is inherently liberatory.[10] The doctrine of non-self elevates important frameworks for understanding the conventional self, alongside the liberated non-self, and the radical freedom inherent in practicing stillness, in which thoughts fall away and the mind/heart transcends dualities.[11]

Selassie identifies the teaching on non-self as ultimately liberative. She credits scholar Andrew Olendzki with illuminating the process of unlearning harmful predispositions and habits:

> Sankharas (mental formations) can be states in our in-the-moment response to experience, sort of the active manifestation of an emotion or a thought. These states are really affected by our *samadhi*, by our meditation practice. But sankharas can also be behaviors, so they can be actions of body, speech and mind and the expression of these states. These have more of a lasting effect—they're not in-the-moment; they become the ways that we habituate. And these behaviors can be really affected by our *Śīla* or ethics, so that if we have ethics around right speech, around right action, they can start to affect our behaviors to match with our aspirations for ourselves and our values. But these sankharas can also become traits. They can become passive manifestations of our emotions as patterns, as dispositions, as tendencies, and these largely are dormant and unconscious. They become our learned or conditioned emotional response and habits, our patterns. And these traits are really supported by *paññā* or wisdom. And that is the wisdom of good friendship and feedback, also the wisdom of continuing this practice, so that we can uncover these unconscious behaviors as we move towards this aspiration of waking up to our freedom.[12]

Blackness, Self, and Non-Self

Rather than thinking of non-self as a destination or ultimate truth, Selassie says, we need to be able to relate to the reality of the self and the truth of non-self at the same time.

> The Buddha was asked if there is a self or non-self. He wouldn't answer because he said "that's not the right question." He pointed to the functional need for connecting or relating to the self. It's not like he walked around and didn't refer to himself or didn't have reference for others. He said those are necessary designations we need to move through the world. There is self, but there's also non-self. . . . He wasn't saying that non-self is

someplace we have to get to and then we can let go of self. He was pointing out that we must develop an understanding of non-self, this is a mark of existence too, in the same way that suffering is a mark of existence. But he also said that there's freedom from suffering.[13]

In connecting and relating to the self, the body is a conduit for liberation. At the same time, Lama Rod Owens, a teacher in the Kagyu Tibetan tradition, relates the metaphysical understanding of self to political, psychological, and spiritual liberation:

In Buddhism, enlightenment isn't the extinguishing of the self. It is the recognition of the self. It's the recognition of the illusion of self. If we did not relate to the self, to this sense of ego, then we wouldn't be able to be in a relationship to people around us. Because everyone in the world communicates through ego. We relate to reality through ego. So if I were to obtain enlightenment—and I hope to at some point—but if I were to obtain enlightenment, I would still be very connected to ego, especially if I'm trying to liberate others from this reality. So it's not the ego, it's not the self that is the issue. It's our relationship [to those ideas]. . . . Our relationship gives meaning to things around us. The thing itself doesn't have meaning. This kind of basic work that I'm always engaged in is this balance between self and non-self, and how that relates to social liberation, and how social liberation ties into ultimate liberation.[14]

For Owens, as well as other Black Buddhist teachers, mindfulness of the body is an essential aspect of liberatory practice. Yetunde states,

In the practices of mindfulness of the body, there's never [a teaching of] "be mindful of the capital S self." . . . So [for some] it somehow has become this interpretation or teaching that the body doesn't exist. But I don't believe that's the teaching because there's so much focus on mindfulness of the body. Those two truths can't coexist with all the focus on meditation and mindfulness of the body—when to eat, how to sit, so I don't believe that no-self means no body. And I think that is destructive teaching actually.

The way that I look at it now is that no self means "try not to become a narcissist." . . . Don't be so focused on ego clinging that you become selfish. When we look at the teachings of the Brahmaviharas on compassion, equanimity, loving, kindness, and sympathetic joy, when you engage in those practices deeply, it makes you selfless; it cultivates selflessness, and so that's really how I see no-self. It means selflessness . . . attention towards the well-being of others.[15]

The fact of constant change—impermanence—of all phenomena, including the self, illuminates that racial constructs of the Black body are empty of substantial meaning. In short, to embrace the teaching on non-self is to recognize that degrading interpretations of Blackness are superficial labels, rooted in ignorance, that historically were exploited for expedient purposes such as land theft and colonization, slavery and forced servitude, and constructing whiteness as intellectually and morally superior to Blackness. In the teaching on non-self, the artificiality of constructed realities is starkly illuminated. To deconstruct the self, not only as a series of always changing and shifting aggregates, but also as a set of degraded images originating from a deluded white supremacist mind, allows practitioners to claim the freedom inherent in dharma teachings. Constructs are simply constructs. They have no basis in reality; nor are they liberating. These constructs form part of the causes and conditions of suffering, but are not hard and fixed facts, eternally believed and internalized. Thus, Black practitioners can shift interpretations of their constructed selves in the movement toward their liberation.

Ruth King, a teacher in the Insight tradition, embraces the teachings on anatta as liberating for people of African descent:

The teachings on anatta—non-self—are an important inquiry for people of color—those of us who've [had] their sense of self ripped away from them or haven't had a chance to shine or be inwardly affirmed in a meaningful way. We question and doubt ourselves. We don't know if we do this because of race or if it's just the human condition.

Self and non-self are wrapped around the Buddhist teaching on ultimate and relative reality. In brief, you need a self (relative reality) to know that you're not a self or to know you are liberated (ultimate reality). In other words, you need the body in order to wake up.

In the Buddhist teachings, non-self is not that you are not a self, it's that you're not a self that you can solidly rely on. The self is constantly changing—a series of processes or aggregate experiences. Change is all there is. When we understand this from our practice, we can soften the grip that identity hardens in our hearts and minds. We can know a deeper freedom, despite conditioning, from the inside out.[16]

For Black teachers with long-term practices, personally relating to dharma teachings can illuminate obscure or potentially threatening passages, especially in a society in which Black people have been dehumanized. Kate Johnson, a teacher in the Insight tradition, says,

What are the deep kind of awakening experiences that we've had, and do we or do we not teach from that place? Some of my most profound experiences in meditation around this [teaching on anatta] have been deep experiences and insights into emptiness and selflessness, and the interdependent, not solid, nature of self. And also the fact [that there is] no central command system for that self, that the mind actually is not that. I don't usually teach that. When I can, my favorite places to teach are within POC [communities], the community of women, and queer communities—that's what I love. And I feel like when I'm in mixed company or when I'm teaching to primarily white audiences I don't often speak about selflessness or anatta because I worry that it's going to be fuel for spiritual bypass.[17]

"Spiritual bypass" refers to using spiritual teachings to avoid psychological and social problems in one's self or environment.[18] For people of African descent, the challenge of relating to non-self is less about "spiritual bypass" and more about relating to language that suggests non-personhood. Denial of Black humanity undergirded laws and social practices during centuries of colonization and formation of the United States as a nation-state.[19] Thus, the language of "non-self" can erect an emotional hurdle that is important to address with nuance. Unique Holland, a long-term practitioner in the Zen and Insight traditions, describes her first encounter with the teachings on non-self. "[We live in a society in which] white people are the norm. There's a racialized class distinction. And so this idea of no self had all of this packaging . . . in a way that was distinct from the kinds of oppression and mask making that was expected of me outside of dharma spaces."[20] The

"norms" to which Holland refers are the constructed norms of whiteness as superior and Blackness as degraded. The teaching on non-self,
for practitioners such as Holland, has the potential to further reiterate
degradation. Yet for Black Buddhist teachers, the liberation found in
the teaching on non-self is akin to the liberation encountered in the
Black Radical Tradition: it is possible to deconstruct the falsely constructed Black body and claim one's (relative) self in positive, affirming
ways. Moreover, in Buddhism, it is possible to affirm one's Blackness as
one—but not the only—stage in the process of spiritual, psychological,
and political liberation. In the practice of letting thoughts fall away,
and entering into meditative concentration, the falseness inherent in
the mundane world fades to background noise, and the experience
of mental stillness arises, even briefly, as the path to liberation. Thus,
dharma practice can be seen as living into the aspirations of the Black
Radical Tradition: practitioners who enter a realm of mental stability
are no longer in reaction to white supremacist constructs and messages.
Rather, they can see the delusions inherent in white supremacy and
observe but do not react to the false constructs inherent within those
delusions.

In their embrace of the teachings on non-self, furthermore, Buddhist
practitioners of African descent elevate core teachings on interdepen-
dency or interbeing. In the Zen tradition, "non-self" is also interpreted
as teachings on interrelationship. Zenju Earthlyn Manuel, a teacher in
the Soto Zen tradition, writes on interrelationship in her meditation
The Way of Tenderness: Awakening through Race, Sexuality, and Gender.
Manuel acknowledges the "profound interrelationship that sustains our
existence" and states that "interrelationship is inherent to living."[21]

> No-self means that other people are involved. That's what no-self means.
> It's not just you. It should say not just yourself, rather than no-self. It
> means no-self in and of itself, like there's nothing happening here. It's
> relational, and that's why I say there's no-self, there's no just you.
>
> No-self has no substance. . . . And so, you have to talk about your
> life back to where you started from: how you're living and who you
> are, so you can understand the suffering. You have to have some[one]
> to study. You can't just walk around, go "there's nobody and there's

nothing and there's emptiness, and so I just sit here and breathe." How long will that last?

I think that no self is really important to understand, especially in Zen, and I talk a lot about it because they [other teachers] use it so much to negate the lived experience, but it's saying it *is* the lived experience. No self is interrelationship. No self is interrelationship, it is interbeing.[22]

Manuel emphasizes that teachings on non-self give practitioners an opportunity to study their own lives: to look within and understand how they arrived at different experiences and identities. Rather than negating the experience of being human, the teaching on non-self is a teaching on learning from one's lived experiences as well as how relate to other persons in an aware and interdependent way. Similarly, Chimyo Atkinson, a former resident monk at Great Tree Women's Zen Center, states,

> To say non-self is kind of negative. [The phrase] is kind of empty because self in my understanding is greater than what we see as contained in this body or what we see is contained in this head. It includes all of your surroundings, everything, all the beings that you are ultimately connected with, because there's the big self. The self that is included in all of this universe. We are not separate from anything. To say self is to separate from all myriad beings that are out there. And that's our big delusion right there.[23]

Understanding the teaching of non-self in relation to the social world, Owens says, fosters deeper understanding of one's own life—as real and in relationship, as a construct and an illusion, and in relation to ultimate reality:

> The ultimate truth is non-self. But the relative truth is self. So one of the things that at least in my practice and also throughout the dharma is that in order for me to earn my experience of the ultimate, I have to actually earn the experience of the relative. So I have to come really close and really solid into what my experience of having a self is. Because once I get really curious in this idea of self, I begin to understand how to actually undo the self, and undo my fixation on the self. I think the self is so

deeply, deeply entwined in a way of being in the world and I have to actually understand the mechanisms of the self in order to transcend the self.

So I can start speaking in ways of very general non-self terms, but actually that's going to be the root of increasing my suffering, of increasing my suffering on the relative, because I just don't understand the self enough in order to move through it or to transcend it yet. But the ultimate is always on the horizon. So I can talk about the self, but I also know at the same time there is no self. This is the tricky part of integrating justice and dharma. Both of these ideas have to be held together. The relative and the ultimate. You can't skip around to either-or. You have to be right with both of those always at the same time, and then that actually begins to help us move more towards the ultimate.[24]

Relative and Ultimate Reality

The ultimate reality to which Owens refers is intimately interwoven with teachings on non-self. The dharma teaching on ultimate and relative reality, known as the Two Truths doctrine, originated with Nagarjuna, an Indian Buddhist philosopher who founded the Madhyamika school of thought.[25] Nagarjuna drew his insights from the words of the Buddha recorded in the Theravada Pali *Tripitika*.[26] In Mahayana Buddhism, the Two Truths teaching explains that relative reality—the material and social world—is fundamentally dualistic. Bodies, mental concepts, emotions and thoughts, and interpersonal and institutional dynamics are believed to be solid, separate, independent entities. Yet once the illusion of separateness is stripped away, meditators access an "ultimate" reality beyond all dualisms. In Mahayana Buddhism, this is known as "emptiness" or "interdependence." In Vajrayana Buddhism, ultimate reality is termed "space," "complete openness," and "primordial purity."[27]

The Two Truths teaching can be supportive for navigating potentially hostile social spaces. Owens states,

How do we actually begin to hold the space for something and nothing at the same time? That's the wisdom that arises. In the absolute I am nothing, but in the relative I am something. So if I don't embrace that and understand that, then I won't know how to let it go. I can be both at the same time. I can be something and nothing. And you can hit extremes. You're sitting in the middle, and you're allowing, you stay present for discomfort, whatever arises. And then your interactions in the world begin to change. . . . You can't move, you can't dodge. You can't dodge the comments, you are running into them and it's wounding. If I see that wall coming up, I just step around it. Because this isn't about me. You don't actually know who I am. Whatever you think I am is an illusion.[28]

Similar to Owens, Spring Washam, a teacher in the Insight tradition, reconciles the relative and ultimate as Two Truths that can be held together at once:

The conventional level will say, my name is Spring, we are in Oakland. . . . And then I can see the universal level like, the quantum level you know look very closely, oh right. It is just the moving particles of my things here and I've had so many mystical experiences of being in that vast space and seeing that so for me, it is easy to navigate those two worlds. To see, yes, for this purpose of my identity, I appear as a Black woman and that is my identity and I will show up and there is a reason. I have this very clear form for a very specific reason in this life. And it is easy for me to not get too mired in the drama because then I can kind of call it back and say, "Well on the great level this is just a story, a chapter in a book, and there is something much vaster holding all of this."

I can relate to the conventional pain that is here and the work that we have to do. Holding those is always a dance, and it has been [increasingly] easier because I *can* hold them. I can get much closer to the suffering, because I can see the impermanent nature of it, yet still be fully present knowing: this is one level of reality. . . . It is two truths, not one or the other, because of impermanence. We are on this grind right now, but this is temporary, this could shift. At any moment it could all change, and so I can get close to the intensity because of my understanding and the trust in impermanence, and also that there is something ultimate in it all.[29]

Washam identifies impermanence, one of the three "marks of existence," as a core teaching for understanding ultimate reality. Furthermore, she finds meaning in the form she embodies in this lifetime: she identifies form, one of the Five Aggregates, in her interpretation of the Two Truths. She embraces her form as a Black woman but does not import all of her identity in her form, even as she lives in a society in which Black people are constantly reminded, indirectly and directly, of their race. In many ways, Washam articulates the approach of the Black Feminist Tradition, in that she validates her Black female body without internalizing its constructed meanings as the primary ways in which she relates to her own existence. She can observe its social significance without adopting conventional interpretations of it. In achieving emotional distance from the ways in which her form is received, she has freed herself of conventionally wrought messages regarding Blackness and womanhood.

The Two Truths that facilitate the mental freedom experienced by Washam are, in the words of Kate Johnson, "inseparable." Johnson explains that "the relative—the relational—and the universal truths arise together. . . . For me that means that you can't transcend nor is it desirable to transcend the relational field because it's actually the relational field that can be a doorway into a deep experience of universal truths, and this means not skipping over the details of who we are and where we are and what our relationships are to each other."[30]

Nuancing embodied experiences is central to the teachings on Two Truths for teachers of African descent. Rhonda Magee, author of *The Inner Work of Racial Justice,* writes that Western Buddhism effectively deconstructs the relative self as a mental construct but does not directly deconstruct the relative self as a *social* construct.[31] Thus, the social reality of Black embodiedness must be explicitly articulated: "There's really some basic truth to the kind of the relative reality, if you will, of our embodiedness. And the fact that however we enter into engagement, whatever we intend, whatever projects we take on, we enter it through the doorways of our own actual lived experience. As far as I'm concerned [there is] no other way into [meditation], because lived experience is always present, creating opportunities and a sense of heritage, a sense of lineage, [as well as] some purpose."[32]

Claiming the importance of one's lived experience and attributing positive qualities to one's Black body, even while holding up the truth of ultimate reality, requires a nuanced approach. For many Black teachers, this interpretative work is fundamentally racial justice work. Justin Miles, a Baltimore-based psychotherapist and Shambhala practitioner, states that dharma teachings give him the tools to see his conditioning as well as alleviate a degree of suffering in his Black community. In cultivating "clarity and mental stability," Miles says he attains the "courage and fearlessness to be able to directly confront those agents that are responsible for helping to perpetuate other people's suffering."[33]

> There is no lasting sense of self based on my own personal understanding and experience of the Buddhadharma. Our lives are not just about adopting and playing out an identity but also relating to something that's much more amorphous and flexible and without stain fundamentally; without blame. [This teaching on non-self] helps me to understand my nature as something that can always be relied on, something that's stable, something that says that I'm just not whoever it is that I've been told to understand myself as. But remember, the Buddha didn't say that there was *no* self. He said there was no *lasting* self. So that also places who I am, in terms of being a Black person, while not to be fixated on or treated as the center of my functioning and being, as an authentic identity born of and based on my relationships with my culture, community, family . . . everything. Our nature shines on the world through a Black lens.[34]

Staying connected to a sense of ultimate reality both reinforces one's social identity as a Black person and minimizes the weight put on it: despite the salience of white supremacist interpretations of the Black body, through Buddhist teachings and dharma practices, Black Buddhists have placed less weight on the historical interpretations of their bodies and more emphasis on seeing the falseness of those social constructs. As white supremacist constructs have fallen away, affirming and uplifting practices of relating to the relative self foster healing and self-confidence. Yet even this level of validation is only one aspect of the path to liberation. As the teachings on relative and ultimate reality demonstrate, living into liberation is recognizing the truth of one's self in relation to a greater truth of ultimate reality, in which dualisms and constructs of relative reality fall away. In the practice of stillness, the Two Truths are held together as a path to liberation, in which human beings are interdependent and yet not dependent upon the meanings created in conventional reality. There is, then, *independence* as well as *interdependence* in a sustained experience of freedom.

The Brahmaviharas

To cultivate the "mental stability, fearlessness, and courage" discussed by Miles, numerous teachers and long-term practitioners uplift the Brahmaviharas as central to their practice. The Brahmaviharas are teachings and practices that include *metta* (loving-kindness), *karuna* (compassion), *mudita* (empathetic joy), and *upekkha* (equanimity). Known as the Four Immeasurables, they are identified as the Four Faces of Love of the Hindu god Brahma.[35] Sharon Shelton, a teacher in the Insight tradition, identifies the Brahmaviharas as heart or love practices:

> During the lifetime of the Buddha, those of the Brahmanic faith prayed that after death, they would go to heaven to forever be with Brahma, the universal God. Brahmanism was an ancient Indian religious tradition, predated to Buddha. One day a Brahmin man asked the Buddha, "What can I do to be sure that I will be with Brahma after I die?" And the Buddha replied, "As Brahma is the source of love, to dwell with him, you must practice the Brahmaviharas: loving kindness, compassion, sympathetic joy, and equanimity."
>
> According to Thai forest monk Thanissaro Bhikkhu, the Brahmaviharas—also referred to as the sublime attitudes—are the Buddha's primary heart teachings. They are essentially four expressions of true love. They're also called immeasurable because if we practice them, if we cultivate them, they will grow and grow every day until they encompass the entire world. Cultivating the Brahmaviharas helps us manifest heart and mind qualities that are again innate in all of us as potential. Metta or loving kindness is our capacity for friendliness or goodwill. Karuna or compassion is our capacity to stay present when faced with pain and suffering. Mudita or sympathetic joy is our capacity for endless appreciative joy and gratitude. And upekkha [or equanimity] is our capacity to be with things just as they are: pleasant, unpleasant, or neutral.[36]

In the three primary lineages of Buddhism, scholars delineate two "wings" that are broadly identified as "wisdom" practices of investigation and concentration, and "heart" practices in the Brahmaviharas. The wisdom practices emphasize examination of what is taking place in one's inner and outer experience. Insight teacher Noliwe Alexander defines the heart practices as a method to cultivate love toward oneself and others as well as achieve inner balance to heal stress and trauma.[37]

The metta (loving-kindness) practice taught in the Insight tradition includes variations on guided meditation techniques that include wishing safety and well-being for one's self, a benefactor, a friend, a neutral person, a challenging person, a person for whom one feels deep enmity, and all beings. Phrases such as "May [I] be safe and protected," "May [I] be peaceful and happy," "May [I] be healthy and strong," and "May [I] live with ease and well-being" are taught alongside techniques to observe the breath and notice inner and outer noise without judgment.

Devin Berry, a teacher in the Insight tradition, emphasizes that metta must be taught alongside awareness of the body, and that self-love is the first meditation in metta practice:

We are really looking at self-love, or metta, more than anything. [We are looking at] compassion for self, more than anything, because of the amount of trauma that we hold in our bodies, and the stories that we have in our heads. We're always engaging in justice and service work taking care of others. During the Deep Time Liberation retreat, it's like, "let's bring it all back here, to this body, to this heart-mind." And we often don't want to do that, because we don't know if we have the capacity to hold all of our own tears or all of our fears. So, we want to reach out for something and someone else and that can make sense and can be skillful means. We're supporting folks in knowing self-love, knowing self-compassion. Because if you have that, and you fill yourself with that, then you can radiate that out to everyone else in the room, and you do it collectively.[38]

Practicing self-love was a theme that arose repeatedly in interviews with Black Buddhist teachers and long-term practitioners. Diane Yaski, who has practiced in the Insight tradition for more than two decades, states that it helped her heal from the pain of divorce and the challenges of parenting.

My metta practice has saved my life. It's what has helped me heal from this basic hate I had for my ex-husband. It's helped me deal with issues that I've had with coworkers. It's helped me deal with myself. It includes

a lot of sending love and kindness to myself, a lot of metta practice to
myself to help me deal with my own personal issues: Just being a human
being and living on this earth, being a woman and being a Black woman,
being a wife and being a mother . . . [feeling] self-doubt. Metta practice
has been everything to me.[39]

Many teachers share that through deep, steady breathing and repeti-
tive phrases, metta practice facilitates the healing of deep familial and
relationship wounds. Joshua Alafia, a Community Dharma Leader in the
Insight tradition, reflects that all four of the Brahmaviharas have been
important for his growth. Metta, Alafia states, is the first step in the path
to embodying the Brahmaviharas.

We can't love until the heart is unlocked. So, metta is the first step. [Ini-
tially] I didn't want to do metta. I had been doing all these Tantric, embodying, bringing deities into the body, all of these aerobic, imaginative
practices. And I was liking the just letting go of all of that and [in Vipas-
sana] just being with, being with, being with, being with. And so then it
was time to do metta, [and] I was like, "I don't have time for metta. I'm
trying to be with." And then having all this time with metta, I started
understanding the wounds of my heart. When we come into the heart-
mind [we can say] "this is what I've been numbing. Oh, this experience
made me do this." I chose romantic relationships with emotionally aloof
women because they triggered this feeling of numbness that I felt when I
felt abandoned and was dealing with emotional aloofness and nonpres-
ence with my father. There it is. In metta it was revealed. The insights of
the wounds of the heart come in metta.[40]

Metta practice, alongside the three other Brahmaviharas, has been
acknowledged as the "crown jewel" of concentration practice.[41] Yetunde
writes,

When practiced thoroughly and regularly, lovingkindness meditation is
an antidote to anger, hatred, rage, and separateness. In essence, loving-
kindness meditation is a practice that involves sitting, practicing mindfulness, and visualization. What is being visualized, generally in sequence
and for predetermined amounts of time, is one's self, someone else who

is loved, someone for whom there is not love or hate (neutral feelings), someone for whom there are intense negative feelings, and then there are visualizations of being at home and throughout various realms in the universe. Each phrase of the visualization is met with an attempt to feel love. Lovingkindness meditation is not to be used as an escape from real feelings that are not akin to love, but are used as a method for transformation over time. The wisdom of having a lovingkindness meditation practice is the knowledge that othering is a part of the human condition and knowing we have choices about how we are going to practice resiliency in the face of persistent ignorance.[42]

The theme of resilience in the practice of metta is central to cultivating the capacity to work with strong emotions, Insight teacher Tuere Sala says:

What I basically begin to understand is that the emotions—when the Buddha would talk about them or when you would look at it in relation to mindfulness or Dharma—the emotions are not about how I feel. The emotions are about capacity, what I can tolerate, what I can hold, how I can hold something or tolerate something. I begin to realize that the emotions, this capacity actually, are necessary in order for the mind to awaken. So that the more we begin to cultivate certain emotional capacities, the more the mind can awaken, the more the mind will be less caught in the closed loop system, and more accessible to whatever the present moment is, regardless of what is arising.

. . . Metta [is] the capacity building emotional energy that supports us to awaken. And without that capacity for kindness, that capacity for friendliness, the ability to stay with difficulty is almost impossible. The ability for us to stay with [is critical]. Let's just look at the current times. It's so difficult right now with so much negativity and so much confusion and fear and overwhelming sense of, oh my god, are we even going to have an earth to live on in 10 years. [In] that degree of overwhelm to the ego, we get stuck back in its system of basically leaving out the details or leaving out the emotional charge. But in the context of an awakened mind, metta is what allows us to be with difficulty, be with it up close and engaged, not having to run away from it or not getting lost in it.[43]

In addition to metta, the cultivation of karuna (compassion) is central to Black Buddhist practices. Shelton reflects that compassion fosters the ability to turn toward harm, such as racism, and work with the feelings that arise in a skillful way:

> Whether it's the suffering we experience ourselves or the suffering of another, compassion is caring about and being present for the pain that we all experience. In the classical teachings of the Buddha, compassion is defined as the heart that trembles in the face of suffering. At times, when we come into contact with pain or suffering, like racism, or injustice or oppression, the reaction is often to turn away, to feel a version, to hate it, to close it down, and maybe even become apathetic. So compassion can be seen as an antidote to this hatred or this aversion, right? We allow our hearts to open to the suffering we come into contact with. In compassion meditation, we practice activating and cultivating that compassion at heart. It's there. We practice activating it, cultivating an awareness of it. We set the intention to care for our own suffering and the suffering of others rather than pushing it away or going to war with it. Now compassion doesn't mean we invite suffering in or become martyrs. But we practice meeting it, even befriending it, when it does show up in our experience.[44]

Shelton also reflects on the importance of the third Brahmavihara—mudita (sympathetic joy)—as a central aspect of cultivating relationships. As a practice of joy that is explicitly oriented toward "sympathy"—the well-being of others—the practice of mudita can facilitate working with difficult emotions such as envy, jealousy, and judgment. Shelton expresses,

> The third heart practice is mudita or sympathetic joy. As I mentioned, mudita is the practice of appreciating the joy and happiness of others. It's the quality of sharing in the experience of joy. We can recognize the impermanence of joy, and really rejoice in the experience, while it is present. Sometimes when others experience some flavor of joy, jealousy or judgment might arise for us. So mudita can be an antidote to this jealousy and envy, allowing us to simply bear witness to celebrate that this other person is experiencing happiness, that joy is here, that joy is present.[45]

Finally, the fourth Brahmavihara, upekkha, is interpreted as equanimity. Interviewees spoke spontaneously about noticing upekkha as an identifiable result of their practice. JoAnna Hardy, a teacher in the Insight tradition, states that oppression and prejudice are the "near enemy" of upekkha and mudita. Hardy identifies upekkha as a practice that "lets people breathe."[46]

Upekkha (equanimity) as the fourth Brahmavihara, is also the seventh factor of awakening and the tenth *Parami* (quality of the heart). It is seen as the sum of the Paramis, which include generosity, integrity, renunciation, energy, wisdom, patience, truthfulness, determination, metta (loving-kindness), and upekkha (equanimity).

Gina Sharpe, a teacher in the Insight tradition, teaches that equanimity is the "culmination" of all the qualities that make up the ten Paramis.

> Equanimity requires us to take a much broader view than our narrow small view that might be totally ego centric, self-centered and narrow. It asks us to take a really wide view of any situation and to balance our hearts and our minds in accordance with circumstances. . . . Our equanimity says I will do everything possible to create the best actions that have the least negative impact and the most positive impact on the world. And I also know I have no control over what happens when those actions interact with all of the other actions in the world.[47]

Indeed, upekkha is closely linked to concentration practices of letting thoughts that arise simply be known without judgment. Betty Burkes, a longtime practitioner in the Insight tradition, reflects that upekkha is the cornerstone of her meditation practice:

> My teacher translates equanimity as "allowing," and it's been such a lifesaver having that language and inheriting the practice through that lens. It's not a preference of one experience over another, especially when we live in a culture that prefers particular experiences, particular bodies over others. . . . The language of "allowing" and the practice of allowing whatever is happening to happen is a steadying, grounding force has been a lifesaver for me, especially the phrases, "oh, and now this" and "now this, but this is the way it is." For so long I didn't want to have whatever experience I was having, joyful or sorrowful. [I have cultivated] the equanimity,

the allowing of my experience, knowing my experience, the experience of my life to happen through me as it is happening. I don't have to control it, I can respond to it, and I can see for what it is and not—and give it space so that there is a spaciousness around it. So that's what I'm feeling right now, just the spaciousness of allowing life to happen. And this is my bodily experience, and hopefully I can carry that with me.[48]

Teachings on observing without judgment foster inner stability, as does the practice of cultivating joy. The historical Buddha referred to joy as one of the seven factors of awakening; it is the inherent result of a steady mind and quiet heart. Owens discusses how he places joy, as well as pleasure, at the center of his practice.

When I go into activist communities, there's this lack of joy. So sympathetic joy actually helps us to deepen joy personally and within groups. So that's one practice I am often teaching. How do we essentially act out of sympathetic joy, allowing ourselves to experience pleasure, happiness, or joy, to sit in that, and then to offer this feeling out to all beings? In doing that we actually deepen our relationship with joy, and it just becomes something that's a part of how we are moving through the day.[49]

Because the Brahmaviharas contain practical strategies for cultivating the four faces of love, Black Buddhist teachers and long-term practitioners emphasize intentional ways of being in relationship while simultaneously becoming more mindful of internal and external realities.

The Satipatthana Sutta *and Awareness Practices*

The *Satipatthana Sutta*, a teaching in the *Middle Length Discourses* of the Theravada Pali canon, provides a core set of instructions for many Black Buddhist teachers and practitioners interviewed for this book. The teachings in the sutta emphasize the "four foundations of mindfulness" practices: contemplation of the body, feelings, mind states, and impermanence. It is considered one of the most detailed instructions for meditation found in the Pali canon and is one of the few suttas to contain instructions without narrative, dialogue, refutation of wrong philosophies, or analysis of doctrine.[50] It contains numerous passages found in other suttas; for that reason, scholars assume that the *Satipatthana Sutta* is a compilation of teachings on mindfulness that incorporate several different discourses.

The first half of the *Satipatthana Sutta* emphasizes the first foundation of mindfulness, contemplation of the body in six stages: three that investigate ordinary bodily movements (breathing, postures, activities) and three that highlight observation of the body (body parts, elements, and corpse reflections). The middle section of the sutta dwells on contemplation of feeling tones, "of the flesh and not of the flesh," that is, feelings associated with the body and feelings associated with mind states. The second half of the sutta emphasizes contemplation of four states of the ordinary mind (lust, hate, delusion, and contracted) and four states of the meditated mind (exalted, surpassed, concentrated, and liberated). In both contemplation of the body and contemplation of the mind states, both parts of the sutta focus on the movement toward greater stillness.[51]

The fourth foundation of mindfulness found in the *Satipatthana Sutta* discusses aspects of suffering and awakening. The aspects of suffering include the Five Hindrances (sensual desire, aversion, sloth, restlessness/worry, and doubt). The sutta then explains the six sense bases (eye, ear, nose, tongue, body, and mind) that illuminate entanglements or fetters that can exist between senses and their objects. Finally, the sutta explains aspects of awakening: the seven factors of awakening (mindfulness, investigation, energy, joy, relaxation, concentration, and equanimity) and the Four Noble Truths.

Investigation of the body is the first foundation of mindfulness. Manuel speaks of all dharma teachings as rooted in contemplation of and connection to the body:

The only way you can ground a teaching, any teaching, any spiritual teaching, is through one's own self, one's own lived experience, and the lived experience is through the body. Buddha himself used his own body and went on a vision quest, to search and discover and to contemplate. And as he was in the forest in the story of when he was getting ready to die, he realized as he was starving. And so, he says, this is not good. He said because if I want enlightenment, I'm going to need this body in order for that to happen. . . . The Buddha, you know, just like Jesus too, both were concerned about suffering when they saw various people aging, and dying. All of these things are embodied lived experiences. And so, they

were interested in what that experience was and they examined it in relationship to suffering. You'll find people studying the Dharma, reading
about it, but not able to integrate it, because it's in their minds, they're just
gathering knowledge rather than looking at their own lives and finding
that particular teaching that speaks to their own lived experience, which
is what I did. I didn't study everything. Everything's interesting, yes, but
I honed in on those teachings that I felt related to my life, which was impacted by systemic oppression.[52]

Awareness of how the body aids liberation is central to Buddhist
teachings. Dawn Scott, a teacher in the Insight tradition, reflects,

> We start out with contemplating the body. And the definition asks us to
> contemplate the body as a body. So, not our ideas about the body or our
> thoughts about the body, not our emotions about the body, not the ways
> that we've been acculturated to relate to our own bodies and the bodies of
> others, but the body as a body.
>
> [You are] relating to the body and seeing it as attractive, or seeing it as
> neither attractive or unattractive, or maybe the practice shows up for you
> as you're connecting with the attractive and unattractive aspects of the
> body. And there's no reactivity where there's a lessening of reactivity.
> There's a balance of the mind. We're neither rejecting or craving, grasping
> after the body. It's composed studying. We're relating to the body as its
> elemental nature, right? We're seeing that the body is empty of a self that
> owns and that can therefore control outcomes, the outcome of how this
> body actually functions. We are seeing into the elemental process nature
> of the body, these four great elements, and then relating to the body as
> mortal.[53]

In its emphasis on inner and outer reality, the *Satipatthana Sutta* is
viewed as an important set of instructions for understanding one's own
racialized experience, teaching about race and racism, and deconstructing privilege. In the 2018 Barre Center for Buddhist Studies "Race and
Dharma" online course,[54] in which a multiracial teaching team employed the *Satipatthana Sutta* as the central text for instructions, Selassie
emphasized the importance of the *Satipatthana Sutta*:

There's no thing called "mind" that's separate from the body and from experience. We're one system. And so we could talk about awareness or we could talk about *Sati* which we translate as "mindfulness" which is the worst translation because "mind" is right in the word. "Remembering" is one of its original connotations and maybe a better translation. The reason why we are remembering the body as part of this practice is because it was never not there. The imagined separation is just revealing what our worldview is, which is the scientific materialist concept of mind and body as separate in Cartesian dualism. So the body is an important aspect of our awareness and our contemplative practice because it's all in our awareness . . . there's so much to be aware of because of all the different parts of the body, and by the body I mean us, our mind, heart, body.[55]

Black Buddhist teachers associate the awareness practices fostered by the *Satipatthana Sutta* with a liberation narrative. In this sense, "liberation" is associated with a state of mind that can rest in the moment without clinging to pleasure or pushing away pain. Scott lifts up the importance of the second *Satipatthana—vedana* or feeling tones—and contemplating feeling "pleasant, unpleasant, and neutral" affects in the body as a practice to help stabilize strong feelings and states of mind:

[In] this second establishment of mindfulness, vedana, we start this inward turn as a refrain that says we're still contemplating internally and externally. We're still caring for the body out of care and compassion, we're still connected to other people through care and compassion. It's an inward turn. It's a shift in our orientation from an outward focus of looking for our happiness through sensory experience and recognizing that "oh, there is happiness that's possible internally." There is a well spring of happiness that can arise from within.

So vedana is the direct experience of vedana in the body. We see its impermanence, it's changing nature and the fact that this body is a subtle and not so subtle source of pain and discomfort. . . . We work with that as we let go, moving at a pace that works for us, this balance. We let go of the body as a source of sensory gratification and learn to depend on and rely on the subtle joy of being in the present moment. And the subtle joy that we come to recognize and really get to know, becomes a foundation for the establishment of wholesome mind states.[56]

Liberation, for many practitioners of African descent, involves practicing skillful ways to work with trauma in the body. It includes delving into traumatizing past experiences and being present with the suffering invoked by trauma. Slowly, over time, these teachers espouse, the ability to sit with suffering and know it fully allows the mind and heart to release layers of pain that clutch memories and experiences like a clenched fist. Berry states,

> Initially, I think everyone needs to actually have a sitting meditation [practice], but [liberation] is actually bringing awareness to whatever it is you're doing. I think for me, a liberation narrative or our collective liberation in using Buddhist tools, really should be focused around awareness of everything that we are doing. . . . Everything is held in the body, it is all here in the body, and so I also want time to integrate it and sit back and just let it be. [In doing trauma work], if the body's got to rock, the body's got to shake, the body's got to cry, all of that needs to happen.[57]

For many teachers and practitioners of African descent, healing work is prioritized alongside social justice work. Alexander associates awareness practices with social action: "If I actually take this practice on, and that is the embodiment of how I live, that's the path I've taken. There's an awareness—there's actually I what would call a 'radical awareness'—of what is happening in the world today."[58]

Awareness practices aid self-understanding as well as intricate social dynamics, says Magee, who employs mindfulness practices to deconstruct social meanings associated with race, class, gender, and sexuality:

> For me, awareness and sort of the practices that I often call mindfulness and compassion practices are partly a vehicle for seeing more clearly who's in the room, including myself. What am I bringing? Who am I meeting? How am I meeting? We know that there are many, many, many, many different dimensions to [awareness], including deep store consciousness or cultural conditionings around gender, sex orientation, race, color. All of the aspects of our lived experience can be both beautiful and

crazy making, both grounding in a certain sense—like this is who I am, this is where I come from—but also can be [painful and limiting] if held too tightly. . . . To me, this is as much a part of awareness practice as anything else: understanding first and foremost my own lived experience and also how I relate to the world through that, and my wanting to be more clear and wanting to be more free in a certain sense.

And so much of who we are, what we become, what our life chances are, and our day to day experience is mediated through our own and other people's sense of who we are based on these characteristics that vary across cultures. So, first is where am I in the world? What are the kinds of characteristics that are meaningful here, that might be differently read if I were somewhere else in the world surrounded by different types of people? To me it opens up a kind of a way of holding or viewing life, to be grounded in awareness, that wherever we are, we're embedded in a social world that is making meaning around our identities.[59]

Without a mindfulness practice, awareness of how we are received by others can guide one's response to oneself. But in understanding the limits of others' perceptions, practitioners can transcend social judgments. In meditation practice, then, the inner and the outer aspects of one's experience are validated. Constructed social identities that perpetuate pain are recognized alongside mindfulness of one's own breathing and bodily organs. Berry says,

The moment I drop that identity [of being a Black man], it's over for me. And at the same, when I'm doing the practice and I've had time to allow the mind to observe the mind, allow the mind to be quiet and allow the heart to open up, those identities either merge or completely fall away. I don't forget them. They just blend in and I really begin to see myself in everyone else and I see everyone else in myself and maybe they don't necessarily see it because of their own ignorance, but it's there. [But] I don't drop my identity as a Black man, as an African American in this country. I cannot and I will not.[60]

The ability to embrace one's reality on the two levels articulated by Black Buddhist teachers and long-term practitioners—relative and ultimate realities, awareness of one's body and one's social realities—creates the mental stability necessary to navigate the racialized fault lines and historical traumas perpetuated in contemporary society. Scott reflects on the contemplation of "mind" in the *Satipatthana Sutta*:

> Seeing the presence of the unwholesome mind states and the absence of the unwholesome mind states . . . without lust, without anger, without delusion, is pointing to the wider way, the wide range of wholesome mind states that arise within our heart and mind, and greed, aversion, and delusion are absent. And then the [*Satipatthana*] *Sutta* also asks us to contemplate more wholesome qualities of mind, a mind that's great, a mind that's concentrated, a mind that's liberated.
>
> In bringing mindfulness to these different states of mind, we're actually starting to get a taste for what a free heart and mind feels like. . . . The whole system on occasion will drop its obsession, will drop its preoccupation with the unwholesome mind states. And again, it's not something that I will. It's the byproduct of having seen the unwholesome over and over and over and over and over again. . . . And on the flip side of that, my heart, mind, body system is actually learning what the wholesome feels like and it's onward leading. It tastes good. So, through this process of this inward monitoring, we're learning, we're teaching our heart, mind, body system where happiness actually lies, what direction happiness is in.
>
> And doing this with *Sati*, a patient, kind, steady, and gentle presence. There's this really wonderful passage in Toni Morrison's "Beloved." There's a character [who is] talking about the 30 mile woman. And he talks so lovingly about her. When I read this passage, I substitute the word 30 mile woman for *Sati*: "She is a friend of my mind, *Sati*. She's a friend of my mind. She gathers me, man. The pieces that I am, *Sati*, she gathers them and gets them back to me in all the right order. It's good, you know, when you got a friend of your mind."[61]

For the Black Buddhist teachers and long-term practitioners whose voices shape this book, investigating the teachings of a constructed, false self as well as investigating one's body, feelings, and mind states lead to an inner stability and awareness that is the experience of psychological and spiritual freedom. The Buddhist practices that have allowed the false, superficial constructs of colonialism and the white supremacist state—and the traumas that result from centuries of harm—to fall away are, for these teachers and practitioners, the practices of liberation. Buddhist practitioners embody the vision for psychological freedom uplifted within Black Tradition, in which their self-identities are no longer mediated by white supremacy.

In cultivating the capacity to see clearly, love themselves and others, meet collective oppression with compassion, and finally attain stillness and non-reactivity within the face of oppression, Black Buddhist teachers and long-term practitioners attain the promise of psychological liberation in the Black Radical Tradition.

6

The Body as a Vehicle for Liberation

Gender and Sexuality in Black Buddhist Writings

Our erotic knowledge empowers us, becomes a lens through
which we scrutinize all aspects of our existence, forcing us
to evaluate those aspects honestly in terms of their relative
meaning within our lives.
—Audre Lorde[1]

The three primary lineages within the tradition of Buddhism—Theravada, Mahayana, and Vajrayana—espouse different teachings with regard
to embodiment, particularly gender and sexuality. This chapter explores
each of these traditions and the meanings for contemporary Buddhists
of African descent, especially those who are drawn to feminine manifestations of the dharma, seek teachings on gender-nonconforming and
transgender embodiment, and embrace queer identity. The first part of
this chapter investigates textual evolutions with regard to gender, focusing primarily on early Buddhist feminine deities and the Mahayana of
Vimalakirti Sutra. It also elaborates the Vajrayana figures of the female
Buddha Tara as well as worldly and wisdom *dakinis*. The second part of
this chapter explores gender, sexuality, and sensuality in the writings of
Audre Lorde and James Baldwin. Finally, this chapter investigates several
elaborations of Lorde and Baldwin in the works of three Black Buddhist
teachers: Sebene Selassie, Zenju Earthlyn Manuel, and Lama Rod Owens.

The Worship of Female Deities in Early Buddhism

In the Theravada Pali canon, twice it is mentioned that female-bodied
persons cannot achieve enlightenment.[2] At the same time, as Buddhist
monks transmitted the Pali canon from oral to written teachings, there
existed a plethora of female deities who were claimed as sacred within

early Buddhist communities. These female deities were upheld as fostering the enlightenment of the male-bodied Shakyamuni Buddha and were also claimed as worthy of worship in their own right.

The pantheon of female deities originated with mother earth, known as Prthivi, or "Vast One," who supported Shakyamuni Buddha on the night of his enlightenment. Scholar Miranda Shaw writes,

> When Mara, the king of the demons, challenged Siddhartha to provide a witness to his worthiness to attain enlightenment, the Bodhisattva stretched forth his golden hand and touched the earth, invoking the one who observes and remembers every event that transpires on her vast body. Responding to her summons, the earth goddess rendered her testimony in world-shaking tones and personally dispersed Mara's armies. In so doing, she created the environment of peace necessary for the Buddha-to-be to enter the subtlest spheres of meditation and attain full spiritual awakening. So crucial was her intervention that she is said to perform the same role in the enlightenment of every Buddha throughout the ages.[3]

Liberation, then, is not solely a quality of seeing impermanence and attaining an unsurpassed level of wisdom and compassion; it is the result of ethical action upon the earth over many lifetimes. The divine earth mother, in response to moral goodness, blesses each person with nurturing support and protection. This maternal energy is spread throughout other spheres in early Buddhist teachings and depictions: Mayadevi, mother of Shakyamuni Buddha; Sri Laksmi, a fertility deity whose image adorns early Buddhist altars; female nature spirits known as "yaksinis"; and Hariti, a deity who was initially a yaksini and assumed stature as a "yaksini queen." Finally, Mahapajapati Gotami, the maternal aunt who raised Siddhartha Gautama (later known as Shakyamuni Buddha), is deified as both the Buddha's caretaker as well as the first female nun, who requested that female-bodied persons be ordained as monastics. In a book celebrating Gotami's plea and subsequent ordination, *Glorious Deeds of Gotami*, it is stated that women have the capacity to attain enlightenment and indeed Buddhahood. It is written that five hundred nuns were so inspired by Gotami that they followed her into enlightenment. She continues to be recognized not as a divine being but rather as a human exemplar, much like the Buddha, who aspired to see clearly the truth of impermanence and to offer compassion for every living being.

Gotami's example was followed by hundreds of female aspirants in the Theravada tradition. The ninth book of the Khuddakanikaya of the Pali Suttapitaka is known as "Verses of the [Female] Elders" or the "Therigatha." Written by approximately one hundred female elders, ostensibly during the lifetime of the Buddha, it contains 522 verses in seventy-three poems. Many of the poems describe the pains of childbirth, marriage, losing a child and spouse, and physical decay due to aging. Other poems contains ecstatic expressions of delight.[4] The "Therigatha" illuminates how, in the Theravada tradition, gender was explicitly recognized and embraced.

Gender Fluidity and Maternal Deities in Mahayana Buddhism

While the Theravada tradition of Buddhism recognizes the significance of gender and recognized female divinity in earth goddesses and Indian goddesses, the figure who retains primary attention is the historical male figure of Shakyamuni Buddha. Theravada Buddhism evolved primarily in the social hierarchies and monastic codes of the monasteries. However, Mahayana and Vajrayana Buddhism—which expanded in universities and lay communities as well as monasteries—evolved gendered images while simultaneously addressing nongendered embodiment in the quest for liberation.

One of the earliest mentions of gender fluidity is found in the *Vimalakirti Sutra*, a first- or second-century Mahayana text. In the seventh chapter, the Buddha's disciple Shariputra converses with a goddess who has appeared. In the ensuing dialogue, Shariputra assumes that a woman would desire to change into male form, should she have the ability to do so:

Shariputra said: "Why don't you change out of this female body?"

The goddess replied, "For the past twelve years I have been trying to take on female form, but in the end with no success. What is there to change? If a sorcerer were to conjure up a phantom woman and then someone asked her why she didn't change out of her female body, would that be any kind of reasonable question?"

"No," said Shariputra. "Phantoms have no fixed form, so what would there be to change?"

The goddess said, "All things are just the same—they have no fixed form. So why ask why I don't change out of my female form?"

At that time the goddess employed her supernatural powers to change Shariputra into a goddess like herself, while she took on Shariputra's form. Then she asked: "Why don't you change out of this female body?"

Shariputra, now in the form of a goddess, replied, "I don't know why I have suddenly changed and taken on a female body!"

The goddess said, "Shariputra, if you can change out of this female body, then all women can change likewise. Shariputra, who is not a woman, appears in a woman's body. And the same is true of all women—though they appear in women's bodies, they are not women. Therefore the Buddha teaches that all phenomena are neither male nor female."

Then the goddess withdrew her supernatural powers, and Shariputra returned to his original form. The goddess said to Shariputra, "Where now is the form and shape of your female body?"

Shariputra said, "The form and shape of my female body does not exist, yet does not not exist."

The goddess said, "All things are just like that—they do not exist, yet do not not exist. And that they do not exist, yet do not not exist, is exactly what the Buddha teaches."[5]

This early Mahayana teaching speaks to the idea of gender fluidity, gender-nonconforming appearance, and nongendered identity: one's gender matters, yet liberation can be found in not clinging to gender. This teaching has important implications in the contemporary period.[6] Myokei Caine-Barrett, Bishop of the Nichiren Shu Order of North America and Chief Priest of Myoken-ji Temple, muses that "there are times that I am not a male or a female or anything, I just am."[7]

Yet even as the Mahayana tradition minimizes the importance of gender, female deities appear throughout the Mahayana texts. Sutras contain depictions of multitudes of goddesses.[8] Maternal deities, such as Parnasavari, Vasudhara, Cunda, Sitatapatra, and Marici, are associated with nature, abundance, healing, and protection. Janguli, the Buddhist snake goddess, functions to protect human beings from snakebites and to offer immunity from poison.[9] An early Vedic deity, Sarasvati, was incorporated into the Buddhist pantheon as a divine female muse for seekers of art, culture, and intellectual pursuits—a feminine counterpart to Manjusri, Bodhisattva of wisdom. The feminine divine energy known as Prajnaparamita, "perfection of wisdom," is embodied in a deity

> who is regarded as the "mother" of all beings who attain enlightenment, for it is her wisdom that engenders liberation. She is the supreme teacher and eternal font of revelation. All who seek illumination must sit at her feet and drink from the stream of teachings that flow from her presence. Thus, Prajnaparamita is the ultimate source of refuge and object of reverence, for only those who prize wisdom above all else may attain it. Even Buddhas and bodhisattvas pay homage to her, because to her they owe their omniscience.[10]

Prajnaparamita's maternal luminosity is second, perhaps, only to the female Buddha, Tara, known as "Mother of Compassion and Salvation." The tales of the origin of Tara are numerous. In one legend, she was born as a human princess, known as "Moon of Knowledge," who sought to attain full enlightenment. Male monastics encouraged her to pray to be transformed into a male body in order to make speedier progress; however, the princess responded that in nonduality, impermanence and emptiness undergird the phenomenal world. Thus, there is no male or female in the realm of enlightenment.[11] Miranda Shaw encapsulates the princess's reply: "She issued the rather pointed rejoinder that 'this bondage to male and female is hollow: Oh how worldly fools delude themselves!' In the presence of the assembled monks she vowed to remain in a female body until all sentient beings are established in supreme enlightenment."[12]

Princess Moon of Knowledge's deep meditation practice—embodied in female form—fostered her capacity for salvation: she attained a capacity to save all beings from their limited perspectives. While the princess disregarded the importance of gendered bodily form, as did Vimalakirti, her female embodiment is noted and, indeed, part of a larger specter of Mahayana Buddhism, in which the female form is linked to maternal insight and compassion.

Princess Moon of Knowledge became known as Tara, the "Savioress" who can defeat all Maras.[13] Shaw writes,

> Princess Moon of Knowledge eventually attained a meditative power known as "Saving All Being." Every morning before breakfast she released millions of beings from their worldly preoccupations; each evening she repeated the feat. Thus, she became known as Tara, "Savioress." In the following aeon, Tara pledged to protect all beings through the universe from harm. Through a power called "Defeating All Maras," she established billions of spiritual guides each day and defeated a billion demons each night.
>
> After ninety-five aeons had passed, a spiritually advanced monk received initiation from the Buddha of the ten directions and became the compassionate Lord Avalokitsvara. The light of all the Buddhas crystallized into a ray of compassion and a ray of wisdom, which united and formed Tara. She emerged from the heart of Avalokitsvara and proceeded to protect beings from the eight inner and eight outer perils. She continued to progress and eventually received consecration from the Buddhas of the ten directions—that is, attained Buddhahood—and became the mother of all Buddhas.[14]

In another myth, similarly, Tara is born from Avalokitsvara—this time from his tears of compassion. From his tears a lotus emerged, and from the lotus blossom, Tara arose to console Avalokitsvara. In Tibetan folklore, from the left teardrop arose Green Tara, and from the right teardrop emerged White Tara.

The cult of Tara emerged in India at the end of the sixth century and beginning of the seventh as part of the evolution of Hindu and Buddhist Tantra.[15] Scholar Rachael Wooten notes that the myths of Tara are rooted in the oldest known religious activities—ancient goddess worship and indigenous shamanism: "Clues about these origins are evident in the language of Tara texts. 'The Twenty-One Praises to Tara' have a strong resemblance to the poetry found in the epic tales of Inanna, the Sumerian Goddess of 4000 BCE. The people of southern India where Tara's tantra likely developed were goddess worshippers, practitioners of sexual yoga, and shamans. The area was so heavily influenced by Sumeria that it has sometimes been referred to as the Sumero-Dravidian culture."[16]

As "Savioress," Tara is a "universal mother who nurtures, assists, and protects all seekers on the spiritual path."[17] Spiritual seekers, as children, take refuge at her feet. She evokes both calm and enlivening energy, confidence as well as mercy. Her maternal energy is likened to a regal queen as well as an affectionate, embracing mother who cares for each and every suffering being seeking healing and salvation. Thus, as protector, savior, and worker of miracles, Tara helps rescue all suffering beings from dangers, obstacles, and worldly troubles. Shaw writes that Tara "deliver[s] them safely to the other shore: spiritual perfection, ultimate peace, Buddhahood." The mantra prayed to her, *Om tare tuttare ture svaha*, is chanted throughout the Mahayana Buddhist world. Buddhist folklore states that invoking Tara's mantra has the power to raise the dead.[18] Shaw states,

> When Tara's Buddhahood is expressed in Mahayana terms, invoking the definition of enlightenment as the realization of universal compassion and transcendent wisdom, Tara is said to embody compassion (*karuna*), which impels her to relieve the suffering of the world, and to command every liberative art (*upaya*) in the service of others. She is also attributed with the complementary quality of perfect wisdom (*prajna*), crowning her character with omniscience. According to the Tantric model of Buddhahood, Tara has integrated emptiness (*sunyata*) and supreme bliss (*mahasukha*) and manifests the five Buddha wisdoms that comprise the totality of enlightenment. She is proclaimed to be utterly transcendent, immersed in ultimate reality, beyond samsara and nirvana, inconceivable and inexpressible. Her being, universal in compass, envelops all that exists and enfolds all living beings.[19]

Thus Tara's embodiment as female, evoking maternal wisdom and care, and her status as a female Buddha are embraced as significant. As a female-embodied Buddha, she is identified as the "Mother of All Buddhas," similar to the ethereal figure of Prajnaparamita, but seen as more interactive and nurturing. Shaw writes that "Tara's ascent in the pantheon coincided with the rise of the Tantric movement, when the doctrine of female Buddhahood was taking shape."[20]

Female Sensuality in Tantric Buddhism

As Mahayana Buddhism evolved and encountered Indian and Tibetan cultures, maternal female goddesses and Buddhas were joined with sensual female deities and spirits. There exist numerous embodied feminine sensual manifestations of deities and spirits within the Tantric, also known as Vajrayana, Buddhist tradition. Karla Jackson Brewer, a Black Buddhist teacher in the Tibetan tradition, describes Vajrayana as a tradition influenced by ancient mother traditions with roots in Africa: "Vajrayana trains us to see the enlightened aspects, the true nature, of everything. It is a path of transformation [that] rejects duality."[21] In Tantra, Jackson-Brewer explains, the ordinary reveals wisdom and liberation. The five "poisons"—pride, envy, ignorance, anger, and desire—that block human enlightenment are transformed into inherent wisdom. Female deities are embraced as couriers of the sacred feminine principle who reveal that, inherent in these wisdom teachings, is the message that human beings are embodied energies of light.

These feminine energies are maternal and can also emerge as wrathful, peaceful, and/or enlightened. Judith Simmer-Brown, a scholar of Tibetan Buddhism, writes that "Tibetan Buddhism developed its own unique understanding of gender,"[22] primarily in evolving the dynamic of "feminine" and "masculine" balance in devotional practices and teachings. The feminine (prajna) in Tibetan Buddhism encompasses spaciousness and limitless capacities to attain the ultimate nature of mind; the masculine (upaya) refers to action, compassion, and confidence to achieve ultimate reality. Thus, the balance of spacious being and fearless striving toward enlightenment facilitates the capacity for enlightenment.[23]

In this tradition, sacred sensuality is often expressed in the gendered body. This is primarily seen in Tibetan images that predominate, especially in the dakinis: goddesses—also identified as "principles"—that emerge as a feminine energy. This feminine energy enters and moves through the emptiness of the meditator's self and functions as a messenger of freedom. The dakinis thus are conduits of wisdom, embodiments of wisdom, and energies that practitioners can invoke and with whom they can create a positive relationship. Jackson-Brewer describes dakinis as messengers that teach through direct action, as energies that take form and transform one's practice. They are identified as protectors on the spiritual path that also wake up the meditator.[24] Tibetan scholar Jan Willis writes that "within Buddhist tantric contexts, dakini is viewed as the supreme embodiment of the highest wisdom itself."[25]

The dakini is a symbol that "stands for ineffable reality itself."[26] Yet, the dakini is more than a singular symbol and more than a feminine deity. According to Jackson-Brewer, Simmer-Brown, and Willis, the dakini represents a kind of "feminine principle," a domain of spiritual experience beyond conventional, social, or psychological meanings of gender. For this reason, Willis says, the dakini is difficult to conceptualize academically and intellectually.[27]

Dakini is a term from Prakrit or Sanskrit that was originally considered to be vulgar. Her roots derive from prepatriarchal Dravidian cultures, known in part for Mother Goddess, yogic, and nature-oriented traditions. Tibetan scholar Sarah H. Jacoby speculates that "along with other classes of female divinities who were later incorporated into Vedic religion, *dakinis* may have descended from indigenous goddess cults whose earliest evidence has been found in the Indus Valley civilizations dating from two millennia B.C.E."[28] The dakini first appeared in Buddhist texts and later in Hindu texts. In Tibet, the dakini evolved from a minor goddess figure to a central symbol of meditative experience in iconography, ritual, and meditation. The word for dakini in Tibetan is *khandro*, which means "she who moves through space," sometimes called a "sky walker," "female sky dancer," "sky goer," and "woman who flies."[29] Jacoby notes that in Tibetan texts, dakinis are also known by the Tibetan name "khandroma."[30]

There are two main kinds of dakinis: worldly dakinis and wisdom dakinis, the latter of which is associated with outstanding female-bodied practitioners. Such female-bodied yoginis are sometimes considered female buddhas, akin to Tara.

> Within dakini realms, worldly dakinis who have no allegiance to dharma are considered powerful and dangerous, capable of cannibalizing victims at whim. These dakinis bear close resemblance to protector dakinis who may not be realized but have sworn allegiance to protect dharma practitioners and serve as allies in meditation practice. Especially important are the completely enlightened wisdom dakinis who guide and instruct the

yogin or yogini. Human dakinis may also be potential spiritual consorts who have the unique ability to accelerate the removal of obstacles for themselves and their partners through sexual yoga.[31]

Willis notes that in Tibetan descriptions of the appearances of dakinis, a clear pattern can be observed: the dakini communicates a Tantric message by prophesying, advising, protecting, or performing the wishes of her companion. Sometimes this is as a sexual partner or consort of the guru. Willis writes: "Manifesting in multifarious forms, 'she' serves as the spur, inspiration, and helpful companion for successfully accomplishing the arduous path of tantric practice."[32] Khandro Rinpoche, a contemporary Tibetan guru, furthermore elaborates: "Traditionally, the term dakini has been used for outstanding female practitioners, consorts of great masters, and to denote the enlightened female principle of nonduality, which transcends gender . . . a very sharp, brilliant wisdom mind that is uncompromising, honest, with a little bit of wrath."[33]

The dakini represents the most intimate aspects of the spiritual path. Simmer-Brown writes, "She is the fundamental nature of the mind; she guards the gates of wisdom for the practitioner and the lineages of tantric teachers; she holds the key to the secret treasury of practices that lead to realization; and she manifests variously in her support of authentic meditation."[34]

The dakini personifies the spiritual process of surrendering expectation and concept, revealing limitless space and pristine awareness. In the Vajrayana Buddhism of Tibet, duality is complementary, not alienating. Dakinis represent the domains conventionally attributed to women, such as embodiment, sexuality, nurturing, and sustenance, and relationship. Furthermore, for dakinis, these domains are transmuted into realms that are not merely conventional but are much more profound than the concerns of daily existence; dakini women serve as models for how obstacles may be turned into enlightenment.

In sacred biographies, the dakini is depicted in a personified manner as an unpredictable, semiwrathful, dancing spirit-woman who appears in visions, dreams, or the everyday lives of yogins or yoginis. Her demeanor changes in various contexts: she may be playful, nurturing, or sharp and wrathful, especially when protecting the integrity of tantric transmission.

She also guards the most private details of the practice, so that only those with the purest motivation are able to penetrate their essence. Without the blessing of the dakini, the fruition of Vajrayana practice is said to be inaccessible.[35]

As a classical symbol, the dakini has two dimensions. In the first, the dakini with all her complexity represents the inner wisdom mind of the Tantric practitioner appearing in concretized form to accentuate obstacles and to indicate the practitioner's inherent wakefulness. In a second dimension, the dakini symbolizes the ancient wisdom of the guru and the enlightened lineages of teachers under whose protection the Tantric practitioner meditates, navigating the perilous waters of the Tantric journey. These two aspects merge when the dakini reveals to the practitioner an ancient wisdom legacy that is simultaneously recognized as the inner wisdom mind of the Tantra practitioner.

Like the goddess in the *Vimalakirti Sutra*, the dakini in her most profound level of meaning is beyond form, gender, and expression, but "she" gives rise to bountiful forms and expressions, which sometimes take the female gender as a way to express "her" essence.[36] Although in the experience of ultimate reality the dakini is beyond gender altogether, scholars note that in the true Tibetan Vajrayana sense the dakini manifests in female-gendered form on various levels. Congruent with teachings in Mahayana sutras and the origins of Tara, the ultimate can express itself in gendered physical bodies and psychological states.

For Tantric practitioners, the dakini is the inner catalyst, protagonist, and witness of the spiritual journey. Simmer-Brown writes, "The *dakini* is the most potent realized essence of every being, the inner awakening, and the gift of the Buddha."[37] Indeed, the dakinis reflect an enlightened, sacred female divinity that is naked, truthful, fierce, active, dancing, wild, and free.

Sensuality and Insight in Contemporary Black Writings: The Dharma of Audre Lorde and James Baldwin

There exists a precedent in Buddhism, then, for engaging the female form in the Mahayana and Vajrayana traditions and for manifesting sensual energy within the Vajrayana tradition. Similarly, an honoring of the female form and of erotic energy can be seen in the pivotal essays of Black Feminist poet Audre Lorde (1934–1992). Similarly, sensual energy is embraced by Black essayist and novelist James Baldwin (1924–1987). In short, while not self-identified dharma practitioners, these writers articulate teachings that point to the experience of direct insight as well as embodied sensual energies. In this way, they can be seen as articulating the dharma. And indeed, as will be discussed below, many Black Buddhist teachers draw upon Lorde and Baldwin to elaborate their teachings of the dharma.[38]

Audre Lorde

In numerous essays in her collection *Sister Outsider*, Audre Lorde uplifts feminine energies and the importance of giving oneself permission to feel.[39] She describes how women's power to enact their own liberation is indelibly connected with the permission to feel; she further identifies women's liberation as rooted in erotic power. Eroticism is more than sexuality or sensuality; it is a creative force that is both deeply attuned to one's inner self and rooted in the messy element of chaos. Lorde identifies the erotic as "a resource within each of us that lies in a deeply female and spiritual plane, firmly rooted in the power of our unexpressed or unrecognized feeling."[40] The patriarchal, rational world amasses its power by oppressing the erotic life force of women, for this erotic power threatens the very tenets through which male power perpetuates itself. For women to embody power, then, is not to adopt the worldview and practices of men—the master's tools will never dismantle the master's house[41]—but rather to choose a different way of being that validates the depth of the interior life: intuition and interior knowing, creative expression, and intimacy with pain that can be used in the service of growth. Lorde attests,

> The erotic offers a well of replenishing and provocative force to the woman who does not fear its revelation, nor succumb to the belief that sensation is enough. The erotic is a measure between the beginnings of our sense of self and the chaos of our strongest feelings. It is an internal sense of satisfaction to which, once we have experienced it, we know we can aspire. For having experienced the fullness of this depth of feeling and recognizing its power, in honor and self-respect we can require no

less of ourselves. For the erotic is not a question only of what we do; it is a question of how acutely and fully we can feel in the doing. When I speak of the erotic, then, I speak of it as an assertion of the lifeforce of women; of that creative energy empowered, the knowledge and use of which we are now reclaiming in our language, our history, our dancing, our loving, our work, our lives.[42]

For Lorde, erotic power is embodied, and women's bodies are claimed as a vehicle for liberation. In privileging women's bodies, Lorde's writings illuminate aspects of Buddhist teachings in all three lineages, particularly the Mahayana and Vajrayana traditions. As seen in the Vajrayana tradition and in contemporary writings by Black Buddhist teachers, erotic energy is part of the path to liberation.[43]

Lorde's writings on the body similarly illuminate teachings in the Theravada tradition. The seven factors of awakening in the Theravada tradition state that awareness and investigation of the body, feelings, mind states, and dharma lead to energy and joy. Lorde points to a similar progression in her experience of eroticism and joy: "Another important way in which the erotic connection functions is the open and fearless underlining of my capacity for joy. In the way my body stretches to music and opens into response, hearkening to its deepest rhythms, so every level upon which I sense also opens to the erotically satisfying experience, whether it is dancing, building a bookcase, writing a poem, examining an idea."[44]

Lorde's emphasis on awareness of the body is seen in a core Theravada text, the *Satipatthana Sutta*, which states that mindfulness of the body is the first foundation of mindfulness. For many Black dharma teachers, Lorde contemporizes what is explicitly stated in all three lineages of Buddhism: awareness of body is essential for the practice of liberation. By honoring the body—its elements and composition, its energies and expressions—Black dharma teachers along with Lorde uplift the body as a vehicle for liberation. Moreover, eroticism is the life force that gives the body its energy; erotic power emphasizes the union between the different aspects of the self—the body, heart, and mind—so that the liberation of the body is inseparable from the liberation of the heart and mind.

Liberation, however, is not solely individualistic; it is communal. In this way, Lorde mirrors central teachings in the Mahayana tradition, which teach that enlightened figures return to earth to assist the liberation of all peoples. Writing in contemporary U.S. society, Lorde deconstructs a myth central to the white, Western, patriarchal world. Liberation is communal and collective and arises from sensual, maternal power. For power to be fully expressed, it must evolve from one's erotic life force to foster deep nurturing, compassionate listening, sharing feelings, and extensive practical support during times of stress.[45] And, in order for communal liberation to be authentic, it must honor differences among people, especially in the feminist movement.

Lorde emphasizes the importance of claiming wholeness in the quest for liberation. In this way, she does not privilege one aspect of her identity but rather integrates her gender, racial, sexual, and class identity into her advocacy for women's freedom. She writes,

> As a Black lesbian feminist comfortable with the many difference ingredients of my identity, and a woman committed to racial and sexual freedom from oppression, I find I am constantly being encouraged to pluck out some one aspect of myself and present this as the meaningful whole, eclipsing or denying the other parts of self. But this is a destructive and fragmenting place to live. My fullest concentration of energy is available to me only when I integrate all the parts of who I am, openly, allowing power from particular sources of my living to flow back and forth freely through all my different selves, without the restrictions of externally imposed definition. Only then can I bring myself and my energies as a whole to the service of those struggles which I embrace as part of my living.[46]

Differences between women are to be named and embraced; indeed, in this way, Lorde is consistent in her orientation toward fearlessness. She refuses to gloss over social meanings that have oppressed women based on their race, class, and sexuality. In this way, too, Lorde's writings mirror dharma teachings that deconstruct false, conventional, seemingly permanent realities. In her quest to recognize, acknowledge, and name the complexity of what is taking place internally and externally, Lorde is advocating for mindfulness of inner and outer realities. Her awareness fosters assertions of the evolution that must take place in the women's movement for all women to be included. "As women, we must root out internalized patterns of oppression within ourselves if we are to move beyond the most superficial aspects of social change. . . . Change means growth, and growth can be painful. But we sharpen self-definition by exposing the self in work and struggle together with those whom we define as different from ourselves, although sharing the same goals."[47] Liberation, then, rests on awareness. It involves rooting out internalized oppression as well as recognizing how women have been divided against each other and taught to fear the expressions of anger that may arise from confrontation. Most importantly, liberation involves pain. Diving into pain—rather than avoiding it—cultivates fearlessness. This fearlessness must be named and verbalized to unmask its repression. This fearlessness is inseparable from strength, and ultimately, freedom. "The strength of women lies in recognizing differences between us as creative, and in standing to those distortions which we inherited without blame, but which are now ours to alter. The angers of women can transform difference through insight into power. For anger between peers births change, not destruction, and the discomfort and sense of loss it often causes is not fatal, but a sign of growth."[48]

Lorde names growth that comes from confronting pain as a survival skill particularly honed by Black people: "One of the most basic Black survival skills is the ability to change, to metabolize experience, good or ill, into something that is useful, lasting, effective."[49] As Lorde focuses on the specific oppressions encountered by Black people, she particularly focuses on internalized oppression. In her essay "Learning from the Sixties," she notes that it is not enough to focus on political and social freedom.

> If our history has taught us anything, it is that action for change directed only against the external conditions of our oppressions is not enough. In order to be whole, we must recognize the despair oppression plants within each of us—that thin, persistent voice that says our efforts are useless, it will never change, so why bother, accept it. And we must fight that inserted piece of self-destruction that lives and flourishes like a poison inside of us, unexamined until it makes us turn upon ourselves in each other. But we can put our finger down upon that loathing buried deep within each one of us and see who it encourages us to despise, and we can lessen its potency by the knowledge of our real connectedness, arcing across our differences.[50]

The self-scrutiny that Lorde points to again and again rests upon training oneself to see clearly the origins of one's anger. Allowing oneself to
feel, rather than repress, allowing oneself to *acknowledge*, rather than deny,
evolves one's power and takes back the weapons from enemies' hands,
especially the weapon of fear. If women are fearless, they cannot be made
vulnerable and enacted upon. "To search for power within myself means I
must be willing to move through being afraid to whatever lies beyond. If I
look at my most vulnerable places and acknowledge the pain I have felt, I
can remove the source of that pain from my enemies' arsenals."[51]

Lorde particularly names the difficult relationships often found
among Black women as important to acknowledge without fear; historically, Black women have been divided against one another but have
feared acknowledging the self-hatred that is internalized and too often
expressed toward other Black women. In order to heal the hatred found
among Black women, Lorde argues that Black women must learn to
mother themselves. Here, too, Lorde expresses core dharma teachings:
in the Insight tradition, the two "wings" of meditation are awareness
(self-scrutiny) and compassion (mothering). "If we can learn to give
ourselves the recognition and acceptance that we have come to expect
only from our mommas, Black women will be able to see each other
much more clearly and deal with each other much more directly."[52] She
further writes:

We can learn to mother ourselves.

What does that mean for Black women? It means we must establish
authority over our own definition, provide an attentive concern and expectation of growth which is the beginning of that acceptance we came to
expect only from our mothers. It means that I will affirm my own worth
by committing myself to my own survival, in my own self and in the self
of other Black women. On the other hand, it means that as I learn my
worth and genuine possibility, I refuse to settle for anything less than a
rigorous pursuit of the possible in myself, at the same time making a distinction between what is possible and what the outside world drives me
to do in order to prove I am human. It means being able to recognize my
successes, and to be tender with myself, even when I fail.

We will begin to see each other as we dare to begin to see ourselves; we
will begin to see ourselves as we begin to see each other, without

aggrandizement or dismissal or recriminations, but with patience and understanding for when we do not quite make it, and recognition and appreciation for when we do. Mothering ourselves means learning to love what we have given birth to by giving definition to, learning how to be both kind and demanding in the teeth of failure as well as in the face of success, and not misnaming either. . . . As we fear each other less and value each other more, we will come to value recognition within each other's eyes as well as within our own, and seek a balance between these visions. Mothering. Claiming some power over who we choose to be, and knowing that such power is relative within the realities of our lives. Yet knowing that only through the use of that power can we effectively change those realities. . . . Mothering means the laying to rest of what is weak, timid, and damaged—without despisal—the protection and support of what is useful for survival and change, and our joint explorations of the difference.[53]

The nurturing that Lorde identifies must first be directed toward oneself, for in the cultivation of self-compassion one develops a more expansive heart that allows one to see the suffering in Black sisters. The tenderness directed toward oneself is a tenderness that is organically offered to others. Lorde's writings on self-compassion and compassion for other Black women position her as a dharma teacher for many Black Buddhist teachers and long-term practitioners.[54] Pamela Ayo Yetunde, who founded an Atlanta-based woman's health center named after Audre Lorde, identifies Lorde as a Bodhisattva—an enlightened being who returned to earth to help others attain enlightenment.[55] Leslie Booker, a teacher in the Insight tradition, describes Lorde's writings as foundational in her process of loving her Blackness.[56] Booker reflects on the construct of Black bodies as inferior to white bodies and asserts that Lorde's rejection of white superiority was deeply influential. For Booker, as for many teachers and practitioners, refusing to internalize those external labels, and being able to turn toward their suffering, is a first essential step to embodying freedom. As Lorde, and Buddhist teachings such as the *Satipatthana Sutta*, honor the elements, composition, energies, and expressions of the body as a vehicle for liberation, the Black body, which has been denigrated, is uplifted and claimed.

There is necessarily a long period of compassionately embracing all the parts of oneself that were degraded and deemed unattractive. The next step in the path to healing is fostering community and extend liberating dharma teachings toward other people, a commitment that Black Buddhist teachers describe as "profound." Booker reflects,

> To me, love is about self—going back to Audre Lorde—it's about self-preservation. You know, it's about honoring this body. It's about honoring the ten thousand joys and the ten thousand sorrows. It's about being with all that arises in the body and not pushing anything away. It is about not fragmenting and leaving parts of ourselves out that we don't love or appreciate, that we think are wrong or bad, or not worthy of our attention and our care. And so, love is inclusive of all the things, whether they be the physical body, our emotional lives, our mental lives, the mental formations that arise. All of that is welcome, our traumas that we have been through, our displacement, our history of enslavement. All of that needs to be loved. My nappy hair and the trauma, the nappy hair growing up, I have such a deep love for all of it, my brown skin, my big nose, my nappy hair, all of that has to be included.[57]

Not only does Lorde identify insight and compassion as essential for personal and communal growth—as do dharma teachings—she distinguishes between pain and suffering. All beings experience pain as endemic to life; pain is inevitable. But Lorde—as do Black Buddhist teachers—makes a distinction between pain and suffering. Pain is an experience often beyond one's control. As aforementioned, Lorde argues that pain can be used for growth. But suffering is different from pain. Lorde notes,

> Suffering [that is distinguished from pain] is the nightmare of reliving unscrutinized and unmetabolized pain. When I live through pain without recognizing it, self-consciously, I rob myself of the power than can come from *using* that pain, the power to fuel some movement beyond it. I condemn myself to reliving that pain over and over and over whenever something close triggers it. And that is suffering, a seemingly inescapable cycle.

And true, experiencing old pain sometimes feels like hurling myself
full force against a concrete wall. But I remind myself that I HAVE LIVED
THROUGH IT ALL ALREADY, AND SURVIVED.[58]

For Lorde, tenderness toward oneself and others is the central orientation toward scrutinizing one's pain, recognizing differences between
women, allowing one's feelings to flourish, and refusing to suffer unnec-
essary psychological terror. In maternal tenderness—first offered toward
oneself and then extended to others—one finds safety, security, and belonging: true refuge. In all traditions within Buddhism, practitioners
take refuge in the Buddha, dharma, and sangha. Numerous teachers
identify taking refuge in the Buddha as taking refuge in an internalized
maternal Buddha figure who cares for all of humanity, and in one's own
awakening heart/mind.[59] Lorde's identification of mothering oneself is
consistent with Buddhist teachings on caring for one's internal landscape in the process of excavating self-hatred, childhood memories, and
negative energies formed by persistent habits.

As Lorde's writings illuminate core dharma teachings and the feminine, maternal, and sensual energies upon which they draw, she demonstrates the synthesis between Buddhism and Black Feminism and her
relevance for contemporary dharma teachers and practitioners. This can
be seen in emerging publications and community-based classes on Buddhism.[60] In her 2020 book *You Belong*, Insight teacher Sebene Selassie
describes the importance of Audre Lorde's influence: "Black music and
arts began to fill my ears, eyes, and body with a different consciousness.
Having never danced much in my life, for me, movement became one
way into what Lorde calls 'the erotic as power.'"[61] Noting that in many
Buddhist communities the erotic is "denied, diminished, dismissed, or
distrusted," Selassie writes, "It was only rereading Audre Lorde's essay
seven years ago that revitalized my aspiration to include the sensual,
sexual, and erotic in my spiritual life. Dance has become a big part of
that . . . embodied awareness rooted in the sensual is central to our
understanding of belonging. If we know how to move (or don't move)
and what we feel (or can't feel), we will have a better understanding of
ourselves. And knowing ourselves is a key to belonging."[62] For Selassie,
dancing, like any practice, involves attuning to the body not through
the intellect but through the senses. Learning to practice *feeling the sen-*

sations of the body, not thinking about what the body is doing, is one aspect of the joy to which Lorde refers. The body, mind, and heart are all connected, but in many places dominated by hegemonic whiteness, people are acculturated to thinking rather than feeling sensations. For Selassie, as for Lorde, the erotic is the sensual connection to one's bodily sensations. Selassie writes, "It can take practice to learn to feel the sensations in the body and stay with the felt sense even as the proliferating mind wants to take over. The body is always in the present moment, here waiting for our awareness to attune to it. Eventually, we begin to understand the difference between thinking about the left foot and sensing the left foot."[63]

In sum, in Lorde's embrace of erotic power as well as her indictment of patriarchy, her celebration of difference, her emphasis on self-scrutiny and self-mothering, and her commitment to fearlessness, she elaborates how inner and outer transformation take place simultaneously.

James Baldwin

James Baldwin, similarly to Lorde, engages the dharma without explicitly naming it as such. As a Black bisexual man writing in the mid-twentieth century, Baldwin observed the rise of the Civil Rights Movement, the Black Power Movement, and the feminist movement. In his renowned book *The Fire Next Time*—which consists of a letter to his nephew as well as an essay reflecting upon racial dynamics in the United States —Baldwin applies direct insights into the fears that arise from delusions in an anti-Black social environment. Specifically, Baldwin addresses the anxieties, projections, and exploitations of white people as they avoid or engage the presence of Black people. Yet Baldwin does not stop at an analysis of the psyche and actions of white Americans; he also celebrates Black people's capacity for love, dignity, courage, and resilience. Furthermore, Baldwin identifies sensual energy as a force to evolve the culture of U.S. white supremacy as it defaults to repression and avoidance of anxious feelings.

Baldwin's analysis of deluded thinking on the part of white people, and the love and stamina required by Black people to survive white supremacy, can be seen in his letter to his nephew. He addresses the terrible, "defeated" lives experienced by so many Black Americans who, like

Baldwin's father, suffered "because, at the bottom of his heart, he really believed what white people said about him."[64]

But Baldwin does not put the onus of internalizing white messages of Black inferiority on his father, or any Black person. Rather, Baldwin squarely indicts white racist society for the damage wreaked on Black psychological states. He states directly to his nephew, "You were born where you were born and faced the future that you faced because you were black and *for no other reason*. The limits of your ambition were, thus, expected to be set forever. You were born into a society which spelled out with brutal clarity, and in as many ways as possible, that you were a worthless human being. You were not expected to aspire to excellence: you were expected to make peace with mediocrity."[65] In so writing, Baldwin does not just focus on the perspectives of white people. He implores his nephew on the following page, "Please try to remember that what they believe, as well as what they do and cause you to endure, does not testify to your inferiority but to their inhumanity and fear."[66] For Baldwin, there is a process of not only stripping away delusions but also cultivating insight, one "wing" of the two wings emphasized in all three Buddhist traditions. Baldwin emphasizes rejecting myths, particularly the religious myths invoked by the Black Christian church as well as the Nation of Islam, which gained credence and thousands of followers in the 1950s and 1960s. For Baldwin, relying on mythological tales rather than cultivating an ability to look at reality directly fails to cultivate the stamina required for sustained dignity under assault.

Stamina requires the capacity to look directly at suffering, including the fact of death. Indeed, myths, symbols, national identity, state violence—all of these foci facilitate a process of avoidance. But if human beings in the United States were to look directly at human suffering and "accept ourselves *as we are*," Baldwin writes, "we might bring new life." Indeed, it is only in the willingness to confront reality, to stare it in the face with insight and compassion, that human beings can embrace the whole of existence, including death:

> Perhaps the whole root of our trouble, the human trouble, is that we will sacrifice all the beauty of our lives, will imprison ourselves in totems, taboos, crosses, blood sacrifices, steeples, mosques, races, armies, flags, nations, in order to deny the fact of death, which is the only fact we have.

It seems to me that one ought to rejoice in the *fact* of death—ought to decide, indeed, to *earn* one's death by confronting with passion the co-nundrum of life. One is responsible to life: It is the small beacon in that terrifying darkness from which we come and to which we shall return.[67]

Indeed, Baldwin's writings evoke the psychological and spiritual strength adhered to—and indeed embraced—by contemporary Black Buddhists.[68] Baldwin's writings on delusion, impermanence, death, dignity, love, and sensuality are deeply resonant for many teachers inter-viewed for this book. He describes the importance of not only stripping away delusions but also embracing deluded white people with love. He writes to his nephew, "You must accept them and accept them with love. For these innocent people have no other hope. They are, in effect, still trapped in a history which they do not understand; and until they understand, they cannot be released from it."[69]

Baldwin's compassion for deluded white people evokes the other "wing" emphasized in all three Buddhist traditions. Indeed, his com-passion for Black despair and danger, and white delusion and fear, il-luminates his broader compassion for people in the United States who suffer as a result of the racist, exploitative origins of the U.S. social order. Baldwin defaults not to rage or retaliation but rather to compassion and love, out of a perspective that the particular suffering wrought on Black and white Americans *can* be seen directly, addressed compassionately, and healed with insight and tenderness.

For Baldwin, the desire of white people to be seen and yet not judged creates a profound tension, an "anguish,"[70] that prevents the capacity for love—of oneself and of Black people. Baldwin writes, "Love tasks off the masks that we fear we cannot live without and know we cannot live within. I use the word 'love' here not merely in the personal sense but as a state of being, or a state of grace—not in the infantile American sense of being made happy but in the tough and universal sense of quest and daring and growth."[71]

Baldwin's admiration for the tenacity and courage of Black people roots his compassionate analysis. Love for Black people, for their capac-ity for survival amid the horrors of Black life in white America, resounds throughout his essay. For Baldwin, Black life is direct and honest. Even with the desire to embrace the myths of the Black Church and the Nation of Islam, Black people bear such profound levels of public and private suffering that the capacity for self-awareness and honesty fosters genuine reckoning and, consequently, dignity. Baldwin writes,

> This past, the Negro's past, of rope, fire, torture, castration, infanticide, rape; death and humiliation; fear by day and night, fear as deep as the marrow of the bone; doubt that he was worthy of life, since everyone around him denied it; sorrow for his women, for his kinfolk, for his children, who needed his protection, and whom he could not protect; rage, hatred, and murder, hatred for white men so deep that it often turned against him and his own, and made all love, all trust, all joy impossible— this past, this endless struggle to achieve and reveal and confirm a human identity, human authority, yet contains, for all its horror, something very beautiful. I do not mean to be sentimental about suffering—enough is certainly as good as a feast—but people who cannot suffer can never grow up, can never discover who they are. That man who is forced each day to snatch his manhood, his identity, out of the fire of human cruelty that rages to destroy it knows, if he survives his effort, and even if he does not survive it, something about himself and human life that no school on earth—and indeed, no church—can teach. He achieves his own authority, and that is unshakable. This is because, in order to save his own life, he is forced to look beneath appearances, to take nothing for granted, to hear the meaning behind the words. If one is continually surviving the worst that life can bring, one eventually ceases to be controlled by a fear of what life can bring; whatever it brings must be borne.[72]

It is in his embrace of resilience that his commitment to embodying sensual energy is directly named. Baldwin addresses the repressed sexuality of white Americans as part of the larger repression of Black people and fears of Black equality. In this way, Baldwin can be seen as evoking the sensual energy named in the Vajrayana tradition. Rather than solely alleviating suffering by focusing on enlightenment, Vajrayana Buddhism evokes particularly practices that evolve joy and bliss as means for attaining liberation. Sensual energy, rather than obscuring the path to enlightenment, provides a direct path to enlightenment. Baldwin names the flowering of sensual energy as a release from fear as well as a practice for respecting and rejoicing in "the force of life":

White Americans do not understand the depths out of which such an ironic tenacity [of Black people] comes, but they suspect that the force is sensual, and they are terrified of sensuality and do not any longer understand it. The word "sensual" is not intended to bring back to mind quivering dusky maidens or priapic black studs. I am referring to something much simpler and much less fanciful. To be sensual, I think, is to respect and rejoice in the force of life, of life itself and to be *present* in all that one does, from the effort of loving to the breaking of bread. . . . Something very sinister happens to the people of a country when they begin to distrust their own reactions as deeply as they do here, and become as joyless as they have become. It is this individual uncertainty on the part of white American men and women, this inability to renew themselves at the fountain of their own lives, that makes the discussion, let alone elucidation, of any conundrum—that is, any reality—so supremely difficult. The person who distrusts himself has no touchstone for reality—for this touchstone can be only oneself. Such a person interposes between himself and reality nothing less than a labyrinth of attitudes. And these attitudes, furthermore, though the person is usually unaware of it (is unaware of so much!), are historical and public attitudes. They do not relate to the present any more than they relate to the person. Therefore, whatever white people do not know about Negroes reveals, precisely and inexorably, what they do not know about themselves.[73]

In this passage, Baldwin touches upon a number of themes that are evoked in the writings of contemporary Black Buddhist teachers: being present, respecting and rejoicing in the force of life, renewing oneself at the fountain of one's own life, trusting oneself and cutting through "a labyrinth of attitudes," becoming aware of historical and public attitudes, and cultivating self-knowledge. These six themes—which, for Baldwin, are rooted in sensuality—arise repeatedly in the writings of three contemporary Black Buddhist teachers who uphold the importance of honoring gender and sexuality within dharma practice.

Gender, Sexuality, Eroticism, and Sensuality: The Body as a Vehicle for Liberation

The three aforementioned contemporary Black Buddhist teachers, writing from different traditions, directly address Baldwin and Lorde's approach to embodied sensuality, presence, and self-awareness. Sebene Selassie, a teacher in the Insight tradition, Zenju Earthlyn Manuel, a teacher in the Soto Zen tradition, and Lama Rod Owens, a teacher in the Kagyu Tibetan tradition all speak to the importance of not only claiming one's racialized, sexualized, gendered social identity but embracing the body as a vehicle for liberatory practice. In much the same way that Baldwin and Lorde embrace joyful, sensual movement and connection, these Black Buddhist teachers speak to the importance of cultivating joyful energy by tapping into the innate wisdom and groundedness of the body.

Respecting and Rejoicing in the Force of Life

Joy, rooted in sensual pleasure, fosters the force of life to which Baldwin refers. Adhering to practices that enhance enjoyment, even bliss, in the quest for an awakened life, is central to Tibetan dharma teachings and, increasingly, Black activist communities in the United States.[74] Baldwin and Lorde's writings offer a precedence for claiming the joy inherent in sensuality. Owens reflects,

> Joy is much more than just being happy; it is experiencing the energy of what I often call bliss. This bliss is an experience of all my distractions falling away and of being left with this profound feeling of freedom. It is the realization of extreme clarity and openness. Many of us experience this during sexual orgasms or highs from substance use. The most authentic experiences of bliss are those that are the expression of deep virtue or goodness, which connects us to an expression of our most nonviolent and loving selves. This bliss, like happiness, is about connection and balance; but it is more about the experience of unity, that there is no separation anymore. . . . I am practicing confidence in my innate capacity to experience bliss, which I ultimately believe is an expression of my true nature.[75]

For Owens, such joy is fundamentally embodied and connected to the earth.[76] It is an energy that brings practitioners closer to an elemental homecoming, akin to the force of life to the identified by Baldwin.[77] Owens recalls the story of Shakyamuni Buddha's enlightenment, when the forces of destruction and death, known as Mara, showered upon the Buddha as he sat under the Bodhi tree. Supported by Mother Earth, Shakyamuni Buddha remained unmoved, even when afflicted. As the earth supported him, he reached down to touch her, signaling, "I have the right to be here." That self-security and claiming of earth mother support, Owens says, foster the capacity for joy. Owens writes, "We are joy. When we take part in that remembering and that stepping into that joy, what we're actually doing is practicing liberation. We're practicing a revolution."[78]

In honoring the earth and one's capacity for joy, ultimately practitioners are honoring their own bodies. Indeed, the body is a vehicle for joyful liberation. In a circular process, then, love of one's body facilitates loving and caring for the earth. Such groundedness, then, is, as Baldwin articulates, "respect[ing] and rejoic[ing] in the forces of life, of life itself." In such care, for body and earth, practitioners can illuminate their natural goodness and inner well-being, their natural state of joy. Indeed, Owens refers to joy as a "natural state" of mind that arises in the practice of meditation.[79]

Sebene Selassie similarly writes that joy is the foundation for dispelling the trauma of living in a racialized, racist society. Selassie recalls the pervasive social messages that linked stereotypical body images in dominant culture to sexual desirability, leading to inhibited movements. Dancing, once awkward, became a way to stop internalizing and repressing natural feelings. The spaces to dance, for Selassie, became avenues for liberated embodiment:

> I first learned to move my body in gay male clubs in my early twenties. These were spaces where I felt free to express myself without worrying about looking seductive or giving the wrong message to men. I could move my body in exploration and freedom, learning what felt good for me. As I came to love hip-hop and R&B in my midtwenties, I learned to dance everywhere. Now I feel comfortable dancing almost anywhere. Sometimes I even do a little jiggle on the subway platform if a song in my earbuds really moves me.[80]

The Erotic as Power

Being present with the body is being *present*, as Baldwin names. This message is foundational in the *Satipatthana Sutta*, a teaching on the four foundations of mindfulness. Selassie reflects, "The mind and body are not truly separate. Those are just words we use to describe our experience of thoughts (and emotions) versus the physicality of life. Our consciousness is not limited to the body or mind; it is a knowing that encompasses both of those and much, much more. . . . 'Embodied' denotes that mind and body are fundamentally not separate. 'Awareness' is the capacity to know both physical and mental/emotional experiences. Embodied awareness leads us to belonging."[81] Selassie echoes Owens in her uplifting of the body as the vehicle for cultivating presence. Owens refers to the practice of paying attention to the body as an "Embodied Approach" to liberation.[82] Both teachers assert that the body can only be in the present—unlike the mind, it does not travel to the past or strive toward the future. Thus, to cultivate presence is to pay attention to the *felt sensations* in the body. Rather than thinking about what the body is doing, both Selassie and Owens describe the importance of being aware of physical sensations, whether these sensations are pleasant, unpleasant, or neutral.

Zenju Earthlyn Manuel, a Soto Zen teacher, writes of the body as nature and as the "the location of awakened experience."[83] Manuel says, "We live within our bodies and therefore perceive life through them."[84] It is not only the practice of deconstructing the social identities laden upon persons and communities, but elevating the body as the site for liberation, that allows for the presence, joy, and innate sensuality named by Lorde and Baldwin. The capacity for feeling deeply, without repression, shame, or inhibition, fosters an inner security that results in self-trust, strength, and dignity.

To be sure, even as Lorde and Baldwin acknowledge joy, they also write of the tremendous pain experienced by Black people. The experience of pain, too, is situated in the body. A practice of embodied awareness leads to the full experience of all emotions, in a container of safety. Manuel writes, "To acknowledge our pain is to recognize the complexity of our bodies as both the place in which we forge meaning for our lives, and the location within which we catalyze liberation."[85] In forging meaning, practitioners begin to *feel* in the safety of refuge—allowing for joy as well as pain to emerge and be embraced.

Indeed, Manuel writes, "It is only due to these bodies in which we live that we can even explore the path to liberation. When we begin to hold an awareness of the body as inheriting nature, then we may begin to experience a liberating tenderness, to have authentic encounters and to reconcile kinship between us."[86] Attending to the body with kindness and awareness facilitates not only trust of oneself but also trust of others. Owens acknowledges the body as a signal for safety and danger: "The body doesn't lie. It always tells the truth. So as I move through the world, I use my body to pick up on cues that my thinking mind can't discern. What is my gut telling me? What is my intuition telling me that I feel in my body? I listen to that information. If I feel relaxed in my body when I am with someone, that's a really good sign. If I feel tension in my body, especially in my gut, when I'm around someone, then maybe that's a clue that something's not right for me."[87]

Paying attention to the body, allowing for suffering to be known, and living into joy foster attunement with one's environment as well as other people. Body awareness is central for such attunement. In a society that privileges thinking, strategy, and the work of the mind, caring for one's body is often disregarded as an afterthought or privilege. Owens— remembering Baldwin—reflects on the importance of rest.[88] Safety with others often emerges with similar aspirations to connect to the body. Owens states, "I'm interested in the level of happiness that is actually about us just being in our bodies or at least having an aspiration to be in our bodies, being connected, being sensitive, being in tune with the world around us despite how hard the world is."[89]

Attunement, for Selassie, Owens, and Manuel, arises from a practice of silent meditation. The writings of all three teachers illuminate that sitting practice is one way in which they resist white supremacy and renew themselves at their own fountains, to use Baldwin's expression. Buddhist practices of meditation allow for suffering to be encountered and known, rather than repressed and rejected. In cultivating the capacity to turn toward burdensome, painful feelings and circumstances, a spaciousness emerges. Each teacher writes about the importance of cultivating spaciousness and inner silence, in order to embrace Blackness, and in order for joy and sensuality to emerge. Selassie writes, "I turned towards Buddhism and Blackness at the same time. I am forever grateful for that synchronicity."[90]

For Manuel, silence allows for constructs to fall away and for a depth of repressed feelings to be known. Her dharma name, "Tenderness," evokes her practice. Manuel writes,

> I allowed tenderness—a gentle opening, a softness of mind and body—to surface. I followed that opening until the way of tenderness unearthed itself as a liberated path. It is a natural, organic, innate medicine, or teaching *within the body* itself. . . . Tenderness does not erase the inequities we face in our relative and tangible world. I am not encouraging a spiritual bypass of the palpable feelings that we experience. The way of tenderness is an intangible elixir for the clogged arteries in the heart of our world. I say that complete tenderness is an experience of life that trusts the fluidity of our life energy and its extension into those around us.[91]

Such tenderness rests, gently, upon the capacity to hold one's own pain, thereby blooming one's capacity for and expression of joy and sensuality. To hold one's own pain, one must cultivate self-trust. For Owens, such trust is rooted in practices that honor the earth as a nurturing mother.

> I trust myself. I trust that I have the ability to experience and feel. I trust that I have the ability to empathize. I trust my ability to change. I trust my ability to embody agency. I trust that I can discern the positive and constructive things the world can offer me as feedback that can help me grow through my suffering. I also trust that I can discern through the bullshit what the world is trying to tell me about myself that has nothing to do with my benefit. This trust in myself doesn't meant that I'm okay all the time, but it does mean that when I am not okay, I can let myself not be okay and I can take care of that not-okayness. This trust is built upon a real acceptance of myself that is supported by intense gratitude. I have to let myself be sick in order to have the space to start working toward being well.[92]

Self-trust, cultivated in the refuge of silence, allows for practitioners to touch into feelings housed in their bodies with safety and care. It fosters known experiences of joy as well as pain. It cultivates self-knowledge. This self-knowledge includes touching into one's sexuality. Owens writes, "No matter what choices you're making in terms of expressing your sexuality, you have to be honest. . . . Sex can then become a profound way that we shape our character and our moral selves."[93] In tandem with self-trust and self-awareness, it is important to address the overarching cultural messages that repress sensuality and sexuality.

Sexuality: Deconstructing a "Labyrinth" of Historical and Public Attitudes

In order to know oneself—one's impulses, feelings, inclinations, habitual behaviors—one must also touch into the felt sensations that arise when making contact with the environment and other people. So often this is difficult, Selassie says, for everyone—we learn to disconnect and dissociate from our bodies. This disconnection, Owens says, is fundamentally rooted in patriarchy and can be particularly acute with regard to sexuality. Owens chronicles in great detail the inhibitions and judgments, particularly in a Black Church upbringing in a small southern town, that arose in his youthful awareness of attraction to other boys. But his embrace of his sexual energies, and his queer identity, came slowly, primarily with support that arose through reading Black queer literature: "The books gifted me such an intense sense of self-worth reading about other Black queer men expressing love for one another."[94]

Cultivating self-knowledge, for Owens, evolved with the support of community. Initially, this community was found in books: not only did he read about love; he absorbed books on politics. Ultimately, the importance of meeting like-minded souls who self-identified as lesbian, transgender, and gender-nonconforming and who articulated radical self-acceptance helped Owens to live into his own self-acceptance. He writes, "I had to start trusting in my own experience of gayness, which felt normal and natural. And as my gayness deepened, it gave way to queerness, which was and is an identity location that articulates not just my expanded attraction to different bodies and gender presentations, but also articulates my radical sexual politics."[95]

Ann Gleig, author of *American Dharma: Buddhism beyond Modernity*, defines queer as a term that has emerged both as an umbrella signifier for a coalition of culturally marginal gender and sexual identities and to delineate a distinct theoretical discourse and academic field that has developed from lesbian and gay studies. Whereas gay and lesbian studies often advocate an essentialist model of sexuality, following the anti-foundational orientation of postmodern and post-structural thought, queer theory disrupts all stable, binary, and fixed configurations of gender and sexual identity and proposes rather that all gendered and sexual identities are discursively conditioned, contingent and ideologically motivated. . . . Recent developments within queer theory engage more with critical race theory, post-colonial thought, and transnational feminism, and call attention to the intertwining categories of race, ethnicity, nation, class, gender and sexuality.[96]

Gleig refers to shifts in sexual and gender identity that embrace a spectrum of fluidity and nonbinary identity; Owens, as a self-identified Black, cis-gendered man who dates men, locates himself within the spectrum of queer identity. So too does Manuel, who writes that "I am bi-sexual at heart but have lived in a same-sex or lesbian relationship most of my adult life."[97] Proponents of queer theory, in pointing to "conditioned, contingent, and ideologically motivated" constructed identities, deconstruct the "labyrinth" of historical and public attitudes to which Baldwin refers.

And, indeed, Baldwin and Lorde are not only uplifting the claiming of one's sexual identity but also pointing to a way of being in which sexual identity is located. For both Baldwin and Lorde, sensuality and eroticism are broad, enveloping energies that move people into the very essence of desire in all facets of life, not simply in sexuality. Selassie illuminates Lorde's approach in her reflections:

When [Lorde] says "erotic," she is not only talking about the sexual—although it includes that—but about our deepest non-rational knowing. It is rooted in the senses and involves a vital connection to the body. She calls it "the power of our unexpressed or unrecognized feeling" or our "creative energy empowered." It allows us to feel fully and live deeply into our experience. The erotic is embodied awareness with an attention to joy, to savoring every moment—not for stimulation but for liberation.[98]

Lorde's references to the erotic, like Baldwin's upliftment of the sensual, foster queer sexuality but are fundamentally about joy, presence, trust, silence, renewal, and self-awareness. Such deep knowing, rooted in a cultivated capacity to feel sensations in the body, leads naturally to liberation.

7

Love and Liberation

Collective Care and Refuge in Black Buddhist Communities

I just love Black people. It starts with that, what we as Black
people touch, when we touch it, the depth of our experience
as being Black in America, the depth of our experience from
our ancestors who—God knows how—survived to get here,
and then survived all the history of enslavement and Jim
Crow and everything. There is the Africanist in us. There is
such a well of depth and presence to represent that we are
people who already had a sense of deep presence, which is
what dharma is about.
—Konda Mason[1]

Love and liberation are at the heart of Buddhism and the Black Radical
Tradition. Buddhism offers wisdom teachings on causes and conditions
and the Four Noble Truths: a recognition of interdependence, impermanence, suffering, compassion, and ethics. Black Radicalism, as a tradition
focused on dismantling exploitative white-supremacist social systems,
fosters a commitment to psychological liberation that deconstructs and
heals internalized white supremacy. While there are marked differences
within these traditions, it is a contention of this book that there are
identifiable overlapping orientations toward understanding and ending
suffering in the emphases on political, psychological, and spiritual liberation. Buddhism, as it has developed in the West, emphasizes clear seeing
and skillfully relating to the conditions of suffering as core aspects of psychological and spiritual liberation. Black Radicalism deconstructs white
supremacy and seeks to dismantle systemic institutions that perpetuate intergenerational trauma. This chapter argues that, in practicing the
dharma, Black Buddhists attain the Black Radical aspiration for psycho-

logical liberation by practicing teachings that foster clearly seeing the false constructs of white supremacy, offering skillful responses to suffering, and cultivating love for Blackness and Black communities.

Practices of Political, Psychological, and Spiritual Liberation
Rage, Violence, and Right Action

Social justice is a central commitment in the lived experiences Black Buddhists. Indeed, nearly all interviewees spoke of their vow to addressing social conditions. Jylani Ma'at, a long-term practitioner in different traditions, uplifts dharma practices as a way of leaning into suffering rather than avoiding it. She asserts that the dharma requires direct responses to socially enacted trauma, especially the phenomenon of racialized violence:

> We are witnessing hangings, lynchings, head decapitation, and burnings. This is very reminiscent of a not-so-distant past. And this to me really challenges my practice, because this is not a "turn the cheek" kind of thing. This is not a "sit on the mat and cross your legs" kind of thing. This is a "get up and do something kind of thing," with compassion for those who obviously are mentally ill, but still holding them fully accountable. And I don't believe that any path that I would be on, any religion that I would participate in, any faith would direct me to be complicit. That's just not who I am, and I don't think that any divine engagement allows for that. . . . And the concept of suffering is not intended to only include people of color, namely Black and Brown and indigenous peoples of America. Joy, safety, and freedom are entitlements for everybody. And to me that is what a full practice is. When you feel free to fully be in it and able to fully address your concerns, your fear, your anger, all of that. I don't think that there's any practice that says you can't be angry and you can't be mad. It's how you respond to things, but that's a human experience. And so what is it that you are asking me to do? Who do you want me to be? And if you are asking me to withdraw and be a void in my spirit, then you don't really want me to show up. And then you are rendering me invisible almost. And we don't have a relationship if that's the case.[2]

Ma'at rejects the suggestion she has encountered from white Buddhist teachers that the role of a Buddhist practitioner is simply to be with suffering, without a commitment to alleviating racism within a white supremacist society. Speaking of police violence against Black men, women, and nonbinary / gender-nonconforming persons, she states,

> That "just be with it"—no, you have to act. That's what the human experi-
> ence is, to have a response. It doesn't have to be a violent response, but
> you do need to respond because otherwise the silence is not living. I have
> to live. And I'm a mother. So I just have somatic responses. I think the
> strong response of Philando Castile's mother is normal. It's appropriate.
> She should not be silenced. Her pain is very real. It's very real and it's
> warranted. And I think if more people could see that, maybe they would
> feel a sense of responsibility to get in the process as well. This isn't about
> others. This is every moment, every person, right now. Right now. . . . It's
> everywhere, and I'm talking about senseless killing that nobody is being
> held responsible for. I don't think there's a church in the nation, or a syna-
> gogue, or a mosque that says let's just accept this violence towards us and
> just be okay with it. And if that is happening, I'm afraid of that, because
> that type of silencing is how we got here. . . . So when I think about activ-
> ism, I feel that the authentic Buddhist tradition is to get up and to be an
> alarmist, and to be active, and to confront things, to bring them out into
> open, to have full sense of awareness, to exact honesty, to also forgive, but
> forgiveness with a sense of responsibility.[3]

The spaciousness cultivated in ongoing dharma practice allows for repressed emotions to arise and be felt deeply. At the time of completion of this book, the trial of George Floyd's murderer is taking place and twenty-year-old Daunte Wright has just been murdered by a white police officer. Black people are again protesting in the streets. The work of dharma practice is to create spaciousness that allows people to confront suffering and honor feelings, individually and collectively, in a context of white supremacist violence.

Such spaciousness also facilitates practitioners to recognize learned childhood coping mechanisms to trauma and to change one's patterns of relating to that trauma. Aishah Shahidah Simmons, a survivor of incest and rape, asks,

How do I move through the trauma and talk about the anger . . . talk about the rage? It's not about denying it. It's not about pretending. It's not about bypassing. It's about not allowing it to control my life. I often hear rage and meditation don't go hand in hand. Or, meditation is about just squashing the rage, as in "don't be angry, just be peaceful."

And yeah, I fully believe that hopefully we can all get there. But what is critical is that we're not dishonest with ourselves and each other. I think there's nothing worse than pretending to not be rageful when we are. And there are many reasons to be angry. What do we do with that rage? How can we channel it so that it doesn't destroy us in the process?[4]

For many Buddhist practitioners, turning toward suffering and acknowledging its causes and conditions is the first step to liberation. Unique Holland, a Zen practitioner, reflects on the lack of acknowledgment of social oppression embedded in her immediate environment and the tools she developed as a response:

Social injustice was very present for me in my everyday life, and it wasn't something that I was ever comfortable with and I always thought about how to resolve it. And in my young teenage years I didn't really get a lot of satisfactory answers from others about why things were the way they were and what we could do about it. We wouldn't talk about the injustices that we face from larger institutions and structures. We were not going to talk about what happens within our Black communities. We were not going to talk about what happens to women. I was observing a lot of [the silences] and was not just really able to identify what was going on. So I carried a lot of anger with me and didn't even understand that it was anger. It wasn't until very recently that I was able to see "oh, that's what that is." And what I've been doing for a very long time was developing a certain set of coping skills that was around just repressing emotion, repressing my own life and perspective and energy.[5]

The practice of repressing emotion to cope with everyday life deeply impacts the nervous systems of oppressed people, according to Order of Interbeing teacher Larry Ward. Not only do dharma teachers strive to translate teachings orally delivered twenty-six thousand years ago, they also endeavor to address the nervous systems of practitioners coping with traumas induced in a modern context. Ward, who self-identifies as a Bodhisattva—an enlightened being who returns to conventional life to help other beings attain liberation—states,

> Our social philosophy is defensively oriented. It is fear based. It is patriar-chal. I'm so excited when I look around the world and see what the young people are doing, what women are doing, indigenous people are doing, as well as anybody else who's awake and wants to be. I'm committed to introducing and sustaining these people as Bodhisattvas, and training them in the deep practices of the Bodhisattva tradition, fostering that new consciousness and giving people practical contemplative skills that they can use to recognize, embrace, deconstruct and reconstruct them-selves and their society. . . . We have got to translate some language that is so embedded in all of us, like "warrior," into spiritual action, because we can't recreate a whole new language for the whole world. A part of that work for me is with poetry and music and song and dance, so that we can have a somatic liberation. Liberation is not complete if it isn't somatic. If the body isn't experiencing itself as vital and alive and full of energy [it is not liberated]. To me, social justice means creating a world in which every person has that opportunity.[6]

The emphasis on somatic liberation is a recurring, spontaneous theme in interviews with Black Buddhist teachers and long-term practi-tioners. Many express frustration at retreats that focus on silent sitting, with few outlets for physical movement. Others point to the different cultural expressions in dharma communities composed of people of Af-rican descent; not only yoga but also music and dancing are embraced as liberatory practices. Kate Johnson, a teacher in the Insight tradition who is also a former dancer, echoes Ward's identification of somatic practices as an aspect of liberation for Black people:

> I think there's one kind of liberation that has to do with the body, and our ability to self-determine what happens to our bodies, like where they move, can go, how we can care for them, how we have access to care, the kind of work that we do. There's something about self-determination in the body that feels like a kind of liberation that I'm really interested in. Another kind is an expressive liberation. This is one that I find particu-

larly challenging in Buddhist spaces, the ability to actually move our bodies in ways that feel genuine, to be able to authentically express ourselves vocally and physically.

They're all kind of interrelated because the freedom to really be able to *feel*, and the access to bodily sensation, might be a result of those kinds of liberation. If we are able to determine where our bodies can move, and how they can move, and where they can go, and be cared for in those spaces, then we can actually feel our bodies and have access to the wisdom that's there, that's in this personal embodied sphere. I think that there are some conditions for liberation. [Those conditions] are about getting our basic needs met, like having water, having food, having love, having rights. I just don't see how without those basic needs met, one could be free to pursue other kinds of freedom. There's a liberation that strikes me as a social liberation. That's what it is to really be known for who we are and know others for who they are, like unknowing and being known somehow. And then I think there's a political liberation that has to also to do with self-determination, but that is at the level of policy. Even in the ways that perception intersects with policy, there could be a real valuing of all bodies, valuing of all lives and a keen awareness of them. But because the historical legacies of violence against particular bodies and lives has been so impactful, our experience today of liberation is not just [about] equal treatment but equity, right? There are some lives that must be protected in particular if all lives are to be valued. I think when it comes to spiritual liberation, the definition I like comes from the Japanese Buddhist tradition of awakening, or liberation as intimacy with all things. For me, this gives a sense of real closeness and affection.[7]

For many Black teachers, the interlocking spheres of spiritual and political liberation cannot be separated. As espoused from the outset in the Black Radical Tradition, liberation is always collective; the Bodhisattva vow as well as the recognition of essential community support engender liberation as a commitment to community. Black Buddhist teachers and practitioners fervently articulate their passion for supporting practical well-being: health and support for bodies, including adequate food and shelter. Interviewees emphasize that spiritual liberation cannot take place without basic support for physical health and wellness. Dalila

Bothwell, a long-term practitioner in the Insight tradition, speaks to the practice of starting to heal oneself and developing capacity to extend healing outward:

> On every retreat there was a moment where I was shutting down. I've lived shut down for more years of my life than not. And [eventually] I was able to be with it, to not feel compelled to move and to try to change an uncomfortable feeling within me. It was so huge for me. So to me that's liberation, because I'm free to be who I am. I'm free to be, to have these experiences move from me. I'm not in control of what arises in this mind body, right? I can respond to it. Of course, there are times when I react with: "now I'm able to respond and I'm able to respond from a place of allowing, of acceptance, and just generally like okay, this is life's experience right now." And so when I feel so, that's on the individual level of this liberation, right?

Bothwell acknowledges that once practitioners find their way into emotional and mental stability, they inevitably seek to teach the path to beings who are suffering: "In so many ways, we have so many people who are wanting to create freedom for others, who are wanting to create some sense of safety in sanctuary and refuge. But we have not found it within ourselves. So liberation looks like everybody having a role and being accepted for their gifts and people accepting their gifts and not trying to change their gifts to look like something else. Freedom is safety to be who we are."[8] The meaning of liberation espoused by Bothwell points to the Black Radical Tradition of focusing on psychological wellness and self-scrutiny; it also uplifts the emphasis on building community. For Bothwell, as for many teachers and practitioners, liberation for oneself is the first step, but it must be extended to create collective safety, sanctuary, and refuge to be *full liberation*. Black Buddhists are not free until all people are free.

Familial Violence and Right Action

Liberation also brings the past into the present; the here and now necessarily includes generations that have gone before. As described at length, Black Buddhists suffer from intergenerational trauma in interpersonal

and institutional contexts. In his reflections on liberation, Kabir Hypolite recalls the importance of reckoning with the past in the present day:

> Liberation, to me, is a very paradoxical term. . . . I mean we're talking
> about going back into slavery times. We're talking about understanding
> the brutality of it all and the tremendous loss. I think of all those slave
> songs and negro spirituals about freedom. . . . I hold them even more
> dear because now, I hear them with the voices of people who either did
> or did not survive slavery. And I wanted to understand and I still have so
> much more to know: Who was here? What was happening? How did the
> events actually unfold? What is the story, what is the thing that was not
> being told about everything that has been done and transpired and that
> creates the fabric of American society today? What echoes are we not
> conscious of? Because to me, liberation is not that someone just came in
> the door and tells you, you're free now, you go. You may be free of your
> physical body, but all the grief, the loss, the scars, the wounds—you're
> still carrying it. And it's that piece that I think we are still struggling
> with and need to be liberated from. . . . You have to sit with it, you have
> to witness it, you have to touch it and taste and smell it. I think the
> irony is that in doing that, we have a certain capacity, if you will, for
> witnessing.[9]

Becoming conscious of the past motivates healing on multiple levels. Practitioners who embrace their trauma seek to shift unconscious
patterns that perpetuate self-harm and collective harm. Those whose
familial relationships have fractured seek to cultivate compassion and
loving-kindness. Simmons, a long-term practitioner initially in the S. N.
Goenka tradition who shifted to the Insight tradition in October 2019,
endured childhood sexual abuse and adult rape. In multiple creative
projects (NO! The Rape Documentary and *Love WITH Accountability:
Digging Up the Roots of Child Sexual Abuse*), Simmons makes visible
the trauma of sexual abuse survivors and her embrace of Buddhism to
heal trauma. She describes the "anchor" that meditation provides, especially in the encounter of rage while sitting: "The bodily sensations that
I experience when I'm enraged are almost unbearable heat, fire, a pit in
my stomach, dry mouth, and also chills. When I am not overcome by
rage, I am aware of it in my body before I can articulate it. If I allow it,

rage consumes me to the point that I am in 100% reactivity mode. Even when, from my vantage point, my rage is justifiable, I cause harm to myself and others when the rage isn't channeled."[10] Simmons highlights the meditative approach of nonreactivity as her rage arises. This stance of observing without reacting is "radical," in her words: a call to "right action" that is rooted in healing. It is critical to face outward toward those who cause harm, but Simmons notes that "the only people we are guaranteed with changing is ourselves." Healing the self facilitates extending healing outward to others.

> It means in each moment to moment to moment to moment I have an opportunity . . . we all have an opportunity to not give innate power away as a result of familial trauma, or other vicious and atrocious forms of oppression—white supremacy, patriarchy heterosexism, socioeconomic challenges, and ableism. For example, I embody multiple identities including, Black-Woman-Lesbian who is also an Incest Survivor and Rape Survivor. All of these identities are marginalized and oppressed in the U.S. and also globally. I am empowered knowing that I have an opportunity to refrain from giving my innate power away in response to these vicious and atrocious forms of oppression. In this *moment to moment to moment* each one of us can experience true liberation from within. This experiential understanding shouldn't ever be misunderstood or misconstrued as excusing or condoning oppression at all. . . . I'm not suggesting that we just, "breathe, observe, calm our mind and not allow these external forces impact you," because often they do impact you.[11]

In meditation, Simmons says, harm is recognized. And yet, even as the meditator acknowledges the full weight of harm, meditation cultivates the capacity to see and act without inflicting further harm.

> As a survivor of both childhood sexual abuse and adult rape, my application of equanimity and *metta* to anti-oppression work are tools to circumvent destroying myself in the process of the work, or becoming the exact systems or entities that I am working to eradicate. This is not an easy feat at all. For me, it is trial and error with tiny glimpses of incremental progress along the way. It doesn't mean pretending I'm not angry. I want to be clear. I still get overcome with rage and despair. I

am a very reactive person. What this practice continuously teaches me is how to work with it.[12]

Black Buddhists take a particular approach to healing intergenerational and intracommunal harm that is both solitary and collective. As Simmons articulates, Black Buddhists whose trauma has led to psychological pain, including rage, depression, and low self-esteem, find refuge in the Buddha, the dharma, and in the sangha, especially in affinity sanghas. Pan-Africanist and Black Power activists built cultural and economic institutions to help protect Black people from trauma inflicted in a white supremacist society. Black Church leaders carried forth the forms of survival, especially worship, music, and food, that aided the uplifting and unity of Black peoples under slavery and segregation. Black Feminists insisted that Black women would no longer silently and disproportionately bear the harm inflicted historically by white and Black men, and white women. The past must be acknowledged in order to be transformed, and as a result, trauma can be healed. Rhonda Magee refers to this spiritual and emotional work as "reconstructing ourselves and the world from a place of deeply valuing every human being."[13] She acknowledges that it will take time for intergenerational healing to take place. And yet this is the path to liberation.

Relating Skillfully to Suffering

A number of Black Buddhist teachers and long-term practitioners spoke of liberation as a practice of relating to suffering skillfully. In Pali, the term *upaya* refers to "skillful means." For Black Buddhist teachers, cultivating the skills of turning toward suffering and seeing it clearly, without personalizing it or being attached to its particular forms, is a practice of liberation. Psychological and spiritual freedom is identified as the ability to relate to suffering without being overwhelmed by it or succumbing to its pain. Noliwe Alexander, a teacher in the Insight tradition, reflects,

I can be a witness because I know what it feels like to be wrapped in and somewhat shackled. It's breaking free of all of that. . . . The possibility of freedom shows up in many ways. . . . I would say being able to turn towards [aversion], not to forget it or to see it and go this way, but actually turn towards it [is liberating]. And for me, sometimes my learning edge is when I do face the hatred and ignorance, when I actually turn towards it. Not that I am attaching myself to it, but I'm not being aversive to it. I'm actually turning towards it for my own liberation, for my own ways of learning and seeing it for what it is, not to make it something else, because we turn towards it in all of its ugliness. I really am turning towards an equanimous mind, being able to see things [clearly]. It's full body, mind, soul, spirit liberation. And just to take the oath, "I'm not liberated till we're all liberated," there's a peace. . . . You have to empower yourself. There is that sense of walking in the world and recognizing there is no box.[14]

For Alexander, the inner strength to embrace suffering facilitates an ability to rise from what psychologist and dharma teacher Tara Brach refers to as a "confined sense of self."[15] Perhaps paradoxically, leaning into pain—rather than avoiding or masking it—and feeling the depth of pain fully illuminate the possibility of a liberated way of being. Stacy McClendon, a dharma teacher at Common Ground Meditation Center in Minneapolis, explains in her dharma talk "The Nature of Mind,"

What we're doing is we're looking at our lives through the lens of dharma, not solely the stories that we know happen in our minds. . . . When I first started meditating, my interest was not in getting to know my mind. . . . I was trying to clean some stuff up, move it along. I thought I knew my mind. It was critical, self-conscious, judging, controlling. I knew it. I had been watching it for decades. It was time to whip it into shape. Enough with watching. It's like acrobatics sometimes; it's just exhausting. Thinking, planning, remembering, scheming, strategizing, fantasizing, embellishing a little bit sometimes, narrating, rehearsing, preparing, commenting, recalling, calculating, and that's before breakfast! But despite all of the activity, the mind wasn't in balance. It was out of shape. All of those controlling thoughts about what I could do to make things differently, I learned that inherent in those thoughts was the belief, this deep core belief, that there is something wrong with the way things are, there's something wrong with the way *I am* right now. And so all of my efforts tightening to control, manage, were out of that place, out of that sense of deficit. Something is wrong. I'm missing something, I don't have enough. What I call the promise of my meditation practice is that I have learned how to relate differently. All of that stuff still happens in my head. What I'm learning is how to relate differently to those old tapes. They're so old, some of them are eight-track tapes. I got vinyl in there. What I'm learning is how to relate differently to those tapes. . . . Acknowledging the conditioning that has resulted in those tapes. And trying to approach the mind, my mind, my heart, with a little kindness, some patience, compassion. When I'm able to do that with myself, I'm better able to do that with other people in the world.[16]

In this freedom is the possibility of dignity and evenness in the face of personal and larger social challenges. One aspect of relating to suffering skillfully, then, is to cease inflicting suffering on oneself.

Radical Black leaders—historically and today—have highlighted a high degree of psychological suffering experienced by people of African descent. Internal freedom, they have argued, emerges when Black people clearly recognize the sources of their oppression. The call for analysis of external conditions that create suffering, and for an ongoing practice of self-scrutiny, aids the practice of liberation. This call has been made from leaders as diverse as Huey Newton of the Black Panther Party for Self-Defense (BPP) and Audre Lorde, a Black lesbian feminist poet. McClendon and Alexander, two Black Buddhist teachers, speak of knowing the mind through skillful means, a practice that leads to psychological liberation. For McClendon and Alexander, the practice of leaning into suffering brings clarity about the origins of suffering—social and psychological—and a confrontation with fear that causes fear to loosen its grip on one's psyche. Such fearlessness, in turn, strengthens personal agency, interpersonally as well as in social activism.

For Black people undergoing intergenerational trauma, psychological suffering is intimately interwoven with socially induced suffering. Katie Loncke, who currently trains in the Rinzai Zen lineage, argues that liberation must be understood through interlocking spiritual and political terms.

Liberation is the cessation of suffering. In a political context it feels like liberation is the freedom from fear from untimely death, or wants, or exploitation. And the way they fit together for me is that I believe that if everyone—if all beings—could experience more freedom from fear, from untimely death, from exploitation, that our Buddha nature would lead us to seek the paths towards the cessation of suffering together. And so it's creating the material conditions so that the spiritual work might have a better chance of happening for more people. . . . Of course, even if we had all of our material needs met, there would still be suffering. The Buddha's beginning of understanding, his seeking to understand suffering and the cessation of it, [demonstrates that]. The Buddha is from a palace. I think that's really profound. And it shows that even if we could achieve our Utopia, there would be questions of birth and old age, and sickness and death, that persist. So I do think it's important to recognize that a more socialistic society or a more fair and compassionate society [still has suffering]. . . . The impulse towards liberation, the impulse towards compassion, and towards healing and justice, I see as just one among our sacred expressions of life.[17]

In political work to alleviate harm—such as protesting racist violence and building community-based organizations—it is also imperative to understand different dimensions of suffering caused by the mind states of greed, aversion, and confusion. Loncke states that alleviating suffering requires leaning into it and knowing it directly, rather than attempting to avoid or transcend it. Similarly, Ward, a teacher in the Thich Nhat Hanh's Order of Interbeing, reflects, "For me liberation is . . . about how I deal with the problem I have. . . . It's in the approach or the way you relate to that problem. It's the way you relate to that problem, and it is also the quality of consciousness. In the Buddha's language, it is wisdom and compassion in heart and mind. You have to look deep enough into that problem outside to first find it inside yourself."[18]

The process of investigating suffering is sometimes explained with the acronym RAIN: Recognition of suffering; Allowing the suffering to be fully felt; Investigating the feelings and realizing that they are impersonal and impermanent; and Not attaching to suffering and subsequently Nurturing one's capacity for tenderness and compassion. The skills cultivated in RAIN practice foster equanimity in the midst of suffering.[19]

In the freedom that comes from allowing feelings to arise, in cultivating wisdom and compassion, there is a natural freedom from mental grasping and obsessive desire. Practitioners who cultivate inner free-

LOVE AND LIBERATION | 243

dom are able to look at the emotions and mind states that arise and pass away and focus on their bodies and breathing as a source of refuge. In this way, they cultivate a stable state of mind that is not altered by conditions, including other people's responses to them. In this way, the Black Radical Tradition's emphasis on psychological independence from internalized oppression in the midst of external conditions of white supremacy is supported, even achieved. In their capacity to meet suffering with psychological balance and nonreactivity, Black Buddhist teachers and long-term practitioners attain the aspiration for psychological independence uplifted in the Black Radical Tradition. Black Buddhists have cultivated methods of working skillfully with thoughts and feelings that facilitate deconstructing internalized white supremacist modes of thinking. A stable state of mind, cultivated in meditation, allows practitioners to see the nature of impermanence, falsely constructed realities, and the instability of constructs of Blackness. As Lama Rod Owens, a teacher in the Kagyu Tibetan tradition, reflects,

> Wherever I am, I'm at home. Home is in my own experience, it's in my own embodiment. So I just reorient myself to understand that home is here in my body and my heart and my own mind. What helps me in terms of going back and forth between different communities and locations is simply, basically, love. And that love, that basic ethic of love, for me, is that we are all suffering, and I understand that we all suffer and we are all making decisions based upon our suffering. And some of these decisions are not informed and others are. I understand that people are doing the best that they can to be happy, and to suffer as little as possible.
>
> So that kind of awareness actually helps me to be really patient and kind. Because I'm also engaged in the same project. So I can move into spaces where people are like, "Why the hell are you here? You don't belong here." I say, "Okay, that's not about me. That's about your own inherited insecurity and discomfort that you are blaming me for." But actually, I've practiced in such a way that I no longer take responsibility for other people's stuff. That comes from a lot of confidence and a lot of self-love, but that's extremely possible.[20]

Owens deconstructs the layers of the emotion of anger and all of the tandem feelings surrounding it. The ability to cultivate a healthy ap-

proach to anger—a "really deep spaciousness"—allows Owens to validate anger and underlying experiences of being hurt, without repressing
and avoiding:

> Anger should never be repressed. . . . So anger gets tricky because we get
> distracted by it, but actually anger is leading us to our woundedness. It's
> in my woundedness that I make a home and I cultivate strategies of heal-
> ing. Once I started taking that kind of responsibility in my experience,
> then the world became much less antagonistic. . . . So think about the
> struggle of other people, and what and how ill equipped so many people
> in the world are to deal with their emotional reality. Allow yourself to
> be patient, but also allow yourself to be critical and direct, and to make
> choices in order to be safe and to decrease violence that you are experi-
> encing in a relationship to other people.[21]

A stable mind allows the emotion of anger to be fully known.
Furthermore, a stable mind fosters freedom from clinging. Leslie
Booker, a teacher in the Insight tradition, identifies such freedom as a
state of liberation:

> I think liberation means being free from clinging, free from attachment,
> free from allowing someone's greed, hatred and delusion to colonize my
> heart and my mind. It means being free to know who I am and not need-
> ing to be anything else. It means not being caught up. It's a spaciousness
> from greed, hatred, and delusion—being able to see [these mind states]
> play out in the world and to turn towards [them] with a sense of com-
> passion. There's a sense of equanimity. There's a sense of clear knowing.
> There's a sense of compassion and empathy. So, I think all these things
> give me a sense of freedom—not getting caught up, seeing the traps that
> are laid out and not falling into them.[22]

Similar to Booker's identification of liberation as freedom from clinging, Ruth King, an Insight teacher and author of *Mindful of Race*, embraces the term "freedom" for the practice of letting go:

> I associate the word "freedom" with moment-to-moment experiences
> we allow to be known and released. For example, we can notice a subtle

shift from the tightness of mental thoughts to its release by giving awareness to the bodily sensations of exhaling the breath. This is a moment of
freedom. Or we can notice an emotion as impermanent by opening our
awareness to noticing its absence. This is a moment of freedom. Such
freedoms are not to be missed, whether a flick, a few seconds, hours, or
days. Freedom is not so much a destination, however allowing such experiences of freedom without attachment are potent and cannot be erased.
Such direct experiences have a cumulative effect on the mind and body.
They deepen our faith, confidence, and inner stability, and they expand
our view and flavor the next moment. In other words, such experiences
flavor more freedom.[23]

In practicing relinquishment of mental grasping, Black Buddhist
teachers understand liberation as moment-to-moment freedom. Bhante
Buddharakkita, a Ugandan monk in the Theravada tradition, explains
liberation in the following ways:

> I understand liberation to be liberation from suffering, liberation from
> all my problems, and all the things. [Liberation is] in the stages actually.
> When you practice mindfulness, and concentrate, and then you suppress
> the five hindrances,[24] you suppress greed and hatred, you can be actually
> liberated at that moment. This what you call a moment-to-moment lib-
> eration. Then there's that kind of liberation that comes when you attain
> deep concentration. . . . Liberation of the mind [is found in] deep con-
> centration. . . . Our wisdom is part of liberation because we are liberated
> from confusion, we are liberated from suffering.[25]

The desire to attain freedom from suffering and the practice of self-
scrutiny initiate liberation. Yet as Bhante Buddharakkita and other
Black Buddhist teachers explain, psychological and spiritual liberation
rest upon training the mind to be still, if only moment to moment. The
ability to recognize strong feelings and powerful mind states, without
getting trapped in or attached to them, results in spiritual liberation.
This moment-to-moment freedom facilitates more spontaneous, joyful
expressions of being and greater ease.

The ability to know and name experiences—the clarity and ease that
arise with experiencing moment-to-moment liberation—is, for Black

Buddhist practitioners, an empowering act of agency. Claudelle Glasgow, a clinical psychologist and teacher in the Shambhala tradition, defines liberation succinctly: "[Liberation is] connecting and seeing what is, and helping others to do the same."[26] It is first an individual experience of cultivating awareness of one's own mind and, in the practice of clear seeing, not attaching to phenomena that arise and pass away.

Similarly, Allyson Pimentel, a long-term practitioner in the Insight tradition, reflects that the capacity to be present with pain without succumbing to terror or anguish is a fruit of meditation practice that is cultivated in calm as well as chaotic moments.

> The greatest gift that I've received from these practices is an increasing, ever-evolving ability to tolerate discomfort. [Being uncomfortable] doesn't mean there's something wrong or bad. It just means that it is the way it is. Now at the same time, there is something wrong and bad with many of the social structures that perpetuate the gross disparities in access and to being treated like a human being in our culture. So, I think it's hard to reconcile, but I also think it's really ripe: this idea that real liberation can come with the straightforward acknowledgement of suffering. On the one hand suffering is here; on the other hand we must ask how we can most skillfully relate to it.
>
> The practice teaches us that pain is inevitable, but suffering is optional. This idea that when we begin to just relate to things as they truly are—without our stories, hopes, fears, fantasies, wishes, ideas, analyses—if we just begin to relate to things as they are, then there's so much possibility for wisdom and love and relief to arrive in those moments.
>
> I have spent so much time in my life struggling with reality, fighting against it, feeling like I don't want things to be what they are. But when I come into contact with something painful and I just name it as such, I've often experienced it as really such a liberation. [After a traumatic accident involving my daughter, I was able to feel and name the overpowering sensations in my body] "this is fear, this is what fear feels like." The instant I said these words, the felt sense of terror associated with the fear completely went away. It re-emerged a nano-second later, but when I named the sensations I was feeling for what they were—"Fear, this is fear"—again, the terror went away. The pain and discomfort were all still there but the suffering was not. And in those breaths when fear was present but

terror was not, I could see a clearer way forward. The taste of freedom, of liberation, is in those sometimes very fleeting moments of clear seeing.[27]

Pimentel's reflections mirror the writings of Black Feminist poet Audre Lorde, who also distinguishes pain and suffering. Indeed, Lorde's writings offer numerous parallel examples of clarifying aspects of Buddhist teachings on suffering and freedom from suffering. For Lorde, suffering is reliving "unscrutinized and unmetabolized" pain in the mind.[28] To be submerged in suffering—to recall experiences over and over without stepping back to recognize how one is being mentally gripped by internalized narratives—is to miss the inherent power embedded in the experience of pain. One can experience pain and be charged and mobilized through it, rather than submerged and defeated by it. But suffering, Lorde says, is when one "condemn[s] oneself to reliving that pain over and over and over whenever something close triggers it."[29]

Many teachers and long-term practitioners are indebted to Black Feminist thinkers such as Audre Lorde.[30] Black Feminism calls for self-scrutiny and healing practices; moreover, Black Feminism grants permission to feel outrage and grief, and to name one's experience of suffering for oneself. Insight teacher Konda Mason states, "I had to let go, and say 'this is,' because that gap between where the suffering exists, is that gap between not accepting what is. We suffer in that space. So we do what we can and if we hold on to the outcome and it doesn't turn out the way you want it to . . . the suffering is so huge. But, if we can do everything we can and let go, [we experience] this mystery of life."[31] For Black dharma teachers and long-term practitioners, the emphasis on being aware of what is taking place, in one's mind-heart as well as in one's social environment, brings direct attention to the here and now, to moments of liberation.

The Truth of the Present Moment

The present moment includes socially induced suffering. Black people experience white supremacist misogynoir and cis-heteropatriarchal heterosexism (including homophobia and transphobia). For Black activists in the United States, the recognition of what is taking place in the present—harm as well as joy—is fundamentally important in the move-ment to establish justice. For practitioner Gretchen Rohr, a former judge in the District of Columbia Superior Court and a Community Dharma Leader in the Insight tradition, being present with suffering is an essen-tial practice.

> Suffering is what's going to get us forward, and [pleasure activism and so-cial justice movements] are reclaiming [freedom] as entitlement to free-dom and liberation *now*. Even in the space of suffering, the whole point of this work is our liberation. We need to taste and touch that now, not wait for an afterlife when we're going to get it. And I think the dharma is just the perfect space for integrating those teachings because . . . I feel like everything that has come from my dharma teachers is that I have the ability to tap into enlightened being right now.[32]

Tapping into an enlightened state of being, what Ruth King refers to as the "ground of us," can be particularly liberating for Black meditators who commit to somatic practices and incorporate devotional rituals into their contemplation. Moreover, for many Black Buddhist practitioners who remain members of church communities, the dharma comple-ments Christian teachings.[33] Many Black Buddhists speak of a reverence for Jesus of Nazareth and Christian ethics, even if they don't affiliate directly with a church.[34]

DaRa Williams, a teacher in the Insight tradition and a trained psy-chotherapist whose focus on intergenerational trauma is supported by indigenous approaches to healing, uplifts the importance of cultivating self-awareness. Williams reflects, "The components of coming to know your own mind and then applying that to whatever the conditions and circumstances and situations are, that's what has me have a great deal of belief and faith that this [dharma practice] is a doorway or a vehicle for transformation for Black folk."[35]

Transformation, for Black teachers and long-term practitioners, is in-evitably focused on cultivating the ability to be present with one's suffer-ing, to recognize difficult mind states such as intense craving, fear, and confusion as well as how society inflicts macro and micro wounds on Black people. The teachings on accepting the truth of "how things are" can be difficult to hear in predominantly white sanghas, especially from white teachers who have been racialized as intelligent, beautiful, and powerful. Loncke, whose training in radical activist communities, and whose tenure as the director of Buddhist Peace Fellowship, has initiated complex analyses of oppression within Buddhist circles, admits to struggling with dharma teachings espoused from white teachers:

> One teaching I embrace is about nonresistance to the *truth* of how things are right now. And when I first encountered this teaching in almost entirely white dharma space, I resisted it a lot. It felt like it was negating a tradition of political resistance to oppression. So, when a white dharma teacher said, "Drop your resistance," it seemed divorced from the political training that I had received. But when I started to realize that it meant was to not resist the truth of how things are, the reality of how things are right now, I started to understand how that is actually key to being able to find a new way for liberation and toward political resistance to injustice and the suffering of oppression. [Experiences] produce pleasant, unpleasant and neutral feeling tones. It gives me the sense of all that's allowable in an experience. And from that place of creativity and possibility, political resistance actually blooms for me, much more than spinning out into frustration and anger that these perceptions and experiences exist in the way that they do.[36]

Loncke is pointing to a shift in consciousness that occurs when meditators focus on their experiences of the present moment and slowly begin to deconstruct the damaging messages that they have internalized. Coming to awareness of one's own perspectives and aspirations, beyond the messages that have influenced one's identity and sense of direction, is an experience of liberation. In seeing the "truth of how things are," one's focus drops away from society's interpretations of worthy and unworthy, and instead the meditator concentrates on phenomena that arise and pass away. Often practitioners articulate the importance of cultivating experiences of safety, belonging, and refuge within one's inner being and community in order to observe impermanent phenomena without reacting. Zenju Earthlyn Manuel, a teacher in the Soto Zen tradition and author of numerous meditations on dharma practice, reflects that conscious embrace of one's own experience and one's relationship to other beings—without trying to change anything—is an act of spiritual liberation.

[Liberation is] *being* free if you have an understanding of consciousness and interrelationship. You understand when you're suffering that there's an interrelationship causing it. It's not just you, it is not just yours, and it doesn't belong to you. Consciousness is that place from how we perceive the world and how we feel about it. I know that whenever suffering arises between people I can withdraw and never return or I can understand the suffering in the context of an interrelationship that is broader than the two people. And when I do have my feelings, "oh that hurt, that's painful, oh God," or anger or whatever comes up for me, I understand that all of the pain is coming from an old consciousness, an old place disrupting the present moment. All pain is ancient. It is stored in the bones, it's a memory, maybe even a memory passed along over generations, of being hurt and rejected, a memory of being not accepted, a memory of being pushed aside, marginalized in society, and those past experiences are stored and can enter our present world. If I can understand that more is working in situations of personal and collective suffering, then I might be more likely to have a sense of liberation even within the suffering. "I've got this." And still we must have feelings. I feel my emotions fully, I have tears, I cry, and I get angry and enraged, but I don't go after the people I feel causing the pain and suffering because I've experienced external battles as exhausting and filled with more suffering. To know the wisdom teachings of the earth and walk with them is liberating. And I don't analyze suffering either. I don't try to fix the suffering in my mind and say, "oh, this is coming from there." I walk with the emotions, give them space, and then love and kindness come through, naturally, as an experience. Then perhaps I might take action based on such spaciousness. I don't work at ending suffering. I let it fade in the deep dive of my practice.[37]

The capacity to cultivate stillness and spaciousness in the midst of suffering is, for many Black Buddhists, an experience of psychological and spiritual liberation.

Inner Spaciousness and Emptiness

Ayesha Ali, cofounder of the Heart Refuge Mindfulness Community, speaks of spaciousness cultivated in meditation as that which allows for inner interrogation and ease: "Reaching in is the first obligation of meditation practice. It is by this practice that I have found space and freedom. I have found a space—one not afforded to me as a Black, female body in this world—to discover my body, my breath, and the contours of my life. It has given me the opportunity to really see the ways in which white supremacy has shaped my vision, my possibilities, even how I might choose to love."[38] The capacity to *be*—and in the process, challenge dominant social constructs of race, gender, and sexuality—arises from an inner spaciousness that expands to emptiness. Myokei Caine-Barrett, Bishop of the Nichiren Shu Order of North America and Chief Priest of the Myoken-ji Temple in Houston, speaks of accessing an inner stillness beyond thinking as an anchor for activism. Jozen Tamori Gibson, a teacher in Vipassana communities and a Soto Zen lay practitioner, uplifts meditation training as the cultivation of spiritual emptiness: being in the present moment.

In cultivating emptiness and heart practices, Gibson determines what is authentic and genuine for themselves and takes refuge in their racialized, gendered body without adopting the meanings associated with it.

I've been fortunate to have been directly impacted by teachers and centers [sangha] that do not separate emptiness and form and liberation. It wasn't the case when I was first introduced to [Buddhism] in Japan, and when I came back to the United States three years later. I was looking for places that were directly talking about emptiness, form and liberation. Being a Black Japanese person, being a Trans NonBinary being who was assigned male at birth (amab), being raised and conditioned in a number of ways, historically ancestrally within the home, we always talk about liberation and freedom. We talk about reconciliation, we talk about redemption, we talk about what it means to actually be seen, heard, and felt as a people in this world. And in my early days of practicing Zen in Japan, the practice itself allowed me to understand for myself. What does it mean to be liberated in this body? Where am I doing so on behalf of others? Am I doing so without the need of being recognized by anyone else? That level of liberation was powerful for me. Powerful. That was only through the practice of emptiness, the practice of knowing that there is no constructed self and that we are constructing ourselves, we are constructing ourselves through name, through words, through relational space. How do we also honor what we have constructed in this relational space? How do we honor what is true?[39]

In the quest for interior knowing independent of external approval or affirmation, Gibson deconstructs the stigmatism that has created painful messages and social divisions throughout their lives; they also cultivate an inner spaciousness that allows for unfolding, relaxing, and transforming internalized oppressions. This inner spaciousness does not refute inaccurate or outdated constructs of Blackness, nor does it convey a new narrative. Rather, the inner spaciousness allows Black practitioners to see the falseness of social constructs—*including their own*—and let them fall away. Instead of replacing white supremacist ideas with Black essentialism, meditators strive to embody an inner awareness of what is taking place in their mind and hearts, without comment or judgment. Simply the act of creating awareness, in emptiness and silence, facilitates a liberated way of being, within oneself and in social environments.

Similarly to Gibson, Sensei Alex Kakuya, a priest within the tradition of Pure Land Buddhism, approaches liberation through a daily practice of cultivating emptiness. After attaining a college degree, joining the military, and moving upward in corporate America, Kakuya embraced Zen. He writes in his blog,

> I dotted all of my Is and I crossed all of my Ts. But happiness remained a mystery to me; like the moon on a cloudy night. I knew it was there, but I couldn't see it. . . . My existential hunger was replaced with a spiritual one. And I stayed up at night wondering, "Will my problems go away if I realize enlightenment?" . . . Once I got a taste of the Dharma, I wanted more. So, I gave away all of my possessions and traveled the country; working on organic farms. For eight months, my life was nothing but meditation, sutra study, and hard manual labor. . . . I respond to my endless hunger for more by taking refuge in the daily activities of life. I strive to live in this present moment; only concerning myself with the problems I find therein. And on the frequent occasions when the undying thirst inside me can't be quenched by mundane life, I light the candles on my altar, and I sit in meditation.

As I watch the candle light dance on my altar, my focus shifts inward to the shining light that we all possess. And I remember that I'm Buddha. I remember that I'm enough. And I don't feel hungry or ashamed anymore.[40]

Self-Love, Collective Love, and Sangha

Loving One's Body, Loving One's Self

Amana Brembry Johnson, a teacher in the Insight tradition, connects the practice of liberation to the practice of honoring the body, recognizing the truth of impermanence and interdependence, and extending love to future generations:

> Our practice is about remembering: remembering to come back to the breath, remembering that we are not our thoughts and experiences, remembering to attend to the body with kind awareness—that the present is the only place where the body resides.
>
> Remembering that we are impermanent beings who are only visiting this realm of materiality for a moment in time, and that there will be others to come after us.
>
> Remembering that our lives, and the earthly experiences of everyone and everything around and above us, below us and within us, are sacred—that we are all part of a jeweled web of interconnection and interdependence.[41]

Black Buddhists reference the necessity of self-love in uplifting love for community and the broader society. Pamela Ayo Yetunde, an aspirant in Thich Nhat Hanh's Order of Interbeing and a Community Dharma Leader in the Insight tradition, states simply that self-love motivates people to take care of themselves. Therefore, it is important to cultivate self-love in the practice of meditation. "Love is an animating forced. It is a liberating force. It is an ethical force. And it's inspiring . . . I don't know what motivates someone to take care of themselves if they don't love themselves. We don't talk enough about love except lovingkindness . . . If we don't have enough love we need to start talking about love and talking about adding the capacity to love as a character perfection. And loving-kindness meditation is a way to cultivate that."[42] Self-love is referenced repeatedly in Black Feminist writings. The Combahee River Collective writes, "Our politics evolve from a healthy love for ourselves, our sisters and our community which allows us to continue our struggle and work."[43] Audre Lorde speaks of Black women loving themselves by mothering themselves: extending tender protection and support to the parts of themselves that they have learned to despise.[44] For many Black Buddhist practitioners, the integration of Black Feminism with dharma practice rests upon embodying teachings on love, specifically the Brahmaviharas. Dolores Watson, a long-term practitioner in the Insight tradition, reflects on the importance of offering love to her own person in the early stages of her meditation practice. "The *metta* practice that we do, sending love first to ourselves, [is transformative]. I remember I did a self-retreat in a retreat center in New Mexico. It was a ten-day retreat and the whole ten days I practiced *metta* to myself. I know that when I heal, I can become a vehicle to heal others. And that's why we have to really embrace love for ourselves, not in an egotistical way, but in a transformative way."[45] For Black people, self-love inevitably involves claiming the beauty of the Black body: the dark skin, phenotypes, and hair textures that originate from the African continent.

So, too, does the practice of taking time to *feel*. For many Black Buddhist teachers, the practice of creating space to feel occurs in creative endeavors. Valerie Mason-John, a teacher in the Triratna community and performance poet, advocates for evolving one's healing process in any kind of art form.

> I really want to say that the going from unworthy to worthy is to find your art form, and that might be through sports. I've just got to the point where actually I've reached out to somebody saying, "I want a voice coach. I want to sing. I think that the next thing for me is to be able to sing and use the voice." So, on a practical level, I would say it's first is asking for help. That's the first thing. I remind people again, the prince [Buddha] asked for help. And it can be so hard to ask for help. . . . And then again what's your art form? Do you love to write? And this isn't about thinking oh I'm going to write and I'm going to have to write these big books and have to perform. Just write for yourself and you can decide what you want to do with it afterwards. If it's singing, sing. If it's dancing, dance. So for

me those are the practical things, to say to somebody "sit down and do it with love and kindness . . . sit and meditate."[46]

Creating space and patience to feel discomfort is inherently an act of self-love that ripples outward, writes Rashid Hughes, cofounder of the Heart Refuge Mindfulness Community in Washington, D.C.:

> Compassion and self-preservation are two critical ingredients of my spiritual practice, and ultimately the keys to my spiritual survival. On my own spiritual path, I've often confused compassion with aggression, intellectualizing discomfort rather than feeling hurt, and over attending to the physical and emotional needs of others. This experience of confusion is relatable for many Black, Indigenous, & People of Color (BIPOC) due to our constant need to survive and simultaneously heal the anti-Black racial and social violence that we live in—not to mention the pressures of the global pandemic and political anxiety of the 2020 presidential election. To combat this, the foundation of my activism must remain centered in my humanity and embodied experience, even when it's uncomfortable.
>
> This practice is not selfishness or passivity; this practice is self-preservation.[47]

In the practice of sitting with one's suffering and cultivating compassion, thereby giving oneself the attention that is often sought from other people, Black dharma practitioners are reminded of their basic goodness. Acharya Gaylon Ferguson, author of *Natural Wakefulness* (2010) and *Natural Bravery* (2016), reminds practitioners that "the view of the Buddha is that we are, all of us, fundamentally whole and complete as we are. In some traditions this is call our basic goodness or 'Buddha-nature.'"[48] Lama Dawa Tarchin Phillips refers to this state of wholeness as "belonging," first to the self and then to humanity and the earth. Reflecting on his daily practice of healing, Phillips writes, "It is a practice to release labels; each day that I sit and hold space for the healing of my own amputation, my body reconnects itself to all mankind ever so slightly more than the previous day. I feel a little less isolated and I deepen my sense of belonging and grace."[49]

Thus the teaching that is embodied by practitioners is to create refuge within themselves. In Buddhist lineages, adherents vow to take refuge in the

Buddha, the dharma, and the sangha with the following phrases: "I take refuge in the Buddha; I take refuge in the dharma; I take refuge in the sangha."

Taking Refuge

Justin Miles, a psychotherapist based in Baltimore and community leader in the Shambhala tradition, offers up the three refuges as a starting place for cultivating self-love. Taking refuge in the Buddha is interpreted in different ways: teachers sometimes reflect on the Buddha as a historical figure who attained enlightenment and serves as a role model for all aspirants. Taking refuge in the Buddha is also seen as an antidote to fear, anxiety, and isolation: by embracing one's own capacity to turn to painful feelings, practitioners embody a fearlessness, as did the Buddha when he encountered the forces of Mara prior to his enlightenment. Thus taking refuge in the Buddha is also an interpretation of "Buddha nature," the inherent goodness that Ferguson references that is fundamental to all human beings. By accessing their Buddha nature, meditators take refuge in their own awakening hearts and minds.[50] Miles reflects on the first precept, taking refuge in the Buddha, as a way to care for one's heart, mind, and body:

> We are working with a practice that helps people to take refuge in whoever and whatever it is that feels sane. It doesn't have to be the Buddha, dharma, and sangha. It could be an ancestor, wisdom teaching from another tradition and a group of supportive friends. . . . Taking refuge also involves a commitment to a sort of self-therapy, where I agree to monitor and engage with the process of how I cultivate suffering for myself (and others) through behavior, speech, and mind. Taking refuge is not passive or an act of disowning our stuff. It's engagement with our relative shadows, a ritual of owning of our shit and looking at our projections. [As teachers], we are asking the meditator to rest in a basic sense of sanity but to also explore the insanity that we all experience through our conditioned fixations and projections, and to take time either on their own or in a therapeutic setting to witness and own those projections, not to create bad feelings or self-judgment but because the thoughts and feelings that we love to push out of our awareness are the things that, if you refuse to see them, stay in charge and run your life. We need to take

time to rest the cycle of suffering. We need to take time to directly look at our suffering as well.

Miles describes the process of taking refuge as a process of inner discernment and awareness of what is taking place in one's body and mind. As a psychotherapist focused on psychological and spiritual liberation, he acknowledges not only that it is important to let thoughts rise and pass away but that knowing the content of one's thoughts is a step in psychological liberation:

> We're taught to let thoughts be as they are and that's good, because we're trying to see the process of thinking while calmly resting in the nature of the thoughts. So that's good. So that's what calm abiding practices are for. But then psychology says, the content of those thoughts is also important, because they are the building blocks of my relative self-sense and identity. Engaging with the content of thoughts as an aspect of taking refuge is important. We should ask ourselves questions about how our minds work. What does my suffering have to do with the thoughts that I have? What are my fixations today? What is my relationship to thoughts? How do I relate to them? How do I believe in them? How do I make meaning of the world? And how do I understand my "self"? And so I'm bringing that into actual daily practice where I take refuge in the Three Jewels but also commit to examining my relative sense of self including the needs of my physical body, my aversion or embrace of wisdom and difficult answers, and the quality of my everyday relationships, sangha or not. It's an act of kindness to attend to both my absolute and relative realities.[51]

The integration of psychology and Buddhism in convert Buddhist communities has been documented extensively.[52] Miles, as a practicing psychotherapist, is particularly focused on the mental health of Black people who have suffered intergenerational trauma. In addition to his private therapeutic practice, he leads a Black Power Meditation Liturgy within his sangha in Baltimore, a predominantly Black city with extreme cleavages between wealthy and impoverished communities. Miles also refers to the liturgy as the Awaken Melatonin chant as he seeks to address the specific needs of his Black community. Like many Black Buddhists who work with incarcerated youth and adults, he embraces the integration of dharma teachings with psychological care, recognizing that internalized racism and self-hatred can be effectively healed only when those difficult feelings are fully present and known by the meditator. Miles concludes, "The Buddha nature can shine through Black people."

Similarly to Miles, Kaira Jewel Lingo, a teacher in the Order of Interbeing, encourages people of African descent to cultivate interior stability even as they invest in community:

> When the Buddha was passing away, his final teaching was to take refuge in ourselves, for each person to take refuge in themselves. He talked about it as taking refuge in the island of self, not in any other person or in any other thing but to take refuge in ourselves.
>
> And so, you know, his original insight when he attained awakening under the Bodhi tree was "ah, all beings can do this. They just don't know it. All the way through." There was a through line from there all the way to the end of his life where the last teaching was, "go do it. You have it. It's not outside of you, it's not in any other person, in any other thing. Take refuge in yourself in the island within." Our own awareness is what we take refuge in, our own strength, our own power.[53]

Lingo further acknowledges the importance of community, particularly in the healing of trauma. Thus it is important for Black people to cultivate collective refuge with one another: "We need each other. We need communities of people who practice embodiment, presence, wisdom, so that's another place of refuge that we have to go for refuge. One of the three jewels is the Sangha."[54] Lingo acknowledges that the experience of trauma can facilitate a depth of awareness that, while painful, can be cultivated as a gift:

> There's an opportunity that this experience of not belonging gives us to actually go deeper to find our own belonging in this island within. . . . Sometimes the experience of being rejected from the outside, being told we don't belong, it can be an opportunity for us to find our refuge, our belonging inside of us. We learn to send our roots down deeper to find the sources of water, the nourishment, wherever we can. If it's not in the upper ground soil, we dig deeper till we find it. This is, I think, the only way

those of us of African descent whose parents, whose ancestors, whose blood ancestors survived slavery. The only way they could have survived was by finding some kind of refuge interiorly.[55]

In creating interior refuge, Jylani Ma'at identifies self-love as a starting place in the process of collective healing. This is especially critical in the practice of extending love to traumatized youth:

I just got to be, show up for myself every day and every moment, and face my challenges in my most authentic way, knowing that I am connected to all things and all people. And that's what I get from [meditation practice]. I have in my Yoruba traditions such an incredible love for all earthly things. You know, that was the first tradition that really talked to me about the dirt, and my relationship with the dirt, and the darkness in the dirt, and the birth of my children, and the burying of the placenta, and the connection like all of that, which is coming from a tradition that is long past for me. But I had loving people who were willing to bring that and make it very alive for me right in Brooklyn, simultaneously learning all these other things. And being in an awakened community around Buddhist principles and taking my children there. So this is synergy with all things. The deepest thing in spirit is to really access a sense of deep love for yourself, because without that you are not hearing anything, you are not even alive enough to practice anything, to embrace anything. There's no space for it. You know, it's just the foundation, that is the container for which I hold everything. And I'm working hard as a mom to show that with my children. And the youth that I work with, incarcerated youth, so many of them are so vacant and so void of even believing that love is healthy. The trauma, the layers are so thick.[56]

For many Black Buddhists, the process of turning toward one's own suffering is, indeed, what it means to practice radical self-love.[57] Kamilah Majied, a practitioner in the Japan-based organization Soka Gakkai International, writes that daily chanting creates a refuge for sorrow. Majied recalls learning to turn toward suffering from the practices embraced by her mother, who found refuge in artists such as Billie Holiday:

To me, "Good Morning Heartache" and many other songs my mother sang, said, "What if we were to turn toward the sadness and welcome it?" To appreciate the part of ourselves that is still hopeful enough to *get* sad and worry. Some of us are hurt beyond sadness or worry. Some of us are stuck in rage, despair, or some pretense that everything is cool. When we can feel sadness or worry, it means we are whole and connected to our hearts. So, I started thinking perhaps when grief arises, we could offer ourselves these meditations:

> *Thank you, sorrow, for showing me how big my heart is and how valuable what I am grieving has been to me.*
>
> *Grief is a window that allows me to look back at all that I have had, all that I have been, and all that I have loved and treasured. I am grateful to be able to grieve such wonderful experiences.*[58]

Majied uplifts the practice of peeling away layers, so that practitioners can access the capacity to feel. At the same time, Venerable Pannavati Bhikkhuni says, it is important to still the mind in order to meet hardship without reacting to it. In this process of taking refuge, Pannavati reflects, less energy is directed outward toward others, while meditators cultivate stillness:

Coming up in my early days I was very much a fighter. We talk about spiritual warriors, but I was a straight up street fighter. I really wanted to change that behavior. Although I was a great spiritual practitioner— devotion was my whole life, I was a walking, talking Bible, I basically memorized it, and I understood it—but I still had not managed to master my own emotions. And that's where meditation helped me. When I got to the place when I no longer had to be afraid of myself, that I would act in some sort of way that I would come to regret just five minutes later, then I knew I was on the right path. That's what meditation has done for me. It's allowed me to take my warring attitude, fighting the world, fighting what's out there. And I'm able to go inside. . . . It has allowed me to go inside and I see my own fear, I see my own insecurity, I see my own ignorance, I see my own hatred, my own lust, I see my own greed, and I'm able to neutralize it inside. And when that happens, then what I see outside changes, it's different. This is how meditation has made such an impact in my life. For once I'm not telling you what you should do. I'm looking at what I need to do to have different eyes through which to see. . . . The BuddhaDharma is powerful, that's all I can say . . . Even when we take refuge in the Buddha, dharma, sangha, there's a notion of a reliance, but it's not a forever reliance. It's a reliance in the beginning to give you some confidence that there is something propping you up . . . when you go through the process, you learn to be a lamp unto your own feet, and a light unto your own path. And you learn that everything you need is resident, is available, within.[59]

In loving one's self—the sorrows, grief, shame, as well as the resilience—Black Buddhists speak of a feeling a deep compassion for the suffering of all peoples. As they identify the depth and nuances of their own suffering, they are able to cultivate an inner spaciousness that can be offered to other people in their suffering. Such spaciousness functions on multiple levels: meditators more frequently access an interior openness and fearlessness; they less frequently internalize the damaging messages inflicted by others; and they embody an inner stability that can be offered to other people who are suffering. In being attuned to the suffering of others, they extend solidarity for "all beings," a central prayer in metta practice.

Cultivating self-love and collective love through metta practice transforms suffering, says Sharon Shelton, a teacher in the Insight tradition. In her dharma talk "The Alchemy of Suffering," Shelton asserts,

The alchemical process of transforming suffering happens when we cultivate an abiding awareness and experience of love in its truest forms, expressed by the Buddha as the Brahmaviharas. Instead of clinging to diluted states of heart and mind, not only can this awareness of the omnipresence of love transform a mind that is suffering, but the practice of loving, the act of loving, the doing of loving can keep waking us up. [It] helps us access, activate, reveal our true inherent nature, when it is unclouded by all the clinging, the aversion, the hatred, and delusion.[60]

Sebene Selassie, a teacher in the Insight tradition, reflects that cultivating mindfulness means simultaneously cultivating compassion, that the two "wings" of dharma seamlessly reinforce one another: "[For] Dipa Ma, mindfulness and kindness were two sides of the same coin.[61] I remember the first time I really understood that in my practice. It was like: 'Oh, I am fully mindful right now because I am really caring and loving this moment and myself.'"[62]

The love that arises can coexist alongside painful emotions, Ma'at says. What matters most are intentions and the capacity for self-reflection.

> I breathe in peace and exhale love. In that exchange, I'm also aware of the fact that I'm code switching, because there's anger in there. There might be some mix of hatred in there. There's a mixture of fear in there. And what I'm doing for myself physically, spiritually, emotionally, somatically is being fully aware of, "Okay, this is where I want to go with it and I want my body to be the vessel of that change so that whatever I do, whatever my response is, is coming out better, but processed." I am fully aware that I am processing it. So when I'm saying "breathe in love," that's with patience and acceptance, and forgiveness. And exhale peace, because that affects my direct entry.[63]

Loving-kindness for oneself and others within awareness practice resounds as a core teaching within Western Buddhist lineages. Many teachers identify self-compassion as the cornerstone of sustained practice. Indeed, the capacity to lean directly into difficult feelings such as anger, selfishness, and jealousy and have compassion for oneself facilitates a process of deep healing that, in turn, fosters intimacy and community building among Black meditators.

This orientation toward converging Blackness with Buddhadharma is echoed by Konda Mason, a teacher in the Insight tradition. She points to a passionate love for Black people collectively as an inspiration for her work:

> I just feel like there is just incredible richness at this combination with adding the dharma to who we already are and jazz of it, it's like the jazz of spirituality. It's hard to describe what you know when Miles Davis is playing . . . [but] we are doing the same thing with the dharma and it is because of our nature, what we have inherited, what we have inherited from those who have come before us, and we are holding all of that. And

so we're holding the pain and we're holding the healing. And I believe that the dharma and what we have already, and bringing that together, just feels like the healing that we and our community need. It is sitting right there. [We can] understand it and actually be a part of that deep [collective] healing, when we heal ourselves.[64]

Cultivating collective support and presence is a foundational practice in the emergence of Buddhism among Black communities. In her description of the intention for holding the Deep Time Liberation retreat focused on healing intergenerational trauma, Alexander says healing must take place collectively:

One reason we needed to bring our focus to those from the African diaspora, is, as more and more of us enter into meditation centers, more and more of us are actually beginning to shift our consciousness from "I" to "we." There's a way in which the sangha can actually allow us to awaken together. It allows us to practice together. It allows us to peel apart, so that we're not really feeling in the silo of our practice but we're actually feeling as though there's a new way. It's incredibly powerful. I think that Deep Time Liberation is going to be the marker for bringing people into their practice. Because they will have already gone through much of the healing that's necessary. [Deep Time Liberation] is really forging a new lens into liberation, individual and collective liberation. It has never been done before like this. . . . We're digging deeper and deeper into the questions: How do we belong? What is our belonging? How do we belong in our families?[65]

The themes of belonging, safety, refuge, and connection are highlighted by Black Buddhist teachers and long-term practitioners. For some Black Buddhists who straddle multiple racial and cultural spaces, dharma practice provides an inner container. Myokei Caine-Barrett states that cultivating a sense of "who you really are" is cultivating refuge and that this is the foundation of practice. As a Japanese Black woman straddling racial and cultural divides, she felt divisions fall away in the practice of meditation. "[Practice] provided me with a tremendous sense of belonging when there was no place that I felt I belonged outside."[66] In stillness, there is belonging. Rev. Merle Kodo Boyd writes,

[Zazen's] stillness can appear passive. It can appear to be the opposite of the action I was raised to see as the solution to injustice and suffering, but gradually I have come to see zazen as one of the most radical actions I can take.

Dogen refers to it as "the backward step." It necessitates a confrontation of a different kind than marches and sit ins demanded. Sitting still, it is impossible to escape the busyness, the amorality of one's mind. What gradually becomes clear is the way the mind works, bouncing from one thought to another, evoking first one emotion and then another. Still and silent, accepting all thoughts, emotions, and sensations no matter how painful or disturbing, zazen is the experience of taking a long unblinking look at oneself. Giving clear nonjudgmental attention to everything, true equality becomes evident.[67]

Inner stillness and collective belonging simultaneously reinforce one another. Creating containers in which Black practitioners feel security, mirroring, and resonance with dharma teachers sets the conditions for taking refuge in the sangha.

Love in Community

Love for others extends from love for oneself, assert Black Buddhist teachers and long-term practitioners. As with other teachers, Lev "Fresh" White, a Community Dharma Leader within the Insight tradition, identifies self-compassion as the first step to a sustained practice in which compassion is extended to the community and the world. By treating every human being as one who carries trauma, White says, it is possible to treat even harmful people with compassion.

We can't have a loving and compassionate world if we are going to be angry and aggressive, because we are creating the world we are in. Compassion is being able to have a clear and deep understanding that there is suffering and that this person is suffering because of traumas, whatever their experience is. And that's where they are causing suffering. So, yes, we definitely need to do something to—we can't relieve their suffering, we can only do that so much for ourselves. But certainly we need to relieve him from his charge of causing suffering to others. And can we do that

with our hearts leading? I think so. I think that we can be more successful in our strategy when we are mindfully loving and compassionate in
creating change. I think it's wise to be compassionate and loving in the
strategies, wherever they are. Otherwise we just set up the same system.
So then we go on causing harm.⁶⁸

The commitment to nonharming is at the root of Buddhist precepts.
Sila, the Pali term that refers to morality, discipline, and restraint, is
elaborated in codes of conduct in which adherents abstain from taking
the life of sentient beings, taking possessions without permission, committing sexual misconduct, lying, and imbibing alcohol. Jozen Tamori
Gibson upholds sila alongside the Brahmaviharas, the four faces of love:

> Love is not harming. Love recognizes greed, hatred, and delusion but
> does not embody [those mind states] at all. Love is able to meet greed,
> hatred and delusion with compassion. Love knows when it needs joy in
> its life, when it can really find joy through someone else's well-being, in
> someone else's great fortune. It is how we move through life in a balanced
> way. I'm talking about the Brahmavihara practice. This love is kindness
> and friendliness as *metta*; compassion as *karuna*; sympathetic joy as
> *mudita*; and equanimity as *upekkha*. That to me needs to be a corner-
> stone practice of the POC community or Black community, the African-
> descended community. All of the Brahmaviharas need to be a primary
> practice for us.⁶⁹

Indeed, the language of love, for many Black Buddhists, evokes the
teachings on the Brahmaviharas: loving-kindness, compassion, sympathetic joy, and equanimity. In the Black Radical Tradition, the Brahmaviharas manifest in the commitment to community uplift and solidarity
with oppressed persons. Bhante Buddharakkita identifies compassion
and solidarity with people throughout the world as universal love:

> One devotes loving-kindness to all beings. . . . For me, life is on two lev-
> els. One is horizontal, the other vertical. Horizontal life that means we
> need to survive. We need to produce. That's why we become monks. So
> we need to work, we need to relate, we need to have a stable family. On
> one level we need this. I have called this horizontal whereby we need to

have a meaningful relationship with whatever relationship we have. This is very important. But there is another dimension in life. And I called that vertical. We need to elevate ourselves. We need to be liberated. We need to really make sure that we have met loving-kindness which is going to uplift us so that we are not only loving our mother or our son, but we actually have universal love, which means liberation.[70]

Love and liberation imply protection: in order for people to feel loved and to be fully liberated, individually and communally, they must feel safe and secure. The affinity sanghas established in some traditions, and the institutional commitment to training Black and queer dharma teachers, support different identities in community, so that healing can emerge. Ralph Steele, a veteran of the Vietnam War, and a teacher in the Insight tradition, speaks to the value of establishing inner and outer protection to create a container for love to emerge:

> It's important to have love and be aware of it, but it is also important to be aware of your boundaries. In other words, it's so important to guard like the Buddha would say, your five senses: eyes, nose, ears, etc., to guard your senses, because if you don't guard, then who else is going to guard them? And the world is not full of love. As soon as we get out of our bed, or walk out of our door, then we walk into a loving atmosphere, and we also walk into a war zone. And so learning love is like [drinking] a cup of tea. It is learning how to use that cup of tea. Sometimes you can share it with another person, sometime you can share it with a group and sometimes you can't share it with nobody except yourself. And by sharing it with yourself then you are exemplifying how things should be.[71]

The interweaving of love for oneself and love for others extends toward protection against harm. Protecting Black bodies is a key commitment in the Black Radical Tradition. As Pan-Africanists and Black Power activists elaborated, the threat of attack against Black bodies is an ever-present danger. The ongoing execution of police violence against Black bodies calls forth a response from Black Buddhists who have cultivated the capacity to face trauma and hold space for Black people who continue to be traumatized by state-sanctioned aggression. Black Buddhists rooted in the Black Feminist Tradition name the disproportionate harm enacted against Black women, who experience exploitation and violence not only from white men and women, but also from Black men. In the commitment to protection, love is a guiding force. Black Buddhist teachers and practitioners identify love for Black people as an energy that arises from compassion and inspiration. The awareness that comes in allowing all feelings to be present facilitates an inner spaciousness and ease, a sense of refuge. That safety in community, that compassion for oneself and others, is at the heart of dharma practice. As Justin Miles reflects,

> Love is helping someone experience beauty, and love is about creating space, or even revealing space, which basically means we are getting out of the way and making room for being. Of the love languages, maybe one could be added is being allowed to be, feeling that I can be, that I'm okay, that nothing needs to change, nothing needs to be altered and yet you're still going to be here. That kind of opening of space is the experience of love itself. . . . We need revolutionary movements that are based on things that transcend our differences, but also make room for our differences. And so we need an atmosphere that allows for all of these perspectives and different ways of viewing things to all be present. But I think, again, if you can create that space and have it all be okay, then the community itself feels like it's okay to be whoever they are, and it's okay that we have conflicts, and we may have the same conversations over and over and over again, but we learn how to have them by trying to see into the other person's perspective. So I think that's also love again.[72]

Miles elaborates a theme—acknowledging difference within community and allowing differences to be present without being threatening. Not only have personal reflections by Black Buddhists emphasized the importance of honoring embodied identity and culture, but teachers of African descent have prioritized the creation of retreat spaces and affinity groups to honor difference. As a Black trans teacher in the Shambhala tradition, Shanté Paradigm Smalls not only commits to teaching Black and queer communities during retreats but also advocates building safe communities within larger sanghas. Smalls believes that these "affinity sanghas" are an expression of a "decolonized dharma":

I do feel like that liberation and love come in community. Practicing together, laughing together, creating together—it's become so clear to me
that going on retreat and just practicing together for sixteen hours a day
is not enough. We need to practice, yes. But building little mandalas together, building these little enlightened societies or "Pure Lands," as our
Pure Land friends would say, building these little communities together
that arise, abide, and dissolve—that's where it's at for me.[73]

Liberated community evolves from individual well-being, from
self-love, and from an ability to create safe collective spaciousness for
authentic expression. The seamlessness of prioritizing one's own well-
being and extending that to others in the community—including the
international community—is at the forefront of dharma interpretations,
healing practices, and solidarity with all suffering peoples. Katie elaborates the interconnection of love and liberation in personal practice,
local sangha, and commitment to working on behalf of suffering peoples
throughout the world:

Love taps into the knowing of our true selves as people who are larger
than the ego-minded self. And this can alleviate some of the fear or de-
fensiveness of needing to protect that which we think makes me-me or
mine-mine. So love is, for me, expansive, relaxing, and powerful. For that
reason, I think of the boundless mind that will protect all beings as a
mother, who at the risk of her life, watches over her own and protects her
only child. And a mother, or a nonbinary parent, or a caretaker doesn't
permissively allow a child to unintentionally cause harm to themselves or
others. I don't think love is permissive.

Lastly, I feel like love and fearlessness are good friends, in that love
leads to fearlessness. Love recognizes that there are important things
to protect beyond ourselves. And fearlessness, those few moments that
I've tasted fearlessness through dharma practice, generates so much
gratitude, so much love for the blessing of existence and contact with
the dharma. . . . Love is so real in revolutionary struggle, it's so beautiful. And [revolutionary struggle] wouldn't be as strong and as mighty
and as powerful as it has been if it didn't have so much love coursing
through it. . . . I think I'm specifically in this moment feeling gratitude
for the love of taking risks for each other in solidarity, a sense of

interconnectedness, that the internationalist Black Radical Tradition has supported.[74]

International solidarity and the practice of clear seeing without judgment combine activist and healing work in unprecedented ways. Many practitioners speak of offering love to themselves through a metta practice and cultivating an inner spaciousness that is sometimes referred to as "emptiness." From this self-love and inner spaciousness extends an outpouring of communal love that responds to the historical and contemporary suffering of Black people and the suffering of peoples throughout the world.

Conclusion

Transformative justice requires us, at a minimum, to ask
ourselves questions. . . . I think this is some of the hardest
work. It's not about pack hunting an external enemy, it's
about deep shifts in our own ways of being.
But if we want to create a world in which conflict and trauma
aren't the center of our collective existence, we have to practice something new, ask different questions, access again our
curiosity about each other as a species.
And so much more.
—adrienne maree brown[1]

This book concludes with a note toward vanguard activists who are
working to abolish the police state and broaden inclusivity and healing within activist communities. It asks, what does this distinct form of
Black Buddhist practice mean for vanguard activists who put themselves
in harm's way, on the front lines, expending extraordinary energy in the
broader struggle for social justice? What does Black Buddhist teachings
mean for self-identified abolitionists, community workers, facilitators,
and movement builders? What do they mean for those who self-identify
as queer, lesbian, gay, bisexual, gender-nonconforming, transgender, or
another term that expresses one's gender and/or sexuality? What does it
mean for those who grew up alienated from their families of origin, a
sense of community, and an experience of protection?

Black Buddhists respond: we are born into certain conditions, and
while we struggle to change the *conditions*, we have the capacity to
change our *conditioning*. Buddhism gives Black people a framework for
naming the conditions of externally wrought suffering, but furthermore,
Buddhism offers teachings that help Black people create inner spaciousness and change habitual patterns. If practitioners can compassionately
see their conditioning and the ways that they continue to hurt them-

selves or inflict suffering on those around them, Black Buddhist teachers assert, then practitioners have capacity to step back and to shift those instinctive habits.

Black Buddhist teachers assert that there is tremendous liberation in changing habitual patterns. These teachers embrace Buddhism as a religious tradition that provides practitioners the prescription, the language, the framework, and the practices so that Black people can be liberated.

While being interviewed for this book, Black Buddhist interviewees talked candidly about the fact of working with trauma: the trauma they inherited and the trauma they continue to live through. Violence against Black bodies is perpetual and sustained. In the United States, the reality of white supremacist violence is ever present and institutionalized. Intergenerational trauma is, correspondingly, deeply lodged in the bodies, patterns, and communities of Black people.

Thus, alongside frontline activist work, there is also internal and intracommunal work that is just as profoundly necessary as frontline activism: the work of deep healing. This is the work of drawing in ancestors and being present with the histories that Black people have inherited, fractured and painful as well as supportive and liberative. It is, furthermore, the practice of embodying joy: committing to healing and resilience and the cultivated capacity to offer loving-kindness to oneself and one's community.

The public collective face of Black people has been that of protest, critique, and moral authority. It is critical to stand against overt oppression, but it is also critical that Black people take the time to heal intergenerational trauma. The teachers and long-term practitioners in this book assert resoundingly that Black people have inner lives, psyches, and hearts that require attending and care. This books elevates the importance of making visible the inner lives of Black people.

In short, the generations of trauma inflicted upon Black people, which Black people often unconsciously perpetuate against one another, will not be healed solely by dismantling patriarchal white supremacy. In exerting tremendous energy against external oppression, without taking the time to heal intergenerational trauma, Black people themselves will continue to perpetuate harm on themselves and those who are closest to them. Black lives matter, in the sense that Black *inner* lives matter as much as Black bodies matter. The teachers and practitioners uplifted in this book assert that by taking the time to heal, to embrace stillness, ancestors, and dancing, Black people bestow upon themselves the generative attention they need to live full lives.

Black Buddhist teachers and practitioners offer myriad relevant interpretations of discourses that are thousands of years old. They point to an embodied dharma of resilience, fortitude, presence, and joy by examining the truths of suffering and the practice of freedom from suffering. They point to the Four Noble Truths and the Noble Eightfold Path, the importance of recognizing causes and conditions of suffering, and the practice of the Brahmaviharas: loving-kindness, compassion, sympathetic joy, and equanimity. And they uplift the body as a vehicle for liberation, understanding the body as a sensual expression of inner abundance.

Black Buddhist teachers and long-term practitioners model for Black folk the courage to face dehumanizing patriarchal white supremacist narratives and recognize the inherent falseness of those constructs. In deconstructing the false constructs of patriarchal white supremacy, they are no longer gripped by them. The very psychological freedom espoused in the Black Radical Tradition is embodied in those who turn toward their suffering and walk into it, determined to be free from it. Black Buddhists live into this psychological aspiration in the Black Radical Tradition. They stand still, unmoved by the *mara* attacking them. In their stillness, they are no longer afraid. Rather, they embody the dignity and authority that arise from fearlessness. The courage to compassionately turn toward suffering and give it spaciousness and refuge is, for Black Buddhists, the practice of liberation.

ACKNOWLEDGMENTS

I am indebted to many, many wise members of multilineage Buddhist and other communities, intellectual, spiritual, and ancestral. I remember, first, my spiritual ancestors Thea Jackson, Annie Ruth Powell, and James H. Cone, who conveyed their love and support for me in numerous ways. I also thank, at the outset, Amana Brembry Johnson, who provided the stunning image gracing the cover of this book.

This book was initially inspired by Rev. angel Kyodo williams, my first interviewee, who has for more than two decades posited a "third way" of engaging activist work. Rev. angel's early insights and her enduring commitment to making the dharma relevant for Black people are elaborated throughout this book.

I am also thankful to the numerous early readers of the manuscript, first and foremost Jennifer Hammer, who is everything I could want in an editor. She provided immediate and clear feedback on draft after draft, challenged me and brainstormed with me for many, many months, and consistently conveyed that this project was a priority. The manuscript evolved beautifully as a result of her careful questions and responsiveness. Also, I am grateful to Martin Coleman for providing careful, always timely assistance bringing this project to fruition.

I also am deeply grateful to Pamela Ayo Yetunde, who read an early draft of the manuscript cover-to-cover and gave me copious chapter-by-chapter feedback. This book expanded significantly in response to her suggestions and encouragement. Ayo invited me to participate in a February 2021 "Black and Buddhist Summit," during which she asked several provocative questions, the responses to which are now part of this book. After conducting more than forty interviews, it was refreshing to be interviewed myself. I gained tremendous perspective on how much I had learned in the process of researching and writing over a four-year period.

Other members of my intellectual community also read full versions of this book and likewise made it much stronger. I am particularly indebted to Sarah Hiatt Jacoby, who read the first three draft chapters and offered enthusiastic feedback, and then read an early version of the full manuscript and gave me tremendous response. I am deeply grateful to Sarah for helping me make connections between Black Buddhist practices and Asian Buddhist practices, particularly in the writings of Ambedkar.

Cheryl A. Giles, Duncan Ryūken Williams, and Larry Yang also read full versions of the manuscript and offered critical and supportive assessments. Duncan and Larry, in particular, offered important perspectives on the dynamics between Black, Asian, and white Buddhist communities and pushed me to expand a narrow but often privileged Black-white dynamic. I am indebted to them for their observations, critical writings, and personal experiences within their respective communities.

Other scholars within the Buddhist academic community warmly embraced me as a new colleague and helped me to contextualize this book within Buddhist studies. I am especially thankful to Ann Gleig, Natalie Avalos, and Nalika Gajaweera, for our enthusiastic conversations and forward looking research projects.

Additionally, I am grateful to Warren Wilson College for providing resources for transcription services and for funding a yearlong sabbatical, during which I completed fieldwork and started writing. I also appreciate Dr. Joseph Oduro-Frimpong, who hosted me at Ashesi University in Ghana for six months of my sabbatical.

This book unfolded as I marinated in the tremendous wisdom of Black Buddhist teachers and practitioners. More than forty interviewees generously offered themselves as conversation partners over the course of two and a half years. I am deeply grateful to all who responded to my queries and took the time to talk with me, and to all of the elders I encountered during the process of researching this book. I am conscious of my own financial and time constraints as a researcher, and I recognize that numerous important voices of our extended community are not uplifted in this book. To anyone who feels overlooked, I apologize profusely. My hope is that there will be many future publications, and that all who self-identify as African descended and practice the dharma feel validated and mirrored in this offering.

Many interviews took place through word of mouth networking. I expanded my network with the help of the steering committee that coordinated "The Gathering I" of Black Buddhist Teachers of African Descent at Union Theological Seminary, October 19–21, 2018: Bishop Myokei Caine-Barrett, Acharya Gaylon Ferguson, Jules Shuzen Harris, Konda Mason, Gina Sharpe, and Rev. angel Kyodo williams. Much of the book took shape as I listened to the reflection of the attendees: Chimyo Simone Atkinson, Merle Kodo Boyd, Jozen Tamori Gibson, Kaira Jewel Lingo, Gyozan Royce Johnson, Ruth King, Dr. Kamilah Majied, Lama Rod Owens, Venerable Pannavati Bhkkuni, Amaragita Pearse, Dawa Tarchin Phillips, Gretchen Rohr, Sebene Selassie, Ryūmon Hilda Gutiérrez Baldoquín Sensei, Ralph Steele, Dr. Larry Ward, Spring Washam, DaRa Williams, Dr. Jan Willis, and Dr. Pamela Ayo Yetunde.

"The Gathering II," which took place over a week at Spirit Rock Meditation Center in October 2019, was one of the most profound experiences of my life. It was during this retreat that I looked around and felt an unprecedented sense of belonging. I am thankful to the coordinators— Rev. angel, Myokei, Konda, and Noliwe Alexander—and for the more than seventy Black Buddhist teachers of different lineages who collectively meditated, talked, sang, danced, and engaged in devotional rituals. I honor Femi Akkinagbe, Joshua Bee Alafia, Laurie Amodeo, Chimyo Simone Atkinson, Rachel Bagby, Devin Berry, Leslie Booker, Martina Bouey, Patrick Brown, Eli Brown-Stevenson, Audrey Charlton, Thomas Davis IV, Alisa Dennis, Mabinti Dennis, Angela Dews, Lawrence Ellis, Acharya Gaylon Ferguson, Jozen Tamori Gibson, Dr. Cheryl Giles, Dr. Claudelle Glasgow, Dr. Shahara Godfrey, Dr. Marisela Gomez, Gloria Gostnell, JoAnna Hardy, Phil Hardy, Rashid Hughes, Karla Jackson-Brewer, Amana Brembry Johnson, Gyozan Royce Johnson, Kate Johnson, Solwazi Johnson, Sensei Alex Kakuyo, Shaka Khalphani, Ruth King, Gina LaRoche, Rhonda Magee, Dr. Kamilah Majied, Zenju Earthlyn Manuel, Vimalasara Mason-John, Stacy McClendon, Satyani McPherson, Justin Miles, Lisa Moore, Rev. Seiho (Clear Peak) Morris, Nobantu Mpotulo, Lama Rod Owens, Dawa Tarchin Phillips, Ericka Tiffany Phillips, Dr. Allyson Pimentel, Rev. Sherrilynn (JyakuEn) Posey, Arisika Razak, Gretchen Rohr, Tuere Sala, Anouk Shambrook, Dr. Shanté Paradigm Smalls, Willie Mukei Smith, Syra Smith, Phoenix Soleil, Ralph Steele, Suryagupta, Dr. Jasmine Syedullah, Alice Walker, Dr. Larry Ward,

Dolores Watson, Fresh "Lev" White, DaRa Williams, Dr. Jan Willis, Dr. Pamela Ayo Yetunde, and Sojourner Zenobia.

I also remain deeply thankful for my cohort from the sixth Community Dharma Leader (CDL6) program: Sharon Shelton, Francesca Morfesis, and Sheila Garrick. Even after the CDL6 program closed due to the COVID-19 pandemic, my little group continued to meet and provide much-needed sangha. They have been cheerleaders and conversation partners who responded enthusiastically when I shared quotes during the early stages of writing this book. I am especially grateful to Francesca, my daily sitting partner.

I furthermore am very blessed to be in a group of Black women meditators as part of the Mindfulness Meditation Teacher Certification program that began in February 2021. I am blessed to train and converse with Aishah Shahidah Simmons, Saundra Davis, Rena Marie Guidry, Glenda Gracia, Dolores Watson, and our mentor, Konda. Aishah in particular has been a constant sounding board.

I feel great gratitude and love for dear friends, near and far, who consistently check up on me: Letitia Campbell, Eleanor Harrison Bregman, Olivia Page, Julie Wilson, and Keaton Hill. I am also grateful for the generous presence of Janelle Railey, who has heard me process ups and downs for many years and has consistently supported my practice.

My family is a steady, amazing support system in my life. They buttress my capacity to balance my practice with parenting two active young children and working as an academic. I remain deeply grateful for the constant generosity of my mother, Jude, and stepfather, John, who have given me time and literal space to commit many hours to writing. I am especially appreciative of their willingness to step in and provide child care, shop for groceries, and open their home to us.

My children offer enduring love and playfulness and help me be a more present, embodied being in the world. Matai, my elder child, invites me to cuddle, read books, and make art on a daily basis. Jaxson, my younger son, ensures that I get on the floor to play every single day. Our regular walks and bike rides in the woods of western North Carolina are a lovely, welcome counterbalance to long hours in front of the computer.

Last but certainly not least, I am grateful to my beloved spouse Ethan. He is my biggest cheerleader. This book came to fruition as a result of his love, dedication, many sacrifices, and abundant encouragement.

NOTES

INTRODUCTION

1 The Buddhist community that contains the largest number of African American practitioners is Soka Gakkai International (SGI), based in Japan. While this book addresses the SGI tradition, it encompasses the thinking of teachers and practitioners of several traditions. A study that emphasizes African American participation in SGI would fill a significant scholarly void.

2 Charles S. Prebish and Kenneth K. Tanaka, eds., *The Faces of Buddhism in America* (Berkeley: University of California Press, 1998); Larry Yang, *Awakening Together: The Spiritual Practice of Inclusivity and Community* (Somerville, Mass.: Wisdom, 2017), 45–49.

3 Embracing African traditions is congruent with elements of the Black Power Movement, especially as it emerged in the late 1960s and early 1970s in New York City and elsewhere. See Assata Shakur, *Assata* (1987; Chicago: Led Books, 2001), 183.

4 Rachel Bagby, *Daughterhood: Sounding Hidden Truths, Ignite Your Freedom* (BookNook, 2016).

5 "Healing Justice" is a framework conceptualized by Cara Page. See https://carapage.co.

6 Charlene A. Carruthers, *Unapologetic: A Black, Queer, and Feminist Mandate for Radical Movements* (Boston: Beacon, 2018), 19–20.

7 Ibid., 25.

8 The concept of "negative liberty" relies on concepts of "freedom from" or interference. According to Robin D. G. Kelley, negative liberty includes the rights to own property, to accumulate wealth, to defend property by arms, to mobility, expression, and political participation. See Robin D. G. Kelley, "Foreword," in Angela Y. Davis, *The Meaning of Freedom* (San Francisco: City Lights Books, 2012), 7.

9 Ibid., 7.

10 Angela Y. Davis, "Race, Power, and Prisons since 9/11," in Davis, *Meaning of Freedom*, 84.

11 Sonya Renee Taylor, *The Body Is Not an Apology: The Power of Radical Self-Love* (Oakland, Calif.: Berrett-Koehler, 2021).

12 I am indebted to Aishah Shahidah Simmons and Francesca Morfesis for helping me to clarify these definitions.

13 Charlene Carruthers, in her reflections of leading police accountability and reparations campaigns in Chicago, states directly: "The emotional, physical, and

spiritual cost of putting our bodies and livelihoods on the line for justice has been high." See Carruthers, *Unapologetic*, 132.

14 See, for example, works as varied as Elizabeth Alexander, *Black Interior: Essays* (Minneapolis: Graywolf Press, 2004), and adrienne maree brown, *Pleasure Activism: The Politics of Feeling Good* (Chico, Calif.: AK Press, 2019).

15 Kevin Quashie, *The Sovereignty of Quiet: Beyond Resistance in Black Culture* (New Brunswick, N.J.: Rutgers University Press, 2012), 4.

16 Ibid., 6.

17 Ibid., 21–22.

18 Quashie distinguishes between "quiet" as an active presence and "silence" as a withholding or absence.

19 Joy DeGruy, *Post Traumatic Slave Syndrome: America's Legacy of Enduring Injury and Healing* (2005; Joy DeGruy Publications, 2017), 8.

20 Peter A. Levine, *Waking the Tiger: Healing Trauma* (Berkeley, Calif.: North Atlantic Books, 1997), 24. He writes: "In order to stay healthy, our nervous systems and psyches need to face challenges and to succeed in meeting those challenges. When this need is not met, or when we are challenged and cannot triumph, we end up lacking vitality and are unable to fully engage in life. Those of us who have been defeated by war, abuse, accidents, and other traumatic events suffer far more severe consequences."

21 Arisika Razak, "The Trauma of an American Untouchable," *Lion's Roar*, March 5, 2021, www.lionsroar.com.

22 Kristin N. Williams-Washington and Chmaika P. Mills, "African American Historical Trauma: Creating an Inclusive Measure," *Journal of Multicultural Counseling and Development* 46, no. 4 (October 2018): 246.

23 Ibid., 246.

24 DeGruy, *Post Traumatic Slave Syndrome*, 94.

25 Williams-Washington and Mills, "African American Historical Trauma," 247.

26 Ibid., 248.

27 Chapter 2 provides extensive investigation into historical traumas inflicted upon African-descended people.

28 Author interview with Gretchen Rohr, October 13, 2019.

29 Author interview with Ericka Tiffany Phillips, November 25, 2019.

30 Author interview with Devin Berry, June 24, 2017.

31 Author interview with Joshua Alafia, May 22, 2018.

32 Somatic practices are increasingly embraced as social justice practices. See Staci K. Haimes, *The Politics of Trauma: Somatics, Healing, and Social Justice* (Berkeley, Calif.: North Atlantic Books, 2019).

33 Berry interview.

34 Author interview with Jozen Tamori Gibson, October 31, 2019.

35 Isabel Wilkerson, *The Warmth of Other Suns: The Epic Story of America's Great Migration* (New York: Random House, 2010), 49–50.

36 Author interview with Kabir Hypolite, March 5, 2019.

37 Author interview with Lama Rod Owens, July 15, 2017. Owens further describes his process of healing intergenerational trauma in an essay, "The Dharma of Trauma: Blackness, Buddhism, and Transhistorical Trauma Narrated through Three Ayahuasca Ceremonies," in *Black and Buddhist: What Buddhism Can Teach Us about Race, Resilience, Transformation, and Freedom*, ed. Pamela Ayo Yetunde and Cheryl A. Giles (Boulder, Colo.: Shambhala, 2020), 44–64.

38 Breeshia Wade, "Blackness, Buddhism, and Trauma" (panel, Black and Buddhist Summit, February 24, 2021), www.blackandbuddhistsummit.com.

39 Mark Epstein, *Psychotherapy without the Self: A Buddhist Perspective* (New Haven, Conn.: Yale University Press, 2007), 43.

40 Polly Young-Eisendrath, "The Transformation of Human Suffering: A Perspective from Psychotherapy and Buddhism," *Psychoanalytic Inquiry* 28, no. 5 (November/December 2008): 548.

41 Alan Roland, "Erich Fromm's Involvement with Zen Buddhism: Psychoanalysis and the Spiritual Quest in Subsequent Decades," *Psychoanalytic Review* 104, no. 4 (2017): 503–522.

42 Franz Aubrey Metcalf, "The Encounter of Buddhism and Psychology," in *Westward Dharma: Buddhism beyond Asia*, ed. Charles S. Prebish and Martin Baumann (Berkeley: University of California Press, 2002), 348.

43 Jeffrey B. Rubin, *Psychotherapy and Buddhism: Toward an Integration* (New York: Plenum, 1996), 83.

44 Ann Gleig, "External Mindfulness, Secure (Non)-Attachment, and Healing Relational Trauma: Emerging Models of Wellness for Modern Buddhists and Buddhist Modernism," *Journal of Global Buddhism* 17 (2016): 2. Gleig notes that some of Korda's podcasts are called "Strategies for Dealing with Fear," "A Safe Container for Anxiety," "Buddhism and Attachment Theory," and "How the Buddha Reparented Himself."

45 See Joseph Cheah, *Race and Religion in American Buddhism: White Supremacy and Immigrant Adaptation* (New York: Oxford University Press, 2011), 1–5. See also Ann Gleig, "Undoing Whiteness in American Buddhist Modernism," in *Buddhism and Whiteness: Critical Perspectives*, ed. George Yancy and Emily McRae (Lanham, Md.: Lexington Books, 2019), 21–42.

46 Larry Ward, *America's Racial Karma: An Invitation to Heal* (Berkeley, Calif.: Parallax Press, 2020), 16.

47 Jasmine Syedullah, "The Unbearable Will to Whiteness," in Yancy and McRae, *Buddhism and Whiteness*, 149.

48 Rod Owens, *Radical Dharma: Talking Race, Love, and Liberation* (Berkeley, Calif.: North Atlantic Books, 2016), 18.

49 Ibid., 18.

50 Sharon Suh, "'We Interrupt Your Regularly Scheduled Programming to Bring You This Very Important Public Service Announcement . . .': aka Buddhism as Usual in the Academy," in Yancy and McRae, *Buddhism and Whiteness*, 3.

51 Rita Gross's groundbreaking text, *Buddhism after Patriarchy: A Feminist History, Analysis, and Reconstruction of Buddhism*, critiqued the sexism espoused in early Buddhist texts and Asian communities. Her work was hailed as pioneering in its efforts to support diversity but nonetheless omitted issues of racism and cultural appropriation. Gross's book was also routinely condemned for taking early Buddhist texts out of context and other omissions. See Hsiao-Lan Hu, "The White Feminism in Rita Gross's Critique of Gender Identities and Reconstruction of Buddhism," in Yancy and McRae, *Buddhism and Whiteness*, 294.

52 Ann Gleig, *American Dharma: Buddhism beyond Modernity* (New Haven, Conn.: Yale University Press, 2019).

53 Yang, *Awakening Together*, 45. Yang defines culture as "the dynamic, ever-changing way in which a group of people lives together, including their conscious and unconscious behaviors, attitudes, norms, values, institutions, and symbols. This collection of characteristics is communicated verbally and nonverbally, transmitted from generation to generation, and constantly created, collected, and transformed in the process."

54 Ibid., 47–48.

55 See chapter 1, "The Tradition of Buddhism: Lineages, Culture, Race, and Liberation," for more details.

56 JoAnna Hardy, "Cultural Appropriation and Spiritual Bypass" (dharma talk, Race and Dharma, Barre Center for Buddhist Studies, April 29, 2019).

57 Nalika Gajaweera, "Sitting in the Fire Together: People of Color Cultivating Radical Resilience in North American Insight Meditation," *Journal of Global Buddhism* (forthcoming). See also David L. McMahan, *The Making of Buddhism Modernism* (New York: Oxford University Press, 2008), 31–33, 36.

58 Two examples are people of color affinity groups and LGBTQIA affinity groups.

59 Ruth King, *Mindful of Race: Transforming Racism from the Inside Out* (Boulder, Colo.: Sounds True, 2018), 46.

60 There has been a dramatic increase in the number of teachers and practitioners of African descent in the Insight/Vipassana community due to concerted efforts by the Spirit Rock Retreat Center and Insight Meditation Society (IMS) to hold POC annual retreats as well as reserve spaces for and fund POC in IMS's three-month retreat. At the time of writing, both of these major retreat centers are holding teacher training programs. POC constitute 90 percent of teachers in training at Spirit Rock and 75 percent of teachers in training at IMS. Larry Yang's research illuminates that prior to the 2020 teacher training, Spirit Rock trained one African American in 2002, one African American and two mixed-race Black in 2010, and two African American teachers in 2016. For a detailed description of the efforts of IMS and Spirit Rock to recruit and train teachers of color, see Ann Gleig, *American Dharma*, 168–172.

61 Black Lives Matter, "About" (n.d.), https://blacklivesmatter.com.

62 Movement for Black Lives' Policy Brief, "End the War on Black Trans, Queer, Gender Nonconforming, and Intersex People" (2021), https://m4bl.org.

63 Michelle Fine, Maria Elena Torre, Kathy Boudin, et al., "Changing Minds: The Impact of College in a Maximum-Security Prison" (Prison Policy Initiative, January 2001), www.prisonpolicy.org.

1. THE TRADITION OF BUDDHISM

1 Hilda Gutiérrez Baldoquín, "Introduction," in *Dharma, Color, and Culture: New Voices in Western Buddhism*, ed. Baldoquín (Berkeley, Calif.: Parallax Press, 2004), 18.

2 Author interview with Joshua Bee Alafia, May 22, 2018.

3 Pamela Ayo Yetunde, "Buddhism in the Age of #Blacklivesmatter," *Lion's Roar*, May 27, 2020, www.lionsroar.com, emphasis added.

4 There are numerous debates on the exact dates of the Buddha's birth and death. John Powers puts the Buddha's birth at 422 BCE and death at 399 BCE (Powers, *Introduction to Tibetan Buddhism*, rev. ed. [Ithaca, N.Y.: Snow Lion, 2007], 515). Richard F. Gombrich argues that the Buddha likely died in 400 or 404 BCE (Gombrich, *Theravada Buddhism: A Social History from Ancient Benares to Modern Colombo*, 2nd ed. [New York: Routledge, 2006], 32). Paul Williams places the death of the Buddha much later, 370 or 368 BCE (Williams, *Mahayana Buddhism: The Doctrinal Foundations* [New York: Routledge, 1989], 9). Scholars of Buddhism agree that the Buddha lived a total of eighty years.

5 Donald W. Mitchell and Sarah H. Jacoby, *Buddhism: Introducing the Buddhist Experience*, 3rd ed. (New York: Oxford University Press, 2014), 47.

6 These teachings will be spelled out in greater detail in chapter 5.

7 Author interview with Valerie Mason-John (Vimalasara), July 11, 2017.

8 Charles Johnson, "Reading the Eightfold Path," in Baldoquín, *Dharma, Color, and Culture*, 127.

9 Mitchell and Jacoby, *Buddhism*, 52.

10 Gombrich, *Theravada Buddhism*, 93. The codes would have been developed at the Second Buddhist Council at Vaisali. See Powers, *Introduction to Tibetan Buddhism*, 515.

11 Gombrich, *Theravada Buddhism*, 3. At the time, Sri Lanka was known as Ceylon.

12 Chapter 5 elaborates how Black Buddhists interpret these core Buddhist teachings.

13 Mitchell and Jacoby, *Buddhism*, 19.

14 Sebene Selassie, "The Five Aggregates" (dharma talk, Race and Dharma Course, Barre Center for Buddhist Studies, April 22, 2018).

15 David Snellgrove, *Indo-Tibetan Buddhism: Indian Buddhists and Their Tibetan Successors* (Boston: Shambhala, 2002), 44.

16 Ibid., 45. See also Powers, *Introduction to Tibetan Buddhism*, 515.

17 Many scholars of Buddhism point to the distinction between Theravada and Mahayana Buddhism as one that centers on the figure of the Bodhisattva. One narrative of historical Buddhism, as a tradition, focuses on critiques of early Buddhism as emphasizing individual enlightenment as an *Arahat* (a solitary

realizer and hearer) as opposed to becoming enlightened but choosing to stay in the realm of sentient beings to help others become enlightened. Some Mahayana adherents called early Buddhism "Hinayana" (lesser vehicle) in contrast with their self-identified "Mahayana" (greater vehicle) interpretation. The term "Hinayana" is considered offensive; adherents of early Buddhism identify their tradition as "Theravada" (the Way of the Elders).

18 James Blumenthal, "Indian Mahayana Buddhism," in *Companion to Buddhist Philosophy*, ed. Steve M. Emmanuel (Hoboken, N.J.: John Wiley, 2013), chap. 5.

19 This is but one example of how Mahayana teachings were adapted to the cultural context of China.

20 Williams, *Mahayana Buddhism*, 55–56, 77.

21 Ibid., 77–78.

22 Ibid., 77.

23 Tendai and Pure Land teachings appeared as schools of thought in Zen shortly thereafter. These three sects became the most visible and well known in China.

24 Heinrich Dumoulin, *Zen Buddhism: A History*, vol. 1: *India and China* (Bloomington, Ind.: World Wisdom, 2005), 97.

25 See chapter 6 for further details on Vajrayana Buddhism.

26 For detailed descriptions of different Buddhist lineages in the United States, see Richard Hughes Seager, *Buddhism in America* (New York: Columbia University Press, 1999) and Charles Prebish and Kenneth Tanaka, eds., *The Faces of Buddhism in America* (Berkeley: University of California Press, 1998).

27 Theravada Buddhism in Burma and Thailand became known as "Insight" in the West and claims a significant number of Black practitioners, due to strategic support from established meditation centers such as the Insight Meditation Society and Spirit Rock Meditation Center. Japanese Buddhist sects, particularly Nichiren Shoshu and Soka Gakkai, claim a significant number of Black adherents, as do Soto and Rinzai Zen sects. Chinese Buddhism, especially Pure Land sects, draw in Black practitioners. Not least, Black practitioners and teachers claim Tibetan Buddhism, namely the Kagyu school and the Shambhala sect.

28 David McMahan, *The Making of Buddhist Modernism* (New York: Oxford University Press, 2018), 5.

29 Joseph Cheah, *Race and Religion in American Buddhism: White Supremacy and Immigrant Adaptation* (New York: Oxford University Press, 2011), 34.

30 Ibid., 33.

31 Ibid., 30–31.

32 Ibid., 23–24. See also Thomas Tweed, *The American Encounter with Buddhism 1844–1912: Victorian Culture and the Limits of Dissent* (Chapel Hill: University of North Carolina Press, 2000).

33 McMahan, *Making of Buddhist Modernism*, 6. He notes that "this new form of Buddhism . . . has been, therefore, a co-creation of Asians, Europeans, and Americans."

34 Ann Gleig, *American Dharma: Buddhism beyond Modernity* (New Haven, Conn.: Yale University Press, 2019), 9.

35 Several of the founders of prominent meditation centers in the United States, in particular Joseph Goldstein, Sharon Salzberg, and Jack Kornfield, who cofounded Insight Meditation Society, studied with Mahasi Sayadaw and Ajahn Chah. Kornfield later cofounded Spirit Rock Meditation Center in Northern California. For reference, see the following books on the development of Insight meditation in the United States: Eric Braun, *The Birth of the Insight: Meditation, Modern Buddhism, and the Burmese Monk Ledi Sayadaw* (Chicago: University of Chicago Press, 2013); Wendy Cadge, *Heartwood: The First Generation of Theravada Buddhism in America* (Chicago: University of Chicago Press, 2005); Charles Prebish, *Luminous Passage: The Practice and Study of Buddhism in America* (Berkeley: University of California Press, 1999), 148–158.

36 Gleig, *American Dharma*, 11.

37 Ibid., 12.

38 Richard Hughes Seager, *Encountering the Dharma: Daisaku Ikeda, Soka Gakkai, and the Globalization of Buddhist Humanism* (Berkeley: University of California Press, 2006).

39 Aishwary Kumar, *Radical Equality: Ambedkar, Gandhi, and the Risk of Democracy* (Stanford, Calif.: Stanford University Press, 2015), 1.

40 Vidhu Verma, "Reinterpreting Buddhism: Ambedkar on the Politics of Social Action," *Economic and Political Weekly*, December 4, 2010, www.epw.in.

41 Sallie B. King, *Socially Engaged Buddhism* (Honolulu: University of Hawai'i Press, 2009), 26.

42 "The Order of Interbeing, Tiep Hien in Vietnamese, is a community of monastics and lay people who have committed to living their lives in accord with the Fourteen Mindfulness Trainings, a distillation of the Bodhisattva (Enlightened Being) teachings of Mahayana Buddhism. Established by Venerable Thich Nhat Hanh in Saigon in 1966, the Order of Interbeing was founded in the Linji tradition of Buddhist meditative practice and emphasizes the four spirits: non-attachment from views, direct experimentation on the nature of interdependent origination through meditation, appropriateness, and skillful means." See Thich Nhat Hanh Foundation, https://thichnhathanhfoundation.org. Nhat Hanh seeks to appeal to Western audiences. He founded the Order of Interbeing (1966) and the Unified Buddhist Church (1968) and later Plum Village, his monastic order in France (https://plumvillage.org).

43 Thich Nhat Hanh, *Love Letter to the Earth* (Berkeley, Calif.: Parallax Press, 2013), 44–45.

44 Ibid., 56.

45 Thich Nhat Hanh, *Being Peace* (Berkeley, Calif.: Parallax Press, 1996), 80.

46 The Dalai Lama, *Freedom in Exile* (New York: HarperCollins, 1990), 202.

47 Ibid., 124, 265. The Dalai Lama describes methods of torture such as "crucifixion, vivisection, disemboweling and dismemberment of victims were commonplace." He notes that as of 1990 "almost one and a quarter million Tibetans lost their lives from starvation, execution, torture, and suicide, and tens of thousands lingered in

prison camps" (149). Furthermore, China continues to produce nuclear weaponry in Tibet and to dump nuclear waste (some of it received from other countries) in Tibetan rural areas, causing environmental destruction and illnesses.

48 Ibid., 227, 268.

49 Ibid., 204–205.

50 Bernie Glassman and Rick Fields, *Instructions to the Cook: A Zen Master's Lessons in Living a Life That Matters* (Boston: Shambala, 1996), 51.

51 Ibid., 93.

52 Ibid., 99.

53 Sociological research by Paul David Numrich illuminated the different forms of practice between immigrants and their descendants, who offered merit and engaged in devotional practices, often in the same buildings as white converts who meditated and engaged in Buddhist philosophical conversations. See Wakoh Shannon Hickey, "Two Buddhisms, Three Buddhisms, and Racism," in *Buddhism Beyond Borders: New Perspectives on Buddhism in the United States*, ed. Scott Mitchell and Natalie E. F. Quli (Albany: State University of New York Press, 2015), 36. See also Cheah, *Race and Religion in American Buddhism*, 7.

54 Hickey, "Two Buddhisms," 40–41.

55 To understand the distinct experiences of young Asian American Buddhists, see Chenxing Han, *Be the Refuge: Raising the Voices of Asian American Buddhists* (Berkeley, Calif.: North Atlantic Books, 2021).

56 Cheah, *Race and Religion in American Buddhism*, 71–76. See also Larry Yang, *Awakening Together: The Spiritual Practice of Inclusivity and Community* (Somerville, Mass.: Wisdom, 2017).

57 Hickey, "Two Buddhisms," 41.

58 Helen Tworkov, quoted in Cheah, *Race and Religion in American Buddhism*, 76.

59 Hickey, "Two Buddhisms," 43.

60 See Cheah, *Race and Religion in American Buddhism*, 77. See also Funie Hsu, "We've Been Here All Along: The Exclusion of Asian and Asian American Buddhists from Conversations on American Buddhism Is Cultural Appropriation," *Huffington Post*, November 29, 2017, www.huffpost.com. Hsu writes, "Rev. Imamura was also speaking quite literally. After their incarceration, his father and mother, Rev. Kanmo and Jane Imamura, established the Buddhist Study Center of Berkeley, where they hosted eminent teachers and welcomed Asian, Asian American, and white practitioners alike. Gary Snyder, Jack Kerouac, and Alan Watts were among the 'countless white Americans' who learned about Buddhism from their study groups. The lectures and events were all free of charge, including the hot tea and pastries set out by Jane Imamura to welcome the attendees. It is important to note that Jane's father, Rev. Issei Matsuura, was one of the first Buddhist priests to be arrested by the FBI and imprisoned at the start of World War II. As a priest, he was viewed as an especially dangerous threat to national security. That the Imamura family would go on to openly and freely share the buddhadharma in America after being imprisoned by the U.S. government for their cul-

tural/spiritual beliefs is a notable example of the ways in which Asian American Buddhists have labored to maintain their practice and make it available to others, despite white supremacy. Yet the Imamuras' historical contribution in cultivating a new generation of American Buddhists—including white Buddhists—were left out of the mainstream conversation on Buddhism. Rev. Ryo Imamura's letter was rejected from *Tricycle* and never published."

61 Hickey, "Two Buddhisms," 44.

62 Cheah, *Race and Religion in American Buddhism*, 77.

63 Ibid., 79.

64 Ibid., 79.

65 Ibid., 66, 79.

66 Ann Gleig writes at length about this phenomenon in an essay on how Buddhist teachings serve people who are in recovery from addiction. See Gleig, "External Mindfulness, Secure (Non)-Attachment, and Healing Relational Trauma: Emerging Models of Wellness for Modern Buddhists and Buddhist Modernism," *Journal of Global Buddhism* 17 (2016): 1–21. See also Gleig, "Wedding the Personal and Impersonal in West Coast Vipassana: A Dialogical Encounter between Buddhism and Psychotherapy," *Journal of Global Buddhism* 13 (2012): 129–146.

67 Hsu, "We've Been Here All Along," 7.

68 The five precepts are to abstain from (1) killing, (2) stealing, (3) sexual misconduct, (4) wrong speech, and (5) the use of intoxicants.

69 Hsu, "We've Been Here All Along," 7.

70 Ibid., 7.

71 Mae M. Ngai, *Impossible Subjects: Illegal Aliens and the Making of Modern America* (Princeton, N.J.: Princeton University Press, 2014); Rima Vesely-Flad, *Racial Purity and Dangerous Bodies: Moral Pollution, Black Lives, and the Struggle for Justice* (Minneapolis, Minn.: Fortress Press, 2017).

72 Duncan Ryūken Williams, "The Karma of a Nation: Racial Reparations from an Asian American Buddhist Perspective" (Buddhism and Race Conference, Harvard Divinity School, March 16, 2021), www.youtube.com/watch?v=8k3sr-5wQWo.

73 Ibid., 34 minutes.

74 Ibid., 34 minutes.

75 Ellen D. Wu, *The Color of Success: Asian Americans and the Origins of the Model Minority* (Princeton, N.J.: Princeton University Press, 2014). Wu argues that Asian Americans were elevated and held up as role models for assimilation and meritocracy, in contrast especially to African Americans.

76 Nanjini Rathi, "Black Lives Matter: South Asian Americans Come to Terms with Own Anti-Blackness," *Indian Express*, June 18, 2020, https://indianexpress.com.

77 Reshmi Dutt-Ballerstadt, "Colonized Loyalty: Asian American Anti-Blackness and Complicity," *Truthout*, June 26, 2020, https://truthout.org.

78 Ivjay Iyer, "Our Complicity with Excess" (Asian American Writers' Workshop, May 7, 2014), https://aaww.org; "Mom, Dad, Uncle, Auntie, Grandfather, Grand-

mother, Family" (Letters for Black Lives, June 7, 2020), https://lettersforblacklives.com.

79 I am indebted to my colleague Dr. Sarah Jacoby, associate professor of religious studies at Northwestern University, for helping me clarify and expand these insights.

80 Interview with Kate Lila Wheeler, March 9, 2021. As a co-coordinator of the Spirit Rock Meditation Center 2016–2020 teacher training program, Wheeler has worked closely with teachers of color to illuminate and shift patterns of patriarchy and racism.

81 Author interview with Larry Yang, March 1, 2021.

82 angel Kyodo williams, *Being Black: Zen and the Art of Living with Fearlessness and Grace* (New York: Viking, 2000), 6.

83 Reissued in 2008, the book's revised title is *Dreaming Me: Black, Baptist, and Buddhist, One Woman's Spiritual Journey.*

84 Jan Willis, *Dreaming Me: An African American Woman's Spiritual Journey* (New York: Riverhead Books, 2001), 149.

85 The teachers who participated in the August 15–20, 2002, retreat are as follows: From the Theravada tradition: Rachel Bagby, Marlene Jones, Ralph Steele, Venerable Suhitananda Dharma. From the Zen tradition: Ryūmon Hilda Guitiérrez Baldoquín, Lawrence Ellis, Sala Steinbach, and angel Kyodo Williams. From the Vajrayana tradition: Acharya Gaylon Ferguson, Choyin Rangdrol, Jan Willis, and Lewis Woods. From the Pure Land tradition: Joseph Jarma and Thulani Davis. Across traditions: Alice Walker and Konda Mason. Author email message with Zenju Earthlyn Manuel and Larry Yang, August 12, 2021. I am indebted to both teachers for their assistance in researching this gathering.

86 Zenju Earthlyn Manuel, *The Way of Tenderness: Awakening through Race, Sexuality, and Gender* (Somerville, Mass.: Wisdom, 2015), 22.

87 Manuel, *Way of Tenderness*, 11.

88 angel Kyodo williams, Rod Owens, and Jasmine Syedullah, *Radical Dharma: Talking Race, Love, and Liberation* (Berkeley, Calif.: North Atlantic Books, 2016), xxi.

89 Ibid., xxvi–xxvii.

90 Williams, *Radical Dharma*, xxxi.

91 Charles Johnson, *Taming the Ox: Buddhist Stories and Reflections on Politics, Race, Culture, and Spiritual Practice* (Boston: Shambhala, 2014).

92 Sheryl Petty, *Ocha Dharma: The Relationship between Lucumi, and African-Based Tradition, and Buddhist Practice* (Movement Tapestries, 2016); Valerie Mason-John, *Detox Your Heart: Meditations for Healing Emotional Trauma* (Somerville, Mass.: Wisdom, 2017).

93 Spring Washam, *A Fierce Heart* (New York: Hay House, 2017), 13.

94 Author interview with Ruth King, May 2, 2018.

95 Ruth King, *Mindful of Race: Transforming Racism from the Inside Out* (Boulder, Colo.: Sounds True, 2018), 1.

96 Angela Dews, *Still, in the City: Creating Peace of Mind in the Midst of Urban Chaos* (New York: Skyhorse, 2018), xvii.

2. FROM THE PLANTATION TO THE PRISON

1 Assata Shakur, *Assata: An Autobiography* (Chicago: Lawrence Hill Books, 1987), 52.

2 Willie Jennings, *The Christian Imagination: Theology and the Origins of Race* (New Haven, Conn.: Yale University Press, 2010).

3 Donald W. Mitchell and Sarah H. Jacoby, *Buddhism: Introducing the Buddhist Experience* (New York: Oxford University Press, 2014), 37–41.

4 Gomes Eannes de Azurara, *The Chronicle of the Discovery and Conquest of Guinea*, vol. 1 (London: Hakluyt Society, 1896), 81. Religion scholar Willie James Jennings notes that Azurara's description is not the first time the words "white" and "Black" indicate something like identity. Their anthropological use in the Iberian and North African regions has an episodic history that extends well before Azurara's utterances. Azurara, however, exhibits an aesthetic that was growing in power and reach as the Portuguese and Spanish began to join the world they imagined with the world they encountered through travel and discovery. Thus, while terms like "race" were not yet used, an aesthetic that furthered distinctions based upon skin color was becoming an authoritative tool for demarcation between peoples. See also Jennings, *Christian Imagination*, 23.

5 Quoted in Luis N. Rivera, *A Violent Evangelism: The Political and Religious Conquest of the Americas* (Louisville, Ky.: Westminster John Knox, 1992), 134.

6 The pope, as monarch, directed the mission of bringing the world to Christ. See R. N. Swanson, "The Pre-Reformation Church," in *The Reformation World*, ed. Andrew Pettegree (London: Routledge, 2000).

7 Quoted in Nicolás Wey Gómez, *The Tropics of Empire: Why Columbus Sailed South to the Indies* (Cambridge, MA: MIT Press, 2008), 291.

8 Quoted in Jennings, *Christian Imagination*, 35.

9 Ibid., 33–34.

10 Some contemporary scholars suggest that narratives of European superiority created trauma in which descendants feel shame for their forebears' destruction and conquest. See Resmaa Menakem, *My Grandmother's Hands: Racialized Trauma and the Pathway to Mending Our Hearts and Bodies* (Las Vegas: Central Recovery Press, 2017).

11 Cornel West, *Prophesy Deliverance* (1982; Louisville, Ky.: Westminster John Knox, 2002), 48.

12 Carl von Linné, "The God-Given Order of Nature," excerpted in *Race and the Enlightenment: A Reader*, ed. Emmanuel Chukwudi Eze (Malden, Mass.: Blackwell, 1997), 13.

13 Mark Larrimore, "Sublime Waste: Kant on the Destiny of the 'Races,'" in *Civilization and Oppression*, ed. Cheryl J. Misak (Calgary: University of Calgary Press, 1999), 101. Larrimore explains that the word *Race* had only recently entered the German language from the French and, when not used for animals (especially

horses), was used interchangeably with words like *Geschlecht, Gattung,* and *Art* to denote kind or lineage. In England and France, it was also used inconsistently.

14 Immanuel Kant, "Of the Different Human Races," in Eze, *Race and the Enlightenment*, 11.

15 Robert Bernasconi, "Who Invented the Concept of Race? Kant's Role in the Enlightenment Construction of Race," in *Race*, ed. Robert Bernasconi (Malden, Mass.: Blackwell, 2001), 24.

16 Ibid.

17 Immanuel Kant, *Critique of Judgment* (Mineola, N.Y.: Dover, 2005), 166–167.

18 Bernasconi, "Who Invented the Concept of Race?," 23–26.

19 Larrimore, "Sublime Waste," 106–107.

20 It is important to note that Kant wrote and lectured on many different peoples, not just Africans, and often placed Americans far below Africans in the hierarchies of peoples he acknowledged.

21 Kant, "Of the Different Human Races," in Eze, *Race and the Enlightenment*, 12.

22 Ibid., 17.

23 Quoted in Robert Bernasconi, "Kant as an Unfamiliar Source of Racism," in *Philosophers on Race: Critical Essays*, ed. Julie K. Ward and Tommy L. Lott (Oxford: Blackwell, 2002), 152, from Kant's unpublished notes (AA, XV/2, p. 878).

24 Ibid., 152.

25 Quoted in ibid., 158; see also Larrimore, "Sublime Waste," 111.

26 J. Kameron Carter, *Race: A Theological Account* (New York: Oxford University Press, 2008), 88.

27 Orlando Patterson, *Slavery and Social Death: A Comparative Study* (Cambridge, Mass.: Harvard University Press, 1982), 7–13. He writes: "A slave could have no honor because he had no power and no independent social existence, hence no public worth. He had no name of his own to defend. He could only defend his master's worth and his master's name. That dishonor was a generalized condition must be emphasized, since the free and honorable person, ever alive to slights and insults, occasionally experiences and responds to specific acts of dishonor. The slave usually stood outside the game of honor." Ibid., 10–11.

28 Angela Y. Davis, "Rape, Racism, and the Myth of the Black Rapist," in *Women, Race, and Class* (New York: Vintage, 1983), 175.

29 Calvin Schermerhorn, *Money over Mastery, Family over Freedom: Slavery in the Antebellum Upper South* (Baltimore: Johns Hopkins University Press, 2011), 4.

30 Frederick Douglass, *Narrative of the Life of Frederick Douglass, an American Slave* (New York: Millennium, 2014), 47.

31 Ibid., 81.

32 Anne C. Bailey, *The Weeping Time: Memory and the Largest Slave Auction in American History* (New York: Cambridge University Press, 2017), 4–5, emphasis added.

33 Mark Thornton et al., "Selling Slave Families Down the River: Property Rights and the Public Auction," *Independent Review* 14, no. 1 (2009): 74.

34 Ibid., 75–76.

35 Katherine McKittrick, *Demonic Grounds: Black Women and the Cartographies of Struggle* (Minneapolis: University of Minnesota Press, 2006), 85.

36 Ibid., 71–72.

37 Ibid., 80–81.

38 Author interview with Konda Mason, November 2, 2019.

39 Andrea J. Ritchie, *Invisible No More: Police Violence Against Black Women and Women of Color* (Boston: Beacon, 2017), xv.

40 Alex Lichtenstein, *Twice the Work of Free Labor: The Political Economy of Convict Leasing in the South* (New York: Verso, 1996), 2.

41 Edward L. Ayers, *Vengeance and Justice: Crime and Punishment in the 19th-Century South* (New York: Oxford University Press, 1984), 151.

42 Douglass A. Blackmon, *Slavery by Another Name: The Re-enslavement of Black Americans from the Civil War to World War II* (New York: Random House, 2008), 90.

43 Lichtenstein, *Twice the Work*, 1–151, esp. 134–135; Blackmon, *Slavery by Another Name*, 56. Over eight decades, there were rarely penalties to industrialists who were leasing former slaves for their mistreatment or deaths.

44 Matthew J. Mancini, *One Dies, Get Another: Convict Leasing in the American South, 1866–1928* (Columbia: University of South Carolina Press, 1996).

45 David M. Oshinsky, *Worse Than Slavery: Parchman Farm and the Ordeal of Jim Crow Justice* (New York: Free Press Paperbacks, 1996), 59.

46 Ida B. Wells, *The Red Record: Tabulated Statistics and Alleged Causes of Lynching in the United States* (1895), www.gutenberg.org. See also Davis, "Rape, Racism, and the Myth of the Black Rapist," 184. Historians speculate that all Black people in the South were directly impacted or knew someone who was directly impacted by lynchings.

47 Davis, "Rape, Racism, and the Myth of the Black Rapist," 185.

48 Ibid., 186. See also Isabel Wilkerson, *The Warmth of Other Suns: The Epic Story of America's Great Migration* (New York: Random House, 2010), 39.

49 A. Philip Randolph, "Lynching: Capitalism Its Cause; Socialism Its Cure (1919)," in *For Jobs and Freedom: Selected Speeches and Writings of A. Philip Randolph*, ed. Andrew E. Kersten and David Lucander (Amherst: University of Massachusetts Press, 2013), 116–122.

50 Wilkerson, *Warmth of Other Suns*, 40–41.

51 Ibid., 9.

52 John R. Logan, Weiwei Zhang, Richard Turner, and Allison Shertzer, "Creating the Black Ghetto: Black Residential Patterns before and during the Great Migration," *Annals of the American Academy of Political and Social Science* 660 (2015): 19.

53 There are numerous volumes documenting this phenomenon. See, for example, Massey and Denton, *American Apartheid: Segregation and the Making of the Underclass* (Cambridge, Mass.: Harvard University Press, 1993).

54 Stewart E. Tolnay, "The African American 'Great Migration' and Beyond," *Annual Review of Sociology* 29 (2003): 221.

55 Sabina G. Arora, *The Great Migration and the Harlem Renaissance* (New York: Encyclopedia Britannica, 2016).

56 George Mumford, "Mind Like a Mirror," in *Dharma, Color, and Culture: New Voices in Western Buddhism*, ed. Hilda Gutiérrez Baldoquín (Berkeley, Calif.: Parallax Press, 2004), 86.

57 Author interview with Bushi Yamato Damashii, July 15, 2017.

58 Movement for Black Lives, "End the War on Black People" (2021), https://m4bl.org.

59 Beth E. Richie, *Arrested Justice: Black Women, Violence, and America's Prison Nation* (New York: New York University Press, 2012), 3.

60 Marc Mauer, *Race to Incarcerate* (New York: New Press, 1999), 142–161; Steven R. Donziger, ed., *The Real War on Crime: Report of the National Criminal Justice Commission* (New York: Harper Perennial, 1996), 24–27.

61 Devah Pager, *Marked: Race, Crime, and Finding Work in an Era of Mass Incarceration* (Chicago: University of Chicago Press, 2007), 11.

62 Jamie Fellner, *Decades of Disparity: Drug Arrests and Race in the United States* (New York: Human Rights Watch, 2009).

63 Joel Dyer, *The Perpetual Prisoner Machine: How America Profits from Crime* (Boulder, Colo.: Westview, 2000), 154, 168, 171. Similar laws that had existed one hundred years earlier had been deemed ineffective, overly costly, unjust, and fuel for dangerous conditions within prisons. States seeking federal funding are required to adhere to truth in sentencing policies in order to receive grants.

64 Other tough-on-crime legislation has been enacted as well. "Three-strikes" statutes mandate that an individual who has committed three crimes must be incarcerated under a life sentence for the third crime. First enacted in California in 1994, three-strikes laws can be applied to nonviolent as well as violent offenses. See Dyer, *Perpetual Prisoner Machine*, 157. The death penalty, like three-strikes legislation, gained widespread public support during the tough-on-crime culture, beginning in the 1970s. Researchers have demonstrated racial bias in capital punishment juries. Legal scholars have demonstrated that the death penalty is largely a means for achieving political popularity, particularly for district attorneys and governors. Despite ample evidence of racism, the death penalty is flourishing once again in the United States. See Stephen B. Bright, "Discrimination, Death, and Denial: The Tolerance of Racial Discrimination in Infliction of the Death Penalty," in *From Lynch Mobs to the Killing State: Race and the Death Penalty in America*, ed. Charles J. Ogletree Jr. and Austin Sarat (New York: New York University Press, 2006), 216; and Mona Lynch, "Stereotypes, Prejudice, and Life-and-Death Decision Making: Lessons from Laypersons in an Experimental Setting," in Ogletree and Sarat, *From Lynch Mobs*, 182–207.

65 Bruce Western, *Punishment and Inequality in America* (New York: Russell Sage Foundation, 2006), xii; Michelle Alexander, *The New Jim Crow: Mass Incarceration in the Age of Colorblindness* (New York: New Press, 2010).

66 Ta-Nehisi Coates, *Between the World and Me* (New York: Spiegel & Grau, 2015), 33.

67 Monique W. Morris, *Pushout: The Criminalization of Black Girls in Schools* (New York: New Press, 2016), 12.

68 Erica Meiners, *Right to Be Hostile: Schools, Prisons, and the Making of Public Enemies* (New York: Routledge, 2007), 6.

69 Ritchie, *Invisible No More*, 73.

70 I clarify my approach to the term "women" by using the words of Andrea J. Ritchie: "While emphatically inclusive of transgender women in the discussion of women's experiences of policing, [this section] does not fully address the experiences of transgender men and gender non-conforming people of color, many of whom are read as feminine by law enforcement officers. Trans men's experiences of policing are largely absent from both mainstream discourses of police violence focused on men, and from efforts to lift up the experiences of women—trans and non-trans—in broader debates around policing." See Ritchie, *Invisible No More*, 12.

71 Ritchie, *Invisible No More*, 104–202.

72 Angela Y. Davis, *Are Prisons Obsolete?* (New York: Seven Stories Press, 2003), 77–83; Richie, *Arrested Justice*, 51–53.

73 Richie, *Arrested Justice*, 26. She states that homicide by an intimate partner is the second leading cause of death for Black women between the ages of fifteen and twenty-five and that Black women are killed by a spouse at a rate twice that of white women.

74 Ibid., 27.

75 Ibid., 32. Richie notes that for Black women intimate violence takes place at the same rates in same-sex and gender-nonconforming relationships as it does in heterosexual dynamics.

76 Ben Beaumont-Thomas, "'No One Cared Because We Were Black Girls': Is Time Finally Up for R Kelly?," *Guardian*, January 17, 2019, www.theguardian.com.

77 Jerhonda Pace, *Surviving R. Kelly*, season 1, episode 6, 29:35.

78 Richie, *Arrested Justice*, 40.

79 Jenny Lumet, "Russell Simmons Sexually Violated Me," *Hollywood Reporter*, November 30, 2017, www.hollywoodreporter.com.

80 Derald Wing Sue, Christina Capodilupo, Gina C. Toino, Jennifer M. Bucceri, Aisha M. B. Holder, Kevin L. Nadala, and Marta Esquilin, "Racial Microaggressions in Everyday Life: Implications for Clinical Practice," *American Psychologist* 62, no. 4 (2007): 271–286.

81 Tiffany Jana and Michael Baran, *Subtle Acts of Exclusion: How to Understand, Identify, and Stop Microaggressions* (San Francisco: Berrett-Koehler, 2020), 16.

82 Joseph Cheah, *Race and Religion in American Buddhism: White Supremacy and Immigrant Adaptation* (New York: Oxford University Press, 2011); George Yancy and Emily McRae, eds., *Buddhism and Whiteness: Critical Perspectives* (Lanham, Md.: Lexington Books, 2019); Larry Yang, *Awakening Together: The Spiritual Prac-

tice of Inclusivity and Community (Somerville, Mass.: Wisdom, 2017); Ruth King, *Mindful of Race: Transforming Racism from the Inside Out* (Boulder, Colo.: Sounds True, 2018).

83 See, for example, Spring Washam, *A Fierce Heart* (New York: Hay House, 2019), 140, and Ann Gleig, *American Dharma: Buddhism beyond Modernity* (New Haven, Conn.: Yale University Press, 2019), 139–175.

84 Washam, *Fierce Heart*, 140.

85 Jack Kornfield, *A Path with Heart: A Guide through the Perils and Promises of Spiritual Life* (New York: Bantam Books, 1993), 247.

86 Gleig, *American Dharma*, 139–175.

87 angel Kyodo williams, Rod Owens, and Jasmine Syedullah, *Radical Dharma: Talking Race, Love, and Liberation* (Berkeley, Calif.: North Atlantic Books, 2016), 118–119.

88 Ibid., 118.

89 Jan Willis, "Buddhism and Race," in *Dharma Matters: Women, Race, and Tantra* (Somerville, Mass.: Wisdom, 2020), 101.

90 Menakem, *My Grandmother's Hands*, 129–130.

91 Bessel van der Kolk, *The Body Keeps the Score: Brain, Mind, and Body in the Healing of Trauma* (New York: Penguin, 2014), 43.

92 Ibid., 44.

93 Ibid., 45.

94 Gyozan Royce Andrew Johnson, "From Butcher to Zen Priest: Radical Transformation through Bloodletting," in *Black and Buddhist: What Buddhism Can Teach Us about Race, Resilience, Transformation, and Freedom*, ed. Pamela Ayo Yetunde and Cheryl A. Giles (Boulder, Colo.: Shambhala, 2020), 123.

95 Cheryl Giles, "They Say the People Could Fly: Disrupting the Legacy of Sexual Violence through Myth, Memory, and Connection," in Yetunde and Giles, *Black and Buddhist*, 42–43.

96 Larry Ward, *America's Racial Karma: An Invitation to Heal* (Berkeley, Calif.: Parallax Press, 2020), 69.

97 Mark Wollyn, *It Didn't Start with You: How Inherited Family Trauma Shapes Who We Are and How to End the Cycle* (New York: Penguin, 2017), 21.

98 Ibid., 24.

99 Ibid., 33.

100 Ibid., 44.

101 Ward, *America's Racial Karma*, 123.

102 Ibid., 89.

103 Ibid.

104 Loretta Graziano Breuning, *Habits of a Happy Brain: Retrain Your Brain to Boost Your Serotonin, Dopamine, Oxytocin, and Endorphin Levels* (New York: Adams, 2016), 34–57. She describes four neurochemicals that, when triggered, can help heal the traumatized nervous system. Dopamine, which triggers joy when one's needs are met; endorphins, which release chemicals that allow the tolerance of

pain; oxytocin, which produces the feelings of being safe with others; and serotonin, which arises when one feels respected by others, all facilitate the healing of
trauma. It is possible to cultivate these neurochemicals and create new pathways
in the brain.

105 Van der Kolk, *Body Keeps the Score*, 116.

3. HONORING ANCESTORS IN BLACK BUDDHIST PRACTICE

1 Rachel Bagby, *Daughterhood: Sounding Hidden Truths, Ignite Your Freedom*
(BookNook, 2016).

2 Queen Afua (Helen O. Robinson), *Sacred Woman: A Guide to Healing the Feminine Body, Mind, and Spirit* (New York: Ballantine Books, 2000), 126.

3 See, for example, Zerihun Doda Doffana, "Sacred Sites and Ancestor Veneration
in Sidama, Southwest Ethiopia: A Socio-ecological Perspective," *Cogent Social Sciences* 5 (2019): 1–16. An ancestor is a "blood- or extended-family member who has
died and made the transition to the spirit-world."

4 Author interview with Bhante Buddharakkhita, June 25, 2018.

5 Judy Atkinson, *Trauma Trails, Recreating Song Lines: The Transgenerational Effects
of Trauma on Indigenous Australia* (North Melbourne: Spinifex Press, 2002), 27.

6 Ibid., 28.

7 Doffana, "Sacred Sites," 7. In southwest Ethiopia, it is believed that the forest, held
as sacred, was willed into existence by an ancestor who subsequently made it
flourish. Doffana writes, "The belief that these sites and trees represent ancestors
is central in the local perceptions of the relationship between sacred groves and
ancestral religion."

8 Atkinson, *Trauma Trails*, 28.

9 Ibid., 29.

10 Ibid., 29.

11 Ibid., 31.

12 Author interview with DaRa Williams, March 9, 2019.

13 Miriam-Rose Ungunmerr Baumann, ""Miriam Rose Foundation: Empowering
Indigenous Futures through Art, Culture, Education and Opportunity" (n.d.),
www.miriamrosefoundation.org.au.

14 Ibid.

15 Atkinson, *Trauma Trails*, 32.

16 Connecting to ancestors through dreams takes place in other parts of the country;
however, qualitative research highlights southern African American communities.

17 Nancy Fairley, "Dreaming Ancestors in Eastern Carolina," *Journal of Black Studies*
33, no. 5 (May 2003): 546.

18 Ibid., 553.

19 Bryson C. M. White, "Death of the Ring Shout: African American Ancestor Veneration, Africana Theology and George Washington," *Black Theology* 12 (2014): 46.

20 Ibid., 47.

21 Luisah Teish, *Jambalaya* (New York: HarperOne, 1985), 68.

22 Ibid., 68–69. Teish details how the Fon people believe that the soul has many layers. At death, the soul rejoins the Goddess and nature. The layer of the soul that is considered spirit/intelligence is handed down from the ancestors and is the guardian of the person. This layer of intelligence blends with the personality of the person to be born. The newly born person is a combination of the ancestor and the new being, along with a blend of physical characteristics. Thus the new person incorporates the physical characteristics of the ancestors, the individual identity, and the protective guardian source. All three elements are oriented toward this new person's destiny.

23 Ibid., 87.

24 Ibid.

25 Atkinson, *Trauma Trails*, 29.

26 See Atkinson, *Trauma Trails*, 57, for sources on human-made trauma versus natural disasters.

27 See chapter 2 for an overview of intergenerational trauma inflicted on people of African descent.

28 Williams interview. She further notes that immigrants from the Caribbean and Africa hold onto their origins because they feel connected to the land. And regarding IFOT, DaRa states, "It is important to note IFOT is a decolonized trauma intervention way of knowing arising out of an indigenous worldview developed by an Indigenous woman in Canada, Shirley Turcotte, and I am just fortunate enough to steward the training and engagement with IFOT and to direct it here in the US."

29 Author interview with Sebene Selassie, May 23, 2018.

30 Ibid.

31 Sebene Selassie, *You Belong* (New York: HarperOne, 2020); Lama Rod Owens, *Love and Rage: The Path of Liberation through Anger* (Berkeley, Calif.: North Atlantic Books, 2020), 75–78; Larry Ward, *America's Racial Karma: An Invitation to Heal* (Berkeley, Calif.: Parallax Press, 2020), 84.

32 Author interview with Ralph Steele, June 13, 2018.

33 Author interview with Shanté Paradigm Smalls, October 29, 2019.

34 Author interview with Myokei Caine-Barrett, May 25, 2018.

35 Author interview with Jozen Tamori Gibson, October 31, 2019.

36 Bagby, *Daughterhood*, location 852.

37 Claudelle Glasgow, "Blackness, Buddhism, and Trauma" (Black and Buddhist Summit, February 24, 2021), www.blackandbuddhistsummit.com.

38 Author interview with Dr. Claudelle Glasgow, October 22, 2019.

39 Author interview with Konda Mason, November 2, 2019.

40 Ibid.

41 Selassie interview.

42 Ibid.

43 Ibid.

44 Author interview with Kate Johnson, May 31, 2018.

45 Kaira Jewel Lingo, "Taking Refuge in Ourselves: Awakening to Wholeness, Belonging to the World" (dharma talk, BIPOC/BAME Colors of Compassion of the Heart of London Sangha, July 12, 2020).

46 Thich Nhat Hanh, *Touching the Earth: Intimate Conversations with the Buddha* (Berkeley, Calif.: Parallax Press, 2004).

47 Author interview with Devin Berry, June 24, 2017.

48 Ibid.

49 *Tonglen* refers to a practice in which a meditator breathes in the pain and suffering of a specific person and breathes out wishes for happiness, well-being, and health. It is fundamentally about an exchange of energy, in which a meditator intends to take on another's suffering and subsequently fill them with joy, happiness, and peace.

50 Berry interview.

51 Ibid.

52 Ibid.

53 Author interview with Kabir Hypolite, March 5, 2019.

54 Author interview with Rosetta Saunders, March 7, 2019.

55 Williams interview.

56 Ibid.

57 Ibid.

58 Author interview with Noliwe Alexander, June 18, 2018.

59 Saunders interview.

60 Williams interview.

61 Hypolite interview.

62 Berry interview.

63 Author interview with Beli Sullivan, March 8, 2019.

64 Alexander interview.

65 Collective statement from the Deep Time Liberation Teaching Team, May 2019.

66 Author interview with Shanté Paradigm Smalls, October 29, 2019.

67 Alexander interview.

68 Zenju Earthlyn Manuel, *Sanctuary: A Meditation on Home, Homelessness, and Belonging* (Somerville, Mass.: Wisdom, 2018), 10.

69 Ibid., 10.

70 Author interview with Larry Ward, June 12, 2018.

71 Kemetic spirituality is rooted in ancient traditions in Egypt.

72 Ibid.

73 Smalls interview.

74 Ibid.

75 Author interview with Zenju Earthlyn Manuel, May 3, 2018.

76 Petty, *Ocha Dharma*, 11–14.

77 Miles interview.

78 Alexander interview.

79 Author interview with Ericka Tiffany Phillips, November 25, 2019.

80 Author interview with Lama Rod Owens, July 15, 2017.

4. TURNING TOWARD EXTERNAL CONDITIONS

1 Steve Biko, *I Write What I Like* (Cambridge: ProQuest, 2005), 68.

2 Ida B. Wells, *The Red Record* (1895), www.gutenberg.org.

3 Garvey was especially inspired by Booker T. Washington, who accepted Jim Crow segregation and promoted the development of Black-owned businesses, technical and agricultural schools, and land ownership. Washington died in 1915.

4 See Eldridge Cleaver, "The Land Question and Black Liberation," in *Eldridge Cleaver: Post-Prison Writings and Speeches* (Washington, D.C.: Smithsonian Libraries, 1969), 63. Cleaver wrote, "Marcus Garvey claimed the continent of Africa for Black people and reasserted Black identification with an ancestral homeland. This marked a major, historic shift in the psyche of black people. It got them over a crucial hump in their struggle up from the white light of slavery into knowledge of themselves and their past. Marcus Garvey gave the ultimate statement of black identity. He went directly to its root, and in doing so he gave black people a firm foundation on which to build."

5 Marcus Garvey, *Philosophy & Opinions of Marcus Garvey*, ed. Amy Jacques-Garvey (New York: Atheneum 1986), 14.

6 Ibid., 14.

7 Ibid., 26.

8 W. E. B. Du Bois, *A W. E. B. Du Bois Reader* (New York: Oxford University Press, 1996), 26–27.

9 A. Philip Randolph, "Keynote Address at Negro Labor Council Convention (1962)," in *For Jobs and Freedom: Selected Speeches and Writings of A. Philip Randolph*, ed. Andrew E. Kersten and David Lucander (Amherst: University of Massachusetts Press, 2013), 142, 144.

10 James Baldwin, *The Fire Next Time* (New York: Vintage, 1962), 25.

11 Martin Luther King Jr., "Letter from a Birmingham Jail," in *A Testament of Hope*, ed. James Melvin Washington (New York: HarperCollins, 1991).

12 Martin Luther King Jr., "Nonviolence and Racial Justice," in Washington, *Testament of Hope*, 8–9.

13 See, for example, Martin Luther King Jr., "A Time to Break Silence," in Washington, *Testament of Hope*, 313–329. King also testified before Congress, calling for a complete restructuring of society.

14 Malcolm X, *The Autobiography of Malcolm* (New York: Random House, 1964/1965), 176–177.

15 Malcolm X, "Message to the Grassroots" (BlackPast, 2021), www.blackpast.org.

16 Malcolm X, "The Ballot or the Bullet" (EdChange, n.d.), www.edchange.org.

17 Stokely Speaks, *From Black Power to Pan-Africanism* (1965; Chicago: Lawrence Hill Books, 2007), 49.

18 Robyn Spencer, *The Revolution Has Come: Black Power, Gender, and the Black Panther Party* (Durham, N.C.: Duke University Press, 2016), 30. "Newton and Seale turned to Marxist theoreticians at home and abroad to explain the poverty they saw all around them. They identified capitalism as the root cause of oppression worldwide and linked the cause of African Americans with Third World liberation movements. They studied anticolonial movements worldwide and tried to apply the tactics of liberation struggle to the African American situation. They were particularly influenced by theories that posited that a small, armed group of dedicated people could lead the revolutionary struggle and that guerilla warfare could be an effective strategy for social change."

19 Ibid., 29. "[Newton and Seale] believed that black America was an internal colony of the United States and that the relationship between the black colony and the 'mother country' was one of pure exploitation of labor and resources. As such, their goal was to create a political vehicle that would raise political consciousness in the black colony and forward the struggle for self-determination there. However, they did not see black self-determination as an end unto itself. They posited that black control of the black nation-state, or national liberation of the black colony, was part of the larger goal to transform America and eventually the rest of the world."

20 Huey Newton, "Fear and Doubt," in *To Die for the People* (New York: Random House, 1972), 79–80.

21 Huey Newton, "The Correct Handling of a Revolution: July 20, 1967," in *To Die for the People: Selected Writings and Speeches* (1992; New York: Writers and Readers, 1995), 15.

22 Ibid., 16.

23 Assata Shakur, *Assata: An Autobiography* (Chicago: Zed Books, 1987), 181.

24 Ibid., 183.

25 C. Eric Lincoln and Lawrence H. Mamiya, *The Black Church in the African American Experience* (Durham, N.C.: Duke University Press, 1990), 92.

26 Ibid., 167.

27 James H. Cone, *A Black Theology of Liberation* (Maryknoll, N.Y.: Orbis Books, 1970), ix. There are, to be sure, many Black theologians publishing on God's care for the dispossessed. As early as 1949, Howard Thurman published *Jesus and the Disinherited* (1949; Boston: Beacon, 1996).

28 Lincoln and Mamiya, *Black Church*, 23–24.

29 There are five other Black Methodist denominations that are much smaller numerically than the three aforementioned denominations. Richard Allen founded the AME Church in 1787 after he, Absalom Jones, and other Black worshippers were pulled from their knees during a church service and told that the gallery they prayed in was closed to Black Christians. In 1796, Peter Williams formed the congregation that became the AMEZ Church after many Black Methodists experienced discrimination and the church refused to fully ordain Black clergy

and allow them to join the conference. In 1822 James Varick was ordained the first bishop.

30 Sandra Richter, "What Do I Know of Holy? On the Person and Work of the Holy Spirit in Scripture," in *Spirit of God: Christian Renewal in the Community of Faith*, ed. Jeffrey W. Barbeau and Beth Felker Jones (Downers Grove, Ill.: InterVarsity Press, 2015), 26. They note that the Hebrew word *ruah* has many meanings—some natural, some supernatural. They ask, which of the hundreds of references to *ruah* as breeze, breath, wind, spirit, mind, capacity, and intellect are actually references to the great God? Biblical translators cannot answer this question. It is worth noting that the phrase "Holy Spirit" (*ruah qodso*) occurs only three times in the Hebrew Bible.

31 Ibid., 35–36.

32 Estrelda Y. Alexander, "The Spirit of God: Christian Renewal in African American Pentecostalism," in Barbeau and Jones, *Spirit of God*, 130.

33 Ibid., 131.

34 Ibid., 133.

35 Ibid., 133–134.

36 Jennifer Leath, a Christian ethicist, describes an emphasis on collectivity in a Christian theological tradition uplifting the voices of Black women, known as "Womanism." Leath argues that collaboration between "Womanist-Buddhist dialogue revives traditional models of collective scholarship, honoring the gifts of community orientation characteristic of both Womanism and Buddhism." See Leath, "Canada and Pure Land, a New Field and Buddha-Land: Womanists and Buddhists Reading Together," *Buddhist-Christian Studies* 32 (2012): 61–62.

37 Rod Owens, *Radical Dharma: Talking Race, Love, and Liberation* (Berkeley, Calif.: North Atlantic Books, 2016), 5.

38 Zenju Earthlyn Manuel, *Sanctuary: A Meditation on Home, Homelessness, and Belonging* (Somerville, Mass.: Wisdom, 2018), 42.

39 Ibid., 37.

40 Jualynne E. Dodson and Cheryl Townsend Gilkes, "'There's Nothing Like Church Food': Food and the U.S. Afro-Christian Tradition: Re-Membering Community and Feeding the Embodied S/spirits," *Journal of the American Academy of Religion* 63, no. 3 (1995): 519–538.

41 Manuel, *Sanctuary*, 43.

42 Jan Willis, "Dharma Has No Color," in *Dharma Matters: Women, Race, and Tantra* (Somerville, Mass.: Wisdom, 2020), 127.

43 Owens, *Radical Dharma*, 4–5.

44 Charlene A. Carruthers, *Unapologetic: A Black, Queer, and Feminist Mandate for Radical Movements* (Boston: Beacon, 2018), 39. She writes, "We are using a hybrid of direct action tactics, traditional field organizing, and spiritual practices."

45 Michelle Wallace, "A Black Feminist's Search for Sisterhood," in *All the Women Are White, All the Blacks Are Men, But Some of Us Are Brave*, 2nd ed., ed. Akasha (Gloria T.) Hull, Patricia Bell Scott, and Barbara Smith (1982; New York: Feminist Press, 2015), 6.

46 Ibid., 7.

47 Audre Lorde, *Sister Outsider* (1984; New York: Ten Speed Press, 2007), 112.

48 Combahee River Collective, "The Combahee River Collective Statement" (Yale University, American Studies, n.d.), https://americanstudies.yale.edu.

49 Ibid.

50 June Jordan, "Notes toward a Model of Resistance," in *Some of Us Did Not Die* (New York: Basic/Civitas Books, 2002), 80.

51 The term "intersectionality" was coined by Black Feminist law professor Kimberlé Williams Crenshaw. See Crenshaw, "Demarginalizing the Intersection of Race and Sex: A Black Feminist Critique of Antidiscrimination Doctrine, Feminist Theory and Antiracist Politics," *University of Chicago Legal Forum* 1989 (1989): 139–167. See also Angela Y. Davis, *Women, Race, and Class* (New York: Vintage, 1983) and *Women, Culture, and Politics* (New York: Random House, 1984).

52 Joy James, "Radicalizing Feminism," in *The Black Feminist Reader*, ed. Joy James and T. Denean Sharpley-Whiting (Malden, Mass.: Blackwell, 2000), 248–249.

53 Angela Y. Davis, "Racism, Birth Control, and Reproductive Rights," in *Women, Race, and Class*, 221.

54 An interpretation of Audre Lorde's works will also be covered in chapter 6.

55 Lorde, *Sister Outsider*, 36.

56 Ibid., 36–37.

57 Ibid., 37.

58 Gloria Watkins (bell hooks), *All about Love: New Visions* (New York: William Morrow, 2000), 233.

59 Gloria Watkins (bell hooks), *Salvation: Black People and Love* (New York: Harper-Collins, 2001), xviii.

60 Watkins, *All about Love*, 67.

61 Ibid., 67.

62 Watkins, *Salvation*, 89.

63 George Yancy, "bell hooks: Buddhism, the Beats and Loving Blackness," *New York Times*, December 10, 2015.

64 Helen Tworkov, "Agent of Change: An Interview with bell hooks," *Tricycle*, Fall 1992, https://tricycle.org. Since the age of eighteen, hooks has embraced contemplative traditions, including Zen Buddhism and the writings of Thich Nhat Hanh.

65 Yancy, "bell hooks."

66 Watkins, *Salvation*, 55.

67 Watkins, *Salvation*, 56.

68 bell hooks, "Toward a Worldwide Culture of Love," *Lion's Roar*, June 8, 2021, www.lionsroar.com.

69 Alice Walker, *Taking the Arrow Out of the Heart* (New York: 37Ink/Atria Books, 2018), xv.

70 Ibid., xv.

71 Ibid., xv.

72 Alice Walker, *In Search of Our Mother's Gardens* (New York: Harcourt Brace Jovanovich, 1983), 237, emphasis added.

73 Walker, *Taking the Arrow Out of the Heart*, xv.

74 Alice Walker, *We Are the Ones We Have Been Waiting For* (New York: New Press, 2006), 103–104.

75 Ibid., 4.

76 Ibid., 93.

77 A Buddhist Resources for Womanist Reflection Consultation, otherwise known as a Womanist-Buddhist consultation, initiated in 2009 by Melanie Harris and Charles Hallisey, evolved into a panel discussion and a series of published essays in which Womanist scholars identified early poems written by marginalized Buddhist nuns and placed them alongside biblical texts containing women's voices that were similarly marginalized. See Melanie L. Harris, "In the Company of Friends: Womanist Readings of Buddhist Poems," *Buddhist-Christian Studies* 36 (2016): 3.

78 Alice Walker, *In Search of Our Mother's Gardens: Womanist Prose* (New York: Harcourt Brace Jovanovich, 1983), xi–xii.

79 Keri Day, "Freedom on My Mind: Buddhist-Womanist Dialogue," *Buddhist-Christian Studies* 36 (2016): 10.

80 Tracey Hucks, "Wombu: An Intellectual Exercise in Womanist and Buddhist Reading," *Buddhist-Christian Studies* 36 (2016): 43.

81 Carolyn M. Jones Medine, "Practice in Buddhist-Womanist Thought," *Buddhist Christian Studies* 36 (2016): 18.

82 Alice Walker, "This Was Not an Area of Large Plantations: Suffering Too Insignificant for the Majority to See," in Walker, *We Are the Ones*, 106.

5. TURNING TOWARD INTERNAL SUFFERING

1 Marlene Jones, "Moving toward an End to Suffering," in *Dharma, Color, and Culture: New Voices in Western Buddhism*, ed. Hilda Gutiérrez Baldoquín (Berkeley, Calif.: Parallax Press, 2004), 45.

2 Author interview with Gretchen Rohr, October 14, 2019.

3 Ibid.

4 Hilda Gutiérrez Baldoquín, "Don't Waste Time," in Baldoquín, *Dharma, Color, and Culture*, 182.

5 Sebene Selassie, "Suffering and the End of Suffering" (dharma talk, Race and Dharma, Barre Center for Buddhist Studies, April 1, 2018).

6 Pamela Ayo Yetunde, "Buddhism in the Age of #BlackLivesMatter," *Lion's Roar*, May 27, 2020, www.lionsroar.com.

7 Pamela Ayo Yetunde, *Object Relations, Buddhism, and Relationality in Womanist Practical Theology* (Cham, Switzerland: Palgrave, 2018), 10.

8 Donald W. Mitchel and Sarah H. Jacoby, *Buddhism: Introducing the Buddhist Experience* (New York: Oxford University Press, 2014), 32–35.

9   *Anatta* is translated from Pali as "non-self" and "no-self." For the purposes of this book, I use the term "non-self" in the text but quote interviewees verbatim in their translation of *anatta*.

10 For example, consider the "one drop rule," in which Blackness refers to any person with one drop of sub-Saharan Black blood. See Christine B. Hickman, "The Devil and the One Drop Rule: Racial Categories, African Americans, and the U.S. Census," *Michigan Law Review* 95, no. 5 (March 1997): 1161.

11 Author interview with Lama Rod Owens, July 15, 2017.

12 Sebene Selassie, "The Five Aggregates" (dharma talk, Race and Dharma, Barre Center for Buddhist Studies, April 22, 2018).

13 Author interview with Sebene Selassie, May 23, 2018.

14 Author interview with Lama Rod Owens, September 14, 2017.

15 Author interview with Pamela Ayo Yetunde, June 6, 2018.

16 Author interview with Ruth King, May 2, 2018.

17 Author interview with Kate Johnson, May 31, 2018.

18 Jack Kornfield, *A Path with Heart: A Guide through the Perils and Promises of Spiritual Life* (New York: Random House, 1993), 247.

19 See chapter 2 for an overview of the dehumanization of Black people.

20 Author interview with Unique Holland, June 23, 2017.

21 Zenju Earthlyn Manuel, *The Way of Tenderness: Awakening through Race, Sexuality, and Gender* (Somerville, Mass.: Wisdom, 2015), 110.

22 Author interview with Zenju Earthlyn Manuel, May 3, 2018.

23 Author interview with Chimyo Atkinson, April 17, 2018.

24 Owens interview, September 14, 2017.

25 A school of interpretation in the Mahayana tradition.

26 The *Tripitika* is the formal term for the Buddhist scriptures of Theravada Buddhism. The scriptures are divided into three sections. In the West, it is known as the Pali Canon, or sometimes colloquially as the Three Baskets.

27 Judith Simmer-Brown, *Dakini's Warm Breath: The Feminine Principle in Tibetan Buddhism* (Boulder, Colo.: Shambhala, 2001), 33.

28 Author interview with Lama Rod Owens, July 15, 2017.

29 Author interview with Spring Washam, June 21, 2017.

30 Author interview with Kate Johnson, May 31, 2018.

31 Rhonda V. Magee, "Taking and Making Refuge in Racial [Whiteness] Awareness and Racial Justice Work," in *Buddhism and Whiteness: Critical Perspectives*, ed. George Yancy and Emily McRae (Lanham, Md.: Lexington Books, 2019), 257.

32 Author interview with Rhonda V. Magee, June 22, 2017.

33 Author interview with Justin Miles, October 20, 2019.

34 Ibid.

35 Gil Fronsdal, "The Four Faces of Love: The Brahma Viharas" (Insight Meditation Center, 2021), www.insightmeditationcenter.org.

36 Sharon Shelton, "The Alchemy of Suffering" (Insight Meditation Community of Washington, September 16, 2020), www.youtube.com/watch?v=ap1jE_oxklE&t=1769s.
37 Author interview with Noliwe Alexander, June 18, 2018.
38 Author interview with Devin Berry, March 6, 2019.
39 Author interview with Diane Yaski, June 5, 2018.
40 Author interview with Joshua Alafia, May 22, 2018.
41 Author interview with Ralph Steele, June 13, 2018.
42 Pamela Ayo Yetunde, "Voluntary Segregation: The Paradox, Promise, and Peril of People of Color Sanghas," in *Black and Buddhist: What Buddhism Can Teach Us about Race, Resilience, Transformation, and Freedom*, ed. Pamela Ayo Yetunde and Cheryl A. Giles (Boulder, Colo.: Shambhala, 2020), 108.
43 Tuere Sala, "Cultivating Awakening Emotions" (dharma talk, Insight San Diego and Worldbeat Productions, September 25, 2020), www.youtube.com/watch?v=y6MfTlf14a4&t=3705s.
44 Shelton, "Alchemy of Suffering."
45 Ibid.
46 Author interview with JoAnna Hardy, June 19, 2017.
47 Gina Sharpe, "The Paramis: Transition from Inner Retreat to Outer Retreat" (dharma talk, The Mountain Hermitage: "Manifesting Spiritual Aspiration by Deepening Practice: People of Color Retreat for Experienced Students," August 23, 2015).
48 Author interview with Betty Burkes, June 28, 2018.
49 Owens interview, July 15, 2017.
50 Bhikkhu Analayo, *Satipatthana Meditation: A Practice Guide* (Cambridge: Windhorse, 2018).
51 Ibid.
52 Author interview with Zenju Earthlyn Manuel, May 3, 2018.
53 Dawn Scott, "Mind" (dharma talk, *Satipatthana Sutta* Course, Barre Center for Buddhist Studies, May 10, 2020).
54 The "Race and Dharma" course was taught through the Barre Center for Buddhist Studies by JoAnna Hardy, Sebene Selassie, Erin Treat, and Brian LeSage, March 25–May 27, 2018.
55 Selassie interview.
56 Scott, "Mind."
57 Berry interview.
58 Author interview with Noliwe Alexander, June 18, 2018.
59 Author interview with Rhonda Magee, June 22, 2017.
60 Berry interview.
61 Scott, "Mind."

6. THE BODY AS A VEHICLE FOR LIBERATION

1 Audre Lorde, "Uses of the Erotic: The Erotic as Power," in *Sister Outsider* (Freedom, Calif.: Crossing Press, 1984), 57.

2 Miranda Shaw, *Buddhist Goddesses of India* (Princeton, N.J.: Princeton University Press, 2006), 150. She notes that "although Shakyamuni Buddha bodied forth the fruition of human potential, his male gender lent a potential qualification and exclusivity to his attainment in the irreducibly gendered discourse of Theravada Buddhism. One result was the Theravada doctrine that a female could not become a Buddha. Although this tenet, mentioned only twice in the voluminous Pali canon, appears not to have been a central one, its presence records one possible reply to the question of whether it is possible to attain the level of Buddhahood in a female lifetime."

3 Ibid., 17.

4 *Therigatha: Selected Poems of the First Buddhist Women*, trans. Charles Hallisey (Cambridge, Mass.: Harvard University Press, 2015).

5 *The Vimalakirti Sutra*, trans. Burton Watson (New York: Columbia University Press, 1997), 90–91.

6 See, for example, Kevin Manders and Elizabeth Marsten, eds., *Transcending: Trans Buddhist Voices* (Berkeley, Calif.: North Atlantic Books, 2019).

7 Author interview with Myokei Caine-Barrett, May 25, 2018.

8 Shaw, *Buddhist Goddesses of India*, 155–165. She writes that goddesses appear in the "Flower Ornament Scripture."

9 There exist snake deities in other Indian traditions at the time in which Janguli was identified. Hindus worshipped Manasa and Jains worshipped Padmavati. All three traditions uphold images of snakes in sculptures of their deities.

10 Shaw, *Buddhist Goddesses of India*, 166.

11 Ibid., 308–309.

12 Ibid., 309.

13 Ibid.

14 Ibid., 309.

15 "Tantra" is a term used interchangeably with "Vajrayana." Both terms refer to a form of Indian and Tibetan Buddhism in which particular practices are uplifted to attain enlightenment.

16 Rachael Wooten, *Tara: The Liberating Power of the Female Buddha* (Louisville, Colo.: Sounds True Press, 2020), 15.

17 Shaw, *Buddhist Goddesses of India*, 306. Shaw refers to Tara as "without doubt the most beloved goddess of the Indo-Tibetan pantheon." She is furthermore likened to the Virgin Mary and sometimes regarded as a "Buddhist Madonna." See ibid., 307.

18 Ibid., 310.

19 Ibid., 316. Tara is identified as offering protection from the eight great fears: lions, elephants, fire, snakes, thieves, drowning, captivity, and evil spirits. See ibid., 318.

20 Ibid., 323.

21 Karla Jackson-Brewer, "Teachings from the Vajrayana Tradition" (Fierce Urgency of Now Workshop, Spirit Rock Meditation Center, October 12, 2019).

22 Judith Simmer-Brown, *Dakini's Warm Breath: The Feminine Principle in Tibetan Buddhism* (Boulder, Colo.: Shambhala Press, 2002), 33. Simmer-Brown notes that the feminine as understood in Tibet is markedly different from the understanding of the feminine and feminism in the Western context.

23 Ibid.

24 Jackson-Brewer, "Teachings from the Vajrayana Tradition."

25 Jan Willis, "Dakini," in *Dharma Matters: Women, Race, and Tantra* (Somerville, Mass.: Wisdom, 2020), 174.

26 Ibid., 174.

27 Ibid., 174.

28 Sarah H. Jacoby, *Love and Liberation: Autobiographical Writings of the Tibetan Buddhist Visionary Sera Khandro* (New York: Columbia University Press, 2014), 135.

29 Ibid., 135. Willis says that these terms can "gloss over" the "tricky and playful" nature of the *dakini*. See Willis, "Dakini," 173–174.

30 Jacoby, *Love and Liberation*, 135.

31 Simmer-Brown, *Dakini's Warm Breath*, 187.

32 Willis, "Dakini," 184.

33 See Dakini Power, "Dakini (Sanskrit): A Female Messenger of Wisdom" (n.d.), www.dakinipower.com. See also Michaela Hass, *Dakini Power: Twelve Extraordinary Women Shaping the Transmission of Buddhism in the West* (Boulder, Colo.: Shambhala, 2013). Khandro Rinpoche was identified as a dakini at the time of her birth. However, human dakinis can be identified in other ways: as having unusual marks or being recognized as a reincarnation of a previous lineage holder.

34 Simmer-Brown, *Dakini's Warm Breath*, 31.

35 Ibid., 8.

36 Jackson-Brewer workshop.

37 Simmer-Brown, *Dakini's Warm Breath*, 42.

38 See Sebene Selassie, *You Belong* (New York: HarperOne, 2020), 61, 98–101; Lama Rod Owens, *Love and Rage: The Path of Liberation through Anger* (Berkeley, Calif.: North Atlantic Books, 2020), 1, 271; and Zenju Earthlyn Manuel, *The Way of Tenderness: Awakening through Race, Sexuality, and Gender* (Somerville, Mass.: Wisdom, 2015), 119–120, 126.

39 See chapter 4 for more extensive interpretations of Audre Lorde's writings.

40 Lorde, *Sister Outsider*, 53.

41 Ibid., 111.

42 Ibid., 54–55.

43 Owens, *Love and Rage*, 190.

44 Lorde, *Sister Outsider*, 56–57.

45 Ibid., 58, 111.

46 Ibid., 120–121.

47 Ibid., 122–123.

48 Ibid., 131.

49 Ibid., 135.

50 Ibid., 142.

51 Ibid., 146.

52 Ibid., 159.

53 Ibid., 173–174.

54 Several Black Buddhist teachers state that they employ Lorde and Baldwin in their practice and dharma teaching. Author email messages with Devin Berry, Noliwe Alexander, Arisika Razak, nialla rose, DaRa Williams, Dalila Bothwell, and Jo-Anna Hardy, August 12–14, 2021.

55 Pamela Ayo Yetunde, "Confessions of a Catho-Easto-Afro Bodhisattva: The (s) heroic Spiritual Journey of Audre Lorde" (class presentation, Shambhala Atlanta POC Sangha, April 24, 2017).

56 Author interview with Leslie Booker, November 20, 2019.

57 Ibid.

58 Lorde, *Sister Outsider*, 171–172.

59 For example, see Tara Brach's interpretation of the practice of taking refuge, *Radical Acceptance: Embracing Your Life with the Heart of a Buddha* (New York: Bantam Dell, 2003), 217–218.

60 As previously mentioned, Selassie, Owens, and Manuel have recently published books citing Lorde and Baldwin. Aishah Shahidah Simmons will teach on Audre Lorde in a "Buddhism and Black Feminism" class at the Barre Center for Buddhist Studies, October 9–November 13, 2021.

61 Selassie, "Turning toward Myself," in *Black and Buddhist: What Buddhism Can Teach Us about Race, Resilience, Transformation, and Freedom*, ed. Pamela Ayo Yetunde and Cheryl A. Giles (Boulder, Colo.: Shambhala, 2020), 80.

62 Selassie, *You Belong*, 102–103.

63 Ibid., 83.

64 James Baldwin, *The Fire Next Time* (New York: Vintage, 1963), 4.

65 Ibid., 7.

66 Ibid., 8.

67 Ibid., 91–92.

68 See, for example, Owens, *Love and Rage*, 163, 225, 271.

69 Ibid., 9.

70 Ibid., 95.

71 Ibid., 95.

72 Ibid., 98–99.

73 Ibid., 42–44.

74 See, for example, adrienne maree brown, *Pleasure Activism: The Politics of Feeling Good* (Chico, Calif.: AK Press, 2019).

75 Owens, *Love and Rage*, 84.

76 Ibid., 80–81.

77 Ibid., 98–100.

78 Owens, "The Dharma of Trauma: Blackness, Buddhism, and Transhistorical Trauma Narrated through Three Ayahuasca Ceremonies," in Yetunde and Giles, *Black and Buddhist*, 61.

79 Owens, *Love and Rage*, 144.

80 Selassie, *You Belong*, 50.

81 Ibid., 76.

82 Owens, *Love and Rage*, 4.

83 Manuel, *Way of Tenderness*, 40.

84 Ibid., 78.

85 Ibid., 79.

86 Ibid., 93.

87 Owens, *Love and Rage*, 199.

88 Ibid., 271.

89 Ibid., 142.

90 Selassie, "Turning toward Myself," 79.

91 Manuel, *Way of Tenderness*, 29–30.

92 Owens, *Love and Rage*, 144.

93 Ibid., 202.

94 Owens, *Love and Rage*, 157.

95 Ibid., 158.

96 Ann Gleig, "Dharma Diversity and Deep Inclusivity at the East Bay Meditation Center: From Buddhist Modernism to Buddhist Postmodernism?," *Contemporary Buddhism* 15, no. 2 (November 2014): 315–316.

97 Manuel, *Way of Tenderness*, 7.

98 Selassie, *You Belong*, 98–99.

7. LOVE AND LIBERATION

1 Author interview with Konda Mason, November 2, 2019.

2 Author interview with Jylani Ma'at, June 17, 2017.

3 Ibid.

4 Aishah Shahidah Simmons, "Rage-Mediation-Action-Healing" (dharma talk, Weekly Dharma Gathering, February 5, 2020).

5 Author interview with Unique Holland, June 23, 2017.

6 Author interview with Larry Ward, June 12, 2018.

7 Author interview with Kate Johnson, May 31, 2018.

8 Author interview with Dalila Bothwell, June 28, 2018.

9 Author interview with Kabir Hypolite, March 5, 2019.

10 Simmons, "Rage-Mediation-Action-Healing."

11 Ibid.

12 Ibid.

13 Author interview with Rhonda V. Magee, June 22, 2017.

14 Author interview with Noliwe Alexander, June 18, 2018.

15 Tara Brach, *True Refuge: Finding Peace and Freedom in Your Own Awakened Heart* (New York: Bantam Books, 2012).

16 Stacy McClendon, "The Nature of Mind" (dharma talk, Common Ground Meditation Center, December 11, 2017), https://cgmc.dharmaseed.org.

17 Author interview with Katie Loncke, June 29, 2019.

18 Author interview with Larry Ward, June 12, 2018.

19 Tara Brach, *Radical Compassion: Learning to Love Yourself and Your World with the Practice of RAIN* (New York: Penguin, 2019).

20 Author interview with Lama Rod Owens, July 15, 2017.

21 Ibid.

22 Author interview with Leslie Booker, November 20, 2019.

23 Author interview with Ruth King, May 2, 2018.

24 The five hindrances include sensory desire, ill will, sloth and torpor, restlessness and worry, and doubt.

25 Author interview with Bhante Buddharakkita, June 25, 2018.

26 Author interview with Claudelle Glasgow, October 22, 2019.

27 Author interview with Allyson Pimentel, June 14, 2018.

28 See chapter 4 for more explanation of Lorde's work.

29 Audre Lorde, *Sister Outsider* (1984; New York: Ten Speed Press, 2007), 171–172.

30 See chapter 6.

31 Mason interview.

32 Author interview with Gretchen Rohr, October 13, 2019.

33 Jan Willis and Emily Cohen, "Across Generations: An Interview with Jan Willis," *Journal of Feminist Studies* 33, no. 2 (2017): 135.

34 Pamela Ayo Yetunde, *Object Relations, Buddhism, and Relationality in Womanist Practice Theology* (Cham, Switzerland: Palgrave, 2018), 54. Yetunde's study on African American Buddhist lesbians found that 92 percent of the women who participated attended Catholic and Protestant churches, including Baptist, Methodist, and Pentecostal denominations.

35 Author interview with DaRa Williams, March 9, 2019.

36 Loncke interview.

37 Author interview with Zenju Earthlyn Manuel, May 3, 2018.

38 Ayesha Ali, "White People, It's Time to Look in the Mirror," *Lion's Roar*, August 13, 2020, www.lionsroar.com.

39 Author interview with Jozen Tamori Gibson, October 31, 2019.

40 Sensei Alex Kakuya, "Confessions of a Hungry Ghost," *Same Old Zen*, January 3, 2021, https://sameoldzen.blogspot.com.

41 Amana Brembry Johnson (dharma talk, Spirit Rock Meditation Center, August 3, 2020), www.spiritrock.org.

42 Author interview with Pamela Ayo Yetunde, June 5, 2018.

43 Combahee River Collective, "The Combahee River Collective Statement" (Yale University, American Studies, n.d.), https://americanstudies.yale.edu.

44 Lorde, *Sister Outsider*, 173–174.

45 Author interview with Dolores Watson, October 13, 2019.

46 Valerie Mason-John, "Closing Session" (Black and Buddhist Summit, February 25, 2021), www.blackandbuddhistsummit.com.

47 Rashid Hughes, "What to Do When Aggression Masquerades as Compassion," *Lion's Roar*, December 21, 2020, www.lionsroar.com.

48 Gaylon Ferguson, "Liberation from Suffering," in *Dharma, Color, and Culture: New Voices in Western Buddhism*, ed. Hilda Gutiérrez Baldoquín (Berkeley, Calif.: Parallax Press, 2004), 97.

49 Lama Dawa Tarchin Phillips, "Belonging," in *Black and Buddhist: What Buddhism Can Teach Us about Race, Resilience, Transformation, and Freedom*, ed. Pamela Ayo Yetunde and Cheryl A. Giles (Boulder, Colo.: Shambhala, 2020), 87.

50 See Tara Brach, *Radical Acceptance: Embracing Your Life with the Heart of a Buddha* (New York: Bantam, 2003), esp. chap. 7.

51 Author interview with Justin Miles, October 20, 2019.

52 See the introduction.

53 Kaira Jewel Lingo, "Taking Refuge in Ourselves: Awakening to Wholeness, Belonging to the World" (dharma talk, BIPOC/BAME Colors of Compassion of the Heart of London Sangha, July 12, 2020).

54 Ibid.

55 Ibid.

56 Ma'at interview.

57 Sonya Renee Taylor, *The Body Is Not an Apology: The Power of Radical Self-Love* (Oakland, Calif.: Berrett-Koehler, 2021).

58 Kamilah Majied, "On Being Laila's Daughter," in Yetunde and Giles, *Black and Buddhist*, 141–142.

59 Venerable Dr. Pannavati, "Finding True Refuge" (interview with Tara Brach, August 26, 2012), www.youtube.com/watch?v=doUHFcpoAOw.

60 Sharon Shelton, "The Alchemy of Suffering" (Insight Meditation Center of Washington, September 16, 2021), www.youtube.com/watch?v=ap1jE_oxklE&t=1769s.

61 Dipa Ma was an Indian teacher who greatly influenced Western meditation practitioners in the 1970s.

62 Author interview with Sebene Selassie, May 23, 2018.

63 Ma'at interview.

64 Mason interview.

65 Alexander interview.

66 Author interview with Myokei Caine-Barrett, May 25, 2018.

67 Merle Kodo Boyd, "A Child of the South in Long Black Robes," in Baldoquín, *Dharma, Color, and Culture*, 103.

68 Author interview with Lev "Fresh" White, November 25, 2019.

69 Gibson interview.

70 Buddharakkita interview.

71 Author interview with Ralph Steele, June 13, 2018.

72 Miles interview.

73 Interview with Shanté Paradigm Smalls, October 29, 2019.

74 Loncke interview.

CONCLUSION

1 adrienne maree brown, *We Will Not Cancel Us: And Other Dreams of Transformative Justice* (Chico, Calif.: AK Press, 2020), 73–74.

INDEX

abolition and abolitionists, 6–7, 114, 136, 271

aboriginal cultures and practices, 98–101

affinity sanghas, 24, 62, 266–68

African Americans, 2; ancestors, 101–2, 112–13; Asian Americans, anti-Blackness and, 59–60; Chinese immigrants and, 58–59; intergenerational trauma, effect of, 13–14; in SGI, 279n1; Third World liberation movements and, 299n18; on U.S. land, 31–32, 103–4, 120, 133–35. *See also* Black Buddhists; Black people

African Communities League, 138

African Methodist Episcopal Church (AME), 149, 299n29

African Methodist Episcopal Zion Church (AMEZ), 149, 299n29

agape love, 141

ageism, 12

Alafia, Joshua, 16–17, 36, 186

"The Alchemy of Suffering" (Shelton), 261

Alexander, Estrelda, 150

Alexander, Noliwe, 14, 118, 121, 124, 126, 133–34; on heart practices, 185; on skillfully relating to suffering, in liberation, 239–41

Alexander VI (pope), 70

Ali, Ayesha, 250–51

All about Love (hooks), 161

Ambedkar, B. R., 49, 60

AME. *See* African Methodist Episcopal Church

American Buddhism, 3, 24, 31, 44–47, 53–57. *See also* Buddhism, in U.S.

American Dharma (Gleig), 26, 227–28

America's Racial Karma (Ward), 24, 94

AMEZ. *See* African Methodist Episcopal Zion Church

anatta (non-self), 8, 33, 40, 115, 172–80, 183

ancestors and ancestral practices: Black body and, 113, 115–17; Black Buddhists, on dharma and, 31–32, 67, 97–100, 103, 105–17, 120–21, 124–25, 134–35; Black Buddhists' familial lineages and, 105–6, 112–13, 120–23, 133–34; Black Radical Tradition and, 136, 168; ceremonies and, 101–2, 105–16, 134–35; deep listening and, 97–98, 100, 135; DTL and, 115–25; guides and, 107–9, 135; in healing intergenerational trauma, 11–14, 100, 105, 114–25; indigenous and aboriginal, 98–101, 103, 120; land and, 98–100, 133–35; rituals and, 109–11, 120, 134–35; shrines and altars to, 125–27; slavery and, 102, 115–16, 118–19, 134–35; venerating ancestors in daily life, 125–27; wisdom of, colonialism and, 102–5; Womanists on, 166–67

ancestral trauma, 123, 125

anicca (impermanence), 7, 172–73, 176, 181, 253

anti-Blackness, in Asian communities, 59–60

anti-Black racism, 6–7, 12, 136

Appeal to the Colored Citizens of the World (Walker, D.), 137

arahant, 37

Aryadeva, 42

73; literature and magazines, 64–67; on Lorde, 209, 214–17, 222; on love, in community, 264–69; on love ethic, 163; on microaggressions, in predominantly white sanghas, 89–91; on mindfulness, of body, 175–76; on non-self, liberation and, 173–77; on non-self, self and Blackness, 174–80; primary lineages of Buddhism influencing, 44; on psychological and spiritual liberation, 196–97, 243, 273; on relative and ultimate reality, 168, 179–83, 195–96; on resistance, to system oppression, 14; on Right Understanding, Three Marks of Existence and, 168, 172–74; on *Satipatthana Sutta*, 168, 190–97; on self-love, 185–86, 253–56, 259, 261, 266–67; shrines of, ancestors and, 125–26; on social justice, 231; in street protests and online activism, 17; on suffering, 169–71, 182–83, 215–16, 231–33; on suffering, as truth of present moment, 247–50; on suffering, relating skillfully to, 239–47; on taking refuge, 255–64; on trauma, 5, 64–67, 232–33, 266; on Two Truths doctrine, 180–83; vanguard activists and, 271–72; on whiteness, in U.S. Buddhism, 111–12; on white supremacy, in U.S. convert Buddhism, 24–25, 27, 89–91; Womanists and, 166–67; Zen teachings and, 62–63

Black Buddhists, on dharma: ancestral practices and, 31–32, 67, 97–100, 103, 105–17, 120–21, 124, 134–35; in Black liberation, 65, 230–31; Black Radical Tradition and, 167; decolonizing, 120; in healing, 65–66, 262–63; intergenerational trauma, racial harm and, 6, 13–14, 23–24, 31, 65–66, 91, 93–96, 124; non-Buddhist traditions and, 127–33; in psychological liberation, 168; Two Truths doctrine and, 182–83

Black children, 18–19, 64, 85–87, 139, 145–46

Black Church Tradition, 2, 32, 239, 299n29; Baldwin on myths of, 218–20; Black Feminists and, 167; Black Liberation Theology and, 147–54; Black Lives Matters activists and, 3–4; collective experiences of, 27; on sexuality, 227

Black Codes, in postbellum southern penal system, 78–79

Black communities: BPP on, 144–47; Buddhism and, 1, 263; communal rituals in, 15; Glassman on, 52; in healing trauma, 258; intergenerational trauma in, 1–2, 11; interpersonal violence, against Black women in, 86–88; love for, 230–31, 262–63, 266–67; Miles, on dharma for, 257–58; psychological liberation in, 32; social isolation in, 14–15; suffering in, 182–83

Black Consciousness, 15, 143

Black dharma teachers, 30, 63, 95–96, 210, 247

Black families, 19–20, 31, 75–77, 138, 162, 236–37

Black Feminists and Black Feminism, 2, 32, 136–37, 239; Black Buddhists and, 254, 266–67; Black Church and, 167; on Black female body, 182; on Black men, 154–57, 159; Black Power Movement and, 154–56; Buddhism, Lorde and, 216; Buddhist-Christian-Feminist love, of hooks, 161–63; on capitalist state, 157–58; in Combahee River Collective, 156–57; dharma, of Lorde, 158–60; on healing, 158–60; meditation of Walker, A., 163–67; on microaggressions, from white feminists, 154–56; on self-love, 254; on suffering and self-scrutiny, 247; Womanism, of Walker, A., 163, 165–67

Black Freedom Movement, 2, 131, 140–43, 155, 167

Black girls, 85–87

Johnson, Charles, 38, 66
Johnson, Gyozan Royce Andrew, 93
Johnson, Kate, 112–13, 182, 234–35
Jones, Beth Felker, 150
Jones, Marlene, 63, 168
Jordan, June, 157
joy, 184, 188, 190, 222–25
Jung, Carl, 22

Kagyu Tibetan tradition, 20
Kakuya, Alex, 252–53
Kant, Immanuel, 72–73
"The Karma of a Nation" (Williams, D.
    R.), 60
karuna (compassion), 184, 188
Kelley, Robin D. G., 7, 279n8
Kelly, R., 87
Kemetic spirituality, 129
Kendall, Mikki, 87
khandas (Five Aggregates), 8, 39–41, 173–
    74, 181
khandro, 206
King, Martin Luther, Jr., 4, 136, 140–43, 152
King, Ruth, 66, 133, 176–77, 244–45, 248
Korda, Josh, 23
Kornfield, Jack, 285n35
Ku Klux Klan, 16, 80
Kumar, Aishwary, 49
Kwanzaa, 15

land: ancestors and, 98–100, 133–35; hon-
    oring, 133–35; U.S., African Americans
    and First Nation peoples on, 31–32,
    103–5, 120, 133–35
Layman, Emma McCloy, 53
Leath, Jennifer, 300n36
Leclerc, Georges-Louis, 71
Ledi Sayadaw, 47
"Letter from a Birmingham Jail" (King,
    M. L.), 140
Levine, Peter A., 12, 280n20
LGBTQIA, 29, 153
libation practices and ceremonies, 129–30

liberation: awareness and, 194, 246, 249;
    Black and Asian solidarity in, 62; Black
    Buddhists on, 65, 230–31, 244–47,
    272–73; of Black women, 156; body in,
    175, 192, 210, 214, 222–27, 234–35, 253,
    273; Buddha on, 35; Christianity on,
    148–51; in community, collective ritu-
    als and care in, 151–54; defining, 6–7;
    ethical action over lifetimes in, 199; as
    freedom from clinging, 244–45; Holy
    Spirit and, 149–51; from intergenera-
    tional trauma, 117, 122, 236–37, 241–42;
    Lorde on, 160, 209–12; love and, 33,
    230, 266, 268; non-self, self and, 175–
    77; non-self and, 173–77; Satipatthana
    Sutta and, 193–94; skillfully relating
    to suffering in, 239–41; somatic, 234;
    stillness and, 34; from suffering, 40–41,
    122, 136, 176, 245–48; Two Truths as
    path to, 183; of women, Lorde on, 209,
    211–12. See also Black liberation; politi-
    cal liberation; psychological liberation;
    spiritual liberation
Lingo, Kaira Jewel, 113, 258
Linnaeus, Carl, 71–72
Lion's Roar, 30
Loncke, Katie, 241–42, 249, 268–69
Lorde, Audre, 32–33, 155–56, 163–64; on
    Black body, 214–15; Black Buddhists
    on, 209, 214–16; Black Feminism, Bud-
    dhism and, 216; on Black women, 158–
    60, 213–14, 254; on body, 210, 214–17;
    on compassion and self-compassion,
    213–15; dharma of, 158–60, 209–17;
    on eroticism and erotic power, 198,
    209–11, 216–17, 228–29; on liberation,
    160, 209–11, 214; on mothering oneself,
    213–14, 216, 254; on self-scrutiny, 159–
    60, 213, 217, 241; on sensuality, 208–17,
    222, 228; on suffering, 215–16, 224, 247
Lotus Sutra, 42
love: Baldwin on, 219; for Black people
    and Black community, 230–31, 262–63,

266–67; of body, 223, 253; Brahma-viharas and, 184–85, 254, 265, 273; in community, 264–69; hooks on, 161–63; liberation and, 33, 230, 266, 268; in meditation practice, 253–54; solidarity and, 268–69; suffering and, 243. *See also* self-love

Love and Rage (Owens), 20

loving-kindness (*metta*), 184–87, 189, 253–54, 261–62, 265–66

lynchings, 80–83, 137

Ma'at, Jylani, 231–32, 259, 262

Madhyamika school, 42, 180

Maezumi, Taizen, 48

Magee, Rhonda, 182, 194

Mahasi Sayadaw, 47

Mahayana Buddhism, 30, 33, 41–43, 164–65, 180, 283n17; gender fluidity and maternal deities in, 200–205; Lorde and, 210–11; *Vimalakurti* sutra of, 198

Majied, Kamilah, 259–60

The Making of Buddhist Modernism (McMahan), 44–45

Malcolm X, 136, 138, 140, 142–44, 266

Manjusri, 202

Manuel, Zenju Earthlyn, 64–65, 127–28, 132, 152–53, 178–79; on body, liberation and, 222, 224–25; on dharma, body and, 191–92; on sexuality, 228; on silence and tenderness, 226; on spiritual liberation, 249–50

Mason, Konda, 78, 109, 230, 247, 262–63

Mason-John, Valerie, 37–38, 66

mass incarceration, 31, 83–84

"The Master's Tools Will Never Dismantle the Master's House" (Lorde), 155–56, 163

maternal deities, in Buddhism, 200–205

Mayadevi, 199

McClendon, Stacy, 240–41

McKittrick, Katherine, 77

McMahan, David, 44–45, 47

The Meaning of Freedom (Davis), 7

Medine, Carolyn Jones, 167

meditation, 2–4, 15–16; attunement, from practice of, 225; drumming and, 118; in healing, 31, 66, 93–94; inner spaciousness in, 250–51, 261; joy and, 223; love and self-love, 253–54; *metta*, 186–87; mindful, at DTL retreat, 120–21; in modernization of Buddhism, 45–46; movement practices in, 17; practices, in U.S. Buddhism, 111–12; Right Livelihood and, 52; rituals and, 109, 111; stillness of, 225–26, 260–61; "streamlined" teachings on, U.S., 30–31; suffering, liberation and, 246–47; Tara's practice of, 202; therapy and, 22–23; *Tonglen*, 114, 297n49; trauma, rage and, 233, 237–39; *upekkha*, 189–90; Vipassana, 47, 111, 115; Walker, A., on, 163–67

Meiners, Erica, 85

Menakem, Resmaa, 91–92

mental formations (*sankharas*), 40–41, 173–74

Metcalf, Franz Aubrey, 22–23

#MeToo movement, 87

metta (loving-kindness), 184–87, 189, 253–54, 261–62, 265–66

microaggressions, 25, 31, 65–66, 83, 88–91, 112–13; from white feminists, 154–56

Middle Length Discourses, 190

Miles, Justin, 129–33, 182–84, 256–58, 267

mind and body, 193, 224, 226, 245, 257

mindful meditation, 120–21

mindfulness, 53, 96, 160; awareness practices and, 194–95; of body, 175–76, 191–92, 210, 224; dharma, compassion and, 261–62; *Satipatthana Sutta* and, 191, 196, 210, 224

Mindful of Race (King, R.), 66, 244–45

misogyny and misogynoir, 7–8, 136, 247

"model minority" status, of Asian Americans, 59–60

monastic codes (*Vinaya Pitaka*), 39

manence of, 176; non-self and, 33, 40,
174–80, 183; therapy, meditation and,
22; Theravada tradition on, 39–40
self-awareness, 10, 66, 219–20, 227, 248
self-compassion, 121, 124, 213–14, 262, 264
self-knowledge and self-trust, 226–27
self-love: of Black bodies, 161–62, 215, 254;
Black Buddhists on, 185–86, 253–56,
259, 261, 266–67; Black Feminists on,
254; of body, 253–56; community and,
268–69; compassion for suffering of
others and, 261, 268–69; hooks on,
161; Lorde on, 215; in *metta* practice,
185–86; Owens on, 243; taking refuge
and, 259
self-scrutiny, 145, 147, 236, 247; Lorde on,
159–60, 213, 217, 241
sensuality: Baldwin on, 208–9, 217–22,
224, 228–29; female, in Tantric Buddhism, 205–8; joy and, 222–23; Lorde
on, 208–17, 222, 228
sexism, 156, 159, 282n51
sexual abuse survivors, 237–38
sexuality, 198, 220, 227–29
sexual violence and exploitation, 17–18,
74, 77–78, 86–88, 93, 157, 237–38
SGI. *See* Soka Gakkai International
Shakur, Assata, 68, 146–47
Shambhala Buddhism, 48, 130–31, 133
Shambhala Center, in New York City, 90
Sharpe, Gina, 189
Shaw, Miranda, 199, 202–4, 305n17
Shelton, Sharon, 184, 188, 261
shrines and altars, 125–27
sila, 265
Simmer-Brown, Judith, 205–8, 306n22
Simmons, Aishah Shahidah, 87, 232–33,
237–38
Sister Outsider (Lorde), 209
Sivaraksa, Sulak, 51
skillful means (*upaya*), 239, 241
slavery, 58, 290n27; ancestors and, 102,
115–16, 118–19, 134–35; auction block

and, 75–78, 83, 135; the Bible and,
148–49; Black Codes after, 78–79;
colonialism and, 68, 103, 136; corporal violence against Black children
and, 18; DTL retreat on, 122–23, 135;
intergenerational trauma of, 75, 77–78,
95–96, 135; intergenerational violence
and, 19; monuments, 122–24; transatlantic slave trade, institution of chattel
slavery and, 73–78, 104, 117, 135, 171;
trauma and, 12–13, 25, 73–78, 91, 103,
171
Smalls, Shanté Paradigm, 105, 125–26,
131–32, 267–68
SNCC. *See* Student Nonviolent Coordinating Committee
socialism, 139
social isolation, 14–15
social justice, 6–7, 51, 194, 231, 234, 271
Socially Engaged Buddhism, 49–51, 60–61
Soka Gakkai International (SGI), 279n1
somatic movements and practices, 17, 23,
234–35
Soto Zen, 43, 127
South Asians, on African Americans, 59
Southern Christian Leadership Conference (SCLC), 141
The Sovereignty of Quiet (Quashie), 9–11
Spirit Rock Meditation Center, 63, 284n27
Spirit Rock Retreat Center, 23, 30, 282n60
spiritual and psychological integration,
21–23
spiritual bypass, 177
spirituality, activism and, 3–5
spiritual liberation, 196–97; consciousness in, 249–50; health and wellness
in, 235–36; political liberation and, 235,
241–42. *See also* psychological liberation and spiritual liberation
Sri Laksmi, 199
state violence, against Black women, 86
Steele, Ralph, 16, 105, 266
Still, in the City (Dews), 66

trauma: ancestral, 123, 125; awareness and, 258–59; Black Buddhists on, 5, 64–67, 232–33; to Black children, in state institutions, 64; Black Feminists on healing, 158; brain, nervous system and, 92–93, 95–96, 233–34, 294n104; childhood, 64, 96, 237–38; of colonialism, 69–70, 103; deep healing, in Black liberation, 20; of gendered and sexualized violence, 17, 74; healing, 20, 237–39, 258–59; of indigenous peoples globally, 103; of lynchings, dislocation, and segregation, 80–83; meditation, in healing from, 66; meditation and, 233; microaggressions and, 88; movement practices, in healing, 17; noncoding DNA and, 94–95; patterns of relating to, 232–33; of racialized violence, 231; rage and, 233, 236–39; slavery and, 12–13, 25, 73–78, 91, 103, 171; stored in body, 91–96, 162; of white supremacy, 162, 239. *See also* intergenerational trauma

Tricycle, 161

Tripitika, 180, 303n26

Trungpa Rinpoche, Chogyam, 48

Truth, Sojourner, 137

Tubman, Harriet, 125–26, 137

Turning Wheel, 64

two Buddhisms theory, 53–56

Tworkov, Helen, 54

Two Truths doctrine, 180–83

ultimate and relative reality, 7, 33, 168, 179–83, 195–96

Unapologetic (Carruthers), 7

"The Unbearable Will to Whiteness" (Syedullah), 24–25

Ungunmerr Baumann, Miriam-Rose, 100

UNIA. *See* Universal Negro Improvement Association

United States (U.S.): black America, as internal colony of, 299n19; Chinese immigrants to, 58; land of, African Americans and First Nation peoples

on, 31–32, 103–4, 133; liberation, of racially and culturally excluded people in, 35; poverty, 141–42; as prison nation, 83–84; racism of, 63, 219; slavery and segregation, in history of, 12. *See also* Buddhism, in U.S.

Universal Negro Improvement Association (UNIA), 138

unsatisfactoriness (*dukkha*), 37, 68, 169, 172

upaya (skillful means), 239, 241

upekkha (equanimity), 184, 189–90

U.S. *See* United States

vagrancy laws, in Black Codes, 78–79

Vajrayana Buddhism, 30, 33, 180, 198, 200; Baldwin and, 220; Lorde and, 210

Valignano, Alessandro, 70

van der Kolk, Bessel, 92–93, 96

vanguard activists, 271–72

Vasubandhu, 43

vedana (feeling), 40, 173, 193

Vietnam War, 141–42

Vimalakirti, 202

Vimalakirti Sutra, 200–201, 208

Vinaya Pitaka (monastic codes), 39

viññāṇa (consciousness), 40, 42–43, 50, 173, 249–50

violence: against Black children, 18–19, 85–87; in Black families, 17–19, 162; against Black women, 17–18, 86–88, 266–67, 293n73; of colonization, 103–5; intergenerational, 19; racialized, trauma of, 231; sexual, 17–18, 74, 77–78, 86–88, 93, 157, 237–38; systemic, 15–17, 20, 65, 86, 231–36; white supremacist, 232, 272. *See also* police violence

Vipassana meditation and practice, 47, 111, 114–16

Visudhimagga (Buddhaghosa), 42

Voting Rights Act of 1965, 141

Wade, Breeshia, 20–21

Waking the Tiger (Levine), 12

ABOUT THE AUTHOR

Rima Vesely-Flad is Associate Professor of Religion and Philosophy and Director of Peace and Justice Studies at Warren Wilson College. She is a Buddhist practitioner in the Insight tradition, a dharma teacher at the Barre Center for Buddhist Studies, and the author of *Racial Purity and Dangerous Bodies: Moral Pollution, Black Lives, and the Struggle for Justice.*